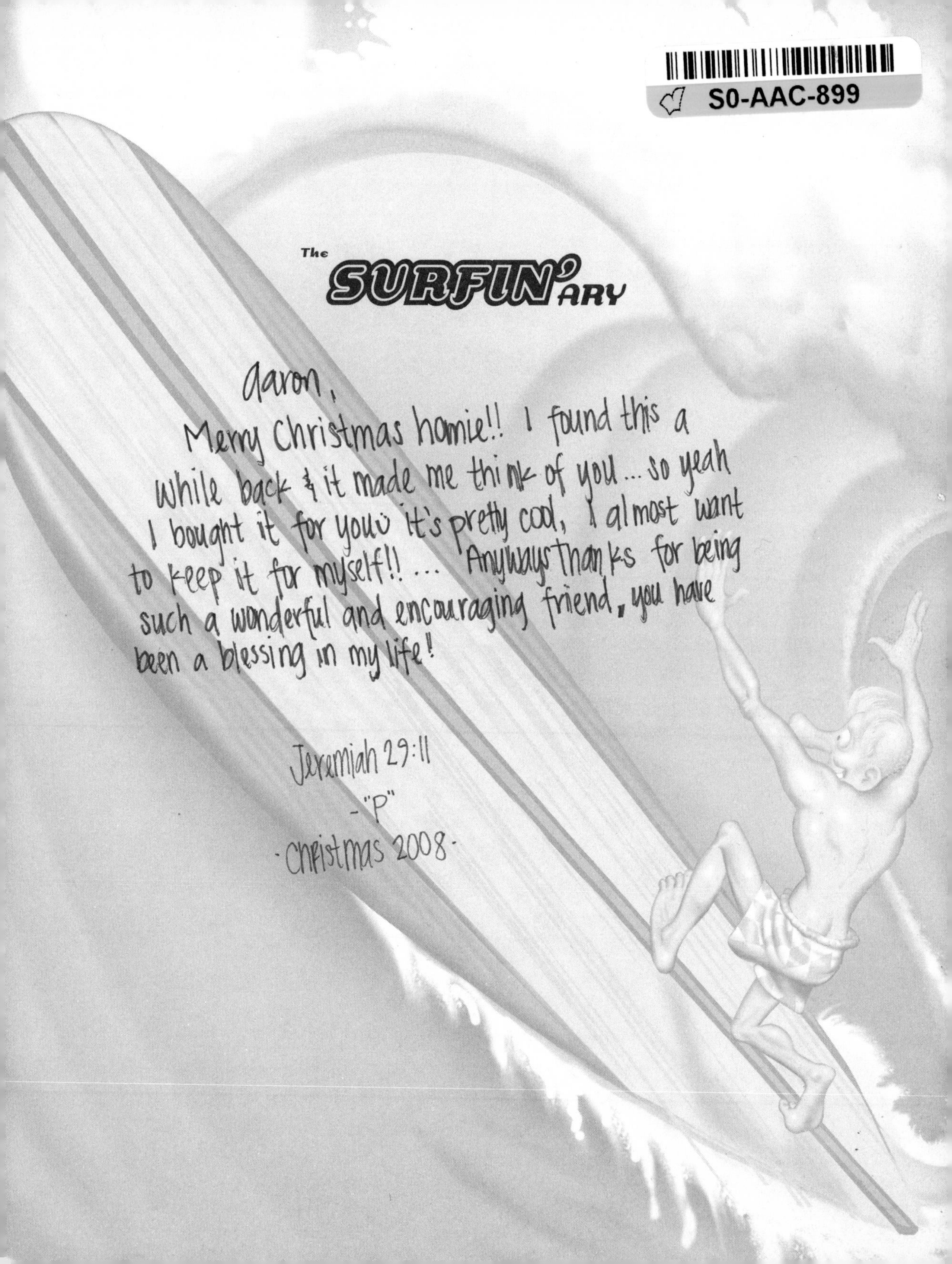

The
SURFIN'ARY

aaron,
Merry Christmas homie!! I found this a
while back & it made me think of you...so yeah
I bought it for you♡ it's pretty cool, I almost want
to keep it for myself!! ... Anyways thanks for being
such a wonderful and encouraging friend, you have
been a blessing in my life!

Jeremiah 29:11

-"P"

·Christmas 2008·

Darrick Doerner duck diving
a wave at Cloudbreak in Fiji

Photo: Copyright © 1995
by Don King

The

SURFIN'ARY

A Dictionary of Surfing Terms and Surfspeak
Revised and Updated Second Edition

Compiled and Edited by **Trevor Cralle**

TEN SPEED PRESS
BERKELEY/TORONTO

Ten Speed Press
P.O. Box 7123
Berkeley, CA 94707
www.tenspeed.com

Permission to use the following copyrighted material is gratefully acknowledged:
Barefoot Adventure movie poster ™ and © 1960 Bruce Brown Films.
"Beach Banter" by Rick Griffin first appeared in "Surfin' Safari Revisited" by Laura Bernstein and Jill Johnson Keeney, published in *New West/CALIFORNIA* magazine, May, 1981.
The Endless Summer movie poster ™ and © 1966 Bruce Brown Films.
"How to be a Surf Bum." From *SurfToons* magazine, © 1967 Petersen Publishing Company. Reproduced with permission.
"An Illustrated Glossary of Surfing Terms," artwork by George Woodbridge with text by Al Jaffe. From *MAD Magazine*, © 1965 by E. C. Publications.
Definition of "Surf" from the *Oxford English Dictionary*. Reprinted by permission of Oxford University Press.
"Real Surfers" by Corky Carroll first appeared in "Getting Air," *Surfer* magazine, 1984. Reprinted by permission of *Surfer* magazine and the author.
Excerpt from "Still Surfin' After All These Years" by Jonathan Kirsch first appeared in *New West/CALIFORNIA* magazine, May 1981.
"Surfish as a Second Language" by Dr. John Cohen first appeared in "Getting Air," *Surfer* magazine, September 1984. Reprinted by permission of *Surfer* magazine.
Excerpts from Wilbur Kookmeyer and Friends (including "The Typical Surf Kid: Past, Present, and Future") © 1985, 1986, 1987, 1988, 1989, 1990 by Bob Penuelas. Reprinted by permission of Universal Cartoon Company and the artist.

Library of Congress Cataloging-in-Publication Data
Cralle, Trevor.
    The surfin'ary : a dictionary of surfing terms and surfspeak / compiled and edited by
Trevor Cralle.-2nd ed.
        p. cm.
    Includes bibliographical references.
    ISBN 1-58008-193-2
1.   Surfing-Dictionaries. I. Title.
GV840.S8 C66 2000
797.3'2'03-dc21

                                                                00-057730

Printed in Canada
1 2 3 4 5 6 7 8 9 10 — 05 04 03 02 01

In Memory of Rick Griffin
(1944–1991)

Art: Rick Griffin

This book is dedicated with
the warmest aloha to my parents,
Bob and Judy Cralle.

Table of Contents

Foreword to the Second Edition

In *Mr. Palomar*, Italian author Italo Calvino writes, "To describe a wave analytically, to translate its every movement into words, one would have to invent a new vocabulary and perhaps also a new grammar and a new syntax, or else employ a system of notation like a musical score."

As it happens, for decades surfers have been doing just this: using, bending, shaping, inventing a rhetoric to articulate both the experience of waves and subjective response to that power, mystery, beauty. There are of course other vocabularies for water—the language of hydrology, oceanography, physics, or meteorology, for example. The vernacular of surfers, however, is based on tribal experience in the ocean, collective days, past and present, beyond counting—this and hunger for a joy deriving from both mastery and submission in the wilderness just off-shore. From such commingling of human and wave comes knowledge, and the erotic pleasure, even hours later on dry land, of carrying an absolutely essential rhythm in blood and bone. Sets and lulls, sets and lulls: truer than clock time.

Surfers also well understand the wit of understatement—the cool of restraint, of course, but also respect for what's beyond words, what can't, or shouldn't, be said. The almost ineffable being . . . the almost ineffable.

The repetition compulsion that is surfing. One wave, another, another. The growing knowledge, in surfers who stay with it, that to surf is to surrender. Other surfers rode the same waves before one began, will ride the same waves after one is gone. Ocean as Ganges.

Surfers as alchemists, transmuting water into words. In his dictionary of surfspeak, Trevor Cralle gives us access to this living dialect, its wit, insight, self-deprecations, appreciations, savorings, hard-won knowledge. Drew Kampion writes in *The Book of Waves:* "The wind speaks the message of the sun to the sea, and the sea transmits it on through waves. The wave is the messenger, water the medium. . . ." And on it goes, through generations of surfers, into Trevor Cralle's labor of love. A book for those who love water, and a book for those who love words.

—*Thomas Farber, author of* On Water, The Face of the Deep, *and*
(with photographer Wayne Levin) Through a Liquid Mirror

-Go"
Rick Rietveld

Foreword to the First Edition

The Surfin'ary is much more than a dictionary. It is a walk down the memory lane of surfing, a time machine that will transport you anywhere in the history of surfing. Sometime in the early sixties I bought my first book on surfing. Since then I have acquired more than 180 books about the culture of surfing. I have been the director of the surfing program at the University of California, Santa Cruz, for seventeen years, and I am on the board of directors of the Surfrider Foundation. I write a regular surfing column for a surfing magazine and consider myself a surfing bibliographer. I am very concerned about preserving and recording the history of surfing, and it is exactly this service that Trevor Cralle has admirably performed for all surfers as well as for the rest of the world. *The Surfin'ary* is an invaluable contribution to the history of surfing.

I rode my first wave (actually the soup) sometime in the latter part of 1961. Almost overnight I became a surf junkie. It wasn't long before my entire lifestyle metamorphosed, and surfing became the focal point of my existence. My vocabulary began to change also. I began to use words like bitchin', Cowabunga!, hang ten, walkin', wipeout, surfari. I began having trouble communicating with my parents and nonsurfing friends; for that matter, I still do. Enter Trevor Cralle. His epic work, six years in the making, defines not only my childhood verbiage from the sixties but also surfing terms from the seventies, eighties, and nineties, as well as ancient Hawaiian terms. This book will be an essential aid in helping surfers and nonsurfers communicate with each other. It will even help surfers communicate with each other. This book could be a college text for a cultural anthropology class!

The wonderful thing about language is that it is always changing. The climate of the nineties and beyond will definitely affect surf talk, creating more new words, words that the surfers of today won't be able to comprehend. Trevor says this is only the first edition and he will continue to record the language of surfers in future editions.

Put this book by your waterbed or beach chair and read ten or twenty pages a day. You can't help but learn something new and entertaining on every page. Get stoked!

—Ward Smith

Santa Cruz, California, March 1991

Note: Ward left the Surfrider Foundation in 1992 in order to found the Surfers' Environmental Alliance (described elsewhere in this book). He also recently collected his 1,000th book on surfing! Ward is still deeply committed to surfing and continues to hear new words almost daily. He would much rather surf the ocean than the Net. And so would you!

Art: David Sirgany

Hana Ho! Preface to the Second Edition

Ahoy, Shaka, Howzit, fellow surfers,

Nearly nine years have passed since the first edition of *The Surfin'ary* came out in August 1991. Since then, I have received, and continue to receive from surfers all over the world, numerous letters that are full of new terms. Many have offered excellent advice and suggestions, which I have incorporated into this newly revised and updated second edition. With over 650 new words, new information added to existing entries, and all the variants of words within a specific entry, there are now close to 4,000 words in *The Surfin'ary*.

This time around, with the advent of e-mail and all of the great surfing Web sites, research and communication were greatly increased. Still, I did not get to everything I wanted to do with the book, i.e., more box features, biographical entries, etc. Some of my boxes of buried treasure I didn't get to cull through, which contained such gems as Michael Girvin's epic paper entitled, "The Philosophy of Rad."

I'm frequently asked if I made up any of the words in this book. Yes, I coined a few and so did some of my friends and many other surfers around the watery globe—they have to start somewhere! My criteria for new or made-up words is simple: If the word fills a surfing void, then it will be considered for inclusion. Some surf words may in fact never be spoken, but they may contribute to some nuance of surf culture that has never been described. Of the 30,000 words that Shakespeare used, he coined six thousand words and only used them once. My father jokingly calls me the "Bard of the Brine" or the "Shakespeare of the Surf" in response to a review of *The Surfin'ary* in *The Oakland Tribune* that referred to me and my book as "The Webster of the Waves." At the same time, I wholeheartedly agree with Tom Farber in the Foreword to the Second Edition, when he says that some aspects of the total surfing experience simply can't be conveyed with words.

*The author
in Baja, 1985*
Photo: Nina Aldrich-Wolfe

d Wave
Jim Phillips

Stinson Beach, California
Photo: Stephanie Gene Morgan

I would also like to point out a major change in the indexing of the second edition. *The Surfin'ary* is now indexed letter by letter within each entry word. The original edition was indexed word by word. So, look closely if you can't find a word, and please send it in to me if it's truly missing!

When this book was first being assembled I had a difficult time conveying to many what it was all about. I still do to anyone who hasn't physically picked it up and flipped through it. Then they see that it's more than just a fifty-word glossary.

It bums me out when I see a surfer who doesn't understand the concept nor the vision of *The Surfin'ary*. As much as I want all surfers to realize that this book is by and for them, some just don't get it. No matter what kind of surfer you are, I'd like to think that there's something here for everyone. I cannot emphasize enough that this book is made by and for surfers.

The Surfin'ary has taken me in many wild and unforeseen directions throughout the surfing world and beyond. Please see the call for submissions under "A Note to the Reader" on page 360 if you would like to contribute anything to the next edition.

Stay Stoked!
    Keep surfing!
        Waves of sunshine!

P.S.
Last year a freelance writer doing an article for a major newspaper in Long Island, New York, called me up and said, "There's not much of a 'surfing culture' is there?"
Yeah, right. Whatever Dude . . .

xiv

Art: The Pizz

Paddling Out: Preface to the First Edition

The Surfin'ary is the first serious attempt at a complete vocabulary of the surfer and the sport of surfing. Surfing and the ocean have always fascinated me. From the time I was born, my parents took me to different beaches up and down the California coast. We rented a house in Newport Beach every summer, where I first saw hip-looking kids hanging out with their surfboards at the beach. Like many surfers, I began wave riding with bodysurfing, and later I graduated to a surf mat. In 1975, at age fourteen, I bought my first surfboard at Santa Cruz—a heavy old nine foot, eleven inch Holden longboard with a laminated wooden skeg. I'll never forget the first time that same summer when I stood up at La Jolla Shores and rode a wave straight into the beach. That feeling of stoke lit a spiritual fire inside me that every surfer can relate to.

I've always enjoyed describing waves and rides and talking surf with my friends. The idea for a surfing dictionary evolved from reading glossaries that have appeared over the years in books about surfing. In the summer of 1984, I began entering those glossaries on a computer in the hope of creating the ultimate surfing glossary. Soon I had around five hundred terms—the seeds of *The Surfin'ary*.

Next I combed through hundreds of back issues of surfing magazines. Another source—an especially entertaining one—was the glossaries on the backs of old sixties surf music albums (not always known for their high degree of accuracy).

I also conducted extensive field research for this book, primarily in California, Hawaii, and Australia. I did additional work in Mexico, the Caribbean, the South Pacific, and Indonesia. Wherever I was—on the beach, at surf shops, out in the lineup waiting for waves with fellow surfers—I carried out interviews.

In 1990, the Australian magazine *Tracks* and Southern California's *Surfer* magazine featured pieces on *The Surfin'ary*. These articles, and flyers I distributed to

The author with his first surfboard at La Jolla (1975)

Photo: Judith Cralle

surf shops, asked surfers to send me their favorite words. This request elicited many strange and wonderful responses. For example, I got a call from a bank teller in Sherman Oaks, California (in the San Fernando Valley), whose friend was an undercover cop posing as a surfer. She wanted to give him a copy of *The Surfin'ary* so he would know what to say and sound hip (scary!). I also received numerous letters from surfers around the world who sent in their local terms.

The need for a surfing dictionary was brought home to me in New Zealand in the fall of 1988. Some kiwi friends, who didn't surf, tried to mimic California surfer talk with sayings such as "Oh, woe, wipe me out—I'm out the backdoor" to mean "No way, you're kidding." "That's old-style Beach Boys talk," they said, as they continued to use expressions like "Wipe me out the back door" to say "See ya later" or "Good-bye."

Along the same lines, an editor at a major East Coast newspaper with international distribution, unsure whether to run a front-page article on *The Surfin'ary*, asked, "Do people in California still surf after Labor Day?" Although some surfers may feel that such ignorance is its own punishment, this editor's misperception made me realize that *The Surfin'ary* might help the media, and other terrestrial professions, understand our surf reality a little better.

Because surfspeak is so totally dynamic and culture specific (or culture bound, as some linguists prefer), its varied meanings and usages can never be fully conveyed to an outsider who hasn't ridden the big one. This kind of action-based knowledge is intimately understood and masterfully used by those who surf. Outside of the surf context, something gets lost in translation and delivery.

The Surfin'ary is intended for all those interested in surfing, including the novice and the nonsurfer who may want to learn about the sport. It is also for the experienced surfer, well versed in surf talk, who is curious to find out what surfers are saying in different parts of the world. Anyone interested in or involved with the ocean should find this a wealth of information. *The Surfin'ary* collects and preserves our rich and diverse global surfing culture. Although there are many great books on surfing, none has focused in such detail on the language of the surfer. This book attempts to chronicle how surfers communicate with each other. Surf's up!

Art: Deano

Second Edition Acknowledgments

Mahalo plenty to my good friend, chief research assistant, linguistic genius, and fellow surfer, Dan Jenkin. Secondly, I would like to thank another good friend, Tom Dalzell, who provided access to his enormous slang library, which should be listed as a national treasure.

It should be recognized that the primary inspiration for *The Surfin'ary* came from the hilarious surf glossaries contained in the Surf Punks record albums, *My Beach, Locals Only,* and *Oh, No, Not Them Again!* Aloha to Drew and Jilly on the Big Island.

Thanks to my many literary advisors, including Lee Micheaux, Lauren Alwan, Briggs S. Nisbet, Mad Monk Jim Crotty, Christian Crumlish, Robert Estes, Marty Frum, Nicki Ittner, Ro London, Lee Quarnstrom, Michael Tarsha, and Tony Wheeler at Lonely Planet.

Thanks also to Jim Thomas and The Mermen, Clayton Horton and "Air Waves" on KSRH in San Rafael, Peter Beall, Brent Beck, Stanley Cardinet, Susan Matthews, Leo Fernekes, Janet Fulrath, Leslie King, fellow lifeguard Kelly Rea ("Backer"), Sandy Roberts and her son Zack, my cousin Holger Sparrevohn, Lori and Michael Shantzis, Pierce Flynn, Reed Foster, and Julie Mott. Perhaps the most enthusiastic spokesperson for *The Surfin'ary* is Paul Damien Russell at Mullethead Surf Designs.

Muchas gracias to the entire Baja Collective, including Amy Baurmann, Cathy Borg ("Borgita"), Elise Brewin, Juan Chico and The Galaxy, Julia Curtis, Gray Douglas Dean, Geoff Evans, Alyson Foster, Shanti Sufi Freedom, Debbie Hailu, Jason Hanchett, Jesse "Word to the Mothership" Hendrich, Nancy I. Kelly, Tamar Kirschner, Eliza Laffin, Laura in the Livingroom, Greg Macchi, Stephanie Morgan, JD Moyer at Loöq, Andrea Orvik, Kevin Parker, Pam Parker, Michaela Parks, Sonal Petal, Liz Phegan ("Estrella del Mar"), Dale Rose, Camille Seaman, Kiakima Simon, Jason Smith ("Señor Limón"), Liz Solomon, and the amigo and fellow pirate, Captain Charles Souza.

Art: The Pizz

Thanks to all at Ten Speed Press, but especially to my project editor, Julie Bennett, who "could smell the cocoa butter and salt air wafting into" her office while reading through the manuscript.

Finally, I would like to honor three wonderful friends who left their mark: my literary agent Lucky Roberts, who taught me so much about the world of book publishing; former Vice President of Ten Speed Press David Hinds, who was as genuine as they come; and my teacher Bernard Nietschmann, who paid me the ultimate compliment by excerpting sections of *The Surfin'ary* and sticking them into the syllabus reader for his "Islands and Oceans" course at U.C. Berkeley. I imagine these three individuals smiling and laughing as they gaze up from the depths of Davey Jones' Locker from beneath the waves.

Art: courtesy of Grant Washburn

xviii

First Edition Acknowledgments

This book is the result of a collaboration among many individuals, including hundreds of surfers past and present, renowned and unknown. Also, without the many books and magazines on surfing, and other published materials, this project would have been virtually impossible. I am deeply indebted to all of the interviewees for their contributions. As much as feasible, I have tried to give credit throughout this book to the various surfers, scientists, writers, and other individuals who made this project a reality. Please consult the sources and credits at the back of the book for a complete listing, including all the photographers and illustrators who have brought the text to life. First and foremost, I wish to thank my parents, Robert Kenner Cralle and Judith Ann Schuyler Cralle, for all of their love, encouragement, and support, which has allowed me the freedom to follow my bliss. Thanks to my dear sister, Heather Stover; my niece and nephew, Cassandra and Cameron; and my bro-in-law, Rick Stover. Thanks to my granny, Margaret Cralle, who used to bodysurf at Redondo Beach even before George Freeth!

I wish to thank my very special friends Ellen Nachtigall and Michelle Anne Stevens. Their encouragement, patience, ideas, and enthusiasm were constant sources of strength while I was working on the manuscript. Michelle, you were in it since day one. Thanks, El, for being a great travel buddy, for all the great concepts, and for coming up with the title, *The Surfin'ary*.

Invaluable advice, comments, and criticism came from the following special consultants and contributing editors: Dan Jenkin ("Paco"), Drew Steele, Amy Agigian, Ben Marcus at *Surfer* magazine, and Pizz. Significant contributions also came from Lisa Hybarger, Mac Reed, Ken Seino, and Ward Smith.

My thanks are also due to the following individuals: Paul McEntyre, Michael Fletcher, Laura Agigian, Gred Histed, Rebecca Fish, Kini Harvey, Jan Thorell, Sherry Carlson, Lulie Haddad, Jawara, Karen Delgadillo, Tom

Art: Jim Phillips

Dodd, Laura Platt, Ken Regalia, Kirk Steers, Dr. James D. Rawls, Mike Peterson, Dan Bush, Valerie Jones, Ira Miller, and The Geneva Brothers—especially Tony Misner and Brian Plotkin.

I wish to thank the students, staff, and alumni of Maybeck High School, especially the class of '79. Thanks to Dave "The Wave" Kinstle, my high school teacher, mentor, travel partner, best buddy, guiding light. Thanks to Kathleen Aldrich, whose English classes I struggled through; she twisted the thumbscrews so tight that I eventually had to write a complete sentence, which made me a better writer.

Special thanks to Professor Barney Q. Nietschmann and Doug Powell at the University of California, Berkeley, for introducing me to the wonderful world of geography. Thanks to Lloyd Austin and all the U.C. divers, especially Scott Cameron and Henry Kaiser.

Many thanks to the California Coastal Commission staff, and especially to Gary Holloway for his boundless enthusiasm and wealth of information. Thanks to Mary Travis and Jo Ginsburg for all the "little lifts." Thanks also to Victoria Randlet, Marty Frum, Lee Micheaux, and Briggs Nisbet.

Lucky Roberts, a hep cat, my publishing consultant and total pal, brought me luck and publication. I also want to thank J. T. O'Hara ("The Queen of Mental Health"), who earned her other title, "The Finder." Thanks to Jim Herron Zamora, whose front-page *Wall Street Journal* article about *The Surfin'ary* set off a wave of media attention and inquiries.

Thanks to Fifth Street Design, first and foremost to Brent Beck, who designed the book and was completely dialed in to the vision, and to Judy Hicks, whose contributions were many. Thanks also to his partner, Jerry Meek, the resident expert in converting a computer-generated manuscript, such as mine, into a typeset book. I also want to acknowledge the efforts of all the people working behind the scenes during the book's production, especially the proofreaders.

I would like to extend a very special thanks to my editor, Carol Henderson. I was a bit skeptical at first when I walked into her home and saw a Mexican Christmas tree ornament in the form of a wooden blue shark dangling in front of her computer screen, with pink legs protruding from the shark's jaws. Did she not like surfers? It turned out to be a very good omen. Thank

Art: Jim Phillips

you, Carol, for all your concentrated energy and wonderful input into this project.

Finally, the crew at Ten Speed, including David Hinds, Phil Wood, George Young, and Sal Glynn, are simply great. Six years ago when I began working on this book, I dreamed that one day Ten Speed Press would publish it. Now this dream has come true.

Photo: Bill Romerhaus

Off-the-Lip:
An Introduction to Surfspeak

stoked: To catch a wave was (and is) to stoke the fires of the heart and soul; hence the terms: to be stoked, the stoked life, degrees of stoke, and pure stoke.

—*John Grissim, Pure Stoke (1982)*

"Hey, bro, Topanga is going off! Yeah, it's pumping, hair balls, man. Totally macking; six feet and offshore." Translation: Yo, dude, a specific surfing location is producing exceptionally large, six-foot-high waves that are big and powerful, like a Mack truck; also, the wind is blowing favorably from the land out to sea—the surf's up!

Ever since the 1959 Hollywood movie *Gidget* made the bohemian life of the Malibu surfer look and sound alluring, surfing terms have trickled into the American mainstream. And since 1961, the songs of The Beach Boys (for instance, "California Girls") have fueled the land-locked dreams of those people who, never having seen the ocean, can only imagine what it's like to "catch a wave" and view the world from a different perspective. Yet the complex language of the surfer has been around for a long time, dating back to ancient Polynesia, where the sport of surfing originated centuries ago.

Surfers have developed a language with a colorful vocabulary of words and expressions. Many of the terms and phrases used by surfers are international in scope, yet they are relatively unknown to people outside the sport.

Why is everyone so fascinated by surfspeak? The sun, sand, and surf combine to form a wonderful fantasy of relaxed pace and gentle sensuality that has captivated people for ages. The popular image of the surfer as a bleached-blonde, blue-eyed, sun-tanned male with salt caked on his eyelids, is held attractive. The romance and mystery of the ocean, with all the potential dangers, such as large sharks (yipes!), that a surfer may encounter, have also been captivating. Big-wave surf pioneer Phil Edwards likened the act of surfing to mountain climbing—only in this case the mountain chases after you. Surf lingo sounds hip. It's free flowing and often humorous.

Surfers don't conform to any particular set of rules. So why should their language? The surfer speaks from the heart with a playful, lazily articulated slang that reflects a laid-back, unhurried life. Standard English does not cover the nuances that surfspeak embraces, such as the term *tube chip* (any tortilla chip that resembles a curling wave).

Surfers have found a way of embracing nature and harmonizing with its flow that is lacking in late twentieth-century pedestrian life. Whereas many individuals are estranged from the natural world, surfers are immersed in it.

The majority of surfing terms spring from California, Hawaii, and Australia, the major wave centers of the world. Modern Hawaiian surfing terms are a mixture of words from the Hawaiian language and Hawaiian Pidgin English. In Hawaiian, bad sores on the feet caused by stepping on coral are called *kakios*. Australian surfers call hammerhead sharks *formula ones*—like the racing car.

1962

Moondoggie: *Didja see that kuk, man? He cut me off just as I was about to hang ten. I was so stoked. It was a bitchin wave.*
Tubesteak: *Yeah, well, that hot dog never takes gas, even on the die. But listen, man, it's gettin' cold, anyway. Wish I had my beavertail. Let's split and get some burgers. We can check out Motherbu on the way.*

Art: Rick Griffin

Surfing Meets the Valley

If you can't surf, at least you can try to talk like a surfer or attempt to dress the part. In 1982, surfing slang moved inland and burst into national—even international—prominence with the hit song "Valley Girl" by Frank Zappa. The tune contained lyrics made up of dialogue overheard by his daughter, Moon Unit, at the Sherman Oaks Galleria shopping mall in the San Fernando Valley, just north of Los Angeles. But as a special language confined to the San Fernando Valley, "Valspeak" is a media myth. The particular accent and slang words associated with Valspeak can be heard among many middle-class teenagers in other suburban areas.

Surfing's been a real trendsetter—surf music, fashion, even the lingo. You know, terms that were developed on the beach to describe waves and rides and other surfers you end up hearing on the sitcoms a year later, like "dweeb." I've heard that word a hundred times on TV, but I made it up a buncha years ago. Or that so-called Valley Girl slang, which is really beach talk that moved a few miles east 'cause the Vals were hangin' out on the beach. "Gnarly," "rad," "radical to the max," it was all beach talk. But now you can walk into a school in Boise, Idaho, and hear kids talking like that.

—*Corky Carroll,* Surf-Dog Dogs and Bitchin' Nights *(1989)*

Surfing spin-off sports, such as skateboarding, windsurfing, and snowboarding, have appropriated surf terms for their specific argots. Surf talk also draws on the icons of popular culture, especially those of TV and film, which everyone can relate to. A casper, as in "the Friendly Ghost," is a fair-skinned tourist who comes out to the beach.

The 1982 movie *Fast Times at Ridgemont High* was the single most important event propelling surf terms such as *dude* and *gnarly* into the mainstream. The film *Under the Boardwalk* introduced *bro* to the movie-going masses. More recent creations, like the Teenage Mutant Ninja Turtles and Bart Simpson have adopted words such as *radical* and *Cowabunga!* (a surfer's exultant cry). Still, the surf slang presented by the media represents only a few grains of sand from the vast beaches of surf lingo.

Terms from the suit 'n tie workaday world brought into an atmosphere of salt air evoke a sense of whimsy. Witness the variation called surf crimes (legalese applied to surfing): "Guy got 'prosecuted' on that wave" (wiped out to the fullest extent).

The ultimate surfing experience—a tube ride, where the surfer gets covered up by a barreling wave—is akin to a religious vision, sometimes described as a whirling cathedral, going to church, or being in the Pope's living room.

Surfers can be very territorial, and their lexicon is full of derogatory terms aimed at people who aren't lucky enough to live near the beach: nonlocals, valleys, inland squids, flatlanders, smog monsters, etc.

Over the years, surfing terminology has evolved. For example, a pipeline (a fifties term) became a tube in the sixties, which became a barrel in the seventies and eighties. Terms have also been adjusted to follow changing surfboard technology, which now enables surfers to

1981

Shaun: *The break was way zooed out, man. I shoulda said later for that. But it was really pumping, hair balls, man. Totally gnarly. Soon as I caught my wave, some goob, probly a valley, cut me off. I sliced his board.*
Scott: *I was watchin', man. The dude's a gyro goon. His board got real dung up. Way rad. I heard to-morrow'll be all mush doggies. Blown out totally.*

Art: *Rick Griffin*

3

execute moves never before attempted, let alone named. The hot surf moves of the fifties and sixties were drop-knee cutbacks, quasimotos, hanging ten, cover-ups, head dips, and soul arches. In the seventies, along with radically shorter boards, came roundhouses, reentries, back-doors, off-the-lips, and snapbacks. Now we're dealing with floaters, aerials, and slashes. Waves have gone from steep to hollow to square and from rolling to tubing to dredging to grinding.

Surfers are keen on abbreviations, as illustrated by the following names for surf spots: J-Bay for Jeffrey's Bay, a famous right pointbreak in South Africa; V-Land for Velzyland in Hawaii, named after the famous surfboard manufacturer, Dale Velzy; K35, K38, and K39, roadside kilo-meter markings where the surf is good in Baja. Other abbreviations include TK for totally killer, nar for gnarly, reo for reentry, and tri, a three-finned surfboard. In Santa Cruz, surfers are breaking new ground in lazy surf talk with minimal-effort expressions like "Zup" (for "What's up"), to which the reply would be "Nuch" ("Not much"); Orange County surfers say "S'later" for "See you later" and "Latronic" for "Later on, dude," which has been shortened even further to "Lonic."

Why are so many surf terms so funny? This may seem like an obvi-ous question. Living at the beach, frolicking under the sun, surfing in the saltwater playground is a totally healthy and positive experience, which breeds true endorphin-induced happiness.

Surfing terms are continually being created afresh. While words like stoke, ripping, and barrel are constants throughout the surfing world, regional conditions and attitudes lead to hundreds of specially encoded sublingos, which don't always spread throughout the global surfing community. Local surfers are the only ones completely immersed in their own indigenous lingo, and they often use slang specifically to keep outsiders at bay.

In Santa Cruz, a group of "Eastside" surfers invented a surfing sublan-guage in the late 1980s that stems from their word *haken*, which means "to go surfing." From that one word they have created a seemingly end-less vocabulary that includes terms like *hakenvesmo* (to surf—with a meal afterwards) and *haken visuals* (getting good barrels). These terms can probably never be fully appreciated by outsiders. The language of the surfer can metamorphose within a sentence. Surfers fool around with different combinations of words and if the result sounds good, they keep it.

Although surf talk may sound simplistic, it has been shaped by a vast and varied set of influences. The earliest known surfing terms came from the Hawaiians, who had words for every aspect of the sport. *Nuumehalani* referred to a surf site on Oahu meaning "the heavenly site where you are alone." *Ahua* was a place close to shore where a broken wave rose and broke again.

A Breakfast Note before Kicking Out

Just as Eskimos have fifty-two different terms to describe various kinds of snow, and desert nomads in the Sahara have numerous terms for all the types of sand, surfers have countless words for waves, from micro to gnarlatious to sucky to burgery. A good rule of thumb for the true surf linguist is that any adjective used to describe your breakfast food can also be used to describe a wave: crispy, crunchy, hearty, tasty, sweet, unreal, and so on.

Misguided dweeby types who perceive surf lingo as juvenile do so, perhaps, because of their own ambivalent feelings. Like any normal human, they yearn for sun, fun, and a fancy-free existence to the beat of nature's rhythms. But, due to career pursuits, the work ethic, or

Art: The Pizz

whatever, they belittle surfing because it doesn't produce wealth and hence is deemed unworthy of adult activity.

True surfers realize how spiritually wealthy the ocean, waves, and they—the riders of ocean and waves—really are. They place their love for this wealth above the desire to make money. These values are seen in expressions like *soul surfing,* to describe noncompetitive surfing for the fun of it, and the *Big Mama,* for the ocean. The surfer's life is attractive to much of the world because it embodies that unbridled, raw, uncontrollable lust for life that so many people who live only to make money have become numb to. It's exactly this joyous youthfulness that keeps surfers, both young and old, in the water and near the ocean.

All of these influences make surfspeak a textured, richly layered language that requires the experience of surfing for its meaning to be fully understood. At the same time, its free-flowing, multitextuality makes it universally appealing and enthralling to all. Fer sure.

Art: Jim Phillips

What Is Surfing?

*surfing: (sur'fing) n. A water sport, in which the partici-
pant stands on a floating slab of wood resembling an
ironing board in both size and shape, and attempts to
remain perpendicular while being hurtled toward the shore
at a rather frightening rate of speed on the crest of a huge
wave. (Especially recommended for teenagers and all others without the slightest regard for either life or limb.)*

—The Beach Boys, Surfin' U.S.A. album liner notes (1963)

Surfing is a thrilling water sport for persons of all ages that has been practiced for centuries. The act itself involves riding across the face of a wave toward the shore while standing on a special board, called a surfboard. Modern surfboards are made of foam and fiberglass and come in various shapes and sizes, from shortboards to longboards and everything in between.

Although the above definition describes surfing at its purest, the sport takes several forms: bodysurfing, the simplest variation, with just a body and a wave (some people wear fins or use a hand-planing device, such as a swimmer's kickboard); bellyboarding, with a small wooden or plastic board; bodyboarding (also called boogie boarding), with a flexible foam board; mat surfing, with inflated rubber surf mats; and kneeboarding, using a smaller, specialized surfboard. Surfers also ride the waves on wave skis, surf skis, and paddleboards and do boat surfing with dories, canoes, sea kayaks, and catamarans. Out on the open ocean, sailboats "surf" down unbroken swells. Surfing spin-off sports include snowboarding on mountain ski slopes, sand-boarding on sand dunes, skimboarding along the shoreline, and windsurfing (sailboarding) on a modified surfboard with a sail. Even skateboarding has its roots in surfing. And now there's kite surfing.

Regardless of the type of surfing, the basic principles are the same. The surfer strokes with the arms, or paddles, toward the shore just ahead of an incoming, unbroken wave. As the wave moves forward and catches up to the surfer, the surfboard (or body, raft, bodyboard, etc.) starts to slide down the face of the wave. At this point the surfer has caught the wave and must stay just ahead of the breaking portion of the wave to maintain the ride; this is done by shifting body weight to maneuver the board in the appropriate direction.

Surfing takes place along all of the coastlines of the world, but California, Hawaii, and Australia are the best-known areas because of their many high-quality surf spots, large surfing populations, and local knowledge combined with advanced design and equipment technology. The most highly regarded surfing spots are usually locations where waves either approach the shore at an angle, break over an offshore reef, or are refracted around a protruding landform, such as a rocky point or a headland.

Surfing is a sport, an art form, a subculture, a social phenomenon, an existential attitude, and a way of life that is worldwide. The popular image of the surfer has changed over the years. The hip but clean-cut surfers in the movie *Gidget* (1959) became the long-haired, pot-smoking Spicoli types in *Fast Times at Ridgemont High* (1982). Today's professional surfer is a mix, and the advertisements in surfing magazines reflect fashion consciousness. Regardless of the image portrayed by the media, however, surfers are a diverse group of individuals who do not conform to any set type.

Surfers feel a special connection to the ocean environment because they are in tune with the rhythms of the sea. It is no wonder humans feel such an attraction to our mother ocean when 98 percent of our bodily fluids are made up of saltwater. The amazing truth is that the sound of the waves crashing and receding is a direct reproduction of the sound of the blood flow heard by a baby in its mother's womb. This rhythm creates a feeling of tranquility for all of us, as it does for the unborn child.

In surfing, we have found a way to use an untapped energy source. As George Leonard notes in *The Ultimate Athlete* (1974), "A surfer takes only the barest minimum of equipment into the sea and prevails—not by opposing but by joining a wave." Surfing is a unique activity because each wave is always changing, so that each ride is a new experience.

Brian Wilson of The Beach Boys probably said it best in 1962 with the line, "Catch a wave and you're sittin' on top of the world." The surfer views the world from a different perspective—from a place high above everyone else:

. . . and for one quick second up there I could see all of Dana Point, Capistrano Beach, the beige hills off inland Omaha, Nebraska, and everything.

—Phil Edwards (1967), on catching a wave

Surfing embodies a multitude of senses and sensations, including the sound of a wave crashing, the thrill of watching someone else get a hot ride; the intoxicating smell of surf wax, neoprene wetsuits, and fiberglass surfboards in a surf shop; and the euphoric feeling of tapping the pure source of an ocean wave.

Art: Rick Stover

There are risks involved when taking off on a big, powerful ocean wave, where one false move can get you pounded into a razor-sharp coral reef or held down beneath the surface for what may seem like an eternity. There are also moments of elation: the rush of adrenaline that you feel when dropping down the steep face of a towering wave—making the drop—and shooting back up to the top of the wave and continuing on a hot ride; and the ultimate in surfing—a tube ride, when the breaking wave that is being ridden curls overhead and engulfs you in a churning liquid cylinder. All of these elements combine to give the surfer that stoked feeling that gives rise to endless hours of storytelling.

> Surfing attracts dedicated cultists who build their lives around their sport—but so does golf. The important distinction between the two is that no one ever stays up late to catch a great golf flick on the late show. No one cruises down Pacific Coast Highway with the radio blasting out a bitchin' golf tune. Indeed . . . there is something very nearly mystical about the lone surfer who spends hours bobbing atop powerful ocean swells just for the chance to thrust himself into the curl of a breaking wave for a few heart-stopping moments. "Surfing is a dance form, and the ocean is like a liquid stage," says one veteran surfer.
>
> —Jonathan Kirsch, "Still Surfin' After All These Years," New West (May 1981)

Surfers all over the world share a reverence for the sensations that surfing evokes. Through this common love of the ocean and the sport of surfing, surfers are able to communicate with one another. Truly, this love is so intense that it crosses borders and bridges cultural gaps that language and governments are unable to span. Reduced to instinctual survival in the surf, we are united with each other at the most fundamental level.

But why do we continually subject ourselves to the potential dangers of the waves? Being out in the ocean stimulates a sensation of extreme vitality that is druglike and addictive. As any surfer will tell you, there's no feeling in the world comparable to gliding on water, taking the alleged steps of Jesus one step further, bringing us closer to the gods of the ocean, and satisfying the soul through a form of art and play as pure as the ocean itself.

A Brief History of Surfing

Long before humans began using surfboards for surfing on waves, marine mammals such as dolphins and sea lions were taking energy out of waves to propel themselves along the front of an advancing wave. The sport and art of surfing originated centuries ago (some claim A.D. 400) somewhere in the Pacific islands, most likely Polynesia. This wave-riding activity was started, perhaps accidentally, by fisherfolk who had to get their ocean-going crafts out and back through the surf. In 1777, British explorer Captain James Cook observed islanders surfing at Matavai Point in Tahiti. Cook also noticed people surfing when he visited the Sandwich (Hawaiian) Islands in 1778.

Beginning in 1821, surfing was almost completely eliminated by European Christian missionaries, who considered it an immoral form of amusement and suppressed it along with much else in the Hawaiian culture. By the time surfing was revived around the turn of the century, there were only a handful of Hawaiian surfers left.

Surfing was "officially" introduced to California in 1907 when the Irish-Hawaiian surfer George Freeth visited from Hawaii to put on some surfing exhibitions at Redondo Beach in Southern California. However, evidence suggests that Hawaiian Prince David Kawonanaokoa surfed Santa Cruz in Northern California in 1885 and was probably the first person ever to surf in California. Hawaiian Olympic swimmer Duke Kahanamoku popularized the sport in California beginning in 1911 and introduced surfing to Australia at Freshwater Beach, Sydney, in 1915.

At first the sport attracted only a limited following, one reason being that early surfboards were fourteen to eighteen feet long and each was constructed of a solid redwood plank weighing up to 150 pounds. Tom Blake invented the "hollow" surfboard in 1928 at Waikiki, reducing the weight to 75–100 pounds. He later contributed another important design feature when he attached a fin (also called a *skeg*) to the underside of a paddleboard in 1935. The birth of modern

Hawaiian man with his family and surfboard by a beach shelter, 1890s
Photo: T. Severin/Bishop Museum

THE DAWN PATROL OF HOMOSAPIEN! HIS EXTINCTION PREVENTED BY LOGIC, REASONING AND INGENUITY! THE THRUST FOR SURVIVAL DREW PRIMORDIAL MAN TO ENACT VERY BASIC URGES, SUCH BASIC URGES AS FISHING AND HUNTING! SUCH BASIC URGES AS CREATING SHELTER AND MAKING FIRE! BUT MAINLY SUCH BASIC URGES AS *SURFING!* BASED ON INTENSIVE AUTHENTIC, SCIENTIFIC, ARCHEOLOGICAL CONJECTURE, THIS STORY ILLUSTRATES ....

THE HISTORY OF SURFING!

Art: Jim Phillips, Surf Crazed Comics

surfing came with the introduction of lightweight balsa boards in the 1940s and the development of polyurethane foam boards in the 1950s, the latter of which changed the sport forever.

The 1959 film *Gidget* set the stage for a string of Hollywood beach movies in the 1960s, which planted a very strong suggestion that the bohemian life of the surfer was just the sort of romantic world a teenager would like to escape to. In the early 1960s came a wave of instrumental surf music that was shortly joined by vocal

Kahanamoku brothers
Moana Hotel, Waikiki, c. 1928
L. to R.: Bill, Sam, Louis, David, Sargent, and Duke
Photo: Tai Sing Loo,
Bishop Museum

groups, led by The Beach Boys, whose anthems spread inland and, fueling the surfing dreams of landlocked people who had never seen the ocean, turned into a national craze that touched the world. Bruce Brown's *The Endless Summer* (1964), a real-life documentary adventure film about two California surfers who traveled around the world in search of "the perfect wave," generated another positive image for surfing.

The wetsuit—a snug-fitting neoprene rubber garment invented in the early 1960s—kept surfers warm and made surfing a year-round activity in temperate waters. The Shortboard Revolution, in the mid- to late sixties, sparked a period of innovative surf-board design that has continued to the present.

Surfers catching
a wave, Waikiki, 1925
Photo: Honolulu Advertiser,
Bishop Museum

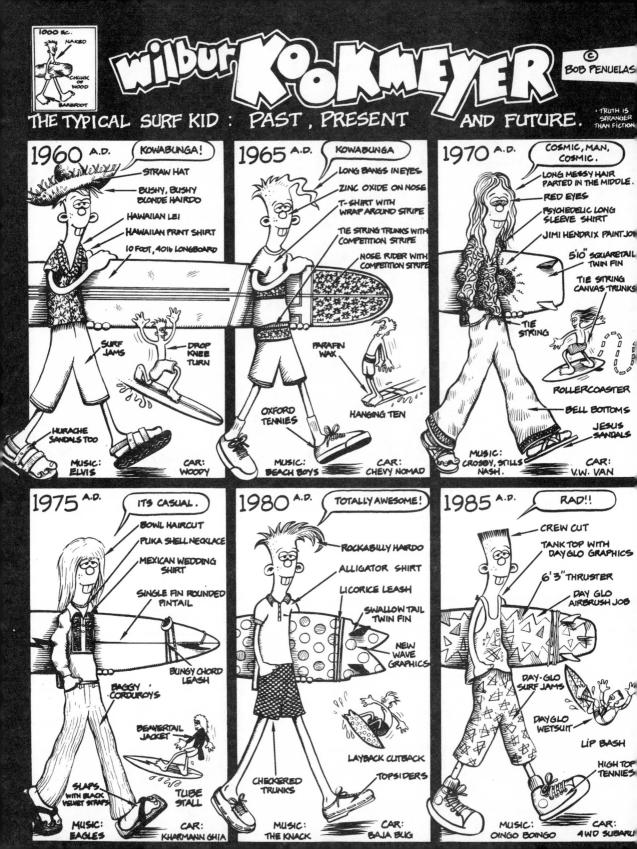

Ancient Hawaiian petroglyph of a surfer

The surf leash, or leg rope, a flexible cord that tethers the surfboard to the surfer's ankle, was experimented with in the late sixties and became standard equipment in the 1970s. The leash made the sport a little safer and accessible to a greater number of individuals; it also opened up many new surf spots where previously a lost board would have been smashed on the rocks. Professional surfing was born in the late 1970s and dominated by the Australians.

The growth of surfing was marked by the commercialism of the 1980s. Surf fashion, which has always set trends, grew into a $2-billion-a-year industry. The bright, often fluorescent, multicolored wetsuits, surf trunks, and T-shirts became the uniform for youth in America. Surf music and longboarding experienced tremendous revivals, and surfing museums began to appear.

The average surfboard weighed about eight pounds and was around six feet in length. In 1981, with the advent of Australian Simon Anderson's revolutionary design for the three-fin surfboard, called the *thruster*, surfing was well on its way into the ultramodern era.

Until the 1980s, surfers were never really known for their social, political, or environmental activism, but that has changed dramatically. The Surfrider Foundation, a California-based environmental watchdog group dedicated to saving waves, monitoring coastal development, stopping ocean pollution, and preserving coastal access, has experienced phenomenal membership growth among surfers since its inception in 1984. Surfers Against Apartheid was a group of professional wave riders who boycotted surfing competitions in South Africa from 1985–1990. The San Francisco–based Surfer's Medical Association was formed in 1985. Australian organizations, also formed during the 1980s, include Surfers for Rainforests and Surfers Against Nuclear Destruction.

Tom Blake with his surfboard, Waikiki
Photo: Bishop Museum

Surfish as a Second Language

Dr. John Cohen, Ph.S. (Doctor of Surfish)
(Excerpted with permission from Surfer *magazine, "Getting Air,"*
September 1984)

Lesson #1

Forget every rule you've ever learned about English.
For most of you, this will create no problem at all.
Examples: See Lessons 2–10.

Lesson #2

Use one adjective as a complete sentence whenever possible.
Examples: Crucial. Random. Critical. Treacherous. Solid. Unreal.
Insane. Bizarre. Cool. Hot. Awesome.

Lesson #3

Add "dude" or "bro" to the end of each sentence that begins with
an adjective.
Examples: Crucial, dude. Critical, bro. Insane, dude. Unreal, bro.

Lesson #4

Modify nouns, verbs and modifiers whenever possible.
Modifiers include: entirely, so, too, totally, super, heavily and sorta.
Examples: Don't say: It was happening at Eleventh Street. Say: It
was so happening at Eleventh Street. Don't say: That flick was
cool. Say: That flick was totally cool. Don't say: It was crowded.
Say: It was super crowded.

Lesson #5

ALWAYS use "way" instead of "very."
Examples: Don't say: These waves are very good. Say: These
waves are way good. Don't say: The tide was very low. Say: The
tide was way low. Don't say: It was very hard when I broke my

arm and couldn't surf. Say: It was way hard when I broke my arm
and couldn't surf.

Lesson #6

Describe waves in terms of cereal.

Examples: The inside was crunchy. It was insanely crispy yesterday. I
just got the tastiest wave! The outside's pretty chewy. It gets tres
mushy when the tide goes in. Tomorrow's gonna be fully scrumtious.

Lesson #7

To save time, abbreviate whenever possible.

Examples: We can hit DT's in the Whaler. Let's cruise the cycles
down to HB. Fresh heiny's in the fridge, bro. Note: Save more time
by calling both the ocean and the waves "it" (e.g., "Howz it look?",
"How was it?", "Let's check it out.")

Lesson #8

Use aggressive verbs whenever possible. Excellent examples of
aggressive verbs include dominate, capitalize, blow out, blow
away, shred, destroy, crank, whip, rip, and zip.

Examples: We dominated the peak all morning. You entirely capitalized on that right. I cranked this screaming bottom turn, destroyed
the lip by cranking a hard cutback, and then I totally blew everyone
out by shredding the inside section and zipping off a reentry before
ripping off a part of my foot on the reef.

Lesson #9

Only talk about subjects you're way familiar with. Safe topics
include the tide, yesterday's waves, tomorrow's swell, the opposite
sex, parties, concerts, racks, and pressure systems.

Lesson #10

To finish off our class, you should be warned not to use Olde Surfish as
it will definitely brand you a geek. Words to avoid include: baggies,
gremmies, combers, breakers, tubular, ho-dads, nay (instead of no),
chicks (try wahinis or ladies), da kine, far out, primo and man.

A Guide to the Dictionary

Anyone opening this book and expecting to find a standard dictionary is in for a surprise. *The Surfin'ary* is really a combination word reference, encyclopedia, and glossary. Even if a single term or phrase could be narrowly defined, I often chose to include several definitions if each gave an intriguing nuance or perspective or drew attention to a different cultural or geographical twist. I also felt free to supplement definitions with "interesting information"—a story or quote or background material to give a term more of a context. In this way I hoped to present a broad picture of the current worldwide surfing subculture, interwoven with some historical notes.

Another unusual feature of *The Surfin'ary* is its fluid form, a reflection of the language itself. You won't find in these pages the rigid constructions—the unrelenting consistency—and the sometimes bewildering complexities of most dictionaries. The emphasis is on usage, not theory, semantics, or etymology. The choice of main-entry words (indexed letter by letter within each entry word in this edition, rather than word by word as in the first edition) is very much rooted in the fact that surfspeak is primarily a spoken language. Consequently the word defined in the dictionary won't necessarily be the "base" form (for instance, an infinitive) but instead may be the form most frequently heard (for instance, an inflection of a verb). So, for instance, you will find *getting a place wired* (a participial form) instead of *to get a place wired* (the infinitive form). A further potentially disconcerting aspect is surfers' irreverent attitude toward so-called standard English. Surfers tend to be as free and easy in their use of the language as they are in every other respect. They play with words, constantly experimenting and improvising, and they don't feel obliged to be constrained by rules or grammar or usage. I hope that the many usage examples will clarify the meaning of terms applied in nonstandard ways.

WHOA! DID JA SEE ME ON THAT INSANE RIGHTHANDER IT WAS GNARLY!! I CAN'T BELIEVE I MADE THAT TOTALLY VERT DROP BLEW ME AWAY, I WAS STOKED!

VALLEY STIX

TOTALLY EXCELLENT UNITS

19

Art: Peter Spacek

AN ILLUSTRATED GLOSSARY OF SURFING TERMS

Before going any further with this article, it will be necessary for the reader to familiarize himself with the Surfer's private language. There is a definite purpose in this language. It was not created for any of the square reasons that many Clubs or Fraternal Organizations have for their mumbo-jumbo. It was not created just to have a silly secret language. The reason for Hip Surfer Talk is more serious and meaningful than that. It's to show off!

"GREMMIE"

A beginning Surfer. Easily recognized because they're the ones who mostly use the idiotic words on this page.

"HO-DAD"

A refugee from the drop-out motorcycle set who takes up Surfing. Easily recognized because they can only dig the pictures on this page.

"DING"

What happens when your surfboard hits something hard.

"BING"

What happens when the something hard your surfboard hits hits you right back.

"ALL-TIME"

A great surf! For example, Hawaii's surf is always all-time! California's surf is often all-time! Arizona's surf is never all-time!

"TAKING GAS"

Losing control and going down — not to be confused with stealing fuel from a parked car to get to beach.

"DOWN"

What happens to a Surfer after "taking gas." He is underwater and is expected to reappear momentarily.

"DROWN"

What happens to a Surfer after "taking gas." He is underwater — not expected to reappear momentarily.

"SAND"

Found in every orifice and pore of a Surfer's body, it makes a gritting sound when he chews or blinks his eyes.

"BULLY"

A big bronze-skinned Surfer who carelessly kicks sand when he walks on the beach.

"SKINNY"

A weak pale-skinned Surfer who usually gets all of the sand kicked by the Bully.

"VAVAVOOM"

A beach bunny who goes off with the Bully, leaving the Skinny—while everyone else wonders what she saw in the Skinny in the first place.

"PUKA"

This is not what a Surfer becomes when the waves go down and up and down and—It's a break in the surface of the board. Not serious.

"COMPOUND FRACTURE"

A break in the body of the Surfer. Also not serious. Unless it's a break in the body of the board. Then it is serious. Only then, it is called a compound puka.

"BIG MAN"

A Surfer who carries his board around during non-surfing weather to give the impression he's hardy.

"WIPE OUT"

To lose a wave. Also what Surfers will probably do to the MAD Magazine offices when they see this article.

With the reader's convenience in mind, I did try to maintain a minimum of consistency in editing the dictionary entries. Basically each entry consists of the term being defined (called the main entry); a part of speech (except for proper names); and one or more definitions. For example:

crank a turn *v.* To lean into a turn at a radical angle.

A term that is a synonym or a shortened form of a term defined elsewhere may simply refer the reader to the other term. For example:

crossover *n.* CROSS STEP.

To find the meaning of *crossover*, look up *cross step*.

The main entry may include more than a single term or phrase. Alternative spellings are separated by *or*, as in the entry "**beach break** or **beach-break** or **beachbreak**." Variant terms are separated by commas: "**geek, geekster, geek-a-mo.**"

For terms with possibly questionable pronunciation, I included a phonetic spelling, as in *tsunami*, on the next page.

The abbreviations for parts of speech are explained in the list following this section. Many words can be used as more than one part of speech. This is especially true of a surfing maneuver, which can be thought of as both a noun—the maneuver itself—and a verb—the action of performing the maneuver. Sometimes both (or all) possibilities are given in the usual position, immediately following the main entry. For example:

walking the dog *v., n.* Moving back and forth on a surfboard to alter speed.

If the different part of speech requires a separate definition, it will be given as a numbered item, usually at the end of the entry, as in *slide*.

slide *n.* **1)** A long track down a large wave from which a safe deviation is usually not possible without wiping out. **2)** A diagonal descent on a wave. **3) sliding** Movement across the face of a

) Magazine, *1965*
:: Al Jaffee
George Woodbridge

wave, as opposed to going straight in with the wave. **4)** *v.* To ride either left or right, on a track somewhat parallel to shore.

Note that item #3 defines *sliding,* a variant of *slide,* but no part of speech is given because it's the same as that of the main entry.

In many entries, a usage example is included, preceded by the word "Usage." For example.

> **beached** *adj.* Totally stuffed from eating. Usage: "I'm so beached, I can't move."

Synonyms are given as "Also called," "Also known," or "Same as" cross-references. A "See" cross-reference indicates that additional or related information can be found at another entry. Some entries, for example *tsunami,* contain both types of cross-reference.

> **tsunami** (sue-NAW-me) *n.* A series of waves (not a single wave) caused by a sudden movement along a large portion of the ocean floor. Means "tidal wave" in Japanese, although the waves it describes have nothing to do with tides. They should not be confused with storm-surge waves. Same as SEISMIC SEA WAVE. See TIDAL WAVE.

The source of a term or definition may be indicated, sometimes together with the place where the term originated and the date the term entered the surfing lexicon. This kind of information always appears in parentheses. Sources are given as abbreviations, keyed to the list that follows this section.

> **abb** *n.* An abnormal person; same as KOOK. See GO-ABB. (San Diego; MVA)

The last element in the definitions portion of an entry may be a frequently encountered variant of the main entry (for instance, an inflected form) or a closely related term not requiring a separate definition.

Following the definitions may be a separate paragraph or paragraphs of additional material; this is the encyclopedic part of *The Surfin'ary.*

The entry for *wave*, for example, includes variants and an interesting observation quoted from another book.

> **wave** *n.* **1)** Undulating or rippling water, the three main natural causes of which are wind, earthquakes, and the gravitational pull of the moon and the sun. (WB) **2)** A moving pulse of energy; a horizontally moving ridge of water the particles of which move in closed curves. **3)** A requisite for surfing. (JRW) —**permanent wave, new wave, ultimate wave**

"Waves are an endless source of fascination for everyone, from scientists to surfers. Who, in watching, is not mesmerized by the ongoing cycles of surge and rush, flow and ebb, storm and calm?"

—*Drew Kampion*, The Book of Waves (1989)

(The full publishing information for *The Book of Waves* may be obtained by looking up the book in the bibliography.)

Sometimes, instead of giving several separate entries and defining each, I lumped together closely related terms under a single main entry. I did this partly to save space, partly because it made finding the variant terms easier, and partly because I just thought it was interesting to see all the variations in one place. For example, item #2 under

Art: Jimbo Phillips

the main entry *evening glass-off* is *evening glass*. Under the main entry *stoked* you will also find *stoke* (noun and verb) and *stoker*, each listed as separate numbered items and defined.

The main typographic distinctions observed in the dictionary are these: **boldface** is used for the main entry, for variants, and for related terms; SMALL CAPS are used for cross-references (indicating that the term is defined elsewhere in the dictionary); and *italic* is used for emphasis (mainly in usage examples, to try to give the flavor of the spoken phrase), for synonyms that aren't defined elsewhere, for "words as words," and for various formal ways of treating particular groups of words (for example, book titles).

A word about offensiveness. Some of the terms and definitions in *The Surfin'ary* may offend some people, but, as Sidney Landau stated in *Dictionaries: The Art and Craft of Lexicography* (Cambridge University Press, 1989), "The lexicographer can only claim to be objectively reporting usage." I compiled the terms and phrases contained in *The Surfin'ary* in a strictly lexicological manner. The inclusion of offensive terms or ideas is by no means an endorsement. Rather, in this age of increasing censorship of artists, musicians, writers, and

thinkers, *The Surfin'ary* attempts to present all that is out there.

I want to make it clear that I do not endorse any localism, sexism, or other shallowness that may exist in the world and that therefore may be documented in this dictionary. Personally, I want to see a world where all living beings, including kneeboarders, women, boogie boarders, sea kayakers, and vals are respected in the ocean and on the earth.

Photo: Jim Phillips

Abbreviations Used in This Work

Parts of Speech

adj.	adjective
adv.	adverb
n.	noun
pl.	plural
prep.	preposition
pron.	pronoun
v.	verb

Sources

(For complete references, please consult the bibliography and the credits list at the end of this book.)

A&B	Rick Abbott and Mike Baker		B&F	Reginal Bragonier, Jr., and David Fisher
A&M	Dennis Aaberg and John Milius		BB	*Body Boarding* magazine
ABC	About.com's Guide to Surfing		BBD	Brian Baird
			BBR	Bernie Baker
AC	Aqua Culture Surf Shop		BC	*Beach Culture* magazine
ADW	Lorrin Andrews		BH	Bob Hasier and Company
AHD2	*The American Heritage Dictionary*, 2nd Ed.		BHP	Katherine Bishop
			BHT	Bob Hightower
AHK	Arthur H. Klein		BLT	Brock Little
AJM	Anthony James Misner		BMS	Ben Marcus
ALN	Matt Allen		BNJ	Benjah
ASKC	Australian Surfing Kit Company		BP	Bob Penuelas
			BSM	Brad Smith
ASL	Australia's *Surfing Life* magazine		BTV	Bob Travis
			C&M	Richard Chester & McCall
ATRL	Ad the Rad Lad		CC	Corky Carroll
B	*Breakout* magazine		CCRG	*California Coastal Resource Guide*

CGL	Chris Gallagher	HJP	Hal Jepsen
CSD	Ted Cassidy	IBN	I. B. Nelson
CVG	Carlos Vidal Greth	IDSM	*The Illustrated Discography of Surf Music*
DBF	Dick Banfield		
DD	Dr. Dume		
DDN	Dennis Dragon	J	Gerry Chalmers
DKM	Drew Kampion	JARR	Phill Jarratt
DM	Desmond Muirhead	JB	Jennifer Blowdryer
DPL	Denny Plyer	JDH	James D. Hart
DS	Drew Steele	JGD	Jay Gould
DSHJ	D. S. Halacy, Jr.	JGM	John Grissim
DSM	Deanne Stillman	JHM	Jared Hermann
DSN	Douglas Simonson	JJV	John Javna
DWK	Dave Kinstle	JKMJ	John M. Kelly, Jr.
ECN	Ellen Nachtigall	JMZ	Julie Moniz
EF	Eric Fairbanks	JP	Jon Pine
ELK	Elkins	JPD	Jack Pollard
ELN	Eric Partridge	JRN	Joe Ryan
EPZ	Eric Penzower	JRW	James R. Walker
ESM	*The Endless Summer* movie	JWN	Jos Walton
		KAH	Kevin Ascher
EWY	Ernest Weekley	KH	Keith Hunter
F&H	Ben Finney and James D. Houston	KSO	Ken Seino
		KTD	Karen T. Delgadillo
FLD	Paul Feldman	L&L	Brian J. Lowdon and Margaret Lowdon
GCD	George Colendich		
GFF	Gary Fairmont R. Filosa II	LH	Lisa Hybarger
GN	Greg Noll	LJE	Lawrence J. England
GS	*Groundswell* magazine	LMY	Lemay
GSM	*Golden Summer* record album	LMZ	*Local* magazine
		LP	Laura Platt
GTM	Grady Timmons	LRI	Lisa Roselli
GTV	Greg Travers	LWK	Tony Litwak
GVS	Don Groves	MBR	Mark Barbour
H&R	Harold Hawkins and Tony Ramarez	MCR	Mac Reed
		MDF	Mary Duffy

MF	Midget Farrelly	RBQ	Robbie Quine
MFM	Marcy Fleming	RBS	Rich Bass
MGE	Matt George	RC	R.C.
MHG	Paul McHugh	RDTW	Ric D. T. Wilson
MLI	Mike Locatelli	RG	Rob Gilley
MM	Mitch McKissick	RHD	*Random House Dictionary*
MMN	Michael Martin	RJS	R. Jones
MNL	Margaret Nicholson	RMN	Runman
MON	Margot O'Neill	RMYN	Dave Romyn
MPN	Mike Peterson	RO	Ron Ortron
MPZ	M. Paskowitz	RPD	Rusty Preisendorfer
MSO	Marcel Soros	RPM	Rosemary Prem
MVA	Michael V. Anderson	RSM	Richard Schmidt
MW	Mark Warren	S&C	David H. Stern and
MWV	*Making Waves* newsletter		William S. Cleary
NAT	Nat Young	S&S	Ken Suiso and Rell Sunn
NHF	Noah Franzblau	SAB	Sunny Abberton
NHMLA	Natural History Museum	SBT	Steve Barilotti
	of Los Angeles County	SCSM	Santa Cruz Surfing Museum
NTS	Non Travis	SFG	*Surfing* magazine
NWT	*New West* magazine	SFR	*Surfer* magazine
OA	*Ocean Almanac*	SGE	Sam George
OED	*Oxford English Dictionary*	SHS	Steven H. Scheuer
P	Paco	SJN	Dr. Scott Jenkins
P&E	Mary Kawena Pukui	SLS	Dennis Salles
	and Samuel Elbert	SMH	Lynn Smith
PDX	Peter Dixon	SP	Surf Punks
PHL	Phil Hellsten	SS	*Sick Surfers Ask The*
PJN	Paul Johnson		*Surf Docs . . .*
PMO	Pamelo Munro	STM	Shaun Tomson
PPJ	P.J.	SW	*Surfing World* magazine
PT	Peter Townsend	SWH	Steven White
PZ	The Pizz	TBB	The Beach Boys
R&D	Rich & Dunc	TDW	Todd Wolf
R&F	Riche Maile and Felix Alfaro	THR	*Thrasher* magazine
RA	Rick Abbott	TJ	Todd Jacobs

TLH	Tex and Lynn Haines	W&B	Tom Wegener and Bill Burke
TMA	Tamara Lipper	WB	Willard Bascom
TMN	Thomson	WCH	Will Church
TRKS	*Tracks* magazine	WLK	Richard Wolkomir
TRN	Tim Ryan	WS	Ward Smith
TWS	*Transworld Surf* magazine	WSF	*Wind Surf* magazine
UTB	*Under the Boardwalk* movie	WVS	Wavescape, South Africa
VAB	Victor Abubo	WW	Woody Woodworth
W	*Waves* magazine	WWK	Wayne Warwick

Santa Cruz
Photo: Trevor Cralle

2000 Jupiter Noseriders
Jupiter, Florida
Photo: Jupiter Noseriders

aaaahooo! or **ahoooooo!** or **AWOOO!**
1) A surfer's hoot or scream when up and riding on a wave. **2)** A yell of encouragement when watching another surfer get a hot ride. (CC) **3)** A call to signal others that an outside wave or set of waves is approaching. **4) aawh wooo!** A scream of appreciation; a mating call of sorts. (MVA)

abb *n.* An abnormal person; same as KOOK. See GO-ABB. (San Diego; MVA)

abbreviated surfing placenames:
Here are just a few of the many shortened names for surf spots that surfers have come up with.

Año = Año Nuevo

Costa = Costa Rica

Diego = San Diego

El Sal = El Salvador

Indo = Indonesia

Mav's = Maverick's

Mendo = Mendocino

Mex = Mexico

Newps = Newport Beach ("Doing scoops in Newps")

Puerto = Puerto Escondido, aka Mexican Pipeline

San Dog = San Diego

above the peak *adv.* A position along the line of the swell, with the breaking wave in front of you. Usage: "I took off above the peak."

accelerate (out of a turn) *v.* To gain maximum speed off a bottom turn in order to climb up the wave face.
—acceleration *n.*

accelerator *n.* In surfboard construction, a material used in conjunction with a catalyst to produce and hasten the internal heat reaction in the liquid resin; part of the curing process. The accelerator used in most polyester resins for fiberglass work is cobalt naphthanate, usually referred to as "cobalt." Almost all resins sold today already contain the required amount of accelerator. (ORB)

accessory man *n.* A guy who always has all the unnecessary accessories like a visor, webbed gloves, multicolored long-sleeve rashguards (under suit), reef walkers, and more—depending on the day. Usage: "Look at accessory man today. He's got everything but the kitchen sink. Oh wait, that's airbrushed on the bottom of his egg." (TWS)

acetone *n.* A highly flammable and extremely toxic cleaning solvent most commonly used to dissolve uncured or uncatalyzed resin from tools and clothing. (ORB)

ache, aching *v.* How you feel after you've been hammered by a wave.

acid drop *n.* Dropping into a wave and having the bottom suddenly fall out, followed by a sense of weightlessness and helplessness. (MVA)

action *n.* Activity. *Action* is almost always used together with another word to form a unified phrase, as in "Check out the swell action."

activator *n.* ACCELERATOR

aerial *n.* **1)** Any maneuver during which the surfer and surfboard leave the water

aerial
Christian Fletcher
Photo: Robert Brown

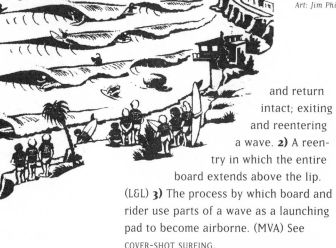

and return intact; exiting and reentering a wave. **2)** A reentry in which the entire board extends above the lip. (L&L) **3)** The process by which board and rider use parts of a wave as a launching pad to become airborne. (MVA) See COVER-SHOT SURFING.

"I think that aerials are the biggest hoax ever perpetrated on modern surfing. . . . They're just trying for aerials on every wave and they don't realize that 99.9% of the photos that they see in the magazines are flying kick-outs."

—*Shaun Tomson (L&L)*

---

aeriollo *n.* A bodyboarding maneuver similar to an el rollo, but executed in a tube.

A-frame barrel *n.* The peeling peak of a wave that pitches out in front of itself, offering left and right tube rides—a wave that goes both ways. Usage: "It was all A-frames." See GARAGED, HOUSES, SHACKED, THROWIN' THE TOOLS IN THE SHED.

afteredge *n.* The trailing edge of a fin.

aggressive *adj.* Said of a surfer who displays a forceful riding style. Usage: "He's really aggressive in the water."

aggro *adj.* **1)** Australian slang for aggressive behavior, usually aggression in the water. (NAT, 1985). **2)** A cross between

aggressive and aggravated. Usage: "That guy looks pretty aggro out there." (JP)

aggrobatics *n.* An aggressive surfing style linked with aerials.

aided forward 360 *n.* A bodyboarding maneuver where the rider spins the board around a full 360 degrees on the wave. The move is initiated by digging a hand into the water. (BB, December 1990)

aided reverse 360 *n.* A bodyboarding maneuver where the rider spins the board 360 degrees back into the advancing wave. (BB, December 1990)

air *n.* **1)** As in "getting air" or "catching air" on a surfboard or bodyboard. See AERIAL. **2)** The vibes in the air. See BAD AIR, GOOD AIR.

airbrush *n.* An artist's tool for applying detailed color to a surfboard—be it fade, graphic, or mural—to create airbrushed art. (MVA)

air buds *n.* Amped up shortboarders.

air drop *n.* Free falling down the face of a wave during a ride. See ACID DROP, ELEVATOR DROP.

air-inhibited resin *n.* A resin that will not completely cure, or set up, in the presence of air. Polyester resin that does not contain wax is classed as "air inhibited." (ORB)

air surfing *n.* Skydiving with feet strapped to a board. Also called SKY SURFING.

alaia board *n.* An ancient Hawaiian board for bodysurfing. (DM)

Aleutian juice *n.* Massive swells originating from the Gulf of Alaska.

all-time *adj., adv.* Great, fantastic, the most, exceptional, the best, primo, first-quality, without equal. Usage: "That was an all-time classic ride."

all-time hooter *n.* An exceptionally good surfer party. (A&M)

all-timer's disease *n.* An affliction that causes surfers to overstate the quality of the surf or overemphasize the radicalness of their surfing ability. Symptoms of all-timer's are wide eyes, arms held far apart, a constantly nodding head, a protruding wagging tongue, and overuse of the word *full-on.* (Santa Cruz and Hawaii; SFR, March 1990)

aloha The Hawaiian word that extends the warmth, friendliness, and pride of the Hawaiian people to their islands' visitors. It has several meanings:

1) Hello. **2)** Welcome. **3)** Good-bye. Usage: "If I'd hit my head on that reef, it would have been aloha." **4)** Love. **5)** A salutation used by surfers everywhere. (GFF) **6)** A feeling toward something, an attitude that reflects the generous feelings implicit in the word *aloha,* as in "the spirit of aloha" or "the aloha spirit."

—aloooohaaaa

aloha print *n.* Fabric used in the production of aloha (Hawaiian) shirts, dresses, etc. Patterns traditionally include such elements as hibiscus flowers, coconut palm trees, outrigger canoes, hula dancers, volcanoes, surfers, waves, drums, parrots, pineapples, islands, or abstract images. Also called HAWAIIAN PRINT.

aloha shirt *n.* The uniform of many surfers. See HAWAIIAN SHIRT.

amp, amper *n.* Someone who's too stoked to surf.

amped, over-amped, amped out *adj., adv.* Overdoing it, overenergetic, making loud or sudden movements. Usage: "This spot is totally amped out."

amped up *adv.* Excited; stoked. Of all the *amp* words, this is the only one with a positive connotation. Usage: "I was so amped up after that ride."

angle, angling *v.* To ride to the right or left across the face of a wave or toward the shoulder of a wave, rather than straight toward the beach. The term *angling* was very popular in the 1940s and 1950s and is still used occasionally.

angle off *v.* To gradually descend the face of a wave toward the right or left. (ORB)

angular 757 fin *n.* A fin with straight, rather than curved, edges and corners, which causes the water to break away cleanly. Same as STRAIGHT-EDGE FIN.

animal *n.* Someone with an aggressive approach to surfing. In the 1960s Nat Young gained the nickname "The Animal."

ankle slapper *n.* A wave that is barely ridable.

ankle strap *n.* A Velcro fastener that secures the surf leash to the ankle. Same as LEASH CUFF.

Anybody home? What you say when paddling out, meaning,"Are there any sharks in the water?" (derived from a Greg Noll story in Hawaii)

"Any waves?" First question a surfer asks another surfer.

aqua boot *n.* Vomiting into the ocean; same as TALKING TO THE SEALS. (LWK)

arc 1) *v.* To turn in an arc-shaped line on a wave. (NAT) **2)** *n.* The line of a turn on a wave.

arch *n.* A back bend used mainly in turns. Also called SOUL ARCH.

arctic *adj.* Used to describe water that is so cold your fingers curl shut and you can't paddle. (P)

arm-dance *n.* The waving of the arms out the car windows on the way to the surf in order to conjure the waves. (South Australia; R&D) See HIGHWAY HAND SURFING.

artificial blonde *n.* A male or female with unnaturally blonde hair from bleach, lemon juice, etc. See PEROXIDE.

Artificial Kookmeyer *n.* A secret spot on the west side of Santa Cruz where you can stand under ocean spray beneath a rock formation and get land tubed. Usage: "Let's go get kooked" or "Kookmeyered."

artificial reef, artificial surfing reef *n.* An underwater structure, such as a pile of cement blocks, used to create waves.

The world's first permanent artificial surfing reef is planned to be constructed off the Ventura County coast at Emma Wood State Beach. When surfing areas are in danger of being spoiled by coastal developers, a reef project can sometimes serve as a bargaining chip to compensate displaced surfers. (FLD)

artificial wave pool *n.* wave pool.

ASP Association of Surfing Professionals, the international organization that oversees surf competitions in the World Tour.

Begun in 1982, the ASP's founding members, led by Ian Cairns, saw the need for standardized criteria that would give consistency to the World Tour. They put together a brief but comprehensive statement: "The surfer who executes the most radical maneuvers in the most critical section of the biggest waves for the longest distance shall be deemed the winner." Note: This rule was amended prior to the 1985–86 season. (L&L) See surfing criteria.

Julie Bennett
Kauai, Hawaii
Photo: Grant Bennett

asphalt surfer *n.* Another name for SKATEBOARDER. The phrase appeared in The Beach Boys' song "It's a Beautiful Day" in the movie *Americathon* (1979). See SKATEBOARDING.

asshole *n.* Everyone else in the water.

Association of Surfing Professionals See ASP.

asymmetrical surfboard *n.* First made by Carl Ekstrom in 1964. See ASYMMETRICAL TAIL.

asymmetrical tail *n.* A surfboard having two different tail shapes to allow for changes in wave conditions; essentially, two boards in one.

ate it *v.* See EAT IT.

atoll *n.* A coral island or group of islands encircling or nearly encircling a lagoon; common throughout the South Pacific. Also called CORAL ATOLL.

Aussie *n.* Someone from Australia; an Australian.

Australia A continent southeast of Asia, between the Indian and Pacific oceans, with a major surfing population. Also called DOWN UNDER or OZ.

Surfing was introduced to Australia at Freshwater Beach, Sydney, in 1915 by Hawaiian Duke Kahana-moku. In 1956 Greg Noll and a few others visited Australia from the United States, taking along some surfing films and boards; their trip became the basis for the modern surfboard movement in Australia. (GN) The Australians are generally credited with the development of the Shortboard Revolution.

Australian Grand Slam *n.* A series of professional surfing competitions, comprised of contests at Burleigh Heads, Bell's Beach, and Narrabeen (near Sydney). See HAWAIIAN TRIPLE CROWN.

avalanche *n.* **1)** What the white water looks like pouring down the face of a wave. **2) Avalanche** An outer reef surf spot on Oahu, Hawaii.

awesome *adj.* **1)** Great, fantastic, as in "totally awesome." **2)** Implying great respect for a given situation or physical achievement. (MVA)

axe *n.* The lip of a wave. "To be given the axe" is to get smacked in the face by a wave.

axed *v.* To be knocked off the surfboard by the wave's lip; a hatchet job. (MVA) **—axed by the lip** Getting smacked by the lip of a wave. (Santa Cruz)

Aye Carumba! (eye-ka-RUM-bah) **1)** A Spanish exclamation meaning, "Wow!" or "Shit!" **2)** What you say when you see a really good-looking person. **3)** What TV cartoon character Bart Simpson utters when he's upside down on a wave.

baby gun or **baby-gun** *n.* A miniboard with big-gun shape characteristics.

back *n.* The backside of a wave.

back attack *n.* A bodysurfing take-off lying on one's back.

backdoor *n.* **1)** A maneuver in which the surfer takes off to one side of or behind the peak in order to traverse the section of the wave where the lip will throw first. **2) going backdoor** *v.* An expression used to describe situations where a surfer is forced to pull into an already pitching barrel from behind the peak. (MW) **3) Backdoor** *n.* A surf spot on the North Shore of Oahu, Hawaii.

back down *v.* To withdraw from a position or commitment, for instance to decide not to take off on a wave. This choice was illustrated in the song "Don't Back Down" by The Beach Boys, which featured the lyrics "Don't back down from that wave."

backhand turn *n.* A turn made with one's back to the wave; the opposite of a forehand turn.

backing off *n.* **1)** The sudden flattening of waves as they move over deeper water, for example over a channel between sandbars (A&B) **2)** A wave action that occurs when a large wave decreases quickly in size. (MM) **3)** The way a wave will flatten out when water depth increases, and then break again inshore. (RA) See BACK OFF, HUNTINGTON HOP.

backlash *n.* A wave action occurring in areas where the depth is uniform.

back off *v.* **1)** When a wave breaks once and then becomes unbroken green water again. **2)** When a wave breaks and then reforms, the white water having "backed off." **3)** When a wave abruptly subsides ("backs off") as it moves into a deep-water trough after crossing an off-shore bar or reef. See RE-FORM. **4)** To change one's mind just prior to takeoff and hold back.

back out, backing out 1) *v.* To pull back rather than continue into a wave that could have been caught; to sit back on the board. **2) backout** *n.* The act of terminating an attempted takeoff by sitting up.

backpaddle or **back-paddle** *v.* When a surfer decides not to take off and backstrokes with the arms to keep from being sucked over the falls.

backpedal or **back-pedal** *v.* To walk backward, foot over foot, from the nose toward the rear of the surfboard. (A&M)

backside *adv.* **1)** Riding with one's back to the wave. (ORB) **2)** To be positioned on a board so that one is turned away from the wave face when riding. **3)** From the surfer's standpoint (while facing the beach), going right with the right foot forward or going left with the left foot forward. (MVA) Usage: "I saw you went backside on that last ride."

backside layback *n.* Leaning backward while surfing with one's back to the wave; sometimes performed in the tube.

backside off the top, backside off the lip *adv.* Turning a surf-

board off the lip of a wave with one's back to the sea.

backside rail grab *n.* Holding the outside rail while going backside in order to keep riding in the mid-face of a wave. See PIG DOG.

backsiders *n.* Surfers who put their right foot forward. See GOOFY FOOT, SCREW FOOT.

backside snap *n.* An intermediate bodyboarding maneuver. (BB) See SNAP.

backspray *n.* Spray picked up from a breaking wave and blown back over the wave by offshore winds; sometimes stings your face.

backup waves *n.* The term competitive surfers use for lower-quality waves that may come at the beginning or end of a set, or merely at random intervals on days when the sets are not well defined; as distinct from SET WAVES. (L&L)

backwash *n.* **1)** Water running rapidly off the beach from a broken wave and frequently colliding in the shallows with incoming water; generally happens on a steep beach. **2)** A wave bounced back out to sea from a steep shoreline. (A&B, ORB) **3)** A wave returning to the ocean after crashing on the beach. (MM)

A backwash may cause a current to run out from the beach; when timed properly it can be used to carry a surfer out into the lineup. It normally occurs at high tide. (MVA)

bad air *n.* The atmosphere created by people who invade your space or burst your bubble. See VIBE. (MVA)

bad-o *adj.* **1)** Describes a surfer with a hipper-than-thou attitude. (CVG). **2)** Really cool. (PZ)

bag, bag it *v.* To quit doing something, get lazy, or take a break. Usage: "I was surfing almost every day last month, but this week I bagged." (SFG, December 1981)

baggies or **baggys** *n.* Large, oversized, loose-fitting, boxer-type swim trunks that are considerably longer in the legs than regular surf shorts and are worn by surfers for show or comfort; usually made of Hawaiian print. (IDSM)

baguio (bah-GHEE-o) *n.* A typhoon or tropical cyclone in the Philippines. See HURRICANE.

bail *v.* **1)** To abandon a ride, usually by diving or jumping off the board. Usage: "I fully bailed." **2)** To leave a place. Usage: "I'm bailing." "Let's bail." **3)** To get out of a current spot or situation. Usage: "How bay. Let's bail this place." (MVA)

bail out 1) *v.* To intentionally get away from, jump off or dive off the surfboard in the face of a coming wipeout in order to avoid getting creamed by a section. **2) bailing out** *n.* When a surfer decides it's time to abandon ship; a survival tactic. (IDSM, A&M) —**bailout** *n.*

"Bail, roach." "Get outta here, kook." (Santa Cruz)

bait wave *n.* See CHASER WAVE.

Baja (BAH-ha) Baja (lower) California, Mexico, a major surf destination for California surfers. See MEXICO.

Baja Bug *n.* A Volkswagen Beetle modified into a surf vehicle; fully equipped for driving off-road on surf trips.

Baja pullover *n.* Classic 1980s long-sleeve hooded surf fashion from Mexico.

bake *n.* **1)** Someone from Bakersfield in California's Central Valley. Usage: "What a bake." **2) full bake** Said of a bake—there's no hope for change. (San Luis Obispo; SWH)

baked *adj.* **1)** Stoned, lit. Nicely high, feeling no pain. Right on the crest. Altered state of mind requiring assistance in functioning, socially hampered. Difficulty operating heavy machinery. Feeling so good that you don't want it to change, but you may also have a complete acceptance of the change going on. Usage: "Man, I'm really baked." **2)** SUNBURNED. **3)** Can also be used to describe someone who's not too bright. See SURFING IN NEBRASKA.

balls to the wall Surfing up against the wall of a huge wave. (CSD)

balsa board, balsa-wood board *n.* A surfboard made of balsa wood.

Balsa wood was first used in surfboards by Lorrin Thurston of Hawaii in 1926. The balsa-wood surfboard built in the early 1930s was laminated with spruce or redwood and weighed sixty pounds.

In the early 1940s the all-balsa board was developed, weighing about forty pounds; balsa strips were added to the mold for reinforcement. Surfboards were constructed primarily of balsa wood from 1949 until 1957. Because boards made of balsa wood were lighter, more people were able to get into surfing.

balsa wood (*Ochroma lagopus*) *n.* A soft, lightweight, porous wood found mainly in Ecuador and parts of tropical South America. Balsa wood is designated "male" or "female" depending on weight, the female being lighter.

Balsero *n.* A person who leaves Cuba on a raft, inner tube, or any makeshift combination.

bamboo board, bamboo surfboard *n.* Instead of fiberglass, shaper/inventor Gary Young from Hawaii and Aussie shaper Frank McWilliams took multiple slivers of bamboo (the strongest natural material on earth and extremely light), and vacuum-wrapped it around a stringerless board, with an extruded closed-cell styrene foam core. The board is finished off with epoxy resin and features unbelievable flex properties. (SFR, April 2000)

Baja pullover
Port-O-Kinst
Playa El Coyote, Baja
Photo: Trevor Cralle

Baja Bug
Art: I.B. Nelson

barney
Numero Uno
La Fortuna, Baja Sur
Photo: Trevor Cralle

banana *n.* ROCKER.

bananabender *n.* A surfboard shape with exaggerated rocker. (Australia; W#8)

bank 1) *n.* An Australian term for SAND-BANK. **2)** *v.* To use white water as a pivot point for directional changes. (MVA)
—**banking** *n.*

bank turn *n.* A carving turn, rolling the board along on one rail or edge. (A&M)
—**bank a turn** *v.*

Banzai! 1) A Japanese cheer or war cry adopted by surfers in the early 1960s. **2)** A gung-ho type of yell given by surfers as they shoot the curl. (IDSM)

Banzai Pipeline A surf spot on the North Shore of Oahu, Hawaii. See PIPELINE.

Barbie, Barbie doll *n.* A plastic doll with an hourglass figure, produced by Mattel Toys in Southern California since 1959. The term is applied to girls with figures or intellects like the doll's. See MALIBU BARBIE.

bare back *adv.* Surfing without a wetsuit; same as TRUNK IT or SKIN IT. Usage: "I went out there bare back today."

barefoot *n.* Normal operating condition preferred by surfers.

barge *n.* An extremely heavy or large surfboard.

barn *n.* A California term for BARNEY.

barnaby *n.* BARNEY.

barnacle *n.* **1)** Someone who is better off sticking to the rocks; same as KOOK or GEEK. (Florida; TDW) **2)** A sharp, rock-encrusting marine organism, which surfers have to negotiate while climbing around rocky coastlines.

barnacle face *n.* OLD SURFER. (Santa Cruz)

barnacopia *n.* A full slew of barneys at the beach.

barnage *n.* Messed up situation. Usage: "What's up with this barnage?"
—**full barnage**

barney 1) *n.* Someone who doesn't surf very well. The term was derived from the Hanna-Barbera cartoon character Barney Rubble on "The Flintstones." Usage: "Get out of my way, ya barney." (SFG, 1989) **2)** GEEK. **3)** *v.* To act like a barney. Usage: "Look at that guy barneying all over the place." (FZ) See FRED. "Spoken like a true barney." "I barneyed so hard I forgot to vote." (P) "B-A-R, N-E-Y" (sung to the Mickey Mouse theme). "*Yo soy* barney" ("I am a barney" in Spanish). "There is *no* culinary barnage in the house." —Jason Smith "I may be a barney, but I'm not Barneyer than thou."—Paco in Baja, 1993

"The '60s 'ho-dad' turned into the '70s 'geek,' who evolved into the '80s 'dweeb.' Today, the put-down of choice is 'barney.' The tourist with the farmer tan and the plastic Party Animal sun visor? Barney. The overzealous kid who cut you off on the best wave of the morning? Little barney. The frat boy who errantly winged a frisbee off the back of your head, interrupting your nap and spilling half your Miller

40

barney cuts *n.* Sharp cuts from barnacles. Usually acquired from exiting the surf via the rocks. (Santa Cruz)

barney log *n.* A piece of firewood that really smokes. (Baja 1993)

barney mobile *n.* Hoopty car.

Barneyo *n.* The homeland of all barneys.

barnita, barnica *n.* Female barney.

barnyard *n.* A derivation of BARNEY—an unskilled or uncool surfer. (Central Florida). Usage: "Why does the swell always come up on weekends? The Inlet was just crawling with barnyards yesterday." —Matt Kechele (SFR) **—barnyard barney**

barometer *n.* An instrument for determining the pressure of the atmosphere; used for judging how the weather and wind will be on any particular day. A change of one-tenth of one degree can mean that a high or low is moving in, accompanied by a major change in weather. (W&B)

barrel 1) *n.* A 1980s term used to describe the breaking motion of a perfect wave; same as PIPE (1960s) and TUBE (1970s). (MW) **2)** A hollow channel formed inside a good wave when it breaks and curls over, as in "wide-open barrel," "pitching barrel," or "sunlit barrel." Surfers crouch down and ride inside the barrel. (JP) **3) get barreled** *v.* To GET TUBED. Usage: "Yeah it was all barreling and everything." (Surfside local, 1990s)

barrel roll *n.* An inverted maneuver made with a bodyboard (or boogie board), using the curling wave to roll with. See EL ROLLO.

barrelitious (barrel-LISH-shish) *adj.* Tasty tubes.

barrelitis 1) Going so long without getting barreled you go into the state of "barrelitis." Characterized by a blank stare, depression, lack of appetite, and the inexplicable desire to go to church. **2)** Getting barreled so many times to the point of exhaustion. (Tavarua, Fiji)

barrier beach *n.* A long, narrow beach created by wave action and separated from the mainland by a lagoon, bay, or river mouth. (CCRG)

bash, bashing *v.* To slam into a wave. See LIP BASH.

basic drop-in rule *n.* See DROP-IN RULE.

bay 1) *n.* A partially enclosed inlet of the ocean. (CCRG) **2)** *adj.* A term applied to the ocean itself when surfers are not satisfied with wave size; indicates a lack of action. Usage: "How bay." (San Diego; MVA)

Bay, the *n.* WAIMEA BAY.

beach *n.* **1)** The spiritual center of the universe, according to surfers. (JARR) **2)** The spot where terrestrial activities take place. **3)** Where surfers like to hang out. **4)** An accumulation of rock fragments subject

barnita
Playa El Coyote, Baja
Photo: Trevor Cralle

barrel
Art: Rick Stover

to movement by ordinary wave action. **5)** Dynamic landform altered by wind and waves in a continual process of creation and erosion. See SANDBAR.

The beach extends seaward as far as ordinary waves move sand particles, or about thirty feet below the low tide level; it extends landward to the edge of the permanent coast, which can be a cliff, sand dunes, or an artificial structure. (WB)

Seasonal cycles of sand deposition and loss dramatically affect the appearance of beaches from summer to winter (the beach profile). Wide and gently sloping in summer, they become steep-fronted and narrow in winter and can vanish overnight, stripped of sand by violent storm waves; most of the sand removed from winter beaches is deposited in offshore sandbars and is returned to the beach by gentle swells during the mild summer months. (CCRG)

beach anxiety n. Not feeling comfortable at the beach for any number of reasons, as in "I have ocean issues." For example, some people are self-conscious about wearing a swimsuit at the beach, or they can't swim, or they're afraid of

sharks, or they sunburn easily, etc. See JAWS, WAVE ANXIETY.

beach babe n. BEACH GIRL.

beach berm n. BERM.

beach betty n. BEACH GIRL.

beach bomber n. A bicycle with fat balloon tires and wide handlebars. Also called BEACH CRUISER or RAY.

beach bonfire n. Often made from driftwood gathered on the beach. A place to TALK STORY.

beachboy or **beach boy** n. **1)** Historically, someone whose livelihood is derived from surfing instruction and outrigger-canoe rides. **2)** Someone who spends time at the beach. **3)** In general, a boy or man who works at the beach. **4)** A male beach attendant (as at a club or hotel). (W9, 1939)

The first beachboy is thought to have appeared at Waikiki on Oahu, Hawaii, soon after the first major resort hotel was completed in 1901. At that time, surfing and outrigger canoeing were in great decline, and the beachboys were largely responsible for reviving these two Hawaiian watersports. (GTM)

"John ('Hawkshaw') Paia could take a ukulele, a chair, and a surfboard, catch a wave, set up the chair, and play the ukulele as he rode in toward the beach."

—Grady Timmons, Waikiki Beachboy (1989)

beach
Monastir, Tunisia
Photo: David Wilson

Pacifica, California
Photo: Trevor Cralle

Beach Boys, The A popular rock music group from Southern California led by Brian Wilson, which, since 1961, has been instrumental in the spread of surfing culture to the rest of the world. Through their song lyrics, they have popularized the California Myth as well as the geography of Californian and Hawaiian surf spots ("All over La Jolla and Waimea Bay . . . Everybody's going surfing!") Drummer Dennis Wilson was the only member of the group who actually surfed.

beach break or **beach-break** or **beach-break** *n.* **1)** Waves breaking on a sand bottom or sandbank in close to the beach, rather than out on the reefs. Powerful beachbreaks include Puerto Escondido in Southern Mexico and Dominical in Costa Rica. Same as SHORE BREAK. **2)** A wide, hot-dog-shaped board designed for small fast waves breaking near the beach.

beach brolly *n.* Australian term for a beach umbrella.

beach bum *n.* A derogatory term for someone who hangs around the beach.

beach bunny or **beach bunnie** *n.* A girl who goes to the beach to watch surfing, usually a nonsurfer or a beginner. Also called SURF BUNNY.

beach chair *n.* Lightweight, fold-up aluminum "lawn chair."

beach coat *n.* GREMMIE COAT.

beachcomber *n.* **1)** Someone who searches the beach for shells and driftwood and other goodies washed up by the sea. **2)** A person who lives on what can be found on beaches or in wharf areas. **3)** A long wave rolling in toward the beach. (AHD2) See COMBER.

beach cruiser or **beach cruizer** *n.* A balloon-tired bicycle. Same as BEACH BOMBER or RAY.

beach dog *n.* A special breed of dog, able to fetch a frisbee or a driftwood stick from the shallows of foamy broken surf; usually an Irish setter or golden retriever with a red bandanna tied around its neck and answering to a name like "Storm" or "Sandy." Same as SURF DOG. See SOGNAR.

beached *adj.* Totally stuffed from eating. Usage: "I'm so beached, I can't move."

beached whale *n.* A derogatory term for an obese male or female. Also called WHALE.

beach etiquette *n.* How to act in a mannerly fashion on the sand and not come off as a complete idiot. An extremely simple skill to develop that includes things like shaking your beach towel off down wind and away from people so the sand doesn't get in their eyes. See also SURF ETIQUETTE.

beach girl *n.* Used to describe an attractive female who clearly lives at or near the beach.

beach girl blonde *adj.* Same as SURFER BLONDE.

beach grem *n.* GROMMET. See GREMMIE.

beachhead *n.* Anyone who hangs around the beach.

The Beach Boys
Brian Wilson
Photo: Rolling Stone

beach house *n.* A surfer's house; usually built right on the beach or within a few blocks of it.

The ocean crashed into the beach again and again, always there behind the music and talk. Its salty smell wafted through the room like a ghost of the ocean, never quite replacing the smell of brewski and of the room itself.

—*Mel Gilden,* Surfing Samurai Robots *(1988)*

beach language *n.* SURF LINGO.

beach law *n.* An area of legal study. See COASTAL ACCESS.

beach party *n.* **1)** A nighttime gathering on the sand, usually with a fire, maybe with somebody playing a guitar, a little drinking and dancing, etc. Popularized in Hollywood surfing movies in the sixties. **2) "Beach Party"** The title song from the first American International Pictures (AIP) beach party flick featuring the former Mouseketeer, Annette Funicello, who was Frankie Avalon's girlfriend in the series. (GSM)

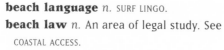

beach party
Adam Ridge and Jason Smith
Playa El Coyote, Baja
Photo: Trevor Cralle

beach party
Maybeck posse
Beach conga in session
Bahia de Los Angeles, Baja
Photo: Trevor Cralle

beach party films *n.* A genre of motion pictures made in the sixties. The title of the first such movie, *Beach Party* (1963), was given to numerous other films produced by several companies. All featured teenage romances on Southern California beaches, where the protagonists were untroubled by parents, school, and most of the realities of life. (JDH)

beach profile *n.* The distribution of sand on a beach and its slope relative to the water. The amount of sand deposited and stripped away changes with the seasons. See BEACH.

beach towel *n.* A huge, colorful terry cloth towel, sometimes striped, that you lay down on at the beach. Not a washcloth, hand towel, or a bath towel; we're talkin' mega-sized.

beach volleyball *n.* A team sport usually played with double partners on a sand court.

beach wagon *n.* A station wagon. (W9, 1935) See WOODY.

beachwear *n.* **1)** Casual clothes. **2)** Boardshorts, bikinis, etc.

beach whistle *n.* A plastic tampon inserter that's washed up on the beach. Usage: "Making a sandcastle is more fun if you decorate it with beach whistles." (TWS, September 1999)

beachy *adj.* **1)** Used to describe anything pertaining to the beach environment, as in "beachy feeling." Usage: "That girl has really beachy hair."

beads up *v.* What surf wax does when it is rubbed evenly on the deck of a surf-

board. The "beads" refer to the small scabs formed by the wax, which give good traction.

beard *n.* **1)** An older surfer. **2)** Someone with ten-year-old surf equipment, a beard, and a hood. (San Luis Obispo; SWH)

beat *adj.* **1)** Used to describe undesirable waves. Usage: "The water's really beat today." (JP) **2)** Feeling worn, not too good. Usage: "Man, I'm feeling mighty beat today." (MVA)

beat a section 1) *v.* To cut ahead of a breaking section of a wave. **2) beating a section** *n.* A scoring move in a surfing contest; same as MAKING A SECTION. Usage: "She received extra points for beating a section."

beaver tail or **beavertail, beavertail wetsuit** *n.* A wetsuit that features a snap-on crotch, the shape of which resembles a beaver's tail. Worn unsnapped—as surfers always wear it—it hangs down like a beaver tail, hence the name. Popular in the 1960s to mid-1970s and now completely out of style.

beef *n.* **1)** What happens when you eat it really bad. Usage (while watching a surf video): "Dude, check out these hot beefs." (LH) **2)** Hawaiian Pidgin for "fight"; as in "You like beef?" or "You won fo' beef?"

beer *n.* The ever-present alcoholic beverage. Löwenbrau is called a LOWIE; Heineken is a HEINI or, in Australia, a GREENIE IN A BOTTLE. (PZ) See PRIMO BEER.

behemoth wave *n.* HUGE MONOLITH.

behind the peak *adv.* ABOVE THE PEAK.

belloomer *n.* A type of bellyboard popular in Australia.

belly *n.* A convex bottom contour of a surfboard. (ORB)

bellyboard or **belly board** *n.* A small surfboard used primarily to ride the waves on your stomach, but it can also be ridden kneeling or standing. (MF) Same as PAIPO BOARD.

bellyboarding *n.* Bodysurfing with the aid of a planing device, such as a small hand-held kickboard or surfboard.

belly rash *n.* BOARD RASH. (Hawaii 1991)

belly surfing, belly womping *n.* BODYSURFING.

bend *v.* The motion characteristic of a wave as it wraps around a point. Usage: "Look at the swell bend."

benny *n.* A person who dresses in the latest surf fashions and is hip on all the local surf lingo, but neither owns a surfboard nor knows how to surf. (New Jersey, NHF, 1985)

Bergwind *n.* A hot dry wind that blows offshore from land to sea on the cusp of winter in South Africa. On the west coast, it blows from the northeast. On the east coast it blows from the north or northwest. Nothing is better than a deep, distant ground swell textured into glassy perfection by a light Bergwind. (WVS)

berm *n.* The steep part of the beach near the water's edge. (A&M) Same as BEACH BERM.

beating a section
Art: I. B. Nelson

betty *n.* An attractive female. Derived from Betty Rubble, a character on *The Flintstones*. It has also been suggested that the term *betty* is named after the character, Betty, in Archie comics.

bettys *pl.* Usage: "Whoa, check out the bettys by the sea wall." See BEACH BETTY, LONGBOARD BETTY, NECTAR BETTY, SURF BETTY.

bicycle *n.* A stance on a surfboard with legs wide apart as though riding a bicycle. (MF)

bicycle surfboard rack *n.* A framework mounted on the rear of a bike for holding a surfboard in an upright position.

biff *v.* Falling and hitting; to get smacked by a wave. (PZ) Usage: "I got biffed on that last wave."

big air *n.* Getting some major altitude above the water. Usage: "I saw you got some big air on that last ride."

big and stormy *adj.* Large, disorganized brownish-colored surf with lots of foam.

big board *n.* LONGBOARD. "On a small board, you make the board perform. On a big board, you perform" —Buffalo Keaulana

biggest waves *n.* Of waves that have been ridden, generally defined as reaching at least the thirty-foot mark.

Of all the records and achievements in the surfing world, none sparks as much controversy as the question of who has ridden the biggest wave. Ace Cool rode a record-breaking thirty-five-foot wave at Outer Pipeline (two miles offshore) on January 5, 1985. The most well-documented big-wave nominees having reached the coveted thirty-foot mark are Buzzy Trent at Makaha, 1958; Greg Noll at Makaha, the epic swell of 1969; and Mark Foo at Waimea, in winter 1986. Only a handful of others are also in contention, among them Peter Cole and the late Eddie Aikau, who bagged thirty-footers in 1969. (SFG, April 1987)

---

big gun or **big-gun** *n.* A surfboard specially designed for large waves; originally an eleven-footer or longer.

big-headed surfer *n.* Someone who thinks he's great. (San Clemente)

Big Mama, the *n.* The ocean. (CVG)

big one, the *n.* A huge wave, as in "riding the big one."

big open face *n.* A large wall to surf across. See WAVE FACE.

big sea *n.* Large, breaking surf; high seas.

big smoker *n.* Jack London's term for a big wave at Waikiki. (1907) He also used the terms *white-headed combers*, *smoking combers*, and *bull-mouthed monsters*.

big south *n.* A large SOUTH SWELL.

big surf *n.* **1)** Extremely large waves. **2)** Waves that create a thunderous sound. See ROAR OF THE OCEAN. **3) Big Surf** The first artificial wave machine, built in

big gun
Derek Ho
Photo: John S. Callahan

big air
Flea, The Lane
Photo: Mike Peralta

Tempe, Arizona, in 1969. Also known as *The Flush*. See WAVE POOL.

big time *adv.* An intensifier roughly meaning anything in high proportions, as in "to eat it big time." (P)

big wave *n.* Large, as in "That was a big wave."

big-wave board design *n.* A design incorporating elongated rail lines and a narrow pointy nose.

big-wave climax *n.* The inevitable scene of every Hollywood surf flick, usually features the underdog and/or hero riding the big one.

big-wave day *n.* When the surf is really up.

big-wave pioneers *n.* The first individuals brave enough to ride the really big waves in Hawaii in the 1950s. George Downing was the first of the modern big-wave riders. Other veterans include José Angel, Peter Cole, Pat Curren, Ricky Grigg, Greg Noll, Mike Stange, and Buzzy Trent.

big-wave rider *n.* Someone who rides the giant surf on the North Shore of Oahu, Hawaii.

big-wave spot *n.* Such as Jaws, Maverick's, Todos Santos, Waimea Bay.

big-wave stability stance, big-wave survival stance *n.* A board position with feet spread apart but toes facing the nose of the board instead of the rail.

Big Wednesday 1) Originally a 1961 surf film by John Severson. **2)** A 1978 Hollywood movie by John Milius. **3)** A specific day in Hawaii in the 1960s when the surf was unusually large. **4)** January 28, 1998, in Hawaii.

biker *n.* Someone who wears full leathers when it's eighty degrees out. (MVA)

bikini *n.* A woman's skimpy two-piece swimsuit, introduced by France's Louis Reard on July 5, 1946, at a Paris fashion show; named after the Marshall Islands atoll, Bikini, where the first announced atomic bomb was tested. Over the years bikinis became smaller, and enterprising girls went topless and created the monokini. (SFG, November 1989) See BUTT THONG, FIO DENTAL, FLOSS.

bikini-bimbo *n.* A derogatory term for a beach girl. See DEBBIE.

bikini contest *n.* Females modeling swimsuits; sometimes featured at surf contests.

billow *n.* A large wave or ocean swell. (AHD2)

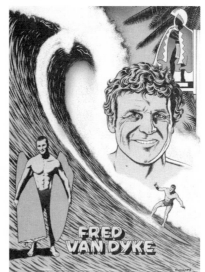

big-wave pioneer
Art: Jim Phillips

blanks
T&C factory, Hawaii
Photo: John S. Callahan

biscuit *n.* WAVE. Part of the breakfast food group of waves, as in "tasty biscuits." Usage: "Mondo biscuit," or "Dude we're getting biscuits." See SAND BISCUIT, SHARK BISCUIT.

bitchin' or **bitchin** *adj.* **1)** A fifties and sixties term for *cool* adopted by surfers; very good, tops, excellent. Usage: "That's a bitchin' surfboard." (PMO) **2)** Anything that is cherry, boss, or neat. (A&M) *Bitchin'* has now been replaced by *rad.* (MVA)

The word *bitchin'*, derived from *bitching*—as in, "Quit your bitching"—may have been coined by Dale Velzy in 1949. While surfing with the Manhattan Beach Surf Club, Velzy was overjoyed after a ride and said, "That was a bitchin' wave," giving the word new meaning and a positive connotation. *Bitchin'* is an example of adolescents' tendency to reverse the meaning of a word so that "bad" means "good," and so on.

---

bite *n.* The way in which a surfboard grabs the wave when turning.

bit surfer *n.* Computer hacker.

black *n.* See CONDITION BLACK.

black ball flag *n.* A flag with a yellow background and a solid black ball in the center, which means "no surfing" in many areas of Southern California, for instance Newport Beach. Some spots allow boogie boards and swimmers to share the same water space but not hardboards, such as a surfboard.

black tide *n.* An oil slick, such as the big Santa Barbara Channel oil spill in 1969, which contaminated more than thirty miles of beaches, and the Huntington Beach spill of 1989.

"EXXON DON'T SURF"

—*1990 California bumper sticker*

---

blank *n.* The polyester-based urethane foam core of a surfboard that the shaper starts out with when making a surfboard. (ORB) Same as FOAM BLANK.

blast 1) *v.* To come off the top of a wave with a powerful maneuver, as in "to blast off the top." **2) blast air** To CATCH AIR. **3)** *n.* A helluva good time.

bleached, bleached blonde hair *n.* **1)** What many surfers acquire naturally from

black tide
Art: Glenn Bering

spending countless hours out in the ocean surfing under the sun. **2)** Lightening of hair the artificial way. See PEROXIDE.

blend, blended lines *n.* The functional unifying of the lines of a surfboard; the FAIRING.

blind *adj.* Riding backward on a surfboard. Usage: "I rode that last one blind."

blisty (BLICE-tee) *adj.* Used to describe surfing conditions—windy, cold, choppy, gray, really big or really small waves. (Marin County, California; BH)

blocky rails *n.* Surfboard rails that have straight, rather than rounded, edges.

blondecease *n.* That moment when the last of the summer's bleached-blonde hair hits the barbershop floor. (SFG, 1990)

blowhole surf *n.* Waves breaking over holes in a lava bottom, which creates a boiling surface. (MF)

blowing *v.* Said of conditions when the wind is strong. Usage: "It was really blowing today." Same as HOWLING.

blown off *v.* What happens to surfers who are lifted by the wind right out of the wave they were riding or attempting to catch—they are literally blown off the wave.

blown out *adj.* Describes conditions when very high onshore winds are ruining the surf, causing waves to be misshaped or rippled and virtually unridable. Usage: "The surf was blown out totally." "Today it was all blown-out surf." See MUSHY.

blow off *v.* **1)** To quit doing something, to abandon it. **2)** To bail on doing something; to flake. (P)

blow-out *n.* A descriptive term for the water surface when it's so badly chopped up by local winds that the approaching ground swells are impossible to ride or are not worth riding. (DSH) See BLOWN OUT.

bluebird *n.* **1)** An extra-big set wave. (SFR, June 1989). **2) bluebirds** An old-time surfers' term for a set of blue waves on the horizon.

blue bottle *n.* PORTUGUESE MAN-OF-WAR. (Australia and New Zealand)

blue juice *n.* A big wave with a lot of energy. (PZ) See JUICE.

blue room *n.* GREEN ROOM.

"**Blue is for water
Water is for waves
Waves are for surfers
and surfers are babes!**"

—*Anonymous*

. . . the "blue room," the silent, revolving cylinder where time melts like a Dali watch.

—*Tom Stevens, The Maui News, October 1983*

Blue Water Task Force *n.* Water quality testing by surfers to keep state and federal standards in check. The program was started by the Surfrider Foundation. See MARINE WATER QUALITY INDEX.

bluff *n.* **1)** A steep headland or cliff along the coast. **2) blufftop** A good vantage point for SURF CHECKS.

board *n.* **1)** SURFBOARD. **2)** A North San Diego County term for a burrito. (LH)

board bag or **boardbag, board cover** *n.* A carrying case for a surfboard to protect it while traveling by car, airplane, camel, etc.

boardhead *n.* Someone who's really into surfing.

board hum *n.* **1)** Vibration of surfboard when riding a wave at high speeds. Caused by damage to fins or a misaligned fin. **2)** Annoying sound a surfboard sometimes makes on a roof rack when traveling in car. See STRAP WHINE.

boardies *n.* **1)** An Australian term for BOARDSHORTS. **2)** Same as SURFIES.

board jousting *n.* See SURF JOUSTING.

boardman *n.* A surfer; same as SURFMAN.

board napping *v.* Laying on your back with your head at the tail of your surfboard and soakin' up some rays while waiting for a set.

Board on Board *n.* Surf sticker on a surfer's car in response to the "Baby on Board" car stickers in the 1980s.

board rash *n.* What you get from lying on a surfboard for long periods of time. (P) Same as BELLY RASH.

board room *n.* A room in a house where surfboards are kept.—**executive board room**

boards galords *n.* Massive QUIVER.

board shape *n.* A design feature of a surfboard that can vary widely. Among the different shapes are BULLET, SPEED, STINGER, etc.

boardshorts *n.* A 1980s term for SURF SHORTS.

board sock *n.* Similar to a BOARD BAG, but no padding.

board speed *n.* The rate at which a surfboard travels over the waves. Can be affected by a number of factors, such as board design (shape and weight) and the position of the board on the wave being ridden.

board surfers *n.* As distinct from BODYSURFERS.

board-to-wave angle *n.* The angle of the surfboard relative to the steepness of the wave.

board wax *n.* SURF WAX.

boatman *n.* Waveski rider. The more affectionate term for someone who rides a PADDLE SKI. See GOATBOAT. (WVS)

boat surfing *n.* Riding the waves or a swell with such ocean crafts as kayaks, canoes, dories, and catamarans.

boat wake, boat wake surfing *n.* Using the wake of a boat to surf. The hull of a fast-moving boat can displace enough water to create ridable waves, with no towline required. All it takes is plenty of horsepower and a delicate sense of TRIM. Hobie Alter once trimmed

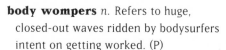

twenty-six miles to Catalina behind a boat. (SFG, April 1987) See WAKE SURFING.

bodyboard *n.* Originally a BOOGIE BOARD, but now includes soft foam boards with a hard plastic or fiberglass covering.

bodyboarder *n.* Someone who surfs using a bodyboard.

bodyboarding *n.* Riding a bodyboard in the surf. Bodyboarders originally rode lying down, but now they occasionally stand up. See BOOGIE BOARD.

bodyroll *n.* A bodysurfing maneuver first done by Buffalo Keaulana in Hawaii in the 1950s. (GN)

bodysurfer *n.* **1)** A surfer who rides the waves with the body alone; swim fins are sometimes used to help propel the bodysurfer through the wave. **2)** Someone who uses the body as a wave vehicle.

bodysurfing or **body surfing** or **body-surfing** *n.* The art of riding the waves without a surfboard, using the body as a planing surface.

Bodysurfing is considered by some to be the purest form of surfing. The sport was invented by marine mammals such as dolphins, seals, and sea lions. Unlike their marine counterparts, however, humans occasionally need to wear swim fins to help them generate enough speed to catch a wave. Three famous bodysurfing spots are Sandy Beach and Makapuu on Oahu's southeast shore in Hawaii and the Wedge at Newport Beach, California.

"I love to body surf, particularly when the water's cold; it really grounds me and wakes me up at the same time."

—*Spalding Gray, Gray's Anatomy (1993)*

---

body wompers *n.* Refers to huge, closed-out waves ridden by bodysurfers intent on getting worked. (P)

body wompin' *n.* Riding waves with the body and usually a pair of fins. Same as BODYSURFING and BELLY SURFING.

bog down, bogging down *v.* To be unable to maneuver or accelerate because of equipment design, lack of skill, or wave quality. Usage: "I was bogged down by the kelp."

bogger *n.* Someone who ends up in a spot on a wave where he or she shouldn't be.

bogulate *v.* To surf poorly. (Eastside, Santa Cruz; R&F) Usage: "I saw you bogulating on that last wave."

bogus 1) *adj.* Describing lame action, a false idea or concept. **2)** Ridiculous, unfair, unbelievable. Usage: "That's completely bogus." "Bogus swell, brah." **3) bogosity** *n.* Usage: "The utter bogosity of that guy taking off on my wave!" **Bog** for short.

boil *n.* **1)** A turbulent patch of water on a developing wave face, usually a couple of feet in diameter, caused by water

bodyboarding
Photo: Woody Woodworth

flowing over an underwater coral or rock outcropping; looks like a pot of boiling water and indicates very shallow water or an underwater hazard. Norwegians have over ten different words to describe submerged rocks. **2)** Circular turbulence caused by tidal surges over shallow reefs. (MVA)

bollockhead *n*. A British term for an individual performing meritorious surfing acts with total disregard for personal safety. (LJE)

bomber *n*. A hard-breaking wave, usually TOP-TO-BOTTOM.

bombora *n*. **1)** An Australian term for an outside break—a large wave breaking beyond the normal lineup. **2)** A huge wave breaking over submerged reefs or rock shelves. (IDSM) **3)** Offshore reef surf, usually big and powerful. (MF) Also called BOMMIE, CLOUD BREAKS, CLOUD BURST. **4)** A deep-water reef well offshore. (NAT, 1985)

bomb out, bombed out 1) *v*. To WIPE OUT. **2) bombout** *n*. Early elimination in a surfing contest. (L&L)

bommie *n*. Short for BOMBORA. (Australia, MW)

bone, bones *n*. Discarded foam rail(s) by the shaper, as in "piles of bones." (Garden City Beach, South Carolina, 1991) Same as RAIL STRIPS.

bone crusher *n*. A big wave that breaks with extreme force. Usage (from the movie *Big Wednesday*): "Gerry Lopez thunders down another Pipeline bone crusher."

boomerang fin
Bobby Owens, 1984
Photo: Bob Barbour

bone yard *n*. The area where waves break. Also known as GRAVEYARD, IMPACT ZONE, SOUP BOWL. (P)

Bongo Board *n*. A short-lived balance-developing toy for surfers in 1963. (SFR, 1963)

bonzer *n*. A type of surfboard with double concaves shaped into the tail area that can be used in conjunction with a multitude of templates and bottom contours. The design also features two short, angled ventral fins and a short-raked center fin placed at the outside edge of the concave. The term "bonzer," which is equivalent slang for "bitchin" in Australia, was adopted by the Campbell Brothers of Southern California in the 1970s for their five-fin surfboard.

boogie board *n*. A soft, flexible foam bodyboard, which can be used in flagged areas. (MW) The original Boogie Board (a brand name) was invented by Tom Morey in 1971. The most widely used surf riding implement of all time, ridden prone and with or without swim fins.

bone yard
Art: The Pizz

"... ain't nothing but a speed bump to a longboarder."

—Longboard Larry

boogie flapper *n.* A derogatory term for a BODYBOARDER. (Santa Cruz)

boomer *n.* A large, heavy-breaking wave, usually unridable. **—booming surf**

boomerang fin *n.* A narrow-based fin shape, which Bobby Owens is credited with adapting from a windsurfer to a surfboard.

bootie juice *n.* Seawater that accumulates in neoprene booties during a session; sometimes mixes with stinky feet, possibly urine, and empties out smelly and lukewarm.

booties *n.* Neoprene rubber surf shoes worn for warmth and grip. (MM) **—hard-soled booties**

born-again surfer *n.* Someone who surfed, then quit (got married, got a job, had a family), but started again in his mid-thirties, thus being "saved" by surfing. The term was coined in the early 1980s by Ward Smith, the coauthor of a cartoon strip of the same name.

boss *adj.* Outstanding, the greatest or best, totally bitchin'.

bottom *n.* **1)** The underside of a surfboard. **2)** The bottom of a wave. **3)** The ocean floor.

bottom contour *n.* **1)** The particular shape of a surfboard's underside, or planing surface. Bottom contours are designed to direct water flow; the various shapes include flat, vee, slight vee, concave, channel concave, channel hull, tri plane hull, hydro hull, belly, chine hull, and hydrofoil stepped. **2)** The shape of the ocean floor, including its reef configuration. (W&B) Also called BOTTOM PROFILE.

bottom out *v.* To come to the end of a drop down the face of a wave from a straight-off position at high speed.

bottom profile *n.* **1)** The contour plan for the bottom of a surfboard. See BOTTOM CONTOUR. **2)** The configuration of the ocean bottom or floor.

bottom turn *n.* **1)** A turning maneuver executed following the takeoff and the drop to bring the rider back onto the wave face. **2)** A turn at the bottom or out in front of the wave, well below the crest of the wave; a turn at the bottom of the wall. **3)** A banking turn off the bottom of the wave used to generate vertical momentum. (L&L) **4)** The initial turn after completing the drop.

bounce, bounce straight in *v.* To shift one's weight up and down on the front of the surfboard in order to keep forward momentum going, as in "bouncing straight into shore." Same as HOPPING.

bouncing off the white water *v.* To rebound off the incoming foam.

bounteous *adj.* Plentiful. You might end a letter: "Sending you bounteous good vibes, ..."

bottom turn
Robbie Burns, Pipeline
Photo: Bill Romerhaus

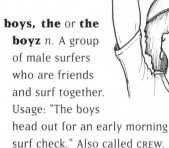

bowl *n*. **1)** A marked, bowl-like concavity on a wave face, a condition often associated with breaking waves that bend or wrap as they move toward shore; sometimes caused by a shallow place in the ocean bottom where a wave breaks with more than usual suddenness and force and is often bigger as well. Two well-known bowls are located at Makaha and Ala Moana on Oahu, Hawaii. **2)** A particular wave shape, caused by reef contour, which is likely to have a close-out section. (L&L) **3)** A wave that, viewed from above, forms a crescent shape. (A&B) Also known as HOOK. **4)** The convex bottom of the forward section of a big-gun surfboard. (MF)

bowl cut *n*. A sixties type of haircut that still looks hip on a surfer; originally created by placing a bowl upside down on someone's head and cutting around it. Also called BOWLY or SURFCUT.

bowleous *adj*. Used to describe a bowly wave or a bowl cut. Usage: "You got bowleous, dude." (San Diego)

bowly 1) *adj*. Used to describe a wave that exhibits bowl characteristics. **2)** *n*. BOWL CUT.

boxed rail *n*. See BOXY.

box jelly *n*. Also called SEA WASP, MARINE STINGER.

box seat *n*. An Australian term for the hottest spot at the takeoff site.

boxy *adj*. Refers to sharp, well-defined edges on the sides of a surfboard, as opposed to smooth, rounded rails. —**boxy rails**

bowl
North Peak, Blacks Beach
Photo: Rob Gilley

boys, the or **the boyz** *n*. A group of male surfers who are friends and surf together. Usage: "The boys head out for an early morning surf check." Also called CREW.

brah or **bra, brudda** or **bruddah** *n*. Hawaiian Pidgin English for brother. Surf brother, surf sista, associate, peer, colleague, friend in liquid solidarity. Usage: "Howzit brah?" "Howzit goin', brah?" Same as BRO in California.

brain wave *n*. A big idea or interesting thought.

"Well, I've had my brain wave for the day."

—Alasdair Middleton, Forge Lodge, Ashburnham, East Sussex, England, September 29, 1997

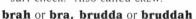

BRATS Acronym for Boca Residents Against Tourists. (Florida; TDW)

break *n*. **1)** The place where waves tumble over and break in shallow water. A wave breaks when the water depth becomes less than one-seventh of the distance between wave crests. (OA) **2)** The action of a wave as the top spills forward down its face. **3)** The area in the surf where the waves are breaking. (MF) See SURF BREAKS. —**break** *v*.

breakaway edge or **break-away edge** *n*. **1)** The trailing edge(s) of a surfboard. **2)** Where the surfboard separates from the water (at its rails, tail, or the afteredge of the skeg).

breaker *n.* Any wave that breaks on its journey to the beach. See PLUNGING BREAKER, SPILLING BREAKER.

breaking *v., adj.* Used to describe a surf spot if it looks good to ride. Usage: "I heard that the point was breaking yesterday."

breaking right, breaking left *adv.* The direction a wave is breaking, as viewed from the water facing the shore.

breaking section *n.* On a wave, any place that's curling over.

breaking wave *n.* A wave is said to be breaking when its top collapses or lip pitches out in front of itself.

break through a section *v.* **1)** To beat or negotiate a wave that breaks in front of you when you are already riding it. See BEAT A SECTION. **2) breaking a section** *n.* A scoring move in a surf contest.

breakwater *n.* A protective device for shorelines that may create a new surf spot or totally ruin an existing one; made with large boulders or steel. See JETTY.

brewery *n.* Synonymous with OUTSIDE, when a set is brewing outside. Usage: "Brewery."

brisk *adj.* Freezing-cold air or water.

bro *n.* Short for brother; a mid-1980s substitute for DUDE. The term was popularized in the Hollywood movie *Under the Boardwalk* (1989). Usage: "Hey, bro." "What's up, bro?" "Later, bro." (Southern California) See BRAH.

broadie *n.* A South African term for SLIDE.

Brobonics *n.* SURFSPEAK. A play on Ebonics; coined by Jeff Weaver (Dirty Monkey) in San Francisco. See SURFONICS.

bro-brah *n.* BRO. (Laguna Beach 1997)

brodad *n.* Someone who overuses the term *bro,* even to the point of calling his mom "bro." A derivative of HODAD. Usage: "Morning, bro. Hey, bro, what's for breakfast, bro?" (P) "My grandma and grandbro are taking me to Hawaii this summer."

brodeo *n.* A barbecue that a bunch of bros are at.

bro in-law *n.* Brother in-law. **—brah in-law**

broken board, busted board *n.* A surfboard broken into two pieces, usually as a result of getting pounded in the surf during a wipeout. Same as SNAPPED BOARD.

"It used to be a big deal if you broke a board in half—a black mark against the surfboard designer—but nowadays, guys go to the Islands and break two, three boards or more riding the winter surf because modern surfboards are lighter and slimmer."

—Greg Noll, Da Bull (1989)

broken wave *n.* A wave that has reached water shallow enough to cause it to curl over from crest to trough and break. As it continues its journey to the beach, it is termed a "broken wave."

broly *adj.* Being cool, nice, or cooperative. Usage (if someone lets you grab a wave): "That was completely broly of you." Or (if someone is uncool): "You're being fully non-broly." (Newport Beach; J)

Bronzed Aussie An Australian group of professional surfers formed in 1976 by Peter Townend, Ian Cairns, and Mark Warren, who thereby introduced the idea of surfers as bankable media superstars.

bro-phonics *n.* The language bros speak. See BROBONICS, SURFONICS.

brotherhood wave *n.* Any wave that you respectfully ride with someone else. Usage: "Brotherhood wave—share it?" (Cowell's, Santa Cruz 1992) See PARTY WAVE.

bro time *n.* Time spent away from your wife or girlfriend. Usage: "Hey, aren't we gonna have a little bro time?" (Benjah, Maui, April 1996)

brown boardshorts material *n.* A really huge wave. (Australia; MW) See CLUCKED.

brush in, brushing in *v.* To work resin well into fiberglass cloth with a brush and spreader made from a stiff piece of plastic. (ASKC; 1965)

BSA British Surfing Association.

BTO (basic takeover) Sending everyone home with a frown (Eastside, Santa Cruz; R&F); the situation when surfers take over a surf spot and hog all the waves.

Bu, the Bu Abbreviation for MALIBU. Also called MOTHER BU.

Bu *n.* A surfer icon with a monthly column in Hawaii's *H3O* surf magazine.

buck *v.* To fight one's way through the surf.

bucket o' nugs Lots of waves. (Eastside, Santa Cruz; R&F)

bucket toss *n.* Hitting the lip. (Eastside, Santa Cruz; R&F)

bud *n.* Dude. Usage: "Hey, bud, let's party." —Jeff Spicoli in *Fast Times at Ridgemont High* (1982)

bugged *v.* **1)** To be annoyed or disquieted. **2)** To be pestered by flies or people at the beach. (MCR)

BUI "Biking Under the Influence" —Isla Vista, California, vehicle traffic infraction. (P)

build *v.* To get stronger. Usage: "Hey, look at that wave build." "The sets are building."

bulgin' *n.* Big swell. As in "A bulgin' on the horizon." (Santa Cruz)

bullet *n.* A shortboard with a well-rounded nose, as opposed to a pointy nose.

bull nose *n.* A 1960s surfboard shape featuring a nose more rounded and wider than the tail. (ASKC)

bum *v.* **1)** To mooch, as in "to bum off one's friends" or "to bum wax." (The question is, if surfers are always bumming wax from each other, who buys it?) **2)** To be down on someone, to be angry with them. Usage: "My girlfriend bummed on me for missing our anniversary to go surf in Mex." See HARSH.

bummer *n.* A let down, total drag; too bad; an unfortunate occurrence. Usage: "Bummer, dude." **—bummers! major bummage**

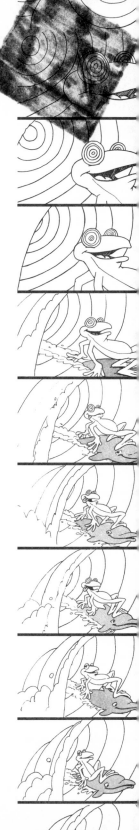

bump, bump on the water *n.* An approaching swell or set of waves. Usage: "Here comes a couple of bumps."

bumper surfing *n.* Riding on the rear bumper of an automobile in a standing position while trying to keep your balance as the car zooms around the streets. (Fresno; AJM)

bumps *n.* A colloquialism for the callused skin on the instep or knees that results from surfing. Also called SURF BUMPS.

bump wing, bump *n.* A marked inward shift of the rail toward the stringer in the tail half of a surfboard, making that half slightly narrower than the front half. Same as WING.

bumpy *adj.* **1)** Very choppy water, as in "bumpy waves." A ride over choppy water would be described as a "bumpy ride." **2)** An ocean condition somewhere between glassy and blown out. (MVA)

buoy *n.* **1)** Someone who floats around, never takes a wave, and is often in the way. Same as DUCK, SOAKER, MALLARD. **2)** A sophisticated weather station that floats around in the ocean. (WS) Outer buoy. **3)** A float moored in water as a warning of danger or as a marker for a channel. (AHD2) See BUI.

buoy reports *n.* Valuable information gleaned from floating weather stations, including wind direction, wind speed, and visibility (meaning the amount of fog or haze in the atmosphere). Buoy reports are broadcast over the RADIO WEATHER CHANNEL. (WS)

burger *n.* **1)** A mushy (shapeless), uneven, bumpy wave. See MUSHBURGER. **2) burgers** A series of such waves. —**burgery** *adj.*

burial at sea *v.* Taking a shit in the ocean; please don't do this. Usage: "Burial at sea, dude." (Punta Chivato, Baja, 1992) See DOCKING A SUB.

Burleigh Heads *n.* A famous right point in Australia, which has been the site of the annual Stubbies professional surfing competition since 1977.

burly *adj.* **1)** Used to describe freezing cold water. Usage: "It's burly out there." (Laguna Beach). **2)** Sometimes used as a substitute for GNARLY. (Santa Monica; JB)

burn, burn up the wave *v.* **1)** To do some really hot moves on a wave. (BP) Usage: "You were really burning it up out there." **2)** *v.* To smoke pot. Usage: "Don you burn?" (Maui 1991). **3)** To cut in front of other surfers.

burn off *v.* Refers to coastal fog that usually dissipates, or "burns off," in the morning or mid to late afternoon on days that are really socked in.

burrito *n.* Traditional Mexican delicacy adopted by surfers with a choice of black, refried, or pinto beans; brown or Spanish rice with saffron; lettuce; cheese; mild, medium, or hot salsa fresca; guacamole; and sour cream—all of which gets folded into a large tortilla. Do not *ever* refer to a burrito as a "wrap"—this is a stupid yuppie disguise. See FISH TACO.

→ Pretty sure you didn't need to see that ☺

"Free burrito upon move in."

—*A surfer's incentive to make a deal,
from a classified ad for an apartment
on Sabado Tarde, Isla Vista, CA (1994)*

burrito money *n.* Pocket change. Usage: "I've just been doing some random gardening to earn a little burrito money."

burying a rail *n.* A powerful maneuver during a high speed bottom turn, where the inside rail of the board is temporarily submerged as the surfer leans into the wave. If going too slow it can dig the rail too deep in the water and can cause you to slow down and fall. See DIGGING A RAIL.

bust a few *v.* To go surfing. (Eastside, Santa Cruz; R&F)

bust through the lip *v.* To pierce through the wave lip as it curls over and then to continue with a reentry or floater, etc.

butter *n.* Girls. (Florida; TDW)

butterfly *n.* A stance on a longboard where the surfer forms a V position by squatting down on the nose of the board with head down, arms straight back and out, and fingers outstretched.

butterfly stomp patch *n.* DECK PATCH.

Butthole Surfers A punk-acid rock group from Texas, formed in the 1980s, that has nothing to do with surfing except having a cool name for a band.

butt surfers *n.* Semiderogatory term for people who surf a WAVE SKI.

butt thong, butt floss *n.* A California term for a G-string bikini. Same as FIO DENTAL, FLOSS, BUN FLOSS.

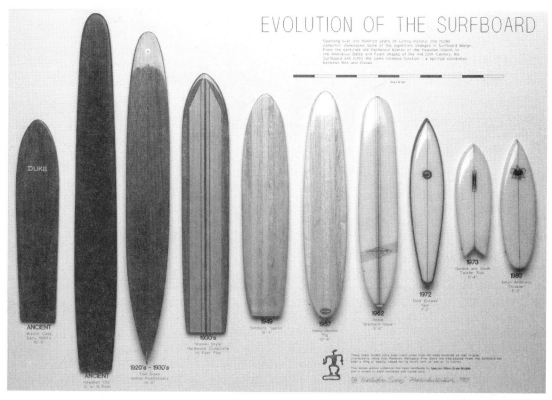

EVOLUTION OF THE SURFBOARD

Art and Photo: Malcolm Wilson

Art: George Woodbridge
MAD Magazine, *1965*

cafard (ka-FAR) *n.* A French term for cockroach, said of a surfer who is badly positioned on the shoulder of a wave and is blocking the passage of others. (WSF; 1989)

Cajon Zone *n.* A derogatory term for inland surfers from El Cajon—San Diego's "valley." *Cajón* is Spanish for "large box, bin, drawer, or locker" (not to be confused with *cojón,* meaning testicle). (RO, P)

caked on *adj.* Refers to surf-wax buildup on a surfboard deck.

Cali *n.* CALIFORNIA.

California *n.* **1)** The Golden State and home of a major surfing population. **2)** An endless summer vacation spot in the eyes of the rest of the world. Usage: "You're so California."

The name *California* was bestowed by the Spanish conquistadors (possibly by Cortéz) after an imaginary island—an earthly paradise—in *Las Sergas de Esplandian*, a Spanish romance written by Montalvo in 1510. Indeed, California was portrayed as an island on early maps. Baja (lower) California in Mexico was first visited by the Spanish in 1533; the present U.S. state was called Alta (upper) California. (WA)

California Current *n.* A cold-water ocean current in the North Pacific that flows southward from the Gulf of Alaska along the west coast of North America.

California Dream *n.* The pot of gold at the end of the rainbow, which many people move to California to find. Means many things to many people. To surfers, it means the California surfing experience.

"California Dreamin'" **1)** A sixties song by the Mamas and the Papas written by John Phillips and Michelle Phillips and containing the line "I'd be safe and warm if I was in L.A." Cover versions were made by America (1978) and The Beach Boys (1986). **2)** A Hollywood movie (1978).

California girl *n.* **1)** The pinnacle of female perfection; typically envisioned as a curvaceous bikini-clad female with blonde hair, blue eyes, and a deep golden-brown tan that is to die for. (AJM, P) **2)** A term popularized by The Beach Boys' 1963 hit tune "California Girls" with the lyrics, "I wish they all could be California girls."

Historical note: Early European explorers described the women they saw along the shores of California as Amazonian. (AJM, P)

California Myth *n.* The belief held by people living outside of California that everyone in California lives at the beach, has a palm tree in the yard, and surfs. These non-Californians also believe that the weather in all of

California is like that in Southern California—sunny and warm.

❦❦❦❦❦❦❦❦❦❦❦

"I think we had a lot to do with the population rush to California. People hearing The Beach Boys' songs envisioned California as sort of a golden paradise where all you did was surf and sun yourself while gorgeous blondes rubbed coconut oil on your body."

—Al Jardine

❦❦❦❦❦❦❦❦❦❦❦

California sun n. There must be something magical in these special sun rays. People always refer to "Sunny California."

California surf sounds, California surfin' sound n. **1)** Instrumental surf music such as that played by Dick Dale, the Belairs, etc. **2)** Vocal surfing music such as those by The Beach Boys, Jan & Dean, and others. See SURF MUSIC.

California surf words n. Used loosely as an umbrella grouping of words like awesome, totally, stoked, gnarly, rad, excellent, etc.

❦❦❦❦❦❦❦❦❦❦❦

"California surf words have made it into my normal conversation."

—Stephanie Gene Morgan (February 3, 2000). Cali-based New York photographer

❦❦❦❦❦❦❦❦❦❦❦

camber n. ROCKER.

canal surfing n. Popular Central Valley activity in places like Modesto, California, where a person is pulled on a surfboard along an irrigation canal by a rope attached to a car. See TOW SURFING.

cane swell n. A big ocean swell generated from a hurricane. (Florida; TDW)

canoe leaping n. Leaping from a canoe with a surfboard in order to ride the wave. (Hawaii) Also called LELE WA'A.

canoe surfing n. **1)** Riding waves in outrigger canoes. (Hawaii) **2) Canoe Surf** A SURF BREAK at Waikiki.

canopy, wave canopy n. The curved overhead crest of a wave.

can or no can Either you decide to go and take off on a big wave or you don't; similar to CHANCE 'EM. (Hawaii; SLS)

Cape Hatteras n. Located in North Carolina, the premier surf spot on the East Coast of the United States. Also called HATTERAS.

Cape Rollers n. Giant waves created off the southeastern coast of Africa. See FOLLOWING CURRENT and OPPOSING CURRENT.

❦❦❦❦❦❦❦❦❦❦❦

Along a stretch of water known as South Africa's Wild Coast, "where the continental shelf abruptly drops away, the Agulhas Current sweeps in hard against this immovable barrier, concentrating the massive southwest flow of water into a relatively narrow stream [that] moves at four to six knots. . . . When storms to the southwest pump waves around the Cape of Good Hope and up into the channel, the wave length of the swell can be shortened dramatically and the wave steepness increased to precipitous angles. Under certain conditions the unusually swift current here actually doubles the height of the waves pushing upstream."

—*Drew Kampion,* The Book of Waves *(1989)*

Captain Goodvibes A cartoon character created by Tony Edwards and featured in Australian surfing magazines such as *Tracks*.

card *n.* An old surfer. (Eastside, Santa Cruz; R&F)

carp *n.* An older surfer that is not as sharp as he used to be.

carve *v.* **1)** To maneuver by digging the rail of one's board into the water while turning, as in "to carve a turn." **2)** To surf excellently. Usage: "He was carving." (NAT, 1985) **3)** To perform constant, controlled maneuvering on a surfboard. (MVA) —**carving** *n.*

carving up the mob An Australian term for a reckless ride by one surfer through a group of surfers or swimmers. See MOB.

casper *n.* A tourist who comes out to the beach with a very pale complexion, looking white as a ghost. The term was derived from the TV cartoon character, Casper the Friendly Ghost. (PZ)

cast a spray *v.* The action of the board hitting the top of a wave and forcing water to fly up in the air. (MM) Usage: "You cast a huge spray on that cutback." See FAN SPRAY.

casual, cas' (kazsh) *adj.* Characteristic of a surfer's mellow attitude. Usage: "Stay casual, man." "It's cas'."

catalyst *n.* **1)** A hardening agent used to make resin set up in the fiberglassing process. **2)** Material added to resin, together with an accelerator, to make it cure rapidly by oxidation. This causes the heat that in turn cures the resin. The catalyst used in most polyester resins is methyl ethyl ketone peroxide, usually referred to as "M-E-K" peroxide—not to be confused with MEK solvent. (ORB)

catamaran, cat *n.* **1)** A twin-hulled sailboat. The modern-day catamaran was designed and built by Woody Brown and Alfred Kumalae at Waikiki in 1948. Fashioned after the giant double-hulled canoes of the ancient Polynesians, it rode the breakers like a surfboard. (GTM)

carving
Kim Mayer
Photo: Mike Peralta

Captain Goodvibes
Art: Tony Edwards

2) A raft consisting of logs or pieces of wood lashed together and propelled by paddles or sails. (W9)

catch air, catching air *v.* Happens when both surfer and surfboard fly off a wave. (MM) Usage: "I totally caught air on that one." Same as GET AIR.

catch a rail, catching a rail *v.* Happens when the down-wave rail of the surfboard catches in the surf and dumps the surfer. See DIG A RAIL.

catch a tip *v.* To dig the nose of the surfboard under water, possibly followed by a wipeout; to PEARL.

catch a wave, catching a wave *v.* **1)** To ride a breaking wave, on a board or some other surf craft or with your body alone. (MF) Same as CRACK A WAVE. **2)** To view the world from a different perspective, as in the line "Catch a wave and you're sittin' on top of the world," from the 1963 song "Catch a Wave" by The Beach Boys.

cathedral-like *adj.* A metaphor for what it's like being in the tube. **—whirling cathedral** *n.*

caught inside *v.* **1)** To be on the shoreward side of a breaking wave, with a mass of foam coming at you. **2)** In paddling out, to have a wave break outside—one of the worst situations to confront a surfer. (MW) **3)** To be unable to make it past breaking waves. (MM)

caveman campfire squat *n.* A bent-knee, squatting-down stance on a longboard with arms stretched out in front as if being warmed over a hot fire. (Malibu; KSO)

channels
Photo: Tom Servais.
Surfer magazine

cavitation *n.* The rapid formation and collapse of vapor pockets in a flowing liquid in regions of very low pressure. When cavitation occurs on one side of a fin, the surfer loses control. (ORB)

chafe, chafing *v.* **1)** To receive an injury or irritation from rubbing against the board while paddling. **2)** To get a rash from a wetsuit rubbing against the skin. See RASH GUARD.

chair *n.* An Australian term for underwater cliffs that create a wave-breaking site.

chalker *n.* A surfer with an all-white board and a black wetsuit; a common sight in the 1970s but a somewhat rare and endangered species today. (Oxnard grommet word, TJ)

chalk people *n.* People who live far from the beach. (Southern California) See CASPER.

chance 'em What you do when you have a 50/50 chance of making it when taking off on a wave—either you go or you don't. (Hawaii; SLS) See CAN OR NO CAN.

channel *n.* **1)** A deep spot where waves ordinarily don't break; usually used for paddling out to the surf. **2)** An entry to a destination over a relatively calm,

caveman campfire squat
Art: Robbie Quine

deeper area of water; an exit over the same area. (MVA) **3)** A gap between sandbanks or reefs. **4) no channel** Describes a condition in which there's no easy way out through the surf. (BP) **5) channels** Grooves in the bottom of a surfboard that function to direct water flow and create lift.

channel concave *n.* A depressed bottom surface of a surfboard with grooves shaped into it.

channel hull *n.* A surfboard bottom contour with channels; a series of flat, concave planes.

channel-sitting *n.* Watching the surf from out on the edge of the break.

channel surf button *n.* Another term for the "scan" or "search" button on a car radio. See LOCAL/VALLEY BUTTON.

channel surfing *n.* Using the TV remote control to quickly switch from one channel to another or flicking back and forth between several programs. Usage: "I channel-surfed last night from about midnight to 3 a.m." (Late 1980s)

chapped *adv.* **1)** The way you feel when you miss a perfect wave. (CVG) **2)** Bummed or depressed. Usage: "I'm chapped because my girlfriend left me." (SFG, 1989)

charge *v.* **1)** A term whose full meaning is obvious when it is said in a burned-out, shaky, laid-back voice ("Chaarrge . . ."); to hit the surf. **2)** To enthusiastically go

surfing. Usage: "Let's charge it, bro, the waves are sweet."

chaser wave *n.* First wave of a set. Generally a smaller, less developed wave than the waves in the middle of the set. Entices you to go after it, thus leaving you right in the impact zone to be worked by the entire set after you miss the wave. Same as BAIT WAVE.

chatter *n.* The sound of water slapping the underside of a surfboard. (MM)

cheater five, cheater five nose rise *n.* A surfing maneuver made famous by Paul Strauch, Jr., in the mid-sixties. (SFR, June 1988) The maneuver involves crouching down on the board while stretching out a leg and hanging five toes over the board's nose, as distinct from walking out to the end of the board in an upright position. Also known as STRAUCH CROUCH.

check out *v.* To look over and observe the surf at one or more spots in order to determine its quality, decide where to go out, etc. See SURF CHECK.

check the surf, checking the surf *v.* The ritual of watching the waves. Surfers do this to determine where to paddle out, but also just to do it even if they're not going out. See SURF CHECK.

cheese feet *n.* The California equivalent of HAOLE FEET.

cherry *adj.* **1)** Boss, bitchin', neat. (A&M) **2)** Said of anything new or in good condition, as in "cherry condition."

chester *n.* Any mascot or companion to ward off evil forces and bring filthy waves. (South Australia; R&D)

chest high *adj.* Said of waves that measure about as high as your chest while surfing.

chewin' the plank *v.* When you get smacked in the face by a surfboard. (Toronja 1993) —**plank chewage, plankage.** Usage: "That wave was a major **plank chewer.**" (Chicha 1993)

chicken carl conditions *n.* Derived from an anonymous Marin County, California, surfer who says the surf is eight feet high when it's really only one foot high.

chicken out *v.* To be overcome with fear; to hold back from catching a steep or high wave. See CLUCKED, WAVE ANXIETY.

chill out v. **1)** Cool it. (MVA) Usage: "Chill out, dude!" **2)** To calm down, to relax. (MM) Usage: "We can chill out at your place."

chine rail *n.* **1)** A rail that is faceted or beveled rather than rounded. (ORB) **2)** A definite edge created by the shaper on the rails of a surfboard where the top and bottom surfaces meet. (MCR)

chinselbogger *n.* Someone who has a weak surfing style. (Eastside, Santa Cruz; R&F)

chip, chip board *n.* The name given to the first all-balsa-wood boards constructed in the late 1940s. Much smaller than the giant planks, they were referred to as potato chips; later, they became known as MALIBU BOARDS.

choder *n.* Mid-1970s Carlsbad term for a policeman. See SLIBITY.

choice *adj.* Great, as in "choice waves."

choiceamundo *adj.* **1)** Said of anything that's cool. **2)** The exhilarating feeling you get when you tube through a wave and flip over its back like an ocean pizza. (Hollywood, Florida)

choke *v.* **1)** To be leery of big surf. **2)** To fail under pressure. (P) **3)** To fail to accomplish one's goal. Usage: "I fell off my board. I choked, big time." (MVA)

chop, choppy *adj.* **1)** A light form of blown out. (MVA) **2)** A term used to describe a certain condition of the water surface, usually when strong onshore winds are blowing. Many little waves are created, making a very bumpy and difficult surface to ride. —**wind chop, choppy conditions, choppy surf, choppy waves**

chopper gun *n.* A special spray gun used for spray-laminating a board by cutting, or "chopping," predetermined lengths of fiberglass roving or strands and depositing them together with catalyzed resin onto the surface of the mold. (ORB)

chubasco *n.* A Mexican hurricane off Baja California producing large south swells that often reach Southern California. —**chubasco lines**

chummin' *v.* Surfing naked with your shorts on your head. (Santa Cruz) See FREE BALLIN'.

churl, churl curl *n.* Gravel in the lip. Usage: "I was in the churl." (1994)

churly-churly *adj.* A churned-up surf carrying a heavy load of sand and gravel that smacks you in the face when you

churly-churly
Art: Rick Stover

walk out into it. Usage: "It's churly-churly today." (San Francisco; RMYN, NTS)

churned, churning *v.* **1)** To be tossed around in a wave. **2)** To take a trip through the washing machine.

churning action *n.* Mean-looking waves. (CC) Usage: "Look at that churning action."

churning cylinder *n.* A gnarly tube.

cigar *n.* **1)** You got it, as in "Cigar, dude!" A skate crossover term derived from "Close, but no cigar." (BHT) **2)** An old term for a wooden surfboard. (G)

clam-shelled *v.* To be engulfed; what happens when a wave closes over a surfer. (W&B) Usage: "I just got clam-shelled."

classic 1) *n.* A perfect surfing day. (MM) **2)** PERFECTION. **3)** Perfect surfing form. **4)** A fantastic day. **5)** The best. **6)** *adj.* Perfect, as in "classic conditions," "classic waves."

clean *adj.* **1)** Good glassy surf conditions (NAT, 1985), as in "clean waves," "clean peeler," "breaking clean." **2)** No sewage present.

cleanup or **clean-up** *n.* **1)** A wave or set of breaks outside of most of the surfers, causing them to lose their boards, thus "cleaning up" the area; a preleash term. **2) cleanup set** or **clean-up set** Large waves that catch surfers off guard, sweeping them into shore. (MM)

climb *v.* **1)** To steer the board up the face of the wave toward the top or crest; climbing the wall. **2)** To lean one's weight on the inside rail of the board to cause it to climb back to the ridge of the wave. Repeated, this act is referred to as climbing and dropping.

climb and drop *v.* **1)** To ride up the face of a wave and back down. (MM) **2)** To steer a rhythmic course up and down the face of a wave. —**climbing and dropping**

Clinton wave *n.* WHITE WATER. (1994)

clocking in the green room A long ride inside the hollow part of a wave. (MM) Same as ROOM TIME, TUBE TIME. Usage: "I saw you clocking in the green room out there."

clocky *n., adj.* Jerky arm movements; used to describe the look of a surfer's arms twirling around to maintain balance. Usage: "That wave went from eight to four because the judges took off half a point for each of those clockies you did on takeoff." (New Jersey and East Coast; SFR, 1989)

closed tail *n.* A design characteristic of a surfboard, featuring a squared-off tail as distinct from a rounded one. Square tail and squash tail are two examples of closed-tail boards.

close haul *n.* A very fast slide when the board-to-wave angle is very small.

close out, closed out 1) *v.* To break all at once along the entire line or length of a wave; applied to waves that become too large to form suitably for surfing. Usage: "The waves are

clam-shelled
Art: Rick Stover

closing out." "It was totally closed out today." **2)** When waves break all the way across a bay or a normally safe channel, rendering a surf spot unridable. **3)** When the waves are so huge that surfers can't paddle out. **4) closeout** *n.* A wave that slams all at once. Usage: "Beware of closeouts." **5) close-out** *adj.* Usage: "It was a close-out set."

Breaking waveл that cloлe out are characterized by a lip that "throwл out" all at once along the entire wall of the wave (aл oppoлed to a lip that gradually peelл off from one лide to the other or from the middle toward either end), thuл rendering the wave unлurfable. Cloлe-out waveл are uлually cauлed by a formleлл bottom profile. When a лpot iл cloлed out, itл лurf iл uлually conлidered too big to ride.

closeout barrel *n.* A tubing wave that collapses before you can successfully surf through the cylinder to daylight.

cloth *n.* FIBERGLASS CLOTH, for example, "20-oz. cloth."

cloud breaks, cloud burst *n.* A large wave (or waves) breaking on an outer reef; same as BOMBORA.

cloud surf *n.* The biggest waves that one can remember.

clubbie *n.* A term often used in letters published in Australia's *Tracks* magazine, referring to members of the Australia Surf Lifesaving Association, usually in a derogatory manner.

clucked *adj.* Afraid, intimidated by a wave. See WAVE ANXIETY.

clueless *adj.* A troublemaker who does not quite understand life. (MVA) Usage: "He's *totally* clueless."

cnoid waves *n.* As waves come in to shallow water, their shape changes to something called a "cnoid," which has a short, steep crest and a long shallow trough—those are what we see as lines of CORDUROY.

coastal access *n.* The ability to get to a beach or surf spot—an issue of vital importance to surfers. Access restrictions have limited surfers' ability to use some surf sites. (JRW) See MEAN HIGH TIDE LINE.

coastal development *n.* Any construction or project that alters the coastline in some way—a potential threat to surfers. Beach-widening projects, small-boat harbor development, and reef reclamation for land all contributes to overcrowding at prime surf sites. (JRW)

coastal terrace *n.* MARINE TERRACE.

coastal zone *n.* The area along the coast where development is regulated and controlled. In California, the boundary of the coastal zone varies depending on the "resources" in the area.

cobalt, cobalt naphthanate *n.* **1)** An accelerator used in POLYESTER RESIN. **2)** An

additive that allows resin to be used at lower temperatures. (ORB)

cobble applause *n.* The tumbling sound made by retreating surf on a cobbled beach, for example at Cape Lookout, Oregon. See PEBBLE CLAP.

coffin, coffin ride, the coffin *n.* A hot-dog riding position on a longboard (under the curl or on the face) with the rider lying stiffly on the back with arms folded across the chest as if in a coffin or with hands pressed together as if praying. (KSO) This stunt was especially popular in the sixties.

cold-water wax *n.* WINTER WAX.

collapsing section *n.* **1)** A portion of a wave that breaks in front of a surfer and turns to white water, making it difficult to continue riding in that direction. (RA) See SECTION. **2)** A beer belly. (IBN)

comber *n.* A long, curling wave. (RHD) Usage: "Would ja look at them there combers, Mabelle." (MVA)

combined seas *n.* A combination of local wind swell and ground swell. (WS)

Coming down! Coming through! A warning cry to anyone who is down the line or taking off in front of you on a wave; usually accompanied by profanity. (A&M) Usage: "Coming down left!" Duke Kahanamoku used to yell "Coming down!" when he caught a wave on his 16-foot, 114-pound, solid koa board. (GTM)

coming off the bottom *v.* When a surfer cranks a bottom turn and shoots back up to the top of the wave.

committed *adj.* When a surfer decides

to turn or take off on a wave, when there's no turning back.

common tit rash *n.* What you get from lying on your board; same as BOARD RASH.

competitive surfing *n.* One of the most subjective of all competitive sports because of the unlimited diversity of waves and conditions that make up the surfing arena. (L&L) Done on both amateur and professional levels. See SURF CONTEST, SURFING CRITERIA, ASP, WCT, WQS.

competitive surfing rules *n.* The rules used to judge surfing contests. These vary throughout the sport, depending on which group or association has jurisdiction over the competition. Generally, surfers are required to ride a certain number of waves in specified time periods called "heats." The surfer who executes the most radical maneuvers in the most critical sections of the biggest waves for the longest distance is deemed the winner. See BASIC DROP-IN RULE, FIRST RIDER UP, RIDER ON THE INSIDE. (LL)

composite *n.* A type of construction using two or more different materials, such as resin and fiberglass. (ORB)

compression ding *n.* A depression in a surfboard, but not serious enough to cause the fiberglass skin to fracture. See DING.

conan *n.* A macho bodybuilder who

conan

Art: Karen T. Delgadillo

can't surf but who tries to impress people on the beach. Taken from the Marvel comic book character Conan, who was played by Arnold Schwarzenegger in the movie of the same name. (South Australia; R&D)

concave 1) *adj.* Characteristic of a bottom contour or planing surface that curves in (is "concave"). (ORB) **2)** *n.* A design feature on the bottom of a board to give extra life. (NAT, 1985)

Condition Black *n.* The state of the ocean in Hawaii and the official Hawaiian Civil Defense alert that declares the ocean off-limits to everyone when the waves are so big that no one is allowed out in the water. Wednesday, January 28, 1998, was such a day. (See video "Biggest Wednesday.")

"When conditions are black, the ocean is in full roar and tourists and watermen stand side by side in slack-jawed respect."

—Surfer *magazine, June 1998*

confused swell *n.* An ocean swell that may be affected by local storms or under the influence of another swell approaching from a different direction. The weather radio sometimes tells us: "Swells are low and confused." See DISORGANIZED.

conservative *n.* A rider who stays away from the curl or the hot part of the wave, taking no chances.

continental shelf *n.* The shallow, gradually sloping area of the sea floor adjacent to the shoreline, terminating seaward at the continental slope. (CCRG) On the East Coast of the United States, the continental shelf stretches far out to sea, diffusing ocean swells into small waves. By contrast, on the West Coast the shelf drops off close to the coast, so that big, powerful ocean swells can approach areas like California with full force and create larger waves.

contour *n.* **1)** The BOTTOM CONTOUR of a surfboard. **2)** The configuration of the bottom of the ocean at a specific surf spot.

controlled *adj.* A requirement added to the ASP scoring criteria in 1985, intended to bring about a switch from extravagant free-form antics that frequently ended in wipeouts to specific and well-defined maneuvers that could be judged more easily. The rules now read "radical *controlled* maneuvers" instead of "radical maneuvers."

cook, cooking *v.* **1)** To surf aggressively, to make fancy moves. Same as RIP, HOT DOG, LACERATE. **2)** (of waves) To offer excellent surfing conditions. See PUMPING. (MVA)

cool *adj.* **1)** Hot. (SP) **2)** Really great, as in "way cool," "so cool," "fully cool," "too cool," "the coolest."

coolacious *adj.* Really super cool. Total valley term. (1992)

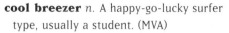

cool breezer *n.* A happy-go-lucky surfer type, usually a student. (MVA)

Coolite *n.* **1)** An Australian brand-name for a Styrofoam trainee surfboard. (MW) **2)** The first board of most Australian grommets, including MR, Rabbit, and Barton Lynch. (SFG, 1989)

coping grab *n.* A wave pool contest move perfected by Scott McCranels for extending wave time after the swell's dribbled out (Allentown, Pennsylvania, 1985, SFR, January 1990).

coral atoll *n.* ATOLL.

coral cut *n.* A deep laceration resulting from a collision with the jagged surface of coral formations. The cut itself is usually not as dangerous as the microscopic bacteria that may get under the skin and cause serious infection. Superficial coral scrapes should be cleaned well. See KAKIOS.

coral reef *n.* An enormous living organism that can produce incredibly clean, tubing surf but is also dangerous because of the razor-sharp cuts that coral can inflict when a surfer is pounded into or dragged over the reef during a wipeout.

cord *n.* SURF CORD. Affixed to the board and strapped to the ankle, a cord allows poor swimmers and poor surfers alike to hop in the ocean; it prevents far more accidents than it causes. Same as LEASH, GOON CORD, SHOCK CORD.

corduroy, corduroy to the horizon, corduroy lines *n.* A strong, straight swell perfectly lined up, like the ribbed cotton fabric used for pants. (BP)

cork *n.* A surfboard that floats too high in the water. (BP)

corkscrew *n., adj.* Spinning action by a bodysurfer when catching a wave. (MF) Usage: "Nice corkscrew action."

corner *n.* A "side bowl," where the wave bounces off the cliff, like at Fingerbowl in Santa Cruz.

corner, cornering *v.* An Australian term for ANGLE—to travel sideways across a wave.

corpuscle *n.* A HELGIE who hangs on the lip waiting for someone to fall. (Eastside, Santa Cruz; SFR, August, 1990)

couch surfing *v.* Crashing around on other people's sofas. (1994) Usage: "I've just been couch surfing at friends' places to save up some money for my next surf trip." Also called SOFA SURFING.

cove *n.* The area beside the point (MVA); a small bay.

covered *v.* To be inside the curl of a wave with water pitching out over one's head. (MM) Usage: "He's totally covered!" (SP)

cover-shot surfing, cover-shot maneuvers *n.* A term used by competi-

couch surfing
Nancy I. Kelly
Photo: Trevor Cralle

tive surfing judges to describe an exhibitionist style of surfing with little regard for technique.

✦✦✦✦✦✦✦✦✦✦✦✦

Surfing magazines and surf photographers have created a tendency among young surfers to indulge in a style of surfing that places little value on making a wave or even completing a particular maneuver, because once they're on the cover they don't care if they fall off in the next frame. The photos that appear in the magazines are simply spectacular wipeouts about to happen in the next frame. (L&L)

✦✦✦✦✦✦✦✦✦✦✦✦

cover-up *n.* GETTING TUBED; the term originated in the sixties and is still in use. A cover-up is similar to a tube ride, where the breaking white water covers the rider. (L&L)

Cowabunga! A surfer's hilarious and exultant shout. As Snoopy says, "That means surf's up!" and who is going to argue with that? (MVA) Surfers adopted the expression from *The Howdy Doody Show* in the 1950s. Sometimes spelled **Kowabunga**. See BANZAI and KOWABONGA.

Cowabunga stokaboka A sixties term for really super stoked. (KSO)

C.R.A.B. (Citizens Right to Access Beaches) Formed in August 1996, C.R.A.B. is dedicated to educating the public on

its rights to use and enjoy our beaches for a variety of recreational pursuits: http://www.americom.net/users/ralphc/

crack *v.* An Australian term for ride. Usage: "Crack a good wave."

crack a surf *v.* To go surfing. (Australia)

crack it *v.* Do it, go for it, go surfing. (A&M)

crank, cranking *v.* **1)** (Of really big waves) To break consistently. Usage: "Unreal, it's cranking out there." (MVA) **2) cranked** *adj.* Used to describe big surf. Usage: "The waves are really cranked." See COOK, PUMPING.

crank a turn *v.* To lean into a turn at a radial angle.

crashing move *v.* Any hot maneuver that scores high in a surfing competition.

craters *n.* Holes in feet from wearing Churchill fins. (Santa Cruz) See FOOT DING.

crazing *n.* Hairline cracks either within or on the surface of fiberglass laminates, caused by stresses generated by excessive heat during cure, removal from the mold, impact, or flexing. (ORB)

cream, creamed *v.* **1)** To be caught by the curl of a wave, thrown off the board, and spun around by the turbulence while being held underwater and tossed aside; a wipeout. **2)** To be beat up; to be crushed to juice in the pilings of a pier. (A&M)

creek skimming *n.* Riding a skim board on a standing wave on a river. (TLH)

crest *n.* **1)** The highest point of a wave before it breaks. **2)** The tallest part of the wave, which usually breaks first. (ORB) Also called WAVE CREST.

crew, the crew n. A group of surfers, for example, "the Santa Cruz crew."

cripple n. A derogatory term for a kneeboarder. Implied in the question, "What's the matter, can't you stand?"

critical adj. 1) The condition when the wave is about to break. 2) Applied to a board with hypersensitive response. 3) Used to describe a very steep, fast-breaking, and difficult-to-ride wave—a "critical" wave.

critical point n. A situation on a wave in which there is no leeway, time, or room for alternatives. See COMMITTED.

critical section, most critical part n. 1) The part of a wave that is very difficult to ride, usually deep within the curl or a very steep section. (L&L) 2) The part right where the wave is breaking.

cross chop n. A water condition created by a crosswind or the convergence of waves. See CHOP.

crosscurrent or **cross-current** n. An ocean current that runs parallel to the beach. (GN) See LONGSHORE CURRENT.

cross curve n. The transverse profile or cross section of a surfboard.

crossover n. CROSS STEP.

cross step, cross-stepping n. The act of walking toward the nose of a long-board, one foot over the other—a stylish move. (A&M, MVA) Same as FOOT-OVER-FOOT WALKING.

crosswind n. A wind that blows directly across the path of a surfer.

crotch delam n. A chemical weathering that occurs to a wetsuit from urination. Over time, the urine eats away at the neoprene and begins to delaminate the suit in the groin region.

crouch n. A leaning-forward, squatting position used to duck into the breaking part of the wave, reduce wind resistance, or obtain better balance on a big-wave drop. See STRAUCH CROUCH.

crowd, crowding v. Not giving another surfer enough space on a wave.

crowded, crowded conditions, overcrowded When there are too many surfers in the water. Usage: "This place gets too crowded!" (SP) See ZOO.

crowd surfing n. Originally called "stage diving," and later, "head walking." Technique mastered by Jello Biafra of the Dead Kennedys in the late 1970s; Vice President Al Gore even tried it on election night 1992. Usage: "Pearl Jam lead singer Eddie Vedder leaps off the

crowd
top: Trestles lineup
Photo: Robert Brown
bottom: beach crowd
Photo: Don Balch

crew
The Domani Brothers in the Mango Lounge Manchester State Beach, California
Photo: Trevor Cralle

stage to crowd-surf in the mosh pit below." (San Francisco Chronicle, October 28, 1993)

"Try not to allow anyone to grab your head in an attempt to surf you by."

—*Russell E. Glaue, on crowd-surfing techniques*

---

crown *n.* A convex curvature, such as under the nose of a surfboard.

crowned deck *n.* DOMED DECK.

crowned rail *n.* CHINE RAIL.

cruise, cruising *v.* To slide across the face of a wave with free and easy turns, nothing tight or radical.

cruisemobile *n.* A Holden station wagon. (South Australia; R&D). See SURF VEHICLE.

crumbling tube *n.* A tubing wave that collapses as the surfer rides through it. In competitive surfing, this kind of tube scores less than a DRY TUBE, where the surfer is completely enclosed. See TUBE RIDE, TUBE SPIT.

cruncher *n.* **1)** A hard-breaking big wave that folds over and is almost impossible to ride (IDSM); same as BOOMER, DUMPER. Also called CRUSHER, CRASHER, BLASTER, WHOMPER, etc. **2)** A ding in a surfboard that can be repaired without a resin filler. To qualify as a "true" cruncher, three circumstances must be present: the fiberglass must be buried in the foam firmly; the glass must not be deeper than 3/16 of an inch; and the area surrounding

the crunch must be solid and attached to the foam. (GCD) See SINKER.

cruzer *n.* Someone who surfs without exerting much energy; a semilazy surfer. (MVA) See CRUISE.

cubal, cubalistic *adj.* Describes when a wave goes SQUARE. (Hermosa Beach body-boarder heard it in Hawaii)

cup *n.* The upward curvature of the front end of a surfboard; the SPOON or SCOOP.

cure *v., n.* In building a surfboard, the changing of the liquid resin to a solid state. Once the resin begins to cure, the process can't be reversed. The technical term for this reaction is *polymerization*. (ORB)

cure time *n.* **1)** The time required for the liquid resin to become hard enough to undergo other processes, such as sanding or finishing, or to cease being tacky or sticky. **2)** Technically, the time required for the resin to reach a poly-merized state after a catalyst has been added. (ORB)

curl *n.* **1)** The curved breaking portion of the wave, curling or pouring over in front of the rest of the wave and creat-ing a space between the main body of the wave and the spilling crest. **2)** The hollow wave face under the lip of a breaking wave. (L&L)

curl line *n.* The path of the wave as it peels from one side to the other.

current *n.* **1)** A body of water that runs or flows, usually in, out, or along a beach or coastline. **2)** Local or large-scale water movements that result in the horizontal transport of water masses and surfers.

curtain *n.* The lip of the wave that comes over the surfer as he/she enters the tube, covering them up from view, as in " . . . and Shane gets it under the curtain."

curtain floater *n.* Surfing across the top of the white water and down the front onto the flats. Usage: "Nice curtain floater, bro."

curve *n.* A surfboard design feature, as in a "curve in the bottom of a board." (NAT, 1985) The way a board is curved affects its hydrodynamics.

custom surfboard *n.* A surfboard built especially to the specifications of a rider. The weight of the surfer and the type of riding to be done are generally taken into consideration.

custom wetsuit *n.* A tailored garment with tapered arms and legs, incorporating various body measurements so that it fits the individual surfer like a glove.

cut *v.* To slide in or move at an angle to the direction of a wave's motion.

cutaway *n.* On the sides of the bow or stern of a surfboard, the section that is removed, or "cut away," in the design stage to permit a smaller board-to-wave angle.

cutback or **cut-back** *n.* **1)** An S-shaped maneuver in which a surfer turns sharply back toward the advancing curl, then turns sharply again to advance once more along the wave face. **2)** A turn toward the breaking section of the wave, or back into the wave. **3)** In competitive surfing, a horizontal change of

cutback
Michio Degawa
Jiro's Point,
Kamakura, Japan
Photo: Courtesy of
Jim Phillips

direction of at least 130 degrees in which the board reverses its original path so that it returns toward the breaking part of the wave. This type of maneuver usually precedes the RICOCHET. The most difficult cutback is to extend far out into the shoulder of a wave, and with no loss of speed, return at 180 degrees in a figure-8 path into the breaking curl. (L&L) **4)** A complete change of direction. (MVA) —**cut back** *v.*, **butt-skimming cutback, cutback radical**

cut down *v.* To surf from the top of a wave to the bottom.

cut downs for old surfers:
"You're so old you can't even remember how to get to the beach."
"You're so old you have to look in the obituaries to see if you're still alive to surf that day."
"You're so old you . . ." etc.

cut it up, cutting it up *v.* Same as RIP, but usually applies to more than one person. (MVA) Usage: "They were really cutting it up out there."

cut off *v.* **1)** To terminate a ride. **2)** To be SNAKED or SHOULDER HOPPED. (RO) Usage: "That dude totally cut me off." **3) cutoff** *n.* An intrusion by someone who doesn't

respect another surfer's right to ride a wave alone. (MVA) **4)** As the Surf Punks say in an album glossary, "Cutting off—valleys usually do."

cut out *v.* **1)** To exit a wave. (MM) **2)** To leave a wave by turning up the face and over the crest. (A&B) Same as PULL OUT or KICK OUT. **3)** To be forced out of a wave by another surfer. Usage: "He cut me out." —**cutout** *n.*

cuttie *n.* Australian slang for CUTBACK.

cyber shaper *n.* Computer shaping machine.

cyber surfer *n.* One who "surfs" the Internet.

cyber surfing *n.* See SURFING AS METAPHOR.

cyclops *n.* A grumpy old longboarder who burns everyone and never looks back. (Eastside Santa Cruz; R&F)

cylindrical *adj.* Describes the shape of a perfectly tubing wave.

Peter Mel
Santa Cruz
Photo: Mike Peralta

76

The Last Surf Shop
Art: Jim Phillips

da kine or **da'kine** (da KINE) **1)** The keystone of Hawaiian Pidgin; you can use it anywhere, anytime, anyhow—very convenient. (DSN) **2)** Another way of saying "whatchamacallit" or "what's-his-name." Usage: "Ey, Michael! Where da kine?" (ECN) **3)** A Hawaiian term for TOTALLY (SP); not to be confused with *the kind,* a California expression meaning "the best." **4)** The word used when you don't use the word, for instance, to describe excellent waves, extremely good weather, or great looks, among other things. Usage: "Da kine waves, brah."

Da kine may be used in innumer-able ways:
Substantive: "Take da kine [broom] and sweep da floor."
Pronoun: Q: "We goin' have one party. I like you come." A: "Where da kine [it] goin' be?"
Adjective: Q: "You think Sam in love with Alice?" A: "Man, he da kine [crazy] 'bout her!"
Suffix: "I see the Oahu-kine surf board and the over-here-kine [on Kauai]."

Excerpted from Elizabeth Ball Carr, Da Kine Talk: From Pidgin to Standard English in Hawaii, The University Press of Hawaii, 1972

Dale, Dick Known as *"King of the Surf Guitar,"* he was the originator of the "surf sound" of surf music in 1958–59. His hits included "Let's Go Trippin'" (1961), recorded live at the Rendezvous Ballroom in Newport Beach. Dick Dale and the Deltones was the name of his band.

"There was a tremendous amount of power that I felt while surfing and that feeling of power was simply transferred from myself into my guitar when I was playing surf music."

—Dick Dale, quoted in Tom Hibbert, Rockspeak! The Dictionary of Rock Terms, Omnibus Press, London, 1983

damsel in distress n. Any female on the beach being pestered by a male dork.
dangle foot n. An old name for GOOFY FOOT.
darryl n. A Santa Barbara term for BARNEY. See DEREL.
Davidson Current A northward flowing, warm-water ocean current located inshore of the California Current along the California coast in late fall and winter. (CCRG)
dawner n. DAWN PATROL. Usage: "C'mon, man, you gotta go for a dawner." (Jim Lucas, Santa Cruz)
dawn patrol n. **1)** An early-morning surfing session. (MM) Some people say of such a session, "Crisp and clean and no caffeine." **2)** Surfing or looking for surf at sunrise. (L&L)

day-after-storm surf *n.* A condition caused by local storms, when waves are typically close together and very uneven in appearance but can be quite large, up to ten feet or more. In California, this happens from November to April. (S&C)

Day-Glo "Radioactive" neon colors, adopted by some surfers and much of the surf industry in the 1980s. Used for fluorescent, overstated clothes, wetsuits, surfboards, zinc oxide, etc.

dead dip *n.* A squatting position in which the surfer leans forward at an exaggerated angle. (IDSM)

dead section, dead spot *n.* A flat section of the wave that limits maneuverability or acceleration. (L&L) Also called DEEP GUTTER.

deal, dealing *v.* When the waves are good. (JP) Usage: "The waves are dealing today."

death *n.* The ultimate—you can't get better. A great wave or an attractive woman can be just like death; after that, you might as well die because it's over. Usage: "That wave was death." "She's death." (Southern California)

This image has been documented in Shakespeare's sonnets, where to die was a euphemism for orgasm. To Jim Morrison of The Doors, sex was an enactment of death.

debbie *n.* A derogatory term for a dumb beach bunny who never gets wet—for example, someone in a bikini contest. (Santa Monica; JB, 1985)

decal *n.* SURF STICKER.

decent *adj.* Used to describe good surfing conditions. Usage: "The waves are pretty decent today."

deck *n.* The top surface of a surfboard.

deck contour *n.* The shape of the top surface of a surfboard. See CROWNED DECK, DOMED DECK.

The different contours also include a flat deck, where the rail turns down quickly, and a deck very blended into rails, where the transition from deck to rail is completely smooth.

deck grip *n.* Adhesive tape strips or shaped pads that act as a WAX SUBSTITUTE.

deck line *n.* The length of the board, as measured along the stringer from the nose tip to the tail of the surfboard. Same as STRINGER LINE.

deck patch *n.* An extra layer of fiberglass cloth laminated into the area of the deck where the surfer lies, kneels, or stands. Its purpose is to avoid excessive dents or knee depressions in the deck. Also called STOMP

80

decoy
Art: Rick Stover

PATCH, BUTTERFLY STOMP
PATCH. (ORB)
**—staggered deck
patches**

deck profile *n.* The outline of a surfboard.

decoy *n.* A FLOUNDER BUOY, who on a crowded day is used by the other surfers as a marker on a slalom course; a spectator. (MCR)

deep, deep inside, deep set *adv.* To be closest too, or actually inside, the curling part of the wave, or the tube.
—deep inside the green room, deep in da tube, deep barrel

deep gutter *n.* The area of deep water where a wave flattens out before it reaches the shorebreak. Also called DEAD SECTION. (L&L) See CHANNEL.

deep peak takeoff, deep takeoff *n.* Catching a wave at its most critical stage. (A&M) See LATE TAKEOFF.

deep setup or **deep set-up** *n.* A deliberate positioning far inside either the tube or the power pocket before accelerating along the wave face.

deep turn *n.* A wide turn carved out near the curl of a wave.

deepwater channel *n.* A safe spot to paddle out.

deepwater wave *n.* A wave coming out of deep water. See BOMBORA.

delamination *n.* **1)** On surfboards, the separation of fiberglass layers from one another or from the foam, as in a "delaminated deck." The condition is most often the result of failure of the foam-fiberglass bond. **2)** On wetsuits, the separation of materials from the neoprene layer. See CROTCH DELAM. **3)** Peeling skin from a really bad sunburn.

delam spots *n.* Areas of delamination on a surfboard where fiberglass has separated from the foam core due to exposure of sun and water seepage through dings over time. (1994)

derel *n.* A term used in a derogatory or joking sense to describe someone who is lacking in intelligence. Short for the word *derelict.* (AC) Usage: "What a derel." See DARRYL.

destructo *n.* The house wrecker in the party scene of the movie *Big Wednesday* (1978). (A&M)

devil winds *n.* See SANTA ANA WINDS.

dewey or **duey** *n.* A nerd. (MVA)

dial, dial in *v.* **1)** To plug in—like a telephone. Usage: "Let's go dial in on some waves." **2) dialed** To be connected or hooked up. Usage: "Ah, dude, your room is fully king, you're so dialed."

dial surfers *n.* People who scan the radio, searching for stations. Usage: "Dial surfers would soon find it because it was on 88.1." (Mark Walsh, 1998)

diamond tail *n.* A surfboard tail design that comes to a point, rather than being more rounded at the end.

dick dragger *n.* Derogatory term for bodyboarder. (TWS, June 2000)

D'YA THINK MAYBE YOU'VE BEEN OUT IN THE SUN TOO LONG ??

delamination
Art: I. B. Nelson

Diego Short for San Diego.

dig a rail, digging a rail *v.* To have the edge or side of the surfboard cut or "dig" into the water. Often occurring when a turn is being attempted, digging a rail may result in a spill. The usual cause is poor positioning on a turn, for instance trying to turn from too far forward. Same as CATCH A RAIL. See BURYING A RAIL.

ding *n.* **1)** A damaged place in the surface of a surfboard, such as a hole, crack, dent, or deep scratch; dingage. See DUCT TAPE. **2)** A surf-related injury, such as a cut on the leg. **3) getting dinged up** *v.* When a surfer gets tossed around by a wave, or when a board has lots of dings. Usage: "I got all dinged up on that wipeout." "My board's all dung up."

ding-ding *n.* The way some Hawaiians refer to a ding. Usage: "You gotta ding-ding, brah."

ding kit *n.* A repair kit for dings, usually containing a small role of duct tape, several grades of sandpaper, and a variety of other things.

ding repair *n.* Patching or filling dings on a surfboard—one of those things in life that no surfer can elude. (GCD)

ding string *n.* A surf leash; so named because using a leash may reduce your chances of dinging up your board.

dip *n.* **1)** GEEK. **2)** A not-with-it kind of chap; a goof. (MM) **3)** *v.* To dip under the lip. See HEAD DIP.

Dirt Surfer *n.* Australian invention specially designed for riding on dirt trails ("dirt surfing") and grass. It features a flexible, pivoting board that has large wheels at both ends.

dirt surfers *n.* Deadheads who have relaxed their standard of personal grooming to the extreme. The joys of living on a tour bus are many, but hot showers aren't one of them. (David Shenk & Steve Silberman, *Skeleton Key: A Dictionary for Deadheads*, 1994)

disco move *n.* Any kook maneuver.

dismo *n.* A person who talks surf, lives surf, dreams surf, but never surfs. (P)

disorganized *adj.* Said of swell or waves that don't line up or break consistently. Usage: "It's pretty disorganized out there." "The swell is small and disorganized" or ". . . a disorganized weather system" (heard on weather radio). See CONFUSED.

dissipate *v.* To flatten or disappear. Waves "dissipate" in size and shape depending on bottom contour and various other factors.

diurnal tides *n.* High and low tides that occur twice daily in many parts of the world, like California. See MIXED TIDES.

dive *v.* To jump head first under and through a wave or bail off the board.

DMA Dimethylanaline—a promoter used in resins.

do a sauna, doing a sauna *v.* To piss in your wetsuit to stay warm while out in the water. (ELN) Same as URINOPHORIA.

docking a sub *v.* When you lose control of your bowels and release a "sub" into your wetsuit. (TWS) See DROPPING ANCHOR.

ding
Photo: Trevor Cralle

Minimigo with amigo
Cabo San Lucas, Mexico
Photo: Leslie King

doggers *n.* Multicolored swimming trunks, ordinarily made of canvas or some other tough fabric.

dogging *v.* Going backside in the pit. See PIG DOG.

dogsniff *v.* When somebody surfs right up close to another surfer from behind, like when dogs sniff each other's asses. Usage: "Dude, that tranny just dogsniffed me again." See RAT HOLING.

dol-fin *n.* A raked surfboard skeg (fin) originating with the hydroplane surfboard and resembling a porpoise's dorsal fin.

dolphin *n.* A playful marine mammal that occasionally joins in on surfing sessions.

domed deck, slightly domed deck *n.* A rounded, rather than flat deck that provides a thicker stringer and increased foam volume (hence more flotation) down the center of the board. (ORB) Same as CROWNED DECK.

dommo *v.* To surf really well—to dominate. Usage: "I dommo Doheny." (SFG, 1989)

dood, doöd, or dööd *n.* Alternative spelling of DUDE. See VALLEY SHEEP.

doom tube *n.* A tubing wave that's so long there is no way out. (BC, Spring 1990)

doormat *n.* Somewhat derogatory, but vaguely descriptive term for a bodyboarder, who seems to hate the term "boogie boarder" more, for some curious reason. (South Africa) In

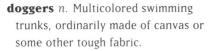

dolphin
Art: I.B. Nelson

Oz, there are a number of interesting variations, such as ESKY LID (cool box lid), TOILET LID, etc. To their credit, bodyboarders usually rise above these insults. (WVS)

dope rope *n.* A derogatory term for SURF LEASH. Same as KOOK CORD, GOON CORD.

dork *n.* Someone exhibiting unacceptable behavior, who doesn't know the unwritten surfer code; a twerp or turkey. For example, a surfer from San Jose or another inland city—from "over the hill"—automatically has dork status. (CVG) Same as KOOK, GEEK. (A&M)

dork out *v.* To blow it. Usage: "Oh, look at that dude, he just dorked out!"

double, doubling *v.* What happens when a wave jacks up in size.

double bubble, double humper, double wave *n.* When a fast outside wave overtakes a slow inside wave, creating a larger and faster compound wave. Same as DOUBLE UP.

double concaves *n.* Design feature near the tail with concave sections on either side of the stringer.

double-ender *n.* A surfboard that is almost symmetrical, with a slightly pointed tip at either end.

double-glassed *adj.* Used to describe longboards that have two layers of fiberglass instead of one.

double-o *n.* double overhead.

double overhead *n.* A wave that is twice as high as the surfer riding it.

double ski *n.* A wave ski designed to be used by two people. (MF)

down the line
Joey Hutson
Salsa Brava, Costa Rica
Photo: Mike Peralta

double spinner *n.* Two consecutive 360-degree body spins on a surfboard. See SPINNER.

double stoked *n.* Twice the stokage—without the caffeine. (Jason Smith, Myers Flat, CA, 1994)

double up *v.* What two consecutive waves do when they meet or join. (L&L) See DOUBLE·BUBBLE. Usage: "Did you see those two waves double up on each other?"

double-wing pin twin fin *n.* A pintail-shaped twin fin with two sets of bumps along the rails.

doughnuts *n.* Very round tubes. (MVA)

dovetailed fin box *n.* A dovetailed slot on the underside of a surfboard for a removable skeg that can also be adjusted fore and aft along the stringer line.

down *adj.* Refers to surf that is flat. Usage: "Surf's down, bro."

down railed *adj.* A surfboard design by Gerry Lopez in which the rail has a lowered outer edge that produces less side spray and higher speeds. (SFR, October 1983) Also called DROPPED RAIL.

—downrails, down rail

down the face *adv.* Surfing from the top to the bottom of a wave.

down the line *adv.* **1)** That portion of a breaking wave some distance away and toward which the rider is projecting his or her track. **2)** The spot to which a surfer maneuvers on a breaking wave. Usage: "The wave started to section on me down the line." "It was all down the line."

"**Surfing is the best sport in the world, bar none. What could be better than riding the ocean's echoes from faraway storms; working a water funnel all down the line? You really find out what true reality is by surfing, by throwing yourself into the middle of all these elements and coming out unscathed.**"

—Llewellyn Ludlow, carpenter-surfer-poet of Mill Valley, CA. Quoted in "Neptune's Children" by Jane Ganahl, San Francisco Examiner, March 10, 1991.

---

down the mine *adv.* **1)** An Australian term for PEARLING. **2)** WIPE OUT. (A&B) Usage: "I went down the mine on that last one."

Down Under *n.* Another name for Australia. Also called OZ, as in *The Land of Oz.*

Doyle board *n.* A brand of soft board used for learning to surf. See SNURFING.

drag *n.* **1)** BUMMER. **2)** A surfboard's resistance to forward motion caused by the shape of its bottom and its breakaway edges.

drag-foot turn *n.* An old-fashioned method of turning long, heavy surfboards by dragging one foot in the water. This maneuver was made famous by a surfer from Hawaii called Scoota Boy. (A&M)

dragging a hand *v.* Letting your trailing hand touch the wave while surfing across it. Same as DRAWING THE LINE.

drastic *adj.* GNARLY; variation on RADICAL. (Santa Monica, 1991)

draw out, drawing out *v.* To extend a turn. Usage: "He was drawing out a high-speed bottom turn." "I saw you carve a drawn-out turn."

draw the line, drawing the line *v.* **1)** To touch the wall of a wave with a finger or hand while surfing across it. Same as DRAGGING A HAND. **2)** To test your limits and push yourself, as seen in the movie *Big Wednesday* (1978): "It's time to draw the line."

dream wave *n.* See PERFECT WAVE.

"Nias is pretty close to my dream wave if the inside section weren't so fat."

—*Serena Brooke,* Surfer magazine, *May 1999*

---

dredge, dredging 1) *v.* The action of strong waves breaking in shallow water, which draw water from ahead of them and suck already shallow water up into their face. Usage: "It was really dredging out there." **2) dredging wave** *n.*

dredging
Photo: Rob Gilley

The big brother of a SUCKEY WAVE. (Australia; MW)

dribble *n.* **1)** Small, powerless surf. **2)** A form of speech favored by surfers who have spent too much time in the sun without a hat on. (Australia; JARR) See TROPPO.

drift 1) *v.* To float in motion with a current, as in a surfer being carried away by a current. **2)** *n.* The sideslip of a surfboard.

drill, drilled *v.* **1)** To be worked—the condition of a surfer who has unsuccessfully negotiated a killer wave. **2)** Used to describe a bad experience, usually with a rough or uncooperative wave. Usage: "Man, that wave really drilled me." (JP)

drip *n.* DIP.

drive, driving *v.* **1)** To accelerate on a wave. (NAT, 1985) **2)** To exert extra effort to trim the board and gain the most possible speed, as in "driving hard off the bottom."

drivey *adj.* Used to describe **1)** A fast surfboard; its driviness. Usage: "Your board is really drivey down the line, mate." **2)** A characteristic of a fast-breaking wave. Usage: "That wave is classic, really drivey."

Doyle board
Jessica Mullany after her first time surfing. El Granada, California
Photo: Stephanie Gene Morgan

drop 1) *v.* To move down on the face of the wave toward the trough. **2)** *n.* The initial downward slide after taking off on a wave. —**taking the drop, heavy drops**

drop in, dropping in *v.* **1)** To slide down the face of a wave immediately after it is caught; to take off on a wave and ride from the top straight to the bottom. **2)** To take off on a breaking wave in front of a surfer already launched, thus cutting the other surfer off. **3)** To refuse to give priority to someone already on a wave. See DROP-IN RULE. **4) drop-in** *n.* Surfing's most offensive behavior, to paddle and then begin to ride on the inside on a wave that someone else is already riding. (MW) Usage: "Don't drop in on meeee!" See RAT HOLING, SNAKING, SHOULDER HOPPING.

dropping in
Photo: Woody Woodworth

Stealing another surfer's wave is the ultimate taboo in surfing, often breached by surfers unfamiliar with the local PECKING ORDER. Some locals yell, "Dropping in!" at intruding surfers to prevent getting snaked. (CVG, BHT)

---

drop-in fade *n.* Stalling the surfboard after catching the wave to let the curl catch up.

drop-in rule, basic drop-in rule *n.* In competitive surfing, the rule that the surfer on the inside at the initial point of takeoff has unconditional right-of-way for the entire duration of the ride. "On the inside" means closest to the breaking curl of the wave. (L&L) See WAVE POSSESSION.

drop-in shout *n.* What you say to alert other surfers that you got the wave and they should pull back or get out of the way, such as "Got it," "Hey! Hey! HEY!" "I'm on it!" "My wave," "Coming through," or, in Hawaii, "Ho! Ho! Ho!" or "Hoooee!"

drop-knee *n.* **1)** A type of turn in which both knees are bent, with the trail leg crossed behind the lead leg and the trail-leg knee dropped closer to the board than the knee of the lead leg. **2)** A bodyboarding position.—**getting up drop-knee**

drop-knee cutback *n.* A dynamic longboarding maneuver involving bend-

drop-in shout
Art: Bob Penuelas

ing one leg in order to turn in the opposite direction. (KSO)

dropped rail *n.* DOWN RAILED.

dropping anchor *n.* Yet another term describing a water-based bowel movement. (TWS, December 1999) See BURIAL AT SEA, DOCKING A SOCK.

dropping off *v.* When a swell begins to weaken from its maximum peak; "Yeah, I heard it **dropped off** over night."

dropping the kids off at the beach Taking a dump on the beach. Please try to avoid doing this! See SAND BISCUIT.

drop-turn *n.* A turn, usually radical, just at the bottom of a drop down the face of the wave.

dry landers *n.* People who never go in the ocean.

dry reef *n.* What you don't want to see as you pull into the barrel. See SUCKING DRY.

dry suit *n.* **1)** A neoprene rubber full bodysuit (sometimes as much as five millimeters thick), which doesn't let water leak in, as distinct from a WETSUIT. Long winter underwear is worn under the suit. **2)** A necessary garment for surfing in places like Maine in the winter.

dry tube *n.* **1)** A tube ride in which the surfer is completely enclosed and emerges without the wave collapsing. **2)** In competitive surfing, a higher scoring maneuver than a CRUMBLING TUBE.

duck *n.* Someone who floats around in the lineup like a buoy. Also called MALLARD.

duck dive *n.* **1)** A maneuver in which the surfer pushes down on the front nose of the board to dive under a breaking or bro-

duct tape
Molly DeCoudreaux's custom duct taped wallet
Photo: Trevor Cralle

ken wave. (JP) **2)** A method of diving with the board under an oncoming wave on the way out through the break. (NAT, 1985)

duck feet *n.* Rubber fins used for bodysurfing, bodyboarding, and kneeboarding.

duct tape *n.* A shiny, silver-colored heavy-duty adhesive tape used for on-the-spot ding repair and a bunch of other things; fixes everything.

"If it can be done with duct tape, it must be done with duct tape."

—Greg Macchi

dude *n.* **1)** A surfing enthusiast, usually of the male gender. Females are sometimes known as **dudettes**. The word was popularized in the 1982 movie *Fast Times at Ridgemont High* by the character Jeff Spicoli (played by Sean Penn). **2)** A lame, outdated valley word; **the "d" word**. See VALLEY SHEEP. (SP, 3). **3)** Another surfer who is your friend. (H&R) **4)** How surfers refer to the other guy, usually because they can't remember his name. (MCR) Usage (various, depending

dry suit
Jack O'Neill with prototype dry suit, Santa Cruz, early 1950's
Photo: O'Neill Inc.

dude
Art: Jimbo Phillips

on inflection or emphasis): "Dude!"
(Hello.) "Hey, dude." (What's happen-
ing?) "Hey. Dude." (Come over here.)
"Killer, dude!" (Awesome.) "Later, dude."
(Good-bye.) "Yo, dude," or simply,
"Dude." (Said to get someone's atten-
tion.) Depending on the inflection
stressed, the word can have a variety of
meanings. If your friend has locked him-
self in the closet, you might say,
"*Dude?*"
"Nice usage of 'dude.'"   —*Trevor Cralle*
Disbelief or agreement: "Oh, no way, dude."
"Duudee—leave my burrito alone."
DOOUOOD or Doo-oo-ood
"Dude, you've got so much gear in here."
          —*Benjah, Love Shack, Santa Cruz, 1991*
"Dude! It's freezing!"
          —*Nate Knight in San Jose, Costa Rica*
"Dude. Whatever, Dude. Get off it, Dude."
          —*Random person on Telegraph Avenue,*
          Berkeley, CA, 1994

"Dude, I'm stoked." or "I'm so stoked,
dude." —**gnarly dude, surf dude,
surfer dude** See DOOD.

dude factor *n.* Number of guys at a
party. (Claytonious, 1993)

dude pack *n.* A condom. Usage: "Oh, no,
I forgot my dude pack. I gotta go to the
pharmacy." (San Fernando Valley)

dude sac *n.* Scrotum.

dude-brah *n.* DUDE. See BRO-BRAH.

dump *n.* WIPEOUT; often refers to bodysurfing.

dumper *n.* **1)** A wave that curls over
steeply as it is about to break, then suddenly washes down into shallow water.
2) A wave that breaks and curls straight
down from the top, dumping the rider.
3) A thick, powerful wave that curls
from top to bottom with the texture of
wet cement. (A&M) **4)** A wave that sucks
out in shallow water and pounds when
breaking. (NAT, 1985)

dune *n.* A big peaky wave.

dweeb *n.* GEEK; a term allegedly coined
by Corky Carroll. Usage: "Look at those
two dweeby-looking types."

dwid *n.* GEEK.

dying cockroach *n.* A supine surfer
who weakly waves arms and legs. (WLK)

surf check
Art: Jim Phillips

early surf *n.* An early-morning surf session. (Australia) —**an early** (Hawaii; GS, April 1990) Usage: "I woke up for an early today at 5 A.M."

earthquake *n.* A trembling movement of the earth's surface that sometimes generates SEISMIC SEA WAVES or TSUNAMIS. See SEISMOGRAPH.

East Coast In surfing, refers to the East Coast of the United States.

east swell *n.* A swell that moves from east to west. (ORB)

east wind, easterly *n.* A wind that blows from east to west. (ORB)

eating reef *v.* Getting munched. (Stockton Ave., Santa Cruz) —**getting reefed**

eat it, eat shit *v.* **1)** To fall off one's surfboard; to WIPE OUT or GET WORKED. (P) Usage: "I ate it somethin' fierce." (GN) **2)** To eat the sand or a piece of your surfboard; to get MUNCHED. (MCR) See LUNCH.

eat the cookie *v.* To wipe out in the white water. (IBN)

eat the rocks *v.* To get crushed into a rocky shoreline, with or without a surfboard.

eat up *v.* Hawaiian Pidgin slang for what happens when a wave swallows a surfer.

ebb, ebb tide *n.* A tide that is going from high to low (ORB); an outgoing tide.

edge *n.* **1)** A design feature on the side or rail of a surfboard. **2)** The portion of a wave that remains unbroken; the SHOULDER. Usage: "I was forced out on the edge."

egg *n.* **1)** A surfboard shape. Refers to the slow rounded shape of a nose, tail, or rail. —**eggy. 2)** A 1960s term for KOOK.

egg board, egg round tail, egg-shaped rounded tail *n.* A surfboard shape featuring an oval tail.

eggroll *n.* A raw novice; same as EGG (1960s), KOOK (1970s), and RUBBERNECK (1980s). There's a heavy PECKING ORDER in surfing; an "eggroll" is anyone who isn't as good as you. (Australia; MW)

E-glass *n.* A specific formula for fiberglass composition commonly used in building reinforcements for boats and surfboards. (ORB)

ego surfing *v.* Searching for your own name on the Internet. (Briggs Nisbet, 1996)

eight ball *n.* Another name for the PRIORITY BUOY used in competitive surfing. See GETTING BEHIND THE EIGHT BALL.

elephant gun *n.* A large surfboard designed especially for big surf, or the heavies; same as BIG GUN.

elevator effect, elevator-shaft drop, elevator-drop takeoff *n.* A sudden fall from the crest of the wave as the result of a sudden drop or elevation in wave height caused by a bottom shoal or depression or by a backwash or doubling.

elevator surfing *n.* The life- and limb-risking practice of riding up and down an elevator shaft on the *top* of an elevator. Generally practiced by East Coast frat boys suffering from alcohol poisoning.

"Then there's the horizontal. In some buildings you can get up to ten elevators in a line. It can take all day for that chance alignment. You could ride the surf from one side of the building to the other and perhaps take in a couple of verticals on the way."

—*The Museum of Contemporary Ideas Web site, New York*

elliptical rail *n.* A surfboard rail that is oval shaped in cross section and that produces a fairly low side spray and more speed than a round rail.

El Niño *n.* An anomalous warming of the ocean surface, associated with a vast fluctuation in atmospheric pressure, that triggers abnormal northward migration of southern species of seabirds and marine life and brings about global changes in weather patterns that have been linked to droughts, severe storms, flooding, and landslides. El Niño,

emergency canoe
Art: Jim Phillips

Spanish for "the Christ Child," got its name because of its periodic appearance around Christmas off the coast of Peru. (CCRG) Both the giant winter surf of 1983 and the occurrence during 1988 of possibly the flattest waves in recorded surfing history were attributed to El Niño. (SFG, March 1990)

el rollo *n.* **1)** Originally a hotdogging longboard maneuver, in which the surfer lies prone and rolls with the surfboard a complete 360 degrees—as seen performed by Corky Carroll and described by Bruce Brown in *The Endless Summer* (1964). Today it is more commonly identified as a bodyboarding maneuver. **2)** A maneuver performed in small surf to exit a wave.

El Spontanio (el spawn-TANE-ee-o) *n.* A squatting position where the surfer looks back between the legs, ordinarily while riding at the nose of the surfboard. In a pure El Spontanio, the fingers must be interlocked behind the surfer's back. The term is a corruption of the Spanish *el espontáneo* (the spontaneous one).

El Telephono (el tel-e-FONE-o) *n.* A hot-dog riding stance invented by Mickey Muñoz in the late 1950s; looks roughly like a bullfighter's classic stance or like someone trying to be thin in a telephone booth crush. The term is a corruption of the Spanish *el teléfono* (the telephone).

emergency canoe *n.* When you have to pull both your feet and arms up on your board, like sitting in a canoe. Usage: "I thought I saw a shark, so I made an emergency canoe." (TWS, December 1999)

emmit, emmits *n.* **1)** A term used by Cornwall surfers to describe tourists or spectators; the old Cornish word for "ants." (England; DMN) **2)** A British DEWEY.

employee surfing *n.* Hiring and firing. See SURFING AS METAPHOR.

Endless Summer A double anthology album of early sixties surfing and hot-rod tunes by The Beach Boys, which was released in 1974 on Capitol Records and thrust the group into a second wave of popularity.

Endless Summer, The Bruce Brown's feature-length film, which followed two surfers around the world in their search for the perfect wave; premiered in Wichita, Kansas, in 1964. Brown was

The Endless Summer *movie poster*
™ & © *Bruce Brown Films, 1966*
Art: John Van Hammersveld

originally planning to fly round-trip to South Africa from Los Angeles, but it turned out to be $50 cheaper to fly around the world, so he went for it and produced what many consider to be the all-time classic surf movie.

The movie sound track was by the Sandals; the album featured the classic instrumental theme of the movie, a mellow surf tune that evoked the feeling of surfing under the sun. The movie poster, done in classic sixties fluorescent colors of purple, orange, and yellow, was created by poster designer John Van Hammersveld; the image has been reproduced on T-shirts.

The following may have been the very first use of the term endless summer:
". . . the slumbrous calm of an endless summer, the glorious tropical trees, the distant view of cool chasmlike valleys, with Honolulu sleeping in perpetual shade, and the still blue ocean, without a single sail to disturb its profound solitude."

—Isabella Bird, "Impressions of Honolulu, 1873,"
from The Spell of Hawaii, *edited by*
A. Grove Day and Carl Stroven
(Mutual Publishing of Honolulu, 1968)

energy *n.* See OCEAN ENERGY.

enforcer *n.* A sixties term for a male surfer with a reputation for being very tough. He usually has a name like "Lunchmeat" or "Heavy Duty"; it's his job to keep the law and order in the water, on the beach, or at a party. (MCR)

enthusi *n.* Enthusiasm. Usage: "C'mon, where's your enthusi?" (Christopher Claiborne, Isla Vista, 1994)

epic *adj.* CLASSIC; something of grand proportions, as in "epic conditions," "epic surf," "an epic day."

epoxy board *n.* A lighter surfboard made out of epoxy resin.

epoxy resin *n.* A thermosetting resin used in boat work and consisting of two parts that, when combined, cure and form into an extremely hard and tough product. Epoxy resins adhere better and shrink less than polyester resins and have generally greater strength; they are also much more expensive. (ORB)

EPS foam *n.* Expanded polystyrene foam that doesn't yellow or break down in sunlight; however, it absorbs more water, and dinged boards must be removed from the sea and repaired immediately.

equatorial tides *n.* Tides of minimum range that occur twice a month when the moon is over the equator. (CCRG) See TROPIC TIDES.

ESA Eastern Surfing Association.

Eskimo roll *n.* **1)** A technique for getting out through a wave by capsizing the surfboard and using the body as an anchor. (MF) **2)** A means of getting past a broken wave. **3)** A method of going under waves when riding Malibus and wave skis. (NAT, 1985)

esky *n.* Australian term for an ice chest; derived from Eskimo. See HAUNTED COOLER.

esky lid *n.* Derogatory term for a bodyboarder. (Australia) See TOILET LID.

evening glass-off *n.* **1)** A late-afternoon surf session that sometimes extends past sunset. Usage: "Let's hit the evening glass-off." **2) evening glass** The calm, glassy surface of the ocean in the evening after the wind has died down. (A&M) See GLASS-OFF.

excellent *adj.* Great, fantastic, exceptionally high-quality, as in "totally excellent," "excellent waves," "excellent conditions," "most excellent." Valley gringo usage: "Hey, ex-SA LAN tay." (Gringo pronunciation of the Spanish *excellente.*)

exit track *n.* The projected path of a surfer steering the surfboard up over the back of a wave in order to terminate a ride.

exostosis *n.* A bone thickening in the ear canal caused by exposure to cold water. Also called SURFER'S EAR.

exothermic heat *n.* The heat given off by the resin during the curing process, or polymerization; caused by the reaction of the accelerator and the catalyst when mixed in polyester resins, and by the hardener in epoxy resins. (ORB)

explosive *adj.* Used to describe a style of surfing characterized by high-speed cutbacks, blasting off the tops of waves, and throwing around lots of spray.

extraction operation *n.* Sending in a game fisherman to catch a rogue shark. (Victoria, Australia; RDTW)

extreme *adj.* RADICAL; pushing the limits while surfing, as in "going to extremes."

Art: Jim Phillips

face *n.* **1)** The unbroken wall, surface, or nearly vertical front of a wave between the crest and the trough. **2)** The front portion of a wave—the part facing the shore—just before it breaks (JP); the unbroken inner curve of a wave. **3)** The desirable part of a wave to surf, as distinct from the white water. Also called WAVE FACE.

face plant *n.* WIPEOUT; a crossover term from skateboarding.

fade *n.* **1)** A move similar to a stall, in which a surfer slows down either to go deeper into the tube or to avoid colliding with another surfer on the same wave who is blocking his or her exit track. See STALL. **2)** Riding toward the curl or hot part of a wave before turning and riding across the face away from the curl; a maneuver used to stay in the hottest part of the wave. **3)** A motion after takeoff that directs the board toward the curl before the bottom turn. (L&L) —**fading to the inside**

fade turn *n.* A turning maneuver used to slow down so that one can wait for the advancing wave to catch up to the board.

fairing *n.* The way in which the contours of a surfboard blend together to produce a smooth appearance.

Fall Down Get Back Ups *v.* When you fall down on top of your board and get back up and keep on surfing. (Siestas and Olas)

falling tide *n.* When the tide is dropping, as distinct from a rising tide.

fall line *n.* The line of fastest descent from the crest to the base of a wave. (Australia; NAT, 1985).

family wave *n.* Any wave surfed together by a parent and offspring, i.e., father and son. (Zippers, Costa Azul, Baja California, 1998). See BROTHERHOOD WAVE, PARTY WAVE.

fan spray *n.* The spray of water a surfer casts when carving a sharp turn on a wave.

farmer john *n.* Sleeveless wetsuit with legs. See SHORT JOHN.

fast *adj.* **1)** As applied to boards, usually means highly maneuverable. May also be used to mean speedy. **2)** As applied to a wave, one that peels off along its length quickly or that travels shoreward at a fast rate. (RA) —**fast surf, fast zippers**

fast-closing adj. Applied to a wave on which the break begins at one end and moves rapidly across the wave line to the other end.

Fast Times at Ridgemont High A 1982 Hollywood movie staring Sean Penn as Jeff Spicoli, responsible for bringing GNARLY and DUDE into mainstream America's lexicon. (SFG, November 1989)

fat *adj.* **1)** Thick, as in a fat wave. **2)** Great, as in "That's so fat." Sometimes spelled *phat*.

fatch *n.* Fat chicks. (possible Newport Beach origin in the 1980s) See NO FAT CHICKS.

fat out *v.* An Australian term for a wave that has become less hollow and fuller, due to a deepening ocean bottom. (MW) Usage: "The wave tends to fat out over by the channel."

97

fat wave *n.* A wave that walls up, looks like it's going to tube, but drops out (loses shape) because of backwash or more water rushing up from behind. (Australia, C&M)

faucet nose *n.* A phenomenon that occurs when you come in after surfing, bend over, and the whole ocean pours out of your sinuses. (MCR) The condition is caused by having water forced up your nose during a wipeout. Same as POST-SESSION NASAL DRIP, NASODRAIN.

fear *adj.* Used to describe scary waves or scary women. Usage: "The waves are fear, it's so good out there." "That girl was fear."

fear factor *n.* An element of surfing, a consequence of big waves, sharks, etc.; something you just have to live with.

"**Courage is resistance to fear, not absence of fear.**"

—*Mark Twain*

"**To be alive at all, involves some risk!**"

—*Big wave surfer Harold MacMillan.
December 30, 1959*

feather 1) *v.* Used to describe the motion of a wave in the instant just before it breaks, when it seems to hang there suspended, or "feathering," just before its lip pitches out. **2) feathering wave** *n.* A wave that does not rise too steeply before breaking. The crest spills over, sliding down the wave face rather than rolling forcefully over. Also called SPILLING WAVE or FRINGING WAVE. (DSH)

feather edge *n.* The edge of a resin-saturated fiberglass material that has been tapered to blend with the adjoining surface, as opposed to ending abruptly. (ORB)

feebletosis *n.* Used to describe weak surfing conditions. (Eastside, Santa Cruz; SFR, August 1990) Usage: "It was feebletosis."

femmie, fem grem *n.* A female GREMMIE. Also called FREMLIN.

fer sure Surfer and valley girl pronunciation of "for sure," meaning totally, definitely, full agreement.

fetch *n.* The distance, or area, over which the wind blows across the water to create waves and swell. The waves may travel out of the particular wind system and cover a long way before reaching the coast as a ground swell. (L&L)

fiberglass, fiberglass cloth *n.* **1)** A woven glass fabric used in surfboard construction; its application is often referred to as a GLASS JOB. **2)** Literally fibers of glass. (GCD) **3)** Glass fibers woven into a cloth and saturated with resin before being used to strengthen the exterior of a surfboard's foam core, or blank. (ORB) **4)** The material that pro-

faucet nose
Art: Rick Stover

fiberglass
Photo: Stephanie Gene Morgan

vides the protective outer coating of a surfboard. (NAT, 1985).

❧❧❧❧❧❧❧❧❧❧❧❧

Fiberglass was invented in a Paris, France, textile mill in 1836, though the term itself didn't come into use until 1936. It comes in weights of four-ounce, six-ounce, etc., per square yard of cloth.

❧❧❧❧❧❧❧❧❧❧❧❧

fiberglass dust *n.* Microscopic bits of fiberglass produced during the shaping process that can be extremely itchy, especially when they work their way under your waistband and into your pants (GN); not good to inhale, either. See GLASS ITCH.

fifty-fifty *n.* A surfboard rail that is rounded or "soft." (MCR)

fill in *v.* When the tide begins to rise. Usage: "The tide started to fill in" or "It'll get better when the tide fills in."

filthy *adj.* HOT, UNREAL, OFF ITS TITS—in other words, totally great. (Australia; MW) Usage: "The waves were filthy out there."

fin *n.* **1)** The vertical projection, or rudder, affixed to a surfboard's bottom near the tail for the purpose of enhancing directional stability and drive. Surfboards can have one (single-fin), two (twin-fin), three (tri-fin), four (quad), or more fins. Also called SKEG. **2)** The dorsal fin of a shark or dolphin.

fin area *n.* The shape or outline of a fin; the surface area of a fin.

fin base *n.* The width of the fin where it meets the board.

fin box *n.* **1)** The three-eighths-inch-thick box that holds the base of removable fins, or skegs; generally made of molded plastic. It was invented by Hobie Alter in 1965. Allows for better water flow at the base of the fins, reducing drag and increasing speed. **2)** The sliding, angled adjustment toward or away from the stringer that allows a board to be adapted to waves of various size. **3)** A plastic channel that the fin slides into. (ORB) See DOVETAILED FIN BOX.

fin canter *n.* The angle of the fin leaned away from the stringer, as distinct from FIN TOE IN.

finger surfing *n.* Navigating telephone message boards by pushing buttons on a Touch Tone phone. ("I made it up." —R. K. Cralle, circa early 1990s)

fin height *n.* The distance from the bottom of the board at the fin base to the top of the fin.

fins
Photo: Trevor Cralle

fin box with removable skeg
Note leash damage is due to lack of rail saver
Photo: Don Balch

fins
Mac Reed Collection
Photo: Trevor Cralle

fish taco
San Quintin, Baja
Photo: David Gelles

finned *v.* To be run over by someone's skeg. (A&M)

fin placement *n.* The distance between the rear edge of the fin and the tip(s) of the tail, usually six or seven inches.

fin rake *n.* The degree the leading edge of a fin is swept back. A fin with more rake has a more drawn-out (longer) turning radius; one with less rake has a more pivotal (shorter) turning radius. See RAKE.

fins, swim fins *n.* Rubber flippers worn on the feet to help kick out and maneuver in bodysurfing, bodyboarding, and kneeboarding.

fin scheme *n.* Same as FIN SETUP.

fin setup *n.* The configuration of fins on the bottom of a surfboard.

fin slot *n.* The track that an adjustable fin slides along in a fin box.

fin toe in *n.* The angle of the fin leaning toward the stringer, as distinct from FIN CANTER.

fio dental (FEE-o-DEN-tal) *n.* Portuguese for "dental floss"—used to describe G-string bikinis. (Brazil) Same as FLOSS, BUTT THONG.

fire, firing *v.* GO OFF, GOING OFF. Another superlative to

describe good surf: "Hey brah, Super's is firing on all cylinders." (WVS)

first break *n.* **1)** The line of breakers farthest from shore on a given day. See ZERO BREAK. **2)** A specific location at a surf spot where the waves break only when they are sufficiently large.

first rider up Refers to a rule adopted by some competitive surfing organizations that gives priority (right-of-way) to the first surfer to stand up on a wave and ride it. All other surfers must yield to that person. See RIDER ON THE INSIDE.

fish *n.* A shortboard with added width and thickness, designed to improve wave catching capability while maintaining performance in small conditions.

fish killer *n.* Someone who FLAPS so hard they knock the fish out. (Santa Cruz)

fish taco *n.* A favorite surf snack consisting of fresh fish fried in lard, wrapped in a warm tortilla, and dressed with a full array of condiments including, but not limited to, salsa fresca, guacamole, and lime. (Baja California, Mexico) See BURRITO.

five-finned board *n.* A surfboard with five fins.

five toes over *n.* HANG FIVE. (DM, 1962)

flagged areas *n.* Swimming areas at beaches where surfboards are prohibited. See FLAGS.

flags *n.* Used to demarcate surfing and swimming areas along a beach and also, at some places, to indicate the condition of the surf. For example, at La Jolla, a **checked flag** denotes a surfing-only

flappin'
Art: Bob Penuelas

100

area; at Newport Beach, a **green flag** indicates light surf; a **yellow flag** means moderate; a **red flag** means heavy, and a **black ball flag** means no surfing.

flail *v.* To make eccentric, often funny, arm and body movements; to surf in a clumsy manner. Usage: "Tommy *flails*." (SFG, 1989)

flailer, flailing dork *n.* What beginning surfers are. (CVG) See FLOUNDER.

flap, flappin' *v.* To make spastic arm movement; to FLAIL. See BOOGIE FLAPPER.

flare *n.* A widened portion of the tail of a surfboard; characteristic of hot-dog boards. This design feature provides greater maneuverability and stability at lower speeds.

flat *adj.* **1)** Refers to surfless ocean or surfless conditions. Usage: "The surf's flat today." **2)** Said of the section of wave that has no power. (NAT, 1985) **3)** A characteristic of some bottom contours or planing surfaces. Usage: "The rocker is very flat in the tail half."

flat calm *adj.* British/Aussie term for total absence of wind. Smooth and GLASSY.

flat deck *n.* The contour or shape of the top surface of a surfboard, where the rail turns down quickly. See DECK CONTOUR.

flatlander *n.* INLANDER.

flatman *n.* Derogatory term for a bodyboarder. See HALF MAN, NO MAN.

flats *n.* **1)** A surfboard shaper's term for the top and bottom of the board. **2)** The area out in front of a breaking wave.

flat spell *n.* A long period—maybe a few days, or even weeks—without surf.

flat calm
Playa El Coyote, Baja
Photo: Trevor Cralle

flat spot *n.* **1)** The relatively horizontal water space between wave crests. Also known as FLATS. **2)** A large COMPRESSION DING.

flatten, flatten out *v.* What a wave does as it passes over a deep spot in the bottom contour. See BACKING OFF.

flex *n.* A measure of how rigid or flexible a surfboard is structurally; considered by many to be the most dynamic action a board exhibits. Usage: "Your board really has a lot of flex in it."

flexible fin *n.* A fin that absorbs, stores, and then releases turning energy by snapping back into line, thus giving the surfboard added thrust through a delayed response.

flick nose *n.* A dramatic increase in the ROCKER near the nose.

flick-off *n.* A maneuver used to kick the board clear of the breaking wave. (NAT, 1985)

flick out *v.* An Australian term for PULL OUT or KICK OUT. **—flickout** *n.*

flip-flops *n.* Rubber sandals. Also called GO-AHEADS.

flipout *n.* A PULLOUT with a somersault.

flip-flops
Photo: Trevor Cralle

flippers *n.* SWIM FINS.

floater *n.* **1)** A maneuver in which the board slides on top of a white water section. **2)** Riding over the white water after a wave breaks, to get back onto the face. (JP) **3)** A move initiated by Cheyne Horan in 1983, where the surfer rides over the falling curtain of a breaking wave. (MW) See CURTAIN FLOATER. **4)** A large, buoyant surfboard.

floater
Vince De La Peña
Photo: Robert Brown

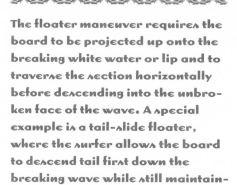

The floater maneuver requires the board to be projected up onto the breaking white water or lip and to traverse the section horizontally before descending into the unbroken face of the wave. A special example is a tail-slide floater, where the surfer allows the board to descend tail first down the breaking wave while still maintaining control. (L&L)

floater reentry *n.* A maneuver in which the surfer heads up into, and comes over with, the breaking part of a wave; allows the surfer to travel over a closed-out white-water section and continue riding. Sometimes called ROLLER COASTER. See CURTAIN FLOATER, FOAM FLOATER.

floaties *n.* Pieces of shit in the water.

floating air biscuits What happens when a surfer farts in a wetsuit and the smell comes right out the neck. (Santa Cruz grommet)

floaty *adj.* Used to describe a surfboard that floats high in the water. Usage: "Your board's a bit floaty, mate." (Australia; ASL, February 1988) See CORK.

flood, flood tide *n.* A tide that is going from low to high. (ORB)

flop out *v.* To exit a wave.

floss, flosser, bun floss *n.* A thong-backed bikini. (Southern California) Same as BUTT FLOSS, BUTT THONG, FIO DENTAL.

flotation, floatation *n.* The ability of a board to float a surfer; its buoyancy.

flounder *v.* **1)** FLAIL. Usage: "You were floundering out there." **2)** To struggle after being pounded by the surf. Usage: "Did you get floundered out there?" **3) flounder buoy** *n.* Someone who is in the way of the other surfers. See BUOY.

flow 1) *v.* To get free stuff from a surf shop. Usage: "Flow me some wax." "Flow me a leash with that board." (Santa Cruz; JMZ) **2)** To move or run freely; to hang loose, make a smooth motion. (RO) Usage: "Surfing is a sport that really *flows.*" **3)** *n.* An incoming tide, as in "ebb and flow"; a FLOOD TIDE.

"Go with the flow. Like a stick floatin' down a creek, and the foam surrounding algae covered rocks. Like urethane bouncing off road debris, a gentle breeze pushing forward. So let it flow and let yourself go!"

—SLAP *magazine, November 1993*

"Don't accept it
Don't reject it.
Just flow with it."

—*Tom Wolfe,* The Electric Kool-Aid Acid Test

Flow Rider *n.* A machine that pumps 10,000 gallons of water per minute to create a standing wave. Created in Big Rock, Texas, in the early 1990s by Tom Lochtefeld, who teamed up with inventor/surfboard builder Carl Ekstrom. Considered to be the best artificial tube on the globe.

Floyd, Floyd wave *n.* Said of walled-out conditions. Derived from the Pink Floyd album *The Wall.* (1994)

fluid *adj.* Smooth. Usage: "Greg really has a fluid style of surfing."

flyaway *n.* Stepping to the tail of the board and wrenching your body and board sharply to get out of a wave.

flying cutout *n.* A cutout in which board and rider fly back over the crest of the wave separately and through the air.

flying kickout *n.* **1)** An exit from a wave in which the surfer kicks the board out from underneath while up in the air. **2)** An attempted aerial that ends in a wipeout. See COVER-SHOT SURFING.

flying swan *n.* **1)** A tandem surf-riding position, with the female sitting on the male partner's shoulders with her arms outstretched. **2)** A bodysurfing position with arms extended outward to the side.

foam *n.* **1)** A chemically produced hard plastic (polyurethane) cellular structure that is shaped into a surfboard; the core of the surfboard. **2)** The frothy aftermath of a broken wave.

The first person to try foam in a surfboard was Bob Simmons in 1950, using polystyrene foam. In 1955, Lorrin Harrison in Capistrano Beach became the first to try polyurethane foam, and in 1956 Dave Sweet in Santa Monica made the first sustained effort to develop polyurethane foam boards. Hobie Alter came out with the first successful polyurethane foam board design in June 1958. Then in 1961 Gordon "Grubby" Clark formed Clark Foam, which is still the largest foam-blank manufacturer in the world. Foam didn't change surfboard design all that much, but it did stabilize and

flying cutout
Brian McNulty, Haleiwa
Photo: Bill Romerhaus

streamline the boards. The same type of board could be made over and over again without worrying about the different weights of wood, bad grain, etc. **(GN)**

foam ball *n.* WHITE-WATER MUSH. (Bolinas)

foam blank, foam block *n.* The basic block of foam from which a board is shaped. Gordon "Grubby" Clark is the person most responsible for the development of the foam blank. (SFR, June 1987)

foam flapper *n.* SPONGE RIDER. (Santa Cruz)

foam floater *n.* A distance-covering floater that originates and ends in the white water. It enhances white-water riding potential by offering an alternative to GROVELING, TRIMMING, or HOPPING. (L&L) See FLOATER REENTRY.

foamie, foamer *n.* An Australian term for a surfboard made of foam. Also known as POLY.

foam pump turns *n.* Maneuvers in which the whole of the surfer's board is behind the section of white water on a horizontal plane. (L&L)

foam rider *n.* Someone who only catches a wave after it has broken and turned into white water.

foam rot *n.* Decay of the core of a surfboard as a result of the board's becoming waterlogged and damaged by exposure to the sun.

foam trim *n.* Efforts, such as hopping or wiggling, aimed at maintaining momentum through white-water sections; carries no point value in surfing competitions. (L&L) Same as GROVELING.

foam turn *n.* Surfing the board up, around, and over a white-water section; an alternative to riding straight or groveling.

foff, foffing *v.* TO GO OFF, but more so; said of waves or surfers. Usage: "Big Rock was foffing yesterday: six feet, glassy and offshore." (North San Diego County; Rob Gilley, 1989)

fog, fog bank *n.* Condensed water vapor in cloudlike masses, which can make good swells bad and bad surf even worse. Variations include **low fog, high fog,** or, if you've been on drugs, **foggy.** Light, onshore winds usually accompany fog and make the surf bumpy and sort of blown out. In very dense fog, though, the ocean is occasionally glassy. See MARINE LAYER. (W&B)

foil *n.* **1)** The distribution of foam on a surfboard, viewed lengthwise from the side; the THICKNESS FLOW. **2)** The thickness cross section of a fin. (ORB)

—asymmetrical foil

following current *n.* An ocean current that is flowing in the same direction that a swell is traveling, thus increasing wave lengths and decreasing wave heights, the opposite effect of an OPPOSING CURRENT. (DKM)

food *n.* Anything from the ocean. Same as GRINDS. See BURRITO, FISH TACO, SHAVE ICE.

football-type S fin *n.* An S-shaped fin with a narrow base.

foot ding *n.* Any bump or scrape on the foot acquired onshore or in the water. See CRATERS, DING.

foam ball
Kevin Parker
Baldwin Park, Maui
Photo: Trevor Cralle

foot-over-foot walking *n*. CROSS STEP, CROSS-STEPPING.

foot paddling *n*. While standing, dipping one foot over the side of a longboard and paddling to increase forward motion.

forehand surfing *n*. Riding with the body facing the wave. (L&L) **—forehand floater**

forehand turn *n*. Making a turn with the body facing the wall of the wave; affords greater stability and control than a backhand turn.

formula ones *n*. Hammerhead sharks. (Australia; MW)

forward roll pullout *n*. A bodysurfing technique for getting off of a wave by somersaulting forward. (MF)

fossil *n*. Someone who is over the hill in the surfing world; one whose heyday is past and who now clings to some hope of regaining recognition. A fossil will sometimes "yarn" (spin yarns) about how great it used to be. (ALN)

four-fin *n*. A surfboard with four fins located near the rails, where they can dig in when the board is leaned on edge. Same as QUAD.

four/three *n*. Refers to the standard Northern California wetsuit, constructed of neoprene panels that are four and three millimeters thick. Always written numerically, "4/3." See MIL.

France The European country that provided surfing with two wonderful inventions: fiberglass and the bikini.

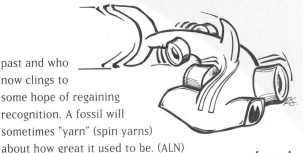

formula one
Art: Rick Stover

French Surf Glossary

"Parlez vous surfer?"

beach: *plage*
jellyfish: *méduse*
ocean: *ocean*
pier: *jetée*
point: *pointe*
reef: *récif*
sea: *la mer*
sea breeze: *brise de mer*
shark: *requin*
snowboarding: *surf de neige*
surf/surfing: *faire du surf*
    (*verb to surf*)

surfboard: *table de surf*
surfer: *surfeur*
surf wax: *cire*
swell: *houle*
tide: *marée*
high tide: *haute marée*
low tide: *basse marée*
wave: *vague*
big: *grande*
small: *petit*
wind: *vent*
offshore: *vent de terre*

frogskins
Art: Rick Stover

freak set *n.* A surprise set of big waves that catches surfers off guard or on the inside. See CAUGHT INSIDE.

Fred Flintstone The name of a Hanna-Barbera cartoon character, which is given to people who can't surf and get in the way. (KSO) Usually just called **fred**; same as BARNEY or WALLY.

free ballin' *v.* Surfing naked. (Santa Cruz) See CHUMMIN'.

freeboard *n.* The portion of the surfboard that extends above the water.

freeboarding *n.* Riding a surfboard while being pulled by a boat. (1960s)

free fall *n.* A mishap that can befall a surfer who is riding high or taking off on a very steep wave and whose surfboard slips out, so that both board and rider fall in midair down the face of the wave. May or may not result in a wipeout.

free-lapping *n.* The process of laying up a rail without trimming it.

free roundtrip ticket over the falls Getting pitched over the front of a wave. (Texas; H&R) See OVER THE FALLS.

Freeth, George (1883-1919) The Irish-Hawaiian who introduced surfing to Southern California. In 1907 Henry Huntington brought him to Redondo Beach and sponsored surfing exhibitions in an effort to boost ticket sales for the Pacific Electric Railroad and to promote a new saltwater plunge. (DM) Freeth's surfing demonstrations at Redondo are generally regarded as the first appearance of the sport on the California coast.

However, see KAWONANAOKOA. A bronze bust of Freeth is located at the foot of the Redondo Beach Municipal Pier.

freeway surfer *n.* A would-be surfer who spends more time driving a car than surfing. (MM) See HIGHWAY SURFER.

freight trains *n.* **1)** Used to describe the appearance of a wave breaking fast in a perfect line down the beach. (MM) **2)** Big, powerful ocean swells. Usage: "Look at those freight trains starting to smoke in."

fremlin *n.* A female GREMLIN.

fringing wave *n.* FEATHERING WAVE.

Frisbee *n.* **1)** A polyethylene plastic flying saucer used by surfers on the beach. First began to be widely marketed in the late fifties and early sixties. *Frisbee* is a registered trademark of Wham-O Manufacturing Company, San Gabriel, California. Also called FRIS or DISC. **2)** A popular device for entertaining surfers at surf movies. **3)** Something to eat off of during surf trips to Baja. **4) ultimate Frisbee** A team sport played in an open area such as a beach or a field.

frogskins *n.* An outfit consisting of a wetsuit and other cold-water articles such as gloves and booties. (Texas; H&R)

frontside *adj., adv.* Riding with the body facing the wave. (ORB) Usage: "She took off frontside."

Frisbee
Photo: Trevor Cralle

frontside layback *n.* An advanced bodyboarding maneuver. See LAYBACK.

frontside under-the-lip snap *n.* An advanced bodyboarding maneuver in which the rider gets under the wave lip and turns sharply.

frozen wave *n.* Snow-covered mountain slope for snowboarding.

full-on *adj., adv.* Complete, entire, total. Usage: "I had the full-on wipeout today." "We were full-on stoked." "That party was a full-on rager." **—full stoke**

full-power drift *n.* A sliding turn on a wave.

full-rail cutback *n.* When you bury the rail of the board in the wave face as you turn back into the wave.

full rails *n.* Thick rails; a surfboard design feature for increasing flotation.

full stick *n.* A longboard that is full-size, as opposed to a routed shortboard.

full suit *n.* A one-piece wetsuit consisting of long sleeves and legs. Occasionally includes an attached hood (attached booties are rare in a surfing wetsuit). Also called STEAMER.

full template *n.* A surfboard that, viewed from above, is wider than normal. See PULLED TEMPLATE.

fully *adv.* Absolutely complete, as in "fully real," "fully stoked," and "The waves were fully throbbing." (SFR, June 1988)

funboard *n.* A combination of short and longboard designs in one board. Designed for playing around on waves, as distinct from a gun or high-performance shortboard. See HYBRID.

functional distance *n.* One of the scoring criteria in competitive surfing; it involves being able to hold one's line (keep moving) through the smallest part of the wave while continuing to do maneuvers. (L&L) See SURFING CRITERIA.

functional maneuvers *n.* In a surf competition, any of certain well-defined maneuvers that can be scored, for example, a floater, cutback, or tube ride.

fun shape *n.* See FUNBOARD.

fun surf, fun waves *n.* Small or medium surf not big enough to make a surfer think twice before taking off or to cause any worry about taking a wipeout. (CC) **—fun surfing**

gale *n.* A grade of storm. Gale-force winds range from thirty-two to sixty-three miles per hour.

gangreeneous (gain-green-e-us) *adj.* A surfer corruption of *gangrenous* that is used to describe a gnarly coral cut, as in "Gangreeneous, dude." (Southern California)

gaper *n.* Wide open barrel. —**gaping barrel**

garaged *n.* A barrel so big you could park your car in it.

garbage *n.* No explanation needed. Usage: "The surf was garbage today." (EPZ)

gargantuan *adj.* Used to describe an immense wave; about the same as HUMONGOUS.

gas money *n.* What every surfer is always trying to dig up in order to get to the beach.

gassed *v.* Getting wiped out on a wave. See TAKING GAS.

gator mini *n.* A shriveled up penis at the end of a cold session. (Santa Cruz)

geek, geekster, geek-a-mo *n.* **1)** A dorky surfer who behaves poorly at the beach. **2)** Originally, a carnival sideshow freak who bit the heads off live chickens. **3) geeky, geeklified** *adj.* Usage: "That's completely geeklified." (RBQ)

gel *n.* **1)** A flake. Usage: "Did you see that guy trying to pick up my girlfriend on the beach today? What a gel." Or, occasionally, "Hey, gel brain, take off on me one more time and I'll carve my initials in your back with my twin fin." **2)** A derelict or do-nothing. (SFG, December

1981) **3)** A stage resin goes through—the physical state in between a liquid and a solid. (GCD) **4)** *v.* To mellow out. (SP) Usage: "Gel, dude."

Gentlemen's Hour, The *n.* That special time of day when you paddle out to a typically crowded spot and find a couple of friendly older surfers. Greetings and salutations are usually exchanged. Usage: "Welcome to the lineup. You've come into The Gentlemen's Hour. Have a few waves." (Malibu)

gerbe (G-air-B-ear) *n.* South African term for shark. (WVS)

getable *adj.* surfable. Usage: "If it's getable, he'll get it." (Bolinas 1997)

get air, getting air *v.* To maneuver the surfboard so that both rider and board leave the surface of the ocean. Usage: "Hey dude, check it out. Did you see me get air?" (MVA) Same as CATCH AIR.

get covered up *v.* To be TUBED. See COVERED.

get "L" *v.* To gain elevation (altitude) on an aerial. (TLH)

get launched *v.* To be catapulted from the board.

get piped *v.* To achieve a tube ride. (WW)

get pitched *v.* To become airborne.

get spun *v.* **1)** To experience the washing machine spin-cycle effect when you're held underwater in the surf after wiping out. **2)** To get closed out for a very long time.

getting a place wired *v.* To figure out how the waves break at a specific surf spot, as seen in the movie *The Endless Summer* (1964). See WIRED.

gibblet
Kimberly Carlson
Ventura, California
Photo: Sherry Carlson

getting behind the eight ball *v.* To paddle around the priority buoy.

getting bombed *v.* What happens to a surfer who gets "avalanched" by a big wave.

getting caught in the white water *v.* When the avalanche-like mass of foaming white water overtakes a surfer from behind.

getting caught inside *v.* Describes the situation when continuously breaking waves prevent a surfer from paddling out through the white water or when one really big wave breaks on a surfer before he or she can paddle over the top. See CAUGHT INSIDE.

getting parked *v.* Getting tubed. For example, you'd pull up to a spot on a good day and say, "There's lots of parking spaces out there." (Corona Del Mar, SFR, January 1992)

getting stuffed in the pit *v.* To be left in the foam because a surfer down the line in front of you has stalled so much that you can't keep moving. (KSO) Usage: "That kook totally stuffed me in the pit."

getting up drop-knee standing up *v.* A bodyboarding maneuver in which the surfer quickly moves from the prone position to kneeling to standing up.

getting way back *v.* To surf deep inside the tube.

get tubed, getting tubed *v.* To ride or shoot a tube.

get worked *v.* To be put on "spin cycle"; to be punished by a bad wipeout. (P) See WASHING MACHINE.

ghost shaper *n.* A shaper working under a master shaper who can't satisfy the demand for his boards alone and must take on help.

ghost wave *n.* A wave that passes unridden as it rolls through the lineup.

gibblet *n.* A surfer between the ages of one and five; too young to be a grommet. Usage: "Look at that little gibblet, he's already ripping over me and he's like two or something." (TWS January 2000)

Gidget 1) The nickname of a real person named Kathy Kohner, whose father wrote a book about her called Gidget, which was a best-seller in 1957. **2)** The main character in the original *Gidget* film (1959), made after the book, and in several derivative films. See TUBESTEAK. **3)** A television series of the same name.

Kathy Kohner got her nickname from the other surfers when she showed up at Malibu Beach, California, in the summer of 1955 to surf. She explained, "I'm so small [they] called me Midget. I got mad. So now it's Gidget. A girl midget. A gidget. Get it?" After her father, Frederick Kohner, wrote a best-selling book about her adventures, her story was adapted into a popular movie called *Gidget*, which gave surfing its first national exposure. The film was shot at Secos, a Southern California surf spot;

Sandra Dee played the starring role, with Mickey Muñoz doing her stunt work.

This was the first of several Gidget films (*Gidget Goes Hawaiian*, etc.) that set the stage for a wave of beach movies in the 1960s. Then the craze hit television, too, with Sally Field starring in a series about fun, fun, fun in the California sun along the shores of Santa Monica. Like the movie, the TV program chronicled the antics of Francine Lawrence (Gidget) and her surfer pals, Jeff Matthews (Moondoggie), Siddo, Larue, and Treasure. The half-hour sitcom aired thirty-two episodes on ABC from September 15, 1965 to September 1, 1966. *The New Gidget*, a TV pilot in the 1980s, starred Don Stroud. According to many, surfing's image suffered irreversible damage as a result of all the Gidget mania. (S&C; JJV)

gilligan *n.* Same as FRED, BARNEY, WALLY, etc.; derived from the character of the same name played by Bob Denver on the TV series *Gilligan's Island*.

gilligan's ball rash *n.* Wetsuit rash. (Santa Cruz)

gitch *n.* Half girl and half bitch; derived from Gitch Anderson in the movie *Under the Boardwalk* (1989).

G-Land An abbreviation for Grajagan (GRAHD-ja-kin), one of the world's hottest surf spots for lefts, on the island of Java in Indonesia.

glass 1) *v.* To laminate resin-saturated fiberglass cloth to a shaped blank. **2)** *n.* short for FIBERGLASS.

glass coat *n.* GLASS JOB.

glasshouse *n.* A smooth ride inside a tubing wave. Usage: "Did you see me pull into that glasshouse?" Also called GREENHOUSE.

glass itch *n.* A skin irritation caused by fiberglass dust. (A&M)

glass job *n.* The application of fiberglass to a surfboard.

glass-off *n.* **1)** A condition usually found in the early morning or evening when the wind dies and the waves become smooth and glassy looking. **2)** A smooth water surface. (MM) **—afternoon glassy slick**

glass-on fin, glassed-on fin *n.* A fin that is permanently affixed to the surfboard, as distinct from a removable fin.

glassout *n.* A day when the surface of the ocean is unruffled and ideal for surfing. See GLASSY.

glassy *adj.* Used to describe an extremely calm ocean surface or wave, usually giving off a glasslike reflection; silky smooth. Glassy conditions usually occur early in the morning when there is no wind.

gliding ability *n.* A surfboard performance characteristic. (L&L) A board's ability to glide through the water is affected by many things, including its shape, weight, and body contour. **—gliding demise**

glass
Gordon Arrendale
Photo: Woody Woodworth

gloss coat, gloss *n.* The thin, final finish coat of resin that is buffed out.

gloss resin *n.* **1)** A thinned resin that has leveling and surfacing agents added to it. **2)** The final coat applied to a surfboard, which is wet-sanded and polished to give the board its smooth, glossy finish.

glue foot *n.* A surfer who almost never falls off the surfboard. (MCR)

gluing up *v.* Joining pieces of foam together, for instance to form the block out of which a surfboard is shaped.

gnar-gnar *adj.* A Laguna Beach term for GNARLY (said in a high-pitched voice). (LWK)

gnarlatious *adj.* Anything that's really cool, huge, or awesome, like a wave. (RBQ) Usage: "Gnarlatious waves today, bro."

gnarly (NAR-le) *adj.* **1)** Treacherous; same as HAIRY. Big waves with glossy faces and clean barrels are considered gnarly. Usage: "In gnarly conditions, watch yourself." (A&M; JP) **2)** A dramatic term for a wave with a real mean streak—the kind of wave that can eat a surfer for breakfast and then use the board as a toothpick. (MW; CVG) **3)** A

term for monster surf. (MM) **4)** According to a Surf Punks glossary, any wave over two feet, or any girl over 120 pounds; **nar** for short. (SP) **5)** Large and dangerous. Usage: "San Onofre was gnarly this morning." (SFG, 1989) "Those were the gnarliest waves out there." (BC, Spring 1990) **6) your gnarlyness** The proper way to address an important dignitary or good friend. **7) get gnarled** *v.* To get thrashed in the surf, as in "all gnarled up." —**gnarly ass, gnarler, total gnarl, gnarliest**

According to Webster's, the word *gnarly,* a variant form of *gnarled,* was used in 1829. Among surfers (with whom the word is most commonly identified), *gnarly* may have first been used at a California surf spot where Torrey pine or Monterey cypress trees grew. Their gnarled roots and branches may have inspired comparisons with the waves.

"I feel so gnarled out."

—*Kiakima Simon*

go-abb *n.* A person like a geek, but not as bothersome. See ABB. (MVA)

go-aheads *n.* Rubber sandals. (GN) Same as FLIP-FLOPS.

goat boat or **goatboat** *n.* A derogatory method of describing a PADDLE SKIER or

WAVE SKIER, the sort of person that goes out in the surf paddling on a canoe that looks like a half-sucked lozenge. The reason why STANDUP SURFERS don't like them much is because goatboats paddle faster. If in the wrong hands, they can also wreak havoc in the water. (Tasmania and South Africa, WVS)

goat in a boat *n.* A derogatory term for a SEA KAYAKER. (Santa Cruz)

go behind A hot-dogging maneuver where one surfer passes over another surfer, and then the surfer who was passed repeats the maneuver. (MCR)

go beyond vert *v.* To surf past the vertical plane.

go for it An expression meaning "Do it!" —take a chance, go ahead and try it. This phrase has been adopted by many, but it was probably popularized by California surfers in the early 1970s. Someone can be said to have a "go-for-it attitude." **GFI** for short. Usage: "Go for it, dude."

go high on the wave *v.* To surf up close to the lip.

going off *v.* **1)** When waves are consistent and breaking smoothly. (JP) **2)** Same as RIPPING, UNREAL, HAPPENING. **3)** Said when someone is shooting along in perfect surf. Usage: "Keith was going off."

going richter *v.* Tearing it up. See OFF THE RICHTER.

going to church *n.* Early sixties expression for GETTING TUBED. (Long Beach, DWK) Same as IN THE POPE'S LIVING ROOM.

go into Zen *v.* When you relax and don't panic during a big wipeout. See HELD DOWN.

Gold Coast A forty-kilometer stretch along Australia's east coast in the state of Queensland, beginning at Southport and ending at Tweed Heads and encompassing such surf spots as Surfers Paradise, Burleigh Heads, Kirra, and Point Danger. Has the finest collection of point breaks in such close proximity anywhere in the world. (NAT, 1986)

gone surf-o *v.* To be crazy over waves; STOKED.

goob *n.* geek.

"Good Vibrations" A 1967 song by The Beach Boys, composed by Brian Wilson; gave rise to such expressions as "getting good vibes." See VIBE.

goof *v.* To perform casual, fun maneuvers on a longboard.

"I like longboarding because you can goof."

—Jay Ward, Powis Beach, 1998

go off *v.* **1)** (of resin) To change from a liquid to a solid. (GCD) See GEL. **2)** (of a surfer) To surf radically. See GOING OFF. Usage: "Yeah, Australia goes off" (said in an Australian accent).

goofy foot or **goofy-foot** *n.* **1)** Riding a surfboard with your right foot forward, left foot back; the opposite of a natural footer. **2)** A left-handed surfer who rides with the right foot forward, left foot back .—**goof, goofy footer, goofy-foot surfer**

Goofy foot is one of the oldest terms still current in surfing jargon, and one never revised: someone who stands on the surfboard with the right foot forward. Most surfers are natural footers, meaning they use a left-foot-forward stance. Some well-known goofy footers are Gerry Lopez, David Nuuiwa, Rory Russell, Tom Carroll, Mark Occhilupo, and Derek Ho.

---

goon *n.* KOOK. The term was derived from a 1930s Popeye the Sailor animated cartoon in which Popeye gets shipwrecked on the Island of the Goonies. (IBN) See GYROGOON. **goonies** Derived from goonie birds on Midway Island.

goonbaa *n.* GOON. (Mark Andre, Carlsbad, California)

grab the rail
Brian Hart
Salza Brava, Costa Rica
Photo: Mike Peralta

goon cord *n.* A derogatory term for a SURF LEASH. Also called a KOOK CORD.

goon squad *n.* A derogatory term for a car full of surfers; about the same as MEAT WAVE.

goop *n.* Liquid resin used for surfacing surfboards.

go-out *n.* A surf session. Also called FULL GO-OUT. Usage: "We can go for the full go-out this afternoon."

go-outable *adj.* SURFABLE. Usage: "It wasn't even a go-outable day." See UN-GO-OUTABLE.

go over the falls *v.* To be picked up by a large dumping wave and carried down its curl. (DHSJ) See OVER THE FALLS.

Got it! What you say to someone down the line who's taking off or dropping in on a wave that you're already surfing on, meaning "This wave is mine." Same as MY WAVE.

gouge *v.* **1)** To hurt oneself while surfing. **2)** To ding a surfboard. **3)** To make aggressive maneuvers on a wave (MM); to carve a large divot out of a wave. (SFG, 1989) Usage: "Did you see me gouge that cutback?"

grabbers *n.* Invading surfers who steal or grab waves from other surfers.

grab-rail aerial *n.* A move in which the surfer grabs the rail while flying through the air; has its functional roots in skateboard ramp riding.

grab the rail, grabbing the rail *v.* A maneuver used by a surfer who is about to be hit by a wave or white water, in which he or she holds onto the outside edge of the board, leans toward the wave, and pulls the board into the wave to keep from being knocked off; allows the surfer to continue on in the curl, through a section, or on the unbroken wave ahead.

grab your board, grab your stick *v.* To pick up your surfboard and go surfing.

grape smuggler *n.* Speedo swimsuit on a male.

grate surfing *n.* Running and sliding on slippery land-based surfaces; works especially well when it's wet. Term coined by Gnarly Charley, San Francisco, November 25, 1997.

graveyard *n.* BONE YARD.

greased *adj.* Wiped out by a wave. Usage: "They just got *greased.*" (Steamer Lane, 1993)

great white shark *n.* Popular name for WHITE SHARK.

green, green wave *n.* An UNBROKEN WAVE. Sometimes referred to as the SHOULDER of a wave.

greenback *n.* **1)** An UNBROKEN WAVE. **2)** A swell that peaks higher and higher but has not yet begun to spill white water down its face. (Australia; AHK)

greenhouse *n.* GLASSHOUSE.

greenie in a bottle *n.* An Australian term for Heineken beer, which comes in a green bottle.

green monsters *n.* Very big waves.

greeno cutback *n.* Where you surf way out on to the shoulder before cutting back into the wave; inspired by George Greenough. (Jacksonville, Florida 1993)

green room *n.* **1)** The space inside of a tube. Usage: "I was deep inside the green room." Same as GLASSHOUSE. It is every surfer's dream to spend even a second or two in that "green room." (GN) **2)** A room painted green. (SP)

"... and these waves throw out over the top of you. Suddenly you're inside this enclosure, a green room, and the wave has broken completely over you. If you want, you can yodel or yell and the noise bounces off the side of the walls. You go on like this for a while, then you go flying out of the other end of this tube into daylight."

—from a Bob Simmons story in Greg Noll's Da Bull (1989).

green waves *n.* Small unbroken waves that are steep enough for riding.

green womb *n.* Inside of a tube. Same as GREEN ROOM. See WOMB.

gremlin *n.* **1)** A beginning surfer. See GREMMIE. **2)** A selfish, undesirable pest who is constantly in trouble and constantly creating trouble for fellow surfers. (DSHJ) **3)** A troublemaker; one whose misdeeds cause surfing beaches to be lost and give surfing a bad name.

—gremlin-devouring tubes English writer Roald Dahl (d. 1990) claims to have coined the word during WW II.

"Gremlins Perverse, resourceful, and mischievous air pixies, or imps, charged with the blame for virtually anything that can go unexpectedly wrong with or in an airplane."

—from "Glossary of Important New Words in the News," Funk & Wagnall's New Standard Encyclopedia Year Book for 1942

gremmer *n.* GROMMET; from the movie *Under the Boardwalk* (1989).

gremmie or **gremmy** *n.* **1)** A fifties and sixties term for a stoked preteen who inhabits surfing beaches and hangs out with, idolizes, and imitates his or her hero. **2)** Either an inexperienced and troublesome surfer or an objectionable nonsurfer who hangs around with surfers and tries to act like them in everything except aquatic skill. **3)** Any kid under fifteen who is stoked out of his or her gourd on surfing. (A&M) **4)** A young, poorly mannered surfer who is a beginner at riding the waves; sometimes a little kid, not necessarily trouble-some. **5)** A young surfer, usually a trou-blemaker, who usually has long blonde hair and baggy pants. **6)** A young and inexperienced surf enthusiast to whom nothing counts in life but a surfboard and waves. **7)** An uncomplimentary term for those who hang around the beach for reasons other than surfing, but less harsh than HODAD. Also called

SURF PUNK. See GROMMET, WEED. —**beach grem, gremmyville**

gremmy coat *n.* Apparel worn by just about every surfer in the sixties on cold winter days. Trench coats, tanker jackets, Goodwill suit coats, Navy pea jackets, moth-eaten fur coats, and ankle-length Luftwaffe officers' coats were especially favored. (A&M) Same as BEACH COAT.

greyzy *adj.* Grey & hazy conditions.

grim situation *n.* **1)** A close call. **2)** Big surf favorable for big-wave riders. —**grim** *adj.*

grind *v.* Getting worked by mean waves, as in **grinded**. (Hawaii, 1991) See SUCK MILK.

grind-down zone *n.* The low spot sur-rounding the actual ding in the surface of a surfboard; an extremely important concept in ding repair. (GCD)

grinder *n.* A power tool used in combi-nation with a #36-grit resin-backed disk to remove fiberglass and resin quickly and efficiently; it can also be turned on edge and used as a cutting tool to open up those dings that are caved in. Attachments such as a power pad or a buffing pad are used for fine sanding and polishing. (GCD)

grinders *n.* Big waves. See POINT GRINDER.

grinding 1) *adj.* Said of powerful waves that are breaking consistently. (MM) **2)** *v.* Used to describe an aggressive rid-ing style. Usage: "You were fully grinding out there."

grinds *n.* Food. Usage: "Let's go get some grinds." or "Killer grinds, brah." (Hawaii) —**grindage** (Jacksonville, Florida, 1993)

116

grinds

Marty Matthews
Punta Chivato, Baja
Photo: Trevor Cralle

gripped *adj.* That frozen feeling right when you're about to take off on a big wave or a steep drop; caused by watching the wave suck out. Usage: "Man, I was gripped." (Jack Barclay)

grit *n.* A cigarette. (Leucadia)

grit cloth *n.* A grit-coated screen used for blending rail contours during the foam-shaping process.

groin *n.* A wall or embankment, constructed at right angles to the shoreline, that projects out into the water. Its purpose is usually to prevent beach erosion, but in some cases it also creates waves for surfing. See JETTY, BREAKWATER.

grom *n.* GROMMET. (Australia; ASL February 1988) —**groms** Usage:"I just had my sixteenth birthday the other day and I was wondering when **gromhood** ends." —Brandt Bacha, Dana Point, California, letter to *Surfing* magazine, March 2000.

grommet *n.* **1)** A young surfer-type person, intent on maximizing beach and in-the-tube experiences. **2)** A sixties Australian term for GREMMIE that has been adopted worldwide and is in current usage. **3)** A trainee surf mongrel on the way to full "surf nazi" status. (MW) **4)** An adolescent or preadolescent surfer. (L&L) **5)** A cheeky young surfer. (NAT, 1985)

grommet snack *n.* Inside waves. See LEFTOVERS.

grommies *n.* GROMMETS.

ground pounder *n.* SHORE POUND. See BEACH BREAK. (PZ)

ground swell *n.* **1)** Large waves generated by distant storms, usually seasonal,

grommets
Soquel High '99
Photo: Mike Peralta

as distinguished from waves formed by local winds. **2)** A swell that originated far away. (MM)

~~~~~~~~~~~~~~~~~~~~~~~~

Surfers prefer a ground swell to a wind swell because it is even, well spaced, and lasts longer. The waves approach the coast in long, parallel lines. Ground swells break best at reefs and points.

~~~~~~~~~~~~~~~~~~~~~~~~

grovel, groveling *v.* **1)** To maintain momentum on a broken wave in an attempt to find a re-formed wave face on which to make further maneuvers. (Australia; L&L) **2)** To extract the last bit of energy out of a wave. (SFG, 1989) Usage: "You were grovelin' on the inside there."

grunts *n.* Food; derivation unknown. (A&M)

117

guaraches (wah-RA-chees) *n.* A Spanish word for leather Mexican sandals with tire-tread soles. Sometimes spelled *huaraches.* Also called MAZATLANS, TREADS.

guava 1) *adj.* A grommet word for COOL. **2)** *n.* A yummy-tasting tropical fruit. (JHM)

guillotine *n.* The wave lip as it comes down and smacks a surfer on the head. Also known as HAMMER.

Gulliver, Gulliver wave *n.* A wave so tiny that you would have to be Lilliputian size to surf it. (Hastings, England, September 22, 1997) Same as MICRO.

gummies *n.* Australian for nonthreatening sharks. See MUNCHIE.

gun *n.* **1)** A long, thin, tapered surfboard for twelve-foot and larger waves, particularly in Hawaii. **2)** A big-wave board; a board designed for big-to-humongous surf, as in a "gun-style board." The old eleven-foot guns weighed forty-five to fifty pounds; they were double-glassed and had heavy, three-quarter-inch redwood sticks in them for reinforcement. By contrast, modern guns are longer, narrower, and lighter. See BIG GUN, ELEPHANT GUN, RHINO CHASER.

gunga *n.* Surf-wax residue that won't come off; the stuff that sticks to your board even after you scrape it. (WCH)

gunlog *n.* Hybrid of a big gun and a longboard.

gunned *adj.* Refers to the size of your board in relation to wave conditions. See OVERGUNNED, UNDERGUNNED.

gunnish *adj.* Used to describe a surfboard that is too long for the rider or conditions. Usage: "Your board's a little gunnish."

gutter section *n.* The unridable inshore white-water area close to shore. —**deep gutter**

gyrator *n.* A sixties term for a gyro. (HJP) —**gyrating for the judges**

gyro, gyro wanker *n.* A derogatory term for an over-displayed surfer—someone who does a lot of wasted arm flapping while maneuvering on a wave.

gyrogoon *n.* A gyrating goon.

gyrospaz or **gyro-spaz** *n.* A derogatory term for someone who wrecks a wave by ripping, slashing, and tearing it up into tiny bits; someone who just really screws up a wave. (SP3) Usage: "Don't gyrospaz on the shoulder."

"You got a perfectly good wave—this guy's just like spazzing all over it, up and down and ripping and slashing and really screwing it up!"

—*Surf Punks,* "Gyrospaz" (1988)

Art: Jim Phillips

hair *n.* Nerve, the courage to take off on enormous waves. A surfer who is exceptionally brave or crazy is known as "having hair." (MVA)

hair ball 1) *n.* A big wave. Usage: "Look at that hair ball!" **2)** *adj.* Wild or radical. (NWT)

hair dry *adj.* Without getting your hair wet. (SFR, 1989) Usage: "I paddled out hair dry."

hair farmer *n.* Long-haired surfer; as in "Look at that weasel-walking hair farmer." (Westside, Santa Cruz)

hair out or **hair-out** *v.* **1)** To chicken out. (JMZ, WCH) Usage: "Don't hair out, bro." **2)** Not committing to a wave or a venture because of fear. (MVA) Usage: "Everyone was completely hairing out." **3) haired-out** *adj.* Scared. (BP) Usage: "I was fully haired-out."

hairy *adj.* Scary, risky, or dangerous; something beyond normal limits, requiring nerve. See GNARLY.

hairy takeoff *n.* When the wave jacks up and starts pitching faster than you can paddle in and get to your feet—and all you can see is red lights flashing—that's a hairy takeoff. (MW)

haken (HAWK-in) *v.* **1)** To go surfing. This is the root of a surfing sublanguage spoken on the Eastside in Santa Cruz. (R&F) **2) haken vees** Surfing waves. **3) hakenveesmo** (hawk-in-VEES-mo) To surf—with a meal afterwards. **4) haken visuals** Getting good barrels. **5) hakenmo sess** (like "session") To go eat.

half men *n.* A derogatory name for kneeboarders because they surf while kneeling instead of standing. (KSO) "Be a man, learn to stand." —Zuma Jay (1982)

hammer 1) *n.* What descends on a surfer when the wave lip comes over and there's nowhere to go. (C&M) **2) hammered** *v.* To be totally immersed in an uncomfortable situation. This baptismal spinning, tossing, and gasping for air while trying to find which way is up is the price a surfer pays for trying to ride juicy waves. (MVA) See WORKED.

handboard *n.* A sixties term for HAND PLANE.

hand gun *n.* A small hand-held device that improves bodysurfing planing speed.

hand plane *n.* **1)** A small bodysurfing device held with the hands out in front of the body to assist in planing. **2)** A small board. (MF, 1967)

hang five, hanging five *v.* **1)** To ride so far up on the nose of the board that the toes of one foot reach over the front end. **2)** To have five toes over the nose of the surfboard. (IDSM)

hangin' eleven *n.* Toes over with a can of Tecate in your hand. (1994)

hangin' head *n.* Surfing prone with head off the front of the board. (Jacksonville, Florida, 1993)

hangin' one *n.* Male surfer surfing naked. See HANG TWELVE, HANG THIRTEEN.

hang loose A Hawaiian term for "everything's cool," usually conveyed by a hand sig-

hanging ten
Wingnut, Santa Cruz
Photo: Bob Barbour

nal called the SHAKA. Usage: "Hang loose, brah."

hang sixteen or twenty *n*. A surfing dog, depending on how you count its toes.

hang ten 1) *v*. To ride so far up on the nose of the board that the toes of both feet are extended over the front end. This involves not only nose riding but also abandonment of the usual diagonal or one-shoulder-forward stance.

2) hanging ten *n*. A hot-dog riding stance reserved for longboards. (A&M) Also called TEN OVER.

hang thirteen *n*. Full package.

hang time *n*. Refers to the time spent in the air during a maneuver. Part-time surf contest announcer Peter Townend borrowed the term from American football. Usage: "Look at that major hang time."

hang twelve *n*. Scrote sack off the front.

haole (HOWL-ee) *n*. (Hawaiian) **1)** A white visitor, resident, or surfer in Hawaii; anyone foreign to Hawaii. Not necessarily a bad thing to be called— depending on who says it. Usage: "Focking haole!" "He's a haole boy."
2) Mainland surfer. (JP) **3)** A Hawaiian valley. (SP3) —**haole boy**

"You're so haole, you don't even know you're haole." (TWS 1999)

Ha means "breath" and ole means "without" or "no." So haole literally means "without breath." Before religious ceremonies, Hawaiians traditionally would cleanse themselves by doing deep-breathing rituals to ready their souls. After 1820, when missionaries arrived with their churches and religious beliefs, the Hawaiians noticed they didn't do breathing exercises before entering a church; they therefore became haoles. (PHL)

haole feet *n*. Tender soles with no callus buildup; comes from not walking barefoot and can be spotted instantly. (Hawaii; MFM, 1982) Same as CHEESE FEET.

haole rot *n*. A fungus on the top part of the back and chest, acquired by surfers visiting Hawaii; curable by applying Phisoderm. (JMZ)

Haole Trolley *n*. Tourist trolleys in Waikiki. (Hawaii, SFR, February 2000)

hapa-haole music *n*. Hawaiian music given a Western tilt to make it more appealing to tourists; it became a national craze when Albert ("Sonny") Cunha performed Henry Kailimai's "On the Beach at Waikiki" at the 1915 Panama Pacific International Exhibition in San Francisco. Johnny Noble, known as the "Hawaiian Jazz King," was a leading figure in *hapa-haole* music; he wrote such popular hits as "Hula Blues," "My Little Grass Shack," and "Hawaiian War Chant." (GTM)

happening *adj*. Cool, great. Usage: "It's a happening spot." "The waves are happening."

hard bottom turn *n.* While turning at the bottom of a wave, really leaning into it so that one's body is nearly parallel to the ocean surface.

hard-breaking *adj.* A wave that breaks with full force. Such a wave can cause problems if not negotiated properly.

hard-core or **hard core** or **hardcore** *adj.* Used to describe intense things, as in "hard-core surfers" or "hard-core locals." May be the most overused word in modern surfing. (SFR, March 1991). Usage: "That's so hard core."

hard planing edge *n.* The squared-off bottom of a surfboard rail.

hard rail *n.* A surfboard rail with a sharper corner and a more defined edge to grab a wave (ORB), as distinct from a round rail. See SOFT RAIL.

harsh 1) *adj.* Severe, unpleasant, irritating. Usage (after a bad wipeout): "That was harsh." **—harsh waves, harsh conditions 2)** *v.* To give someone a hard time. Usage: "She fully harshed on me."

hasake or **hasaki** *n.* From the Arabic *khasakay*, a diamond-shaped 12- to 13-foot-long wooden board 3½ to 4 feet wide at the center and weighing 130 to 155 pounds. Used in Israel for paddling out and riding small surf back in with a hand paddle. (AHK)

hassle, hassling *v.* To compete to gain the inside position at takeoff and thereby the right-of-way; same as HUSTLE. (CC, L&L) In competitive surfing contests, this practice has been virtually eliminated by the use of the priority buoy system.

haunted cooler
Baja Collective, Mexico
Photo: Trevor Cralle

hateful *adj.* Miserable. (LH) Usage: "It was such a hateful night."

Hatteras Short for CAPE HATTERAS.

haunted cooler *n.* Any ice chest that creaks when you slowly open the lid. When the creaking stops, you look at each other and together everyone says in a deep, low vampire voice, "Haunted cooler." Or, stating the obvious, "Dude, how haunted is that cooler?" "So haunted." (Baja, 1998) See ESKY.

Have a Hawaiian Day A warmer, tropical alternative to "Have a Nice Day."

have a surf *v.* Australian for going surfing.

"I dig having a surf."

—Shirley Strachan, Tracks magazine, July 1976

Hawaii 1) The surfing mecca of the world, known collectively throughout the surfing community as "the Islands." **2)** A volcanic chain

CCRREEEEK

Art: Rick Stover

of islands including Kauai, Oahu (home of Honolulu, Waikiki, and the North Shore), Maui, and Hawaii ("the Big Island"). **3)** The fiftieth state of the United States.

British explorer Captain Cook named this archipelago the Sandwich Islands in 1778. It was a U.S. territory from 1900 until it became a state in 1959. The name Hawaii is possibly derived from the native word for homeland Hawaiki or Owhyhee. (WA)

Hawaii Five-O A TV detective show filmed on location in Hawaii and starring Jack Lord. Theories as to where the famous wave at the beginning of each show was shot include Sunset Beach (the film was flopped) or Ala Moana; however, it was probably shot at Rockpile, just west of Ehukai Beach Park. (BB, February 1991) The show's opening theme song (recorded in March 1969) became the Ventures' second biggest hit, reaching #4 on the charts. (GSM)

Hawaiian A Polynesian language. See "Pronunciation of Hawaiian" on the next page, and see Appendix A for a list of ancient Hawaiian surfing terms.

Hawaiian Glossary Hawaiian Pidgin doesn't have an orthography; there are no written words with the proper letters according to standard usage. For example, sometimes you see "brah" or "bra" for brother.

"Eh . . ." Hey.

garens Guarantee(d), a sure thing.

hana ho One more/one more time. "Hana ho!"

mahalo plenty Thanks very much.

moani Hawaiian for gentle sea breeze.

ono, onolicious Delicious.

poki (POE-KEY) Raw ahi surf snack mixed with sesame seeds, green onions, and coconut cream.

pau Done, finished, over, as in "Are we pau?"

pupus Food/snacks.

whatevahs Whatever.

Hawaiian luau n. See LUAU.

Hawaiian music n. Vocals combined with ukulele, slack key guitar, steel guitar, and drums; the music often takes its inspiration from the beach. The popularity of Hawaiian music reached a peak in the 1930s, owing largely to Harry Owens, whose 1935 song "Sweet Leilani" became the #1 hit nationwide. (GTM) See HAPA-HAOLE MUSIC.

Hawaiian Pidgin, Hawaiian Pidgin English An English-based dialect widely spoken in Hawaii, called "pidgin" for short. Examples are *brah, bra,* or *brudda* for "brother." See DA KINE.

Hawaiian print n. ALOHA PRINT.

Hawaiian pullout n. Going to the nose of the surfboard and sharply twisting one's body, right or left depending on the wave, in order to pull the board out of the wave. Also called ISLAND

Hawaiian shirts
Trevor Cralle and
Stanley Cardinet
Photo: Unknown

PULLOUT. See STANDING ISLAND PULLOUT, SQUATTING ISLAND PULLOUT, and SITTING ISLAND PULLOUT.

Hawaiian shirt *n.* A short-sleeved, loose-fitting, open-collar shirt originally worn in Hawaii and adopted by many surfers the world over; made of light-weight fabric. Business attire in Hawaii. Worn untucked. Anybody who wears 'em tucked just doesn't get it. Same as ALOHA SHIRT. See ALOHA PRINT.

Hawaiian shirts were originally made of silk or rayon, and later of cotton or polyester—the latter never worn by surfers except to be tacky at a party. The shirts feature colorful, often bold designs—a visual vocabulary including palm trees, romantic beaches, tropical jungles, airplanes, bamboo, volcanoes, exotic flowers, surfing

"Pack your Trash"
in Hawaiian,
translated by Rell Sun
Art: Jim Phillips

Pronunciation of Hawaiian

Hawaiian is a language of the Polynesian language family. It has just twelve letters: all of the vowels *a, e, i, o,* and *u,* and the consonants *k, h, l, m, n, p,* and *w.* Traditionally, each vowel is pronounced separately, and each is pronounced the same as in Latin or Spanish:

English	Spanish	Hawaiian
a is "ah" as in "father"	or "taco"	or "Makaha"
e is "a" as in "way"	or "peso"	or he'e nalu"
i is "e" as in "beat"	or"hijo"	or "malihini"
o is "o" as in "flow"	or "dos"	or "moana"
u is "oo" as in "dude"	or "bruja"	or "naiu"

In modern-day Hawaiian, combinations of vowels, such as *ai, ei, ou,* and so on, are usually sounded together. Thus, *ai* becomes "i," as in "like"; *ei* becomes "ay," as in "way"; *ou* becomes "au," as in "owe." Consonants are pronounced the same as in English. When *w* is used as the first letter of in a word, as in *Waikiki,* it is pronounced like the *w* in "warm." In the middle of a word, as in *Ewa, w* is usually pronounced as "v."

scenes, pineapples, drums, outrigger canoes, and images from Polynesian legend. The functional use of creative colors and the amazing artistic renderings in these shirts capture the simplicity and spirit of Hawaii.
As the saying goes: "Speak softly and wear a loud shirt."
—Anonymous

CAUTION
HAZARDOUS WAVES

ROCKY POINT IS OCCASIONALLY HIT BY RANDOM WAVES OF GREAT SIZE WHICH CAN CARRY AN ADULT OFF THIS SHORELINE.

ENTER AT YOUR OWN RISK
ROCKY POINT

hazardous seas
Rocky Point, Big Sur
Photo: Trevor Cralle

Hawaiian style *adj.* Same as ISLAND STYLE.

Hawaiian time *n.* Late. (SP) Same as ISLAND TIME.

Hawaiian Triple Crown In professional surfing, the Pipeline Masters, the Big Wave Classic at Waimea Bay, and the World Cup at Sunset Beach. All of these contests are held annually around December on the North Shore of Oahu, Hawaii. See AUSTRALIAN GRAND SLAM.

hawt *adj.* Surfer pronunciation of HOT. (Oceanside, California, 1980s)

hazardous seas *n.* Term for dangerous ocean conditions commonly heard on WEATHER RADIO storm broadcasts.

hazelwood *n.* Anyone unable to maneuver a watercraft, be it a surfboard, a motorboat, or an oil tanker, and who as a result causes great damage. This eponym may have been derived from Joseph Hazelwood, captain of the Exxon *Valdez*, the tanker that ran aground in the fall of 1989 off of Alaska, causing a massive oil spill. (AJM)

head cock *n.* Looking back over your shoulder while surfing. (Siestas and Olas)

head dip *n.* While riding a wave, bending the head to touch the wave or white water. If your head gets wet from the wave, you've done a successful head dip.

head-high *adj.* Used to describe a wave that's about six feet high. —**head-high wave**

headland *n.* A point of land, usually high and with a sheer drop, extending out into the ocean; a promontory. (CCRG)

headstand *n.* Standing on your head during a surf ride—a hot-dog maneuver performed on a longboard.

head surfing *n.* CROWD SURFING, as in the "No Head Surfing" sign at Slim's nightclub in San Francisco.

head wave *n.* See OCEAN WAVE.

heat *n.* A specified time period in which to perform maneuvers on waves in a surf contest.

heavies, the heavies *n.* **1)** Very big waves, from twelve to twenty-five feet high and over, usually found in Hawaii. —**the local heavies, big locals 2)** Big-name surfers in the sixties. (A&M)

heaving *adj.* GOING OFF, FIRING, SICK. See MORNING SICKNESS.

"Rosarito was heaving and so were we."
—Keith Hunter, after a trip to Baja, 1997

heavy *adj.* Intense, as in "heaviest surf spot" or "That was heavy."

heavy surf advisory *n.* Broadcast alert over the weather radio that surfers love to hear.

hectic *adj.* Pretty NAR. (SP3)

hectic gnarler *n.* A really good-looking girl. (Santa Barbara, California)

heel cracks *n.* Flip-flops slap against heel and dry it out so it cracks the skin; can be painful. Prevention includes applying moisturizing lotion, using a pumice stone when you bathe, and—heaven forbid—wearing socks and shoes.

heels over *n.* A hard-to-pull-off longboarding maneuver that involves walking out to the end of the board, turning around, and hanging the heels over the nose tip. (KSO)

heenalu or **he'enalu** or **he'e nalu** (hay-ay nah-LOO) *n.* Hawaiian for surfing.

heini *n.* Heineken beer. Also called GREENIE IN A BOTTLE (in Australia).

held down, held under *v.* **1)** Refers to wiping out and getting tossed around beneath the sea, when a few seconds can seem like an eternity. (CC) **2)** To be prevented by the force of a breaking wave from coming up quickly for air—an unpleasant situation. Happens when a surfer is caught in the white water or caught inside. After a wipeout, being

Hebrew Surf Lingo

If you're planning on surfing in Israel, here are some key terms:

fin: *herev*
glassy: *shemen* ("oil")
high pressure: *rama*
jetty: *shover galim*
low pressure: *sheka*
surfboard: *galshan*

surfing: *glisha*
tube: *tzinor*
wall: *kir*
wave: *gal*
wax: *sheava*

wind directions:

Eastern: *Mizrahit*
Western: *Maaravit*

Southern: *Dromit*
Northern: *Tzfonit*

Note: *Jora* ("septic tank"), which is used to describe a closeout wave, is also used to describe a bad "washing machine" wipeout.

(Adapted from Ben Rac's Surfing in Israel website: http://www.angelfire.com/mo/bellz/index.html)

trapped underwater and unable to surface for air as a wave passes overhead. Usage: "It felt like I was held down for over a minute." See GO INTO ZEN, HOLD DOWN.

helgermite *n.* HELGI. A young local who surfs. Like a tiny parasite on kelp. (Santa Cruz)

helgi *n.* A Santa Cruz word for a young, enthusiastic, "surf-stoked" wave rider. (CVG); a GROMMET.

helicopter, helicopter spin *n.* A THREE SIXTY turn (L&L); has nothing to do with being rescued from the surf by a helicopter on the North Shore of Hawaii.

heli-surfing *n.* A kind of surfing that requires the help of a helicopter to lower the surfer into a remote or out-side break.

hella *adj.* A strengthening adjective used to increase the force of a word, as in a "Hella fine chick." Usage: "Dude, it's hella good out there." **—hella bunk** (not cool, messed up).

helper fin *n.* A smaller fin.

hero *n.* A sixties term for anyone who thinks he's better on a surfboard than he is. (IDSM)

hideous, hiddie *adj.* **1)** Offensive to the senses, and especially to sight; exceed-ingly ugly. **2)** Morally offensive; shock-ing. Usage: "Scott's Reef, Oregon, is sur-fable up to 5', but at 8-12', the place is hideous." "The waves are pretty hiddie today." (SFG, 1989) See GNARLY, HAIR BALL.

high, high pressure system, high pressure *n.* A climatic condition char-acterized by warm weather, less turbu-lent air, and winds that blow clockwise around the weather system's center, in contrast to a low pressure system, in which winds blow counterclockwise around the center. (W&B)

high-energy winter waves *n.* Powerful seasonal waves generated by very large faraway storms.

high-flying backside reentry *n.* A surfing maneuver where the surfer, with back to the wave, leaves the water with the board and returns.

high surf conditions *n.* HEAVY SURF ADVISORY.

high tide *n.* When the sea level is at its highest mark. **—high tide line, high tide mark**

highway hand surfing *n.* Same as ARM-DANCE.

highway surfer *n.* **1)** A HODAD who goes to the beach and spends all his time driving up and down the highway with a surfboard sticking out of the car. (ASKC, 1965) **2)** Someone who spends all his time in the car and never gets to the surf. **3)** A POSER whose surfboard stays on the roof rack. (A&B) Same as FREEWAY SURFER. **—highway surfie** (Australia)

hips *n.* The portion of a surfboard between its midpoint and tail; measured twelve inches from the tail.

hit a wave, hit the surf *v.* To ride a wave or go surfing. Usage: "Let's hit the surf."

hittin' 1) *adj.* Used to describe something of extreme goodness. For example, after a session Sambro is hungry, and when

given a steaming hot bowl of home-cooked beans, he takes a bite and exclaims, "Dude! These beans are hittin'!" **2) hitting** *v.* Usage: "There's a big swell that's supposed to be hitting tomorrow."

hodad or **ho-dad** or **hoedad, hodaddy** *n.* **1)** A derogatory term for a non-surfer. See GREMMIE. **2)** A surfer who rarely goes in the water but still talks, acts, and dresses as if he were a minor god of the sport; a fake; a show-off. (DSHJ) Same as POSER. **3)** A greaser, sort of a hot rodder with long hair and side-burns. **4)** A street person as opposed to a beach person. Such a person usually spends a lot of time riding around in a lowered car. (A&M) **5)** A hood from the back streets, generally driving a hopped-up car; may or may not be a surfer. **6)** An antisurfer hoodlum, often just an ill-mannered beach bum who doesn't surf but loiters around the regular surfers; an undisciplined, antisocial character. **7)** An all-out, nonsurfing surf bum-a person with questionable motives. **8)** Anyone the surfers don't like. (IDSM) **9)** An unknown surfer, a stranger to the lineup.

hold, holding *v.* Refers to the ability of a surfboard or fin to grab onto a wave. Usage: "My board was holding the wave face." **—holding power** *n.*

hold down *n.* The force of a breaking wave that prevents you from swimming up for air. Usage: "Oh man, the hold down was horrendous." See HELD DOWN, TWO-WAVE HOLD DOWN.

hold one's line *v.* To hold one's position on a wave. Usage: "Hold your line—I'm coming through!"

hold up *v.* **1)** What waves do when, because of an offshore wind, they continue longer before breaking. Usage: "Look at that wave hold up." **2)** To stall the board during a ride and then continue the ride. **3) held up** To be lifted by an offshore wind while taking off on a wave. (RA) See HUNG UP.

hollow *adj.* **1)** Used to describe an extremely concave wave, or a fast, deeply curling, plunging wave. **2)** A descriptive term for a cylindrical wave. (NAT, 1985) See TUBE.

hollowback *n.* An East Coast term for a DUMPER. (DSHJ, 1965)

hollow out *v.* What happens when a wave begins to peel over into a tube.

hollow surfboard *n.* A surfboard with its core or insides removed. In 1926 surfer-swimmer Tom Blake, a Waikiki waterman originally from Wisconsin, accidentally invented the hollow surfboard when he was trying to replicate a sixteen-foot board and drilled the wood full of holes. After sealing the holes, he found that he had created a lighter, longer surfboard that was well suited for paddleboard racing. His discovery revolutionized surfboard design. (GTM)

hondo *n.* A derogatory term for nonlocal, or anyone living inland from the beach. Usage: "Did you see all those hondos at our break today?" Or, occasionally, "I think all you **inland hon-**

dos should take the next bus back to Anaheim." (SFG, December 1981) Same as INLANDER, FLATLANDER, VALLEY.

honing *v.* When waves are huge and breaking at an accelerated rate. (MM) Usage: "The waves are honing up the coast."

honker, big honker *n.* A really big wave. (DPL)

hood *n.* A neoprene rubber head covering for surfing in cold water. (MM) See SQUID LID.

hooded *n.* Full wetsuit with a hood attached.

hook *n.* **1)** The curling part of the wave, BOWL. **2)** The innermost ridable part of a tubing wave. See CURL, POCKET. **3)** *v.* To ride the best part of the wave. Usage: "I hooked into the meaty part of the wave."

hook up *v.* **1)** To fix or set someone up. Usage: "I can hook you up with a wetsuit." **2)** To meet someone. Usage: "We can hook up over at Dave's apartment."

hoon *n.* Someone who tends to compensate for a lack of surfing ability with eye-catching performances in the car park. (Australia; MW)

hot batch
Art: Jim Phillips

hoot *v.* Howling and yelping approval and encouragement to anyone on a wave.

Hoota! The yell of a surfer who's stoked. (A&M)

hooter *n.* A really great party. Usage: "That was a real hooter."

hootin' *adj.* GOING OFF. Usage: "It's hootin' out there." (Mark Warren, 1993)

hooting *n.* Calling or shouting that compliments the quality of a ride or a wave. (Australia; L&L) See SURFER HOOTS, AAAAAHOOO!

hop, hopping it back and forth *v.* To bounce the front of the board up and down and from side to side in order to extend a ride on a wave that is petering out. See GROVELING.

horrendous *adj.* Used to describe a large or difficult wave. (DBF) Usage: "That was a horrendous wave."

hose *v.* CREAMED. Usage: "I just got hosed by that wave."

hot *adj.* **1)** COOL. (SP) Usage: "Wow, hot ride." "Look at those hot chicks." **2)** A slang expression applied to a good-quality wave. (NAT, 1985) **—hot waves**. **3)** Used to describe a batch of resin that goes off fast, or quickly changes from a liquid to a solid. Yes, resin will get *hot!* (GCD)

hot batch *n.* A mixture of surfboard resin catalyzed for quick setting, left over in a laminating bucket, creating heat, cracking, smoke (cyanide gas), and in very hot mixtures, bursting into flames.

hot coat *n.* **1)** A fast-drying coat of resin applied between the fiberglass lay-up and the finish sanding. **2)** The resin layer that is sanded to blend and refine the contours of a board. (ORB) Also referred to as SAND COAT.

hot curl *n*. **1)** A 1930s term for a challenging, fast-breaking wave. **2)** HOT-CURL BOARD.

hot-curl board *n*. **1)** The name of Hawaiian surfboards designed from 1950 to 1955 for big-wave (hot-curl) riding. Such boards are fast and maneuverable. Also known as HOT-SLOPE or HOT-SHAPE BOARDS. (AHK). **2) hot-curl redwood board** A plank of solid redwood with no fins, used in the 1930s; the tail comes down in a V shape, the bottom is rounded, and there is no scoop in them. (GN)

hot dog *n*. **1)** Applied to a fancy and tricky style of surfing and also to the board design best suited to that style. **2)** A wide and heavy board. (IDSM) **3)** *v*. To show a great deal of ability in the surf, usually demonstrated by fancy turns, walking the nose, and taking chances. **4) hot-dogger** *n*. A surfer who is skilled in, and devoted to, fancy and tricky riding (DSHJ); one who exhibits tricky footwork and generally a snappy style of board riding. **5) hot-dogging** *n*. Fast maneuvering on small surf. (L&L) **—hot-dog maneuvers**

hot gooper *n*. A fast-drying resin made by adding an extra catalyst or cobalt.

hot little section *n*. A fast and fun section of a wave to ride. See INSIDE ZIPPER.

hot sand *n*. The sun-baked surface of a beach—yowch!

hot-shape board, hot-slope board *n*. HOT-CURL BOARD.

"Hottest 100 Yards" *n*. Nickname given to small stretch of Newport Beach circa 1980, where locals Danny Kwock and others were among the first to sport neon airbrushed boards and matching trunks. (SFR, January 1990)

hotties *n*. **1)** Good waves. **2)** Great surfers.

houge (HO-ghee) *v*. To scarf down food after you surf. (San Clemente) Usage: "Let's go houge." See HAKEN-VEESMO and HAKENMO SESS, listed under HAKEN.

houses *n*. BARRELING. Usage: "It was houses, brah." (Hawaii) See SHACKED.

howling *adj*. Strong, as in "howling winds."

How's the surf? How are the conditions? One of the first questions a surfer asks another surfer. See ANY WAVES?

Howzit brah? Hawaiian Pidgin expression meaning, "How's it going, brother?" See BRAH.

huaraches (hwah-RA-chees) *n*. GUARACHES.

huevos (HWAY-vos or WAVE-os) *n*. Spanish for "eggs," but a cross-cultural surfer homonym for waves. See OLAS. (P)

Huey 1) The Australian kahuna (NAT, 1985) **2)** The legendary god of the surf. (MM)

huge *adj*. **1)** Said of a wave that's bigger than large. **2) huge monolith** *n*. A gargantuan wave; Mount Everest, massive, mega-enormous—Hawaiian style. (MM, CC) Same as BEHEMOTH WAVE.

human lure *n*. What a surfer feels like in sharky waters—not a nice feeling. (Australia; MW)

human lure
Art: Rick Stover

humongous *adj.* Used to describe waves. When the surf is bigger than big, it's huge; when it's bigger than huge, it's humongous. Same as GARGANTUAN. See BROWN BOARDSHORTS MATERIAL. (MW)

humpers *n.* Medium-to-large unbroken waves.

hung up *v.* **1)** To be tottering on the upper lip of a wave, usually held there by the updraft of a strong offshore wind. See HELD UP, listed under HOLD UP. **2)** To have the skeg of one's board get caught in kelp.

Huntington Beach Surfing Walk of Fame Dedicated in May, 1994, each inductee receives a granite stone placed in the sidewalk extending from the corners of Pacific Coast Highway and Main Street in Huntington Beach, California. Catagories include: Surf Pioneer, Surf Champion, Surfing Culture, Local Hero, Woman of the Year, Honorary Inductee, and members on the Honor Roll.

Huntington Hop *n.* A typical bouncing maneuver used to make it through small waves; the term originated at the Huntington Beach Pier in California, where the annual OP Pro surf contest is held.

"When the swell is small there is an outside section followed by a deep gutter where the wave flattens out before it reaches the shorebreak. Often surfers will have to straighten off and bounce their board through this dead section to reach the inside. This has become so commonplace that the technique has become known as the 'Huntington Hop.'"

—*Michael Martin, "Surfing for the Judges" in* Competitive Surfing: A Dedicated Approach *(1988)*

hurricane *n.* A powerful, destructive storm, stronger than a tropical storm, that starts over water and has winds rotating counterclockwise at speeds in excess of seventy-two miles per hour. Such winds develop in low pressure areas and are usually accompanied by very high tides. A storm's diameter may range from 150 to 300 miles. Hurricanes are assigned such names as "Gilbert," "Hugo," or "Ewa." A storm of this magnitude is called a *hurricane* in the Caribbean Sea and the Atlantic, a *cyclone* in the Indian Ocean, and a *typhoon* in the China Sea and most of the Pacific. In the Philippines, it is called a *baguio.* (GVS, OA)

hustle *v.* HASSLE.

HV (high velocity) fin *n.* A fin designed to control and stabilize the natural drifting tendency of channel bottom boards; invented by Australian shaper Kym Thompson.

hybrid, hybrid board *n.* A surfboard that ranges from seven to nine feet with a mixture, or cross, of several designs, attempting to give it some of the floatation and paddling of a longboard as well as the performance of a shortboard.

hydro *n.* HYDROPLANE SURFBOARD.

hydrocoffin *n.* A wave that encloses, and then breaks on, a surfer.

hydrofoil step, hydrofoil stepped *n.*, *adj.* HYDROPLANE STEP.

hydro hull *n., adj.* A bottom contour designed to channel water away to give maximum planing.

hydro-ironed *v.* To get flattened by a close-out set. (Pedro Point, Pacifica; BTV) Usage: "I just got hydro-ironed."

hydroplane step *n.* An area on the front of a longboard designed especially for nose riding.

hydroplane surfboard *n.* A sixties surfboard incorporating a hydroplane step to produce both the highest possible speed and quick-turning maneuverability.

hydrothermal ceramic technician The job description of a dishwasher, a position commonly held by some surfers. When said with the proper delivery, the title earns instant respect from almost anyone (especially gullible surfers).

hydrothermal ceramic technician
Art: Mr. X
©2000 Mullethead Surf Designs

ice chest *n.* A insulated, plastic rectangular container with a hinged lid that keeps surf snacks cold. See ESKY, HAUNTED COOLER.

ice cream headache *n.* A piercing pain in the head resulting from ducking under freezing cold water while paddling out. (MM)

ice cube tube *n.* A curling cold-water wave. (P)

ice surfing *n.* A hybrid sport done on frozen lakes around the world, mixing the speed of ice boating with the agility and power of windsurfing. The ice board is similar in size and shape to a big skateboard. Most boards have two blades in the back for stability and either one or two blades in the front to control the steering. Just like the wheels on a skateboard, the blades on an ice surfing board are mounted on flexible "trucks" so the rider can control the steering by leaning forward or backward while standing sideways on the board.

IGOM (eye-GOM, like "Tom") *adj.* Immediate Go Out Material. Checking the surf from the cliff, you turn to your friend and say, "Eye-gom." (Jackson Rahn, Santa Cruz)

impact zone *n.* **1)** The area directly in front of a breaking wave, where the falling lip strikes the water or the beach; the place where the breaking wave lands and exerts maximum force. (NAT, 1985) **2)** The area where a wave first breaks. (ORB)

in-betweeners *n.* Small waves that come in between sets. (SFG, March 1990)

inboard *adj.* The side of a surfboard nearest the wall of a wave. Usage: "I was really leaning on the inboard rail."

inconsistent *adj.* Said of waves that do not break at regular intervals. Usage: "The waves were totally inconsistent today." See DISORGANIZED.

indicator *n.* **1)** A wave (or the place where it breaks), seaward of the usual takeoff point, that provides an indication of the size and shape of waves moving into the lineup zone. Rincon's Third Point is a good example. **2)** An outside wave that breaks over a shallow reef or sand bank and backs off, indicating that a wave or set is approaching. **3)** A surf spot outside of (seaward of) the spot you are riding that can be used to gauge approaching waves. **4)** A sign that a set of waves is approaching. (NAT, 1985)

Indo Australian slang for Indonesia.

Indonesia *n.* A republic in the Malay Archipelago, comprising hundreds of islands (including Bali and Java), each with its own culture, language and dialect; has many excellent surf spots. See "Speaking Indonesian" on page 136.

information surfing *n.* Navigating the info revolution through the libraries of the world; digital superhighway.

injected molded fin *n.* A fin with a perfect foil. (SFG, February 1990)

inlander *n.* A derogatory term for anyone who isn't lucky enough to live within walking distance of the beach. See VALLEY.

Speaking Indonesian

The country [of Indonesia] is so diverse, a Western Indonesian can be as unintelligible to an Eastern Indonesian as both would be to an English-speaking surfer. Fortunately for travelers, Bahasa Indonesia is the official language of the country. It is taught in schools, used on television, street signs and in newspapers, and makes it possible for a traveler to learn one tongue, and make himself understood whether he's in Timor or Sumbawa (Paul King, *Surfer* magazine, January 1991). Bahasa Indonesian is a very easy language to learn. Here are some useful words and expressions for the traveling surfer to know:

beach: *pantai*
big: *besar*
channel: *saluran*
fast: *cepat*
high tide: *air pasang*
low tide: *air surut*
ocean: *lautan*
offshore winds: *angin darat*
onshore winds: *angin laut*
peak: *puncak*
point: *titik*
reef: *karang*

shoulder: *bahu*
small: *kecil*
sunscreen: *anti panas matahari*
surfboard: *papan bersilancar*
surfer: *pesilancar*
surfing: *bersilancar*
surf wax: *lillin*
swell: *gelambang*
tube: *lengkung*
wall: *tembok*
wave: *ombak*

Thank you: *Terima kasih*
You're welcome: *Termia kasih kembali*
I'm sorry: *Maaf*
You're a good surfer: *Kamu pesilancar yang baik*
I'm stoked: *Saya bahagia*
I'm bummed: *Saya kecewa*
I come from . . . : *Saya datang dari . . .*
I am here to surf: *Saya disini untuk bersilancar*

(Adapted from PK in SFR, January 1991)

inland invader *n.* Anyone who travels to the beach from deep inside the interior. Same as VALLEY, FLATLANDER.

inland squid *n.* A derogatory term for a surfer who doesn't live near the beach. (MM) See SQUID.

inland surfer *n.* **1)** Anyone who has to travel a great distance to get to the surf. **2) Inland Surfers** An organization based in Phoenix, Arizona, whose slogan is "Real surfers don't need water." (DS)

Inland Surfers Association (ISA) A Southern California organization.

in position Said of a surfer who is in the right spot to catch a wave.

insane *adj.* Really great, usually used to describe the surf. Usage: "It was totally insane." "It was an insanely hollow wave."

insepia (in-sa-PEE-a) *n.* Riding on the nose of a board with one foot forward and both hands stretched out in front. (Australia; ASKC, 1965)

inshore *adj., adv.* Refers to either the beach or the area of water just off the beach, or the area inside the break.

inside *n., adv., prep.* **1)** That portion of the white-water surf zone that is landward of breaking waves. **2)** The area between the breaking waves and the shore. (MM) **3)** Shoreward of the breaking waves. (NAT, 1985) See CAUGHT INSIDE. **4)** Toward the shore or near the shore. **5)** Toward or close to the curl. If two surfers catch the same wave, the one closest to the curl on takeoff is inside. (MF) **6)** Completely within the curling part of the wave, as in "inside the tunnel" or "inside the barrel"; IN THE TUBE. (A&M)

inside break *n.* Surf breaking shoreward of a larger outside (seaward) spot. See OUTSIDE BREAK.

inside of a tube Being completely covered by the curl of a wave—one of the supreme thrills in surfing. (A&M)

inside rail *n.* The edge of the board closest to the wave face. (L&L) See OUTSIDE RAIL.

inside reef *n.* A surf spot located shoreward of the outside break; usually smaller surf. (GN) See OUTSIDE REEF.

inside section, inside wave *n.* A wave that is shoreward of the main break. The waves inside the main break are often smaller and easier to ride.

inside zipper *n.* A really quick inside wave that is small but fast and fun. (KSO) See ZIPPER.

instabro *n.* Someone who tries to sound cool, usually by giving a big wave of the hand and saying, "Hey, brooo." (J. Lofty Crew) See BRODAD.

intense, totally intense *adj.* Extreme. Usage: "A repo man's always intense."

interference penalty *n.* In accordance with ASP rules, a surfer judged to have interfered with another surfer is scored on only three rides instead of four. (L&L)

interference rule(s) *n.* In competitive surfing, very strict prohibitions about hassling—crowding or impeding—an opponent. The ASP rule book has twelve

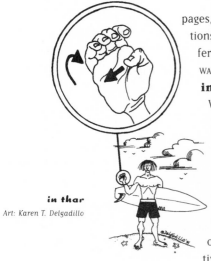

in thar
Art: Karen T. Delgadillo

pages, complete with illustrations, devoted to the interference rule. (L&L) See WAVE POSSESSION.

internal heating *n.* Warmth generated by pissing in a wetsuit. (PZ) See URINOPHORIA, PETER HEATER.

International Surfing Association (ISA) The worldwide amateur organization of competitive surfing.

Internet surfing *n.* See SURFING THE INTERNET.

in thar Anything that's cool—the way it is "in there," or inside a tube. The expression can also be accompanied by a hand gesture, with fingers curled over like a breaking wave and thumb pointed in, as if getting tubed. (Santa Cruz, RPM) Usage: "That's in thar." "In thar!"

in the curl Refers to surfing inside of a barreling wave; GETTING TUBED.

in the Pope's living room Refers to a good ride in a good barrel. (JP) Jock Sutherland made this term infamous. Same as being in the GREEN ROOM or GOING TO CHURCH. Usage: "I was hangin' with the Pope." or "I was cold hard chillin' with the Pope." (Factorisimo, 1994)

in the tube Inside a barreling wave; TUBED.

in-the-tube 360, in-the-tube forward 360 *n.* A bodyboarding maneuver

in which the surfer spins fully around while riding in the tube. An **in-the-tube reverse 360** is currently under development.

in the tube time *n.* See TUBE TIME.

in the tunnel 1) *n.* IN THE TUBE. **2) getting tunneled** *v.* Same as GETTING TUBED.

in the womb IN THE TUBE. Same as being in the GREEN ROOM or GREEN WOMB. See WOMB.

inverted air *n.* A bodyboarding maneuver that involves turning upside down when catching air.

ISA 1) International Surfing Association. **2)** Inland Surfers Association.

island *n.* **1)** A piece of land completely surrounded by water but not large enough to be called a continent or continental island; the result of volcanic action or coral formations. **2)** Unquestionably the best place to look for big surf, for some part always points straight into the swell. (W&B) One side of the island is always offshore!

island fever *n.* The feeling that you've spent too much time on an island and it's time to go. Usage: "After two

in the Pope's living room
Art: Rick Stover

months on that place I was starting to get island fever."

island pullout *n.* A exit from a wave identified with the first surf riders from Hawaii to popularize the sport in California and elsewhere; performed by grasping the nose of the board, swinging the stem shoreward, and pulling the board back through the wall of the wave. See HAWAIIAN PULLOUT, SITTING ISLAND PULLOUT, STANDING ISLAND PULLOUT.

Islands, the *n.* The cool way to say HAWAII. (MVA) But what if you're from Fiji?

island style *adj.* Laid back free and easy in Hawaii. Same as HAWAIIAN STYLE. See ISLAND TIME, HAWAIIAN TIME.

island time *n.* The pace of the tropics: forget being in a hurry. Foreigners learn patience in the tropics. Same as HAWAIIAN TIME. See MAÑANA.

ISP International Surfing Professionals—a now-defunct organization.

Israel and surfing See HEBREW SURF LINGO.

it Pronoun used to refer to the surf. Usage: "It [the surf] was so good out there."

Italian Surf Terms

beach: *spiaggia*
coral reef: *banco di corallo*
falling off onshore wind: *scaduta di libeccio*
high tide: *marea alta*
hollow wave: *onda scavata*
jellyfish: *medusa*
jetty: *molo*
low tide: *marea bassa*
onshore wind: *libeccio*
point: *molo*
reef, cliff: *scogliera*

rocky: *scoglioso*
seafood: *frutti di mare*
sea urchin: *riccio di mare or echino*
shark: *squalo or pescecane*
surf: *surf*
surfboard: *tavola di surf*
surfer: *surfista*
tide: *marea*
wave: *onda*
wind: *vento*

jack, jack up *v.* **1)** (of waves) To suddenly gather water and gain elevation in moving from deep into shallow water. (MW) Usage: "The wave really jacks up on the inside." "Look at that wave jacking." **2)** The motion of a wave when it suddenly lifts up just before breaking. Usage: "I saw you smack a jacking six-foot lip." **—jacking, jacking up**

jam *v.* **1)** To block the ride of another surfer. (MF) **2) jamming** To dance or groove to reggae music.

jams *n.* Very colorful swim trunks, almost knee-length and usually loose to the point of bagginess. Dave Rochlen started the jams trend in the early 1960s with the original Surf Line Jams, which were brightly colored Hawaiian-print trunks, cut just above the knee; every surfer wore them. (GN) See BAGGIES.

Jan & Dean Jan Berry and Dean Torrance, a sixties rock 'n' roll music group known for their songs about surfing and cars. Among their hits was "Ride the Wild Surf" (September 1964), the title song from the film of the same name starring Fabian and Tab Hunter. See SIDEWALK SURFIN'.

Japan The Asian country responsible for manufacturing some forty thousand surfboards per year in its surfboard factories. Also known for Nippon's surf-hungry populace and for fast-changing typhoon conditions. See the Japanese surf glossary on the next page for the local lingo.

jacking
Photo: Rob Gilley

Japan boards *n.* Small-wave boards that are super wide, super thick, and blocky. The name derived from a series of Japanese events held in tiny surf; the boards were made for one thing—riding dribbly white water to shore. (SFG, February 1986)

Jaws 1) In case you were on Mars in the mid-seventies, there's this nasty shark off Martha's Vineyard, see . . . **2)** A best-selling novel by Peter Benchley about a New England beach community terrorized by a great white shark. **3)** Steven Spielberg's 1975 movie based on Benchley's novel.

Jaws was the biggest box-office powerhouse of all time, if you exclude movies with spaceships or ghosts; it featured the $2 million mechanical man-eating shark nicknamed "Bruce." This movie—more than any other single event—greatly fueled people's fear of sharks and drove many individuals away from the ocean, scaring them for life (hence "The

Jaws Syndrome"). John Williams provided the music, which won an Academy Award for Best Original Score. **(SHS)**

Art: Jim Phillips

"Breathes there a soul brave enough to go near the beach after seeing this film?"

—*Arthur Cooper*

"Ever since *Jaws*, I really haven't enjoyed being in the ocean."

—*Randy Mishoe, Sunset Beach, North Carolina*

Jaws *n.* Also called *Peahi* (Hawaiian for "beckon"), this massive underwater ridge is located half a mile offshore the north

shore of Maui. Tow-in surfing pioneered here by Laird Hamilton and Buzzy Kerbox during the winter of 1992–93.

"Jaws isn't just a location, it's a theoretical wave that manifests itself in real life. It's almost a spiritual entity, a sleeping giant that sometimes awakens and beckons surfers."

—*Joel Achenback*, National Geographic, *November 1998*

jaws board *n.* A surfboard design.
jazz 1) *n.* Talk; business, miscellaneous thoughts, as in "all that jazz." **2)** *adj.*

Japanese Surf Glossary

Japanese Surf Cake label
Art: Jim Phillips

beach: *nama*
channel: *suiro*
ocean: *umi*
peak: *mine*
point: *sentan*
reef: *anshou*
sand: *suna* (US slang) or *yuuk*
sea urchin: *uni*
shark: *same*
shoulder: *kata*
surf: *isonami*
surfboard: *naminoriita*
surfer: *isonami nohito*
surfing: *nami nori* or *safin*
surf wax: *isonami no mitsurou*

swell: *fukure*
tide: *shio*
high tide: *manchou*
low tide: *kanchou*
tube: *kuda*
typhoon: *taifuu*
wall: *kabe*
wave: *nami*
big wave: *ooki nami*
small wave: *chiisai nami*
wind: *kaze*
offshore wind: *okini no kaze*
onshore wind: *riku ni mukau no kaze*

(Translations by Aya Nagao)

ENGLISH CONVERSTAION

お気楽英会話
台風の波のことならオマカセ！

どうやら台風の接近で、少しずつウネリが大きくなってきている、ある週末のことです。

Swells are getting bigger.

「うねりが大きくなってきたね」

Yea. Typhoon is on a way.

「うん、タイフーンがこっちに向いているからね」

Surfbeat are becoming short period.

「サーフビートの周期も短くなってきたしね」

What is shrfbeat?

「サーフビートって何？」

Don't you know a surfbeat?

「サーフビートを知らないの？」

Surfbeat is period of set waves.

「サーフビートは、セットでやってくる波のことなのだ」

What is set means?

「セットってどんな意味？」

Set is a group of swells coming in period.

「セットは、周期的にやってくる波のグループのことなわけ」

Hey .! Are you real surfer?

「オイ、オマエ本物のサーファーか？」

Of course .! I can ride a wave.

「勿論！ 僕は波に乗れるものね」

But real surfer must know about surt.

「でも本物のサーファーなら、波のこと知らなくっちゃ」

Hey big sets are comig

「オイ、大きなセットが来はじめたぜ！」

Let's go out .!

「さあ、海に入ろうぜ！」

Wait .! Watch a couple of sets and check a period to find out a timing of paddle out.

「待った！ セットをもう少し見て、セットの周期をチェックして、パドルアウトのタイミングを見つけないとね」

Tha's right.

「そうだね」

How long?

「どのくらいの間？」

A couple of sets.

「いくつかのセットが来るまでね」

そんな会話が続いているうちに、波はどんどん大きくなり、セットの間隔も短くなってきたようです。それに波は、クローズアウト気味になってしまいました。

Oh no. waves are getting junk.

「アリャー、波が悪くなっちゃった」

この言葉を残して、2人のサーファーは、いつの間にかそのビーチを離れていきました。

台風といわず、カリフォルニアでもハワイでも、オーストラリアでも、初心者の会話というのはこんなものなのでしょうね。

だから、もし波が大きくてビビッてしまった時には、このくらいの英会話もキメてから、どこか波の小さいところに移動するか、帰りましょ。でもちょっと情けないかナア〜〜〜。

GLOSSA-RY

TURN OFF [təːn ɔːf]
　栓などをひねって止める。テレビなどを消すこと。幻覚剤を止めること。そらすこと。

TURN ON [təːn ɔn]
　TURN OFFの反対。幻覚剤などをやること。夢中になること。

TURN OUT [təːn aut]
　追い出す、ひっくり返す。前乗りしたサーファーを波から追い出すこと。

TURN OVER [təːn óuve]
　ひっくり返すこと。転覆、転倒、折り返し。

TWINFIN [twin fin]
　フィン（スケッグ）が2つあるボードデザイン。70年代前半に普及し、やがてトライフィンが出現するまで、人気を博した。

UNDERTOW [ʌ́ndətou]
　波打ち際で、寄せた波が返す時にできる海底の流れ。この流れは長くても数メートルほどのもので、あわててしまうとパニックになりやすいので注意。ともかく海の、そして波の動きを知ることなのだ。

UNDULATION [ʌndjuléiʃən]
　波形、波紋、波動のこと。

UP AND DOWN [ʌp ən daun]
　波のトップからボトムへ。そしてトップへとターンを繰り返してライディングするテク。

UPSET [ʌpsét]
　ひっくり返す。負かす。混乱する。

UPWARD [ʌ́pwəd]
　上部へ、上向きに（波のトップへ）ライディングすること。

V-BOTTOM [V-bɔ́təm]
　サーフボードのテール寄りのボトムの断面が、V字形になっているデザイン。

VEGEMATE [vébʒimeit]
　オージーの大好物？ のペースト状の食べ物。

From Japan's Surfin' Life, *1990*

Art: Jim Phillips

Having a good time. Usage: "I was jazzed."

J-Bay An abbreviation for Jeffrey's Bay, a famous right point break west of Port Elizabeth, South Africa. Sometimes spelled **Jay Bay**.

jello arms *n.* Limp limbs from excessive paddling. (MM) Same as RUBBER ARMS.

jellyfish *n.* **1)** Any marine coelenterates of the class Scyphozoa, characteristically having clear purple or blue umbrella-like floats between two and twelve inches in diameter but with tentacles—containing stinging cells—that may extend down for fifteen or twenty feet. There are some four thousand varieties. They sometimes infest near-shore waters during the summer months. One treatment after an encounter: apply meat tenderizer to the sting. See SEA WASP. **2)** Jellyfish, a beach game invented by Dan Jenkin in 1994 at Montara Beach, California, where you and your buddies float on your backs just outside the impact zone with no self-propulsion allowed. The object of the game is to drift, like a jellyfish, into the breaking surf, get continuously worked and be the last one to wash up on shore.

jelly roll *n.* A 1950s hairdo, generally seen on ho-daddies or low riders. The hair is combed up on either side so that it spills over in the front and is glued to stay in place with Butch wax. (A&M)

jet *v.* To make a quick disappearance. (TMA) Usage: "Let's jet."

Jet Ski
Wave jumping
Photo: Woody Woodworth

jellyfish
Purple striped jellyfish
Art: Andrea McCann

Jet Ski *n.* **1)** Useless ocean polluter. (DS) **2)** A loud and obnoxious motorized craft resembling a snowmobile and used to race around the water surface and spew totally offensive, smelly gasoline fumes around surfers. **3)** Has evolved into an essential tool for surf living rescues as well as the main vehicle used for TOW-IN SURFING. Also called WAVE RUNNER.

jetty *n.* **1)** A structure projecting into the sea, usually made of cement, steel, or large blocks of hard rock. **2)** A shoreline protective device intended to stabilize the beach and keep it from washing away, or to protect the entrance to a harbor. A jetty may destroy an existing surf spot (such as Dana Point) or create a new one, such as 56th Street in Newport Beach—one of the finest **jetty set-ups** known to mankind. (W&B)

jetty break *n.* A specific type of surf break created by the presence of a jetty. (KH)

jetty jumping *v.* Walking out on a jetty to jump off and avoid a long paddle out on a winter day. Usage: "Let's jetty jump

jetty break
Art: Jim Phillips

144

today, it's too cold to paddle out."
(Northeast US)

joneser *n.* See JONESING.

jonesing *v.* Craving—how a frustrated surfer feels when begging for a great wave. (CVG)

juice *n.* **1)** The energy or power of a wave. **2)** Big, powerful surf. Usage: "Those were pure juice," **3)** In Hawaii, pure, unsweetened island juice. Usage: "Lotta juice, brah." **—pure juice, blue juice**

jungle rash *n.* An itching and chafing of the testicles from continual wearing of wet boardshorts. (Australia)

junk, junk surf, junky waves *n.* **1)** Choppy waves created by local winds. When the surface is chopped up, the

jetty
Photo: Woody Woodworth

approaching swells are harder to ride. **2)** Surf that is barely ridable. (DSHJ) Usage: "It's pretty junky out there."

junker *n.* A competitive surfing term for a ride that the judges score so low (a 1.5, for instance) that you toss it from your overall score. Also called THROW-OUT WAVE. See SURFING CRITERIA.

Art: Jim Phillips

kacked *adj.* Tired, wrecked, out of it. Usage: "I'm kacked." —**kacked out** (Ocean City, New Jersey) See SPENT, TAPPED.

Kaha Huna The mythical Hawaiian goddess of surfing. (IDSM)

Kahanamoku, Duke (1890-1968) The "father of surfing." Duke Paoa Kahinu Makoe Hulikohola Kahanamoku, known to most as Duke, was a Hawaiian Olympic swimmer (a gold medalist in the hundred-meter freestyle in Stockholm, Sweden, in 1912 and in Antwerp, Belgium, in 1920). He popularized surfing in California (on a visit in 1911) and introduced surfing to Australia at Freshwater Beach, Sydney (in 1915). A bust of "The Duke" is located at the foot of the Huntington Beach Pier in California. The first Duke Kahanamoku Invitational Surfing Championships were held at Sunset Beach, Oahu, in 1965.

"I have never seen snow and do not know what winter means. I have never coasted down a hill of frozen rain, but every day of the year where the water is 76, day and night, and the waves roll high, I take my sled, without runners, and coast down the face of the big waves that roll in at Waikiki. How would you like to stand like a god before the crest of a monster billow, always rushing to the bottom of a hill and never reaching its base, and to come rushing in for

half a mile at express speed, in a graceful attitude, of course, until you reach the beach and step easily from the wave to the strand?"

—*Duke Kahanamoku in* Waikiki Beachboy
by Grady Timmons (1989)

Kahoona The self-described surf bum in the movie *Gidget* (1959).

Kahuna **1)** A Hawaiian witch doctor adopted by modern surfers as an imagi-

Duke Kahanamoku
Photo: Surfer Magazine

nary surfing god. **2)** The god of sun, sand, and surf. **3)** A Hawaiian priest of mysterious powers and rites. **4)** The only surf god, which true surfers make sacrifices to when the surf is flat. (H&R)

kahuna tuna *n.* KOOK.

kakios (ka-KEY-os) *n.* A Hawaiian word for very bad sores on the feet from stepping on coral; the coral sand gets into the sores and becomes infected. (GN)

kaks *n.* **1)** A derogatory term for San Jose surfers; they don't surf, they just "kak." (Santa Cruz) **2) kak** A term for dick.

kamaaina (KAH-ma-EYE-na) *n.* **1)** The Hawaiian name for Island residents who either were born in Hawaii or have lived there twenty-five years or more. **2)** An old-timer to the waves of Hawaii; someone experienced in surfing the big waves. See MALIHINI.

kamikaze or *kami-kaze* *n.* **1)** A planned wipeout, done on purpose with no hope of saving the board or avoiding the swim. **2)** Riding the board at the nose with arms held straight out to each side. (IDSM) **3)** Any daredevil feat. **4)** A Japanese word literally meaning "divine wind" but used to describe Japanese air pilots in World War II who were assigned a suicidal crash. (1945)

    kamikaze run *n.* A suicidal take off on a big dumper; usually ends in a bone-crushing wipeout. (A&M)

Kawonanaokoa, Prince David The Hawaiian who was probably the first person ever to surf in California (in Santa Cruz in 1885). See FREETH.

kayak *n.* A canoe with a light frame covered with skins, canvas, marine ply, or fiberglass; sometimes used to ride waves. A kayak is paddled with a double-bladed paddle, the paddler sitting in a hole in the deck with only his or her trunk visible. **—sea kayak, ocean kayaking**

K-cloth, K-glass *n.* A special fiberglass developed by John Kershaw of Kno-Naw Corporation.

K-den Hawaiian Pidgin for "OK, fine, everything's cool—I'll see ya later." (VAB)

keckin' air *v.* CATCHING AIR. (Santa Cruz; WCH) Usage: "I saw you keckin' air out there."

keel fin *n.* WINGED KEEL.

Keep surfing 1970s slogan that still holds up today. You don't hear many people say, "Keep golfing."

kelp *n.* Seaweed; a large brown algae that grows off the Pacific coast, usually giant kelp (*Macrocystis pyrifera*) or bull kelp (*Nereocystis leutkeana*).

"Good kelp" grows in thick stands a quarter mile to a mile offshore, in water fifteen to fifty feet deep. It dissipates wave shock further from shore and cuts down wind chop while allowing strong swells to pass, so that protected surf stays glassy even when onshore winds are blowing.

kelp
Giant kelp
Art: Andrea McCann

"Bad kelp" grows in water so shallow that it can slow down the speed and shape of a wave. It often interferes with a surfer's ride by catching the skeg and inducing a surprise wipeout. (S&C; SFR, March 1991) Usage: "I kept getting hung up on kelp out there."

~~~~~~~~~~~~~~~~~~~~~~~~~~

kelpbed kid *n.* Beginners who go out and sit in the kelp at the hot spots. (Santa Cruz)

kelphead *n.* **1)** A beginning surfer who spends most of the time with his or her head in the kelp. (San Diego; LP, 1981). **2)** A person lacking any knowledge of the ocean or the waves. (ATRL)

kelpie or **kelpy** *n.* **1)** A malevolent water spirit in Scottish legend, usually having the shape of a horse and causing or rejoicing in drownings. **2)** A sheepdog of a breed originating in Australia. (AHd2)

kelp monster *n.* California mythological sea beast that reaches up and grabs the passing fin of a surfboard, stalling the ride or causing the surfer to wipe out.

kelp mooring *n.* While sitting on your board and you grab a kelp stipe to hold your position in the water.

kelp skeg *n.* A shallow, raked fin designed for riding over kelp. (MCR)

kevlar *n.* An aramid fiber cloth that is lighter and more durable than fiberglass. (ORB)

kick *n.* The rocker, or curvature of the nose or tail area. **—nose kick, tail kick**

kicked *adj.* Turned up or scoop-shaped—used to describe the nose or tail of a surfboard.

kick five *n.* A longboarding maneuver, in which the surfer goes out to the nose of the board, hangs five with one foot, kicks the other foot out in front of the tip of the board, and then shuffles back. (KSO)

kickoff or **kick-off** *n.* The act of kicking the board out in front of a bailout.

kick out *v.* **1)** To pull out of a wave by jamming or kicking the back foot down on the tail section, a motion that lifts and pivots the nose of the board out of the wave and back over the wave crest. **2)** To flip the board over or through the back of a wave while falling off the tail of the board into the wave—a last ditch effort to keep from losing the board. **3)** To leave a wave abruptly in order to avoid losing, or damaging, the board or to avoid wiping out. (IDSM) **4)** To deliberately exit over the back of a wave while maintaining board control. **5)** Loosely, to ride back over the crest of the wave. Also known as CUT OUT, FLICKOUT, PULL OUT.

—kickout or **kick-out** *n.*

kick stall *n.* A hot-dogging maneuver in which a surfer shifts all of his or her weight to the tail of the surfboard, causing it to stall, and then quickly shifts forward again, retrimming the board. (MCR)

kelp monster
Art: Rick Stover

kill *adj.* KILLER. Usage: "That would be kill if your brother let me borrow his board." (Santa Cruz grommet, 1992)

killer *n., adj.* **1)** A complimentary word, meaning awesome or great, as in "Let's go get some killer slices [pizza]." Usage (said of an excellent wave): "That was a killer wave." (JP) Or (said of a great ride): "Killer, dude." **2)** Can also mean something bad. Usage (after a wipeout): "That last wave was a killer." **3) killer wave** *n.* Either a good or bad wave. **4) Killer Dana** A famous surf spot that no longer exists.

killer board *n.* A board on a wave with no rider; same as LOOSE BOARD.

killing it, killin' it *v., adj.* Surfing good. When you're ripping hard. Usage: "You were killing it out there today."

kind, the kind *n.* A Southern California expression for the best. See DA KINE.

King Neptune *n.* The king of the ocean in Roman mythology. See NEPTUNE'S REVENGE.

"When old King Neptune's raising Hell and breakers roll sky high, Let's drink to those who can ride that stuff and to the rest who are willing to try."

—"Doc" Ball

"Neptune! Bless us with Fat Tubes."

—Graffiti on the inside of "La Casita Bonita," a driftwood teepee at Goat Rock Beach, California, July 1996

kite surfing *n.* You start by lying on your back in the water with your feet in the footstraps of your board. Have the board in front of you with the kite hovering high above you. Steer the kite into the "power zone." You will be lifted out of the water and pulled forward onto the board. You need to know how to water start. You are attached to your board with a leash. You also need to have a tether of webbing or rope to connect the bar or control handles to your harness. (Maui) See SURF KITE.

kneebangers *n.* Real long shorts.

kneeboard *n.* A surfboard, usually short (five to six feet in length), ridden on the knees. (NAT, 1985)

kneeboarder *n.* A surfer who rides a kneeboard.

kneeboarding *n.* Surfing on the knees on a specialized board. The rider can maintain a compact and stable position, good for quick, radical maneuvers, and tube riding.

knee dragging or **knee draggin'** *v.* Catching a knee on the wave while surfing. (JWN)

kneeling dents *n.* KNEE WELLS.

kneeling patch *n.* Extra sheet of fiberglass cloth applied to the center deck of a board to prevent kneeling dents; same as DECK PATCH.

kneeling position *n.* A paddling position on a longboard.

kneelo *n.* An Australian term for a kneeboard rider. (NAT, 1985)

kneemen *n.* KNEEBOARDERS.

knee pad *n.* Extra padding on the knee section of a wetsuit.

knee paddle, knee paddling *n., v.* Stroking through the water with the arms while balanced in a kneeling position on a longboard.

kneerider *n.* KNEEBOARDER. (SFR, 1989)

knee slapper *n.* A very small whitewater wave. See ANKLE SLAPPER.

knee wells *n.* Pressure marks on the deck of a longboard caused by excessive knee paddling. (MCR); same as KNEELING DENTS.

knobs *n.* KNOTS.

knock with both elbows An Australian saying meaning to bring enough beer to a party—that is, both arms full. Usage: "Yeah, come on over at eight—and remember to knock with both elbows." (BMS)

knot *n.* An international measurement of speed equal to one nautical mile, or 6,076.115 feet (1,852 meters), per hour; of interest to surfers because it is used to measure wind speed. For example, in a calm sea or glassy conditions, wind speed is less than one knot, whereas a gale ranges from thirty-four to fifty-five knots. (WB, AJM)

knots *n.* **1)** A buildup of excess tissue caused by friction between the body and the surfboard. Also called SURF KNOBS or SURF BUMPS. **2)** Calcium deposits over the knees and on the feet where the knees and feet come in contact with the board in a kneeling position. See VOLCANO.

The medical term for knots is Osgood-Schlatter disease (also known as housemaid's knee). A nonmalignant condition, it can be very painful for beginning surfers or for those just returning from a long absence. It's particularly common among young surfers.

---

kona (KO-nah) *n.* Hawaiian for the leeward side of an island, for example, the Kona Coast of the Big Island.

kona wind *n.* A south wind in the Hawaiian Islands, generally onshore at most of the beaches with a southern exposure, where it causes mushy surfing conditions. Occasionally, however, it blows offshore and makes it glassy on the North Shore.

kook or **kuk** *n.* **1)** A rank beginner; a know-nothing; someone who is generally blundering, out of control, and in the way or who gets into trouble because of igno-

knock with both elbows
Art: Rick Stover

rance or inexperience. **2)** A lame surfer, rule breaker, idiot; same as GOOB, GEEK, UNLOCAL, VALLEY. Sometimes called HODAD or GREMMIE. **3)** Someone who imitates others badly. (MF) **4)** Anyone who doesn't know how to surf. (H&R) **5)** One who practices **kookism**—a pseudo surfer, fake, goon, pretender, wannabe, beginner, novice, etc. (BP) **—longboard kook** (W&B), **kookish maneuvers, overkooked**

〰〰〰〰〰〰〰〰〰〰

Kook is an especially derogatory term, applied specifically to someone who lives inland. Kooks are always getting in the way of "real" surfers, letting their boards get away and sometimes crashing into other surfers. Kook spelled backwards is still kook.

〰〰〰〰〰〰〰〰〰〰

kook box *n.* A 1940s term for a paddleboard or hollow surfboard used by lifeguards; so named because you felt like a kook on them. (GN)

kook cord *n.* A derogatory term for a surf leash; same as VALLEY LIFELINE.

kooked out, kooking out *v.* See DORK OUT.

kook maneuver *n.* A stupid move, such as taking off in front of another surfer. (IBN)

Kookmeyer, Wilbur A cartoon character introduced in 1986 in Bob Penuelas's cartoon strip, "Maynard and the Rat" in *Surfer* magazine. Wilbur is a young beach kid, the quintessential wannabe and the epitome of what it's like to be a kook—whether it's surfing, hanging out with the cool group, or trying to impress the most beautiful girl on the beach.

kook repellent *n.* A novelty spraycan product by Runman; the successor of Silly String. Works best on yourself.

kookster *n.* A spazzy kook.

kooky 1) *adj.* Having the characteristics of a kook. Usage: "This really kooky guy just cut me off." **2) Kooky** A character on the 1960s TV series *77 Sunset Strip.*

Kowabonga The cry of the legendary Chief Thunderthud (played by Bill Lecornec) on *The Howdy Doody Show*

Art: Bob Penuelas

(1947-60). This all-purpose expletive and greeting was coined in 1949 by Eddie Kean at a script meeting. Surfers eventually turned the term into "Cowabunga!"

~~~~~~~~~~~~~~~~~~~~

"Kowabonga was a nonsense word that originally meant an expression of anger, like 'dammit!' But the way Bill first said the line, it sounded more like a exclamation of surprise, and that's mostly the way we used it. Years later, Baby Boom surfers weaned on Howdy Doody would scream 'Kowabonga!' on an ecstatic wave, which evolved into Cowabunga! Young officers in Vietnam, incredibly, used it as a battle cry."

—Stephen Davis. Say Kids! What Time Is It?
(Boston: Little, Brown, 1987)

~~~~~~~~~~~~~~~~~~~~

Kowabunga! or **Kawabunga!** COWABUNGA.

kracka-pow!! The sound a surfboard makes when it goes flying off a roof rack as you drive away. (GCD) See RACK FLYER.

K35, K38, K39 Roadside kilometer signpost markings in Baja California, Mexico, where the surf is good.

kuk n. Hawaiian for shit. Possible origin of KOOK.

frozen wave
Art: Jim Phillips

lacerate *v.* To tear up a wave (BP); to make aggressive maneuvers on a surfboard. Same as COOK, RIP.

lagoon *n.* A shallow body of water separated from a larger bay or from the ocean by a landform such as a sand spit or reef (CCRG); used to gain access to surf spots.

laid-back *adj.* Relaxed. Used to describe someone's style in the surf or an attitude on land. Usage: "He's really laid-back."

Lake Atlantic The surfers' name for the flat summer conditions in Florida. (TDW)

lake surfing *n.* When the conditions are right, surfing on a lake, e.g., Lake Michigan.

laminate *v.* To apply resin over fiberglass during surfboard construction.

laminating resin *n.* The base resin used in applying fiberglass cloth to a shaped blank.

land breeze *n.* A light wind blowing offshore.

landlocked *adj.* **1)** The state of being too far inland to reach a beach in a reasonable amount of time, for instance, from Kansas or Bolivia. **2)** Also used to describe nonsurfers. (JP)

"There's no life east of I-5."

—*California bumper sticker sold at surf shops in the early 1980s*

landmine *n.* A surfer on the inside during NIGHT SESSIONS. (Hawaii, SFR, February 2000)

lands end *n.* The extreme seaward tip of an island or promontory.

Land Shark The *Saturday Night Live* TV skit involving a Jaws-like great white shark posing as a delivery person.

land tubed *v.* Anything onshore that you can stand or squat under that resembles a barreling wave, such as a natural rock formation like WAVE ROCK in Australia. See ARTIFICIAL KOOKMEYER.

"Real surfers surf gaping huge bushes hanging ominously over the sidewalk."

—*The Parker Brothers, letter to Surfing magazine, January 1992, Kaneohe, Hawaii, via Mojave Desert*

land yacht *n.* A really big station wagon used to transport surfers and boards to and from the beach. (LWK)

La Niña *n.* The cooler sister of EL NIÑO. This cold water phenomenon produces the opposite effects of El Niño, such as abnormally high atmospheric pressure over Tahiti and low pressure over Australia.

lap line *n.* The edge of laminated fiberglass cloth, usually trimmed. (ORB)

last wave *n.* **1)** Refers to the previous wave, as in "Did you see me on that last wave." **2)** The last wave of the session. See ONE MORE, STRAIGHT IN.

late, lates, lato *n.* LATER, BAIL, etc. As in Let's go: "Let's lates." Saying good-bye

leash cups aplenty
Photo: Bob Barbour

to a friend: "Lates, Bu." Wipeout: "He totally lates it." (Santa Cruz)

late drop, late drop-in, late take-off *n.* Catching a wave as it starts to break, a move that usually ends in disaster because the wave has already started to crash.

later, lates, late "See ya later."

lateral drift *n.* The motion of a surfer carried in a cross current. See LONGSHORE CURRENT.

later for that "Forget it." (MLI)

laters, later ons LATER.

latronic (lay-TRON-ic) "Later on." This expression was possibly derived from Mike Latronic; it has been further simplified to **lonic**. (North San Diego County; LH) Usage: "Latronic, dude."
—latron (LAY-tron)

latrons LATRONIC. (San Diego)

launched *v.* To be thrown or catapulted off a board up over the back of a wave; same as PITCHED.

lava tube *n.* A hollow cave carved out of lava rock; generally refers to submarine caves beneath surfing spots.

leash cuff
Photo: Trevor Cralle

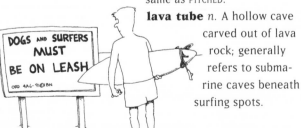

DOGS AND SURFERS MUST BE ON LEASH
ORD 4AL-91018N

Art: I. B. Nelson

layback *n.* **1)** A stalling cutback maneuver in which the surfer, instead of carving an S-turn, jams into a skidding slide while leaning back toward the curl, then allows the body's momentum to return him or her to an upright posture before continuing along the wave face. **2)** A 1980s maneuver in which the surfer is surfing backhand and leans way back on the wave face. (NAT, 1985) See BACKSIDE LAYBACK.

lay down surfing *n.* BODYBOARDING.

layforward *n.* Surfing maneuver opposite of a LAYBACK. See PIG DOG.

lay up *v.* To place a sheet of fiberglass over a foam blank and trim it to fit. See LAP LINE.

Lazor Zap *n.* A wide-tailed surfboard popularized by Cheyne Horan; it had a brief tenure. (SFG, February 1986)

leanback *n.* A backward-leaning stance on a surfboard.

leap-off-and-catch When a surfer terminates a ride, swings back over the top of a wave, and lands prone on the surfboard in position to paddle back out. (AHK, 1967)

leash *n.* SURF LEASH.

leash cuff *n.* Velcro secured around the ankle of your TRAILING FOOT.

leash cup *n.* A small, round cup laminated into the tail section of a surfboard and finished with a cross-pin, to which the surf leash is attached. Same as PLUG.

leash loop *n.* A small piece of a fiberglass product called a rope that is laminated to the rear deck of a surfboard and used to attach a surf leash.

ledge *n.* **1)** An underwater formation, usually a reef, that causes incoming swells to jack up quickly and pitch forward in a powerful, thick lip. (MW) **2)** part of a wave. **3) ledgier wave** *adj.* See WAVE LEDGE.

leeward *n., adj.* Refers to the protected side of an island, where the wind is calm and the surf is small or nonexistent; the opposite of WINDWARD.

left *n.* **1)** Any wave breaking in such a manner that a surfer taking off must turn to his or her left to stay ahead of the curl. **2)** A wave that breaks from left to right, as viewed from the shore, or from right to left, as viewed from the water looking toward the beach. (ORB, MW) Surfers always define left and right from their vantage point out in the water, facing the shore. —**left hander** or **left-hander**

leftovers *n.* Smaller waves after a big SET has rolled through. See GROMMET SNACK.

left point *n.* A point break that produces waves that break to the right.

left slide *n.* A ride where the surfer slides to the left on a wave that is breaking from right to left.

legalese grommetspeak *n.* See SURF CRIMES.

legend *n.* An Australian term for someone who rides a Mal, or longboard. (R&D) Usage: "The place was full of legends."

leg rope or **leg-rope, leggie** *n.* An Australian term for a SURF LEASH.

lei *n.* Hawaiian fresh-flower, hand-strung necklace worn at various occasions. Sweet smelling fragrances come from *plumaria* and other tropical flowers. Placed around surfer's necks during awards ceremony at surfing competitions. Also called a **flower lei**.

length The dimension of the surfboard from the tip of the nose to the tip, or tips, of the tail.

let down *v.* (of a wave) To break. Usage: "The lip let down on his head."

"Let's Go Trippin'" The instrumental surf tune by Dick Dale that was the first acknowledged surf music hit. (PJN) In the late fifties and early sixties, *trippin'* was another word for surfing.

lifeguard *n.* A person trained in lifesaving who watches over the beach and ocean area, rescues people from drowning in the surf, patrols up and down the beach in a jeep, and sits in a tower and scopes out the scene with a pair of binoculars. This individual is a keen observer of the beach scene and a good source for local surf conditions.

lift *n.* **1)** The force created when the water flow is faster across one side of a fin than the other. (ORB) **2)** ROCKER.

lifted rail *n.* A surfboard rail whose outer edge is above the center line of the side rail.

lightning *n.* Get out of the water! Saltwater is *highly* conductive.

Lifeguard tower
Oahu, Hawaii
Photo: Camille Seaman

lifeguard
Art: Rick Stover

lei
Pukani at mid-winter luau with island kine flowah lei. Flanked by Gretchen Walker and Anda Abramovici.
Photo: Elise Brewin

Lilo (lie-low) *n.* Australian brand name for an inflatable vinyl SURF MAT. No Aussie ever talks about a raft.

line *n.* **1)** A long line or set of waves. Usage: "I can see some lines wrapping in from the south." or "The lines are stacking on the horizon." **2)** A wave that forms a steep, long wall of water, ordinarily making for an extremely fast ride. **3)** A strong, well-developed swell that is pumping in toward shore like a freight train. **4)** The contour of a surfboard.

> "A wave is a blank canvas, and you're able to draw on it whatever wild lines you want."
>
> —Body Boarding *(December/January 1990)*

line up *v.* **1)** (of surfers) To sit in the lineup. **2)** (of waves) To start to break evenly. Usage: "The waves are lining up nice." **3)** To keep track of one's position in the water in relation to two fixed land objects, called **lineups**. (GN) Usage: "I was lining up with the palm tree and your car."

lineup
Summer 2000
Cowell's, Santa Cruz
Photo: Trevor Cralle

lined up *adj.* Used to describe long, even swells. (NAT, 1985) **—lined-up waves**

lineup or **line-up** *n.* **1)** The place in the water where the surfers gather to pick up waves; the takeoff area. **2)** The area where surfers straddle their boards waiting for waves to begin curling. (B&F) **3)** The point where the waves are consistently starting to break. (A&B) **4)** The term used to describe the wave and swell formation at a surfing location. (NAT, 1985)

lining surf *n.* A wave that stretches a long distance from end to end and often provides a lengthy ride. (MF, 1967)

lip *n.* **1)** The top edge of the wall of a breaking wave. **2)** The fringing crest of a wave that is starting to break. **3)** The part of a wave that comes over first when the wave breaks. (ORB) **4)** The leading edge of a clean-breaking wave. (MW) **5)** The pitching crest of a hollow or semihollow wave. (L&L) **—wave lip, thick lip**

lip attempt *n.* Any attempt to perform an off-the-lip maneuver.

lip bash or **lip-bash** *n.* Snapping a turn off of the wave lip. (SFR, October 1983). Usage: "Nice lip bash."

lip floater *n.* A surfing and bodyboarding maneuver in which the surfer glides over the wave lip.

lip-launched *adj.* When the wave lip pitches you out and dumps you in front of the advancing wave. Usage: "I got lip-launched." (1994)

lipnar *n.* Bleeding sun and salt cracked chapped lips. (Frigate Bay, St. Kitts,

West Indies, 1994) Not to be confused with NARLIP.

lipper *n.* Any off-the-lip maneuver. (Santa Cruz)

lip-slasher, lip-slamming *n.* Surfing off the lip.

lip slide *n.* Floating the board across the wave lip. (SFG, March 1990)

lip smack *n.* See OFF THE LIP.

liquid smoke *n.* The effect when an offshore wind rips the tops off of waves, giving the spray a smoky, jet-blown appearance.

liquid sunshine *n.* What they call rain in Hawaii. See PINEAPPLE JUICE.

littoral drift *n.* The relocation of sediment as a result of two factors: its transport by a longshore current and its wave-induced deposit on the beach. (CCRG)

lit-up *adj.* What it feels like to be stung by a Portuguese man-o'-war—your skin's on fire. (Florida; TDW)

live *adj.* Great, awesome. Usage: "That was live."

loady *n.* Someone who's more interested in smoking weed than surfing. (San Clemente)

local, locals *n.* **1)** Anybody who lives in a particular area and surfs it the most. (ORB) **2)** Inhabitants of a private beach area; must live within two miles of the ocean. (SP) **3)** Anyone who's been there a day longer than you. (MW) **—local heavies**

localism *n.* **1)** Territorial defiance in defense of a surf spot. The activity was born in 1779 when angry Hawaiians killed Captain James Cook at

Kealakekua Bay. (SFG, November 1989) **2)** When surfers who frequently ride the same surf break act like jerks to those who don't. (MM) **3)** An attitude that can easily be identified by the warnings that are painted on signs and fences. "If You Don't Live Here, Don't Surf Here." "No Unlocals." "Warning! Windansea May Be Hazardous to Tourists!" "Valley Go Home!"

**If You Think You Can
Just Pull Up And
Paddle Out, You're
Wrong. Our Localism
Is Still in Full Force**

—SSL (Silver Strand Local), c. early 1992,
lifeguard tower, Silver Strand Beach, Ventura

local knowledge *n.* **1)** Knowledge about a particular surf break—which way the wave breaks best, where the easiest access is, what tide works best, etc. (SFR, July 1990) A lack of local knowledge can sometimes be partially made up for in enthusiasm. **2)** Having all the information about a surf spot. See WAVE KNOWLEDGE, WIRED.

local/valley switch *n.* The name surfers give to the "local/distant" button on a car radio that improves reception. (DBF, 1981)

local wind *n.* Wind caused by factors in the immediate area, rather than by well-developed storms coming from afar.

*local
Cocles Beach, Costa Rica
Photo: Mike Peralta*

longboard skateboard
Cori Schumacker
Twin Peaks, San Francisco
Photo: Mike Peralta

Local wind conditions kick up surf that is generally weak and very short-lived, with wave periods very close together. See SEA BREEZE, WIND SWELL.

locies (LO-keys) *n.* LOCALS. (North County, San Diego)

locked *adj.* Surfing in the perfect spot on the wave, as in "staying locked."

locked in *v.* **1)** To be in a position on a fast-closing wave, trimming just ahead of the curl, so that there is no choice but to drive straight across the wave's face as fast as possible to avoid being wiped out. **2)** To be in a position where it is impossible to pull out even if you wanted to. **3)** The situation when a surfer is caught on such a fast-moving wave that he or she is forced to hang on to the board for dear life. (IDSM) **4)** To be positioned in the perfect spot on the wave—that is, inside the curl. (MM)

locos *n.* LOCALS. Regulars or residents of a given location or surf spot. (Hawaii)

log *n.* **1)** A very heavy surfboard. **2)** A long surfboard. (JP) **3)** A longboard. (MM) **4)** Any board over seven feet and weighing over fifteen pounds. (H&R)
5) logger An old MALIBU. (NAT, 1985)

logjam *n.* **1)** The situation when there are too many longboards on the same wave. **2)** Constipation; the opposite of TOURISTA.

logman *n.* LONGBOARDER.

lone-star session *n.* Surfing all by yourself. (RMN)

longboard *n.* A surfboard eight to ten feet long, used during the forties, fifties, and sixties and revived in the eighties.

A longboard provides more flotation than a shortboard because it contains more foam. It also paddles and catches waves more easily, and is more stable in big, fast, bumpy surf. In addition, the longer rail line gives control. Longboards are known for gliding, carrying speed, and keeping their momentum through slow or mushy sections of a wave.

longboard betty *n.* Female surfer who rips on a longboard.

longboard club *n.* A group of surfers who have organized to promote longboarding.

longboarder *n.* A surfer who rides a longboard.

longboard skateboard *n.* A much longer skateboard made for cruising free and easy; very popular in the 1990s.

longboard valley kook *n.* Derogatory term for LONGBOARDER.

long crested swell *n.* A swell that produces large waves.

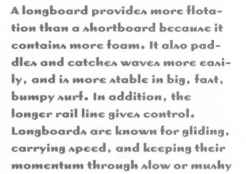

log
Charles Souza
Photo: Camille Seaman

longboards
Coco y Flaco, Mexico
Photo: Kirwin Fox

longboarder
Art: Jim Phillips

longboard betty
Liz Solomon
Santa Rosaliita, Baja
Photo: Trevor Cralle

longest functional distance, functional length of ride *n.* **1)** In professional surfing, the longest possible distance that a surfer can ride along the horizontal plane in the judges' field of vision while performing maneuvers. The length of the ride is both the least important and the most controversial aspect of the scoring criteria. See SURFING CRITERIA. (L&L) **2)** The length of the ride. **3)** Continuing to perform functional maneuvers for the maximum distance that the wave allows. Riding for the maximum distance does *not* mean riding straight in with the white water (groveling).

long hair *n.* A heavy-metal surfer. Usage: "He's a long hair." (San Clemente)

long john *n.* A sleeveless wetsuit with full-length legs. See SHORT JOHN.

long-line drive *n.* A long, fast ride on a hot wave.

longshore current *n.* A stream of water flowing parallel to and near the shore; caused by waves hitting the beach at an oblique angle. (CCRG) This current often carries a surfer down the coast during a session, making it difficult to paddle out or line up.

loomer *n.* A big wave suddenly appearing outside.

loop *n.* A surfing and windsurfing maneuver in which the surf craft is ridden through a complete circle in the air or in a wave.

looper *n.* A wave that curls or throws out in front of itself, often breaking over a surfer to create a ride in the tunnel.

loose 1) *adj.* Used to describe a board-handling characteristic, as in "loose and responsive." **2) looseness** *n.* The maneuverability of a surfboard. (L&L)

loose board *n.* An incoming surfboard with no rider! Also called KILLER BOARD.

lost at sea *n.* Last seen or last known location before disappearing forever. Famous watermen who were lost at sea include Eddie Aikau and José Angel.

louie *n.* Someone with a ripped tank top who rides a motorcycle or drives around in a jacked-up pickup truck with fluorescent shocks and a Local Motion decal. (Newport Beach)

loungeboarder *n.* LONGBOARDER. (1994)

lovelys *n.* Good-looking girls, as in "scopin' on some lovelys." (North San Diego County)

low, low pressure, low pressure system *n.* Unstable moving air and winds that blow counterclockwise around the center of the system, in contrast to a high pressure system, in which the winds blow clockwise around the center. Low pressure systems make surf, highs don't. (W&B)

low-energy summer waves *n.* Fun surf that never gets very big.

lowk *n.* LOCAL; a term used in the movie *Under the Boardwalk* (1989).

low tide *n.* A lowering of sea level. Some spots break best at low tide; some break only at low tide.

low tide
Bolinas, California
Photo: Stephanie Gene Morgan

lurker
Art: Keith Hunter

luau *n.* A Hawaiian feast and party with music and hula dancers.

lull *n.* **1)** A period in which there is no constant roll of waves breaking on the bank. **2)** The period between sets when the waves are smaller or nonexistent. (ORB) **3)** A long wait between waves. (MM) **4) major lull** A longer than normal wait between sets, which often means that a bigger set is coming next. (L&L)

lumps *n.* Recognizable swell shape that will form surfable waves. (Santa Barbara)

lumpy *adj.* Used to describe the uneven surface of a wave; not CLEAN. "The waves were a little lumpy." (1994)

lunch *v.* HAMMERED or WORKED. (MVA) Usage: "I got completely lunched out there."
—**lunch time** (SFG, October 1987)

lurker *n.* **1)** Someone from the idwest who lives at the beach, doesn't work or go to school, drinks a lot of beer, has a tattoo, scams to get by, mooches off girlfriends or lives off a trust fund, may or may not surf. **2)** A Sunset Boulevard type (Hollywood, Los Angeles), who rides a skateboard or a beach cruiser. These characters lurk around, going from place to place to look for drugs, a free meal, a sack of herb, or parties. (Mission Beach, Newport Beach, and Huntington Beach)

Santa Cruz Surfing Club 1941
Photo: Ed Webber
Courtesy of Harry Mayo,
Santa Cruz Surfing Museum

PACK YOUR TRASH

PLEASURE POINT NIGHT FIGHTERS

Art: Jim Phillips

Maalaea, Maalaea Pipeline (ma-LAY-ah) *n.* A spectacular surf site located on the south shore of Maui, Hawaii, and known as the "fastest wave in the world"; breaks fast only a few times a year. Threatened by a harbor expansion project, the Protect Maalaea Coalition is fighting to save this endangered surf spot.

mack, mack out *v.* To eat enthusiastically and without inhibitions, usually after a surf session. (P) Same as SHOVEL, MOW. Usage: "Let's mack."

macked *v.* To be smacked by a big wave. (SWH) Usage: "I got completely macked."

macking *v.* When huge waves roll in, big and powerful as a Mack truck. (RQN) Usage: "The waves are fully macking."

magazine shot *n.* See COVER SHOT SURFING.

magic board, magic stick *n.* Everyone has had one or more surfboards that performed above all others. That's the magic board.

mainland *n.* Not in the islands.

mainlanded *adj.* A temporary condition for a visiting island surfer to California. Usage: "Hey, Benj, sorry we didn't hook up while you were mainlanded."

major *adj.* BIG TIME, as in "a major lull."

major hang time *n.* A long floater. Usage: "Look at that major hang time." See HANG TIME.

major hazard *n.* Any hidden obstacle that can suddenly derail a surfer, such as a storm drain, underwater cables, or submerged rocks. See BOIL.

major maneuvers *n.* In competitive surfing, the outstanding or eye-catching moves that most influence a judge's score. They are (in descending order of degree of difficulty): tube ride, cover-up, reentry, cutback, ricochet, floater, and bottom turn. (L&L) Also see METHODS OF FINISH, MINOR MANEUVERS, and TRANSITIONAL MANEUVERS.

makable wave *n.* Any wave that's fairly easy to catch. —**makeable takeoff**

Makaha A Hawaiian beach and surf spot on Oahu that is famous for its backwash and awesome bowl (the Makaha bowl).

Makaha board *n.* A board designed in the 1950s, especially for riding through the Makaha bowl. The design featured a pointed tail and a flat bottom, which were supposed to help the board glide across the flat part of the wave and thus enable the surfer to make it through the bowl. Another distinctive design element was the sharp breakaway edge on the bottom of the tail block.

make a section 1) *v.* To surf through a particular section of a wave to another section. **2) making a section** *n.* A scoring move in a surf contest.

makeitaudible (make-it-audible) To ride in and out of a big barrel; the term was coined by Nathan Fletcher. May have to do with yelling as you ride in and out of a tube, or with the sound that you

macking
Art: Rick Stover

165

mallard
Art: Rick Stover

hear inside the wave. Usage: "Makeitaudible, dude."

make waves, making waves *v*. To catch a wave and ride it. "Surfers don't make waves they ride 'em" —California bumper sticker (1989)

Mal, Mal-rider *n*. Australian slang for a malibu board, or longboard.

Malibu 1) A Southern California coastal community known for its beaches and surf spots. **2)** The place where anti-valley sentiments originated. **3)** The birthplace of the Malibu board.

Malibu Barbie *n*. A label given to a girl with the IQ of a Barbie doll. See BARBIE. Usage: "She's such a Malibu Barbie."

Malibu board, Malibu or **malibu** *n*. A lightweight balsa board designed by Malibu surfers Matt Kivlin and Joe Quigg.

The Malibu board was developed in the late forties and early fifties, when it was ridden mainly at Malibu Beach, California, and referred to as a "chip board." It was based on the Simmons theory of reducing weight, but it went one step further by improving the shape and thus the maneuverability of the board. Originally made of balsa wood (plywood in Australia), the modern Malibu is constructed of foam and fiberglass and is from eight-and-a-half

to ten-and-a-half feet long. Also called MAL (in Australia), ZIP BOARD, and LONGBOARD.

malihini (MAH-le-HEE-nee) *n*. A newcomer to the Hawaiian Islands. Newcomers to the sport of surfing are also referred to as malihinis. See KAMAAINA.

mallard *n*. A KOOK; someone who floats around out in the lineup like a duck. (San Clemente)

mañana *n., adv.* Spanish for "morning," "tomorrow," or "in the near future." An important concept and state of mind that is necessary to grasp and accept when traveling in Baja and other Spanish-speaking areas south of the Mexican border. Same as HAWAIIAN TIME or ISLAND TIME.

—mañana method, mañana time

In his book *Demon Box* (New York: Viking Penguin, 1986), Ken Kesey says the Arabic version of mañana is bukra f'il mish-mish ("Tomorrow, when it's the season of the apricot.")

Malibu
Photo: John S. Callahan

mane *n.* Spray thrown aloft from a breaking wave, caused by an offshore wind. See LIQUID SMOKE.

maneuverability *n.* How well a surfboard turns on a wave. For example, a shortboard is more maneuverable than a longboard.

man-made waves *n.* Artificially produced waves, like those at Big Surf in Arizona. See WAVE POOL.

man-on-man *n.* A system introduced to professional surfing by Australian Peter Drouyn at the inaugural Stubbies Contest at Burleigh Heads, Australia, in 1977. Although having two surfers in the water was a breakthrough then, it is now standard practice in competitions, except in the big waves of Hawaii. The catch in the system is that inside positioning is the key to dominating the man-on-man heats, making them more of a paddle race than a surfing contest. (L&L) See PRIORITY BUOY.

manson *n.* **1)** A psycho surfer. Usage: "Some manson snaked Johnny-Boy at Beach Park, and did a cutback right into him." (Sunset Beach Surf Shop, Hawaii; SFR, 1989) **2)** A term used by shortboarders to describe out-of-control longboarders. (RJS)

marauder *n.* A sixties term for a reckless surfer. (IDSM)

marine layer *n.* **1)** Fog and low clouds that frequently form along coastlines in late spring and early summer; caused by the mixing of cold, upwelling water with warm air. Although the cold, opaque marine layer blocks the sun at the beach, a short distance inland the fog ends and it is hot and sunny. (California; W&B) **2)** An inverted climatic condition that pervades certain coastlines.

marine stinger *n.* See SEA WASP.

marine terrace *n.* **1)** Uplifted sea floor that was cut and eroded by wave action, forming a flat plain edging the ocean. **2)** A good spot for a surf check. (CCRG) Also called COASTAL TERRACE, WAVE-CUT BENCH.

marine water quality index California state standards specify levels of fecal coliform bacteria in swimming areas should not exceed 200 per 100 ml. water. Stay out of the water for three days after a heavy rain to avoid getting sick. See BLUE WATER TASK FORCE.

massive *adj.* Used to describe waves that are really superbig.

mat *n.* SURF MAT.

Maui cruiser *n.* Rusted-out large American car that somehow keeps chugging along from surf spot to surf spot. See SURF VEHICLE.

Maverick's *n.* Northern California big wave surf spot offshore of Pillar Point. Named in 1961 after "Mac" McCarthy's dog, Maverick, a white German shepherd. Surfed alone for more than fifteen years by Half Moon Bay's Jeff Clark. The spot was brought into the surfing limelight with big surf on January 29, 1991. Site of Hawaiian big wave rider Mark Foo's tragic death on December 23, 1994. The

media frenzy put big-wave surfing and Maverick's in the world spotlight. Also called **Mav's** or **Mavz**.

Maxi-pad cowboy n. A derogatory term for a bodyboarder, so called because the bodyboard resembles an absorbent feminine pad in shape. (Hawaii)

max out v. **1)** To be over the limit, over the top. Usage: "The huge swell maxed out." **2)** Used to define the upper limit of a particular wave. Usage: "This wave maxes out at two meters." (MW)

Maytag v. To get SPUN. "We got Maytaged." See SPIN CYCLE.

Mazatlans n. Mexican sandals with tire-tread soles; same as GUARACHES.

McDonald's tray n. Cafeteria-type plastic tray used for bodysurfing planing aide. First used by Hawaiians in Waikiki and now used by many a surfer around the world. On Oahu, frequent "borrowing" of these trays caused the fast-food restaurants to drill holes into them.

mean adj. Nasty but good. Usage: "Those waves look pretty mean."

mean high tide line (MHTL) n. The highest point that the tide reaches on the shore. In California, and certain other areas of the globe, the beach is public property up to the mean high tide line, even on a so-called private beach posted with "no trespassing" and "keep out"

Maytag
Art: Rick Stover

signs. This means that a surfer may walk along the beach (up to the MHTL) in order to reach a surf spot; it's always smart, though, to respect the property owner's land.

mean wave height n. See WAVE HEIGHT.

mean wave period n. See PERIOD.

meat wave n. A carload of valleys. (SFR, August 1990)

meaty adj. **1)** Used to describe the part of a wave with the most energy. Usage: "I saw you trim through that meaty section." **2)** Big, thick and powerful, as in a "meaty wave."

meditating n. See YOGA MANEUVERS.

medium tide n. **1)** Somewhere in between high and low tides. Some spots break best during a medium tide. **2)** A tide that doesn't get superhigh.

mega adj. An intensifier, as in "mega-enormous waves" or "mega-tubular."

mellow adj. **1)** Relaxed, laid-back, enjoying a kicked-back pace. Usage: "Don't harsh my mellow." (Don't marsh my mellow.) Or, "That really harshes my mellow." (Darcey, 1992) See GEL. **2)** Used by jazz musicians in the 1930s to describe their scene; it was *mellow.*

3) Used by East Coast types, quite fairly, to ridicule California's "laid-back" pretensions. "If I start to get too mellow, I ripen and rot." —Woody Allen, *Annie Hall* (1977). Or, "When Californians use leaf blowers, life is less mellow." —*The Wall Street Journal* (December 4, 1990).

4) "Mellow Yellow" A 1966 pop song by Donovan Leitch.

Mellow had an established slang usage among surfers and other beach kids well before the word became associated with the hot-tub-and-long-hair crowd. The surfing connection may have been initiated by Mark M. Wagner when he was a junior at La Jolla High School; his poem "Day Chant" (published in Surfer magazine, March 1970) featured the line, "Let's hug the mellow day and come back again tomorrow!"

"In Orange County, California, in 1981, wanting to be mellow is like wanting to be dead."

—Kief Hillsbery, "Clockwork Orange County," Outside magazine (August/September 1981)

mellow out *v.* **1)** To relax, veg. **2)** "Cool it!" Usage: "Mellow out, dude!"

meltdown, the meltdown *n.* A phenomenon you experience when it's low tide, really hollow, and you take acid drops off of waves. (Ocean Beach, San Francisco; BTV)

melting lines *n.* Well-harmonized contours of a surfboard.

menehune *n.* (meh-NAH-who-KNEE) Hawaiian word for junior division in a surfing competition—usually eleven to thirteen years of age. Named after the Hawaiian mythological little people.

mersh *adj.* Mushy surf. (1993)

message in a bottle *n.* What every surfer longs to find washed up on shore.

methods of finish *n.* Any of several maneuvers used to end a ride. In competitive surfing, they are (in descending order of degree of difficulty): KICKOUT, PULLOUT, STEPOFF, and UNCONTROLLED. (L&L) Also see MAJOR MANEUVERS, MINOR MANEUVERS, TRANSITIONAL MANEUVERS.

Mexi, Mexican blanket *n.* A multicolored, thick woven blanket made from cotton, wool, or mixed fibers. Used by many surfers as a beach mat, bed spread, couch throw, seat cover, curtain, rug, or simply to keep warm after a cold water sesh.

"Hola, hola, I gotta you blankets. How many, how many? What color? Almost free. Check five more."

—Muy Caro, Mexican blanket vendor from Mulege, Baja

Mexican hurricanes *n.* Storms off Baja that bring short-term south to southwest swells to the California coast. Also called CHUBASCOS.

Mexico, Mex A major surf destination, especially among California surfers. See "Spanish for the Mexico-bound Surfer," page 242. Also see BAJA.

Mexi-gringo surf drawl *n.* The lingo of Spicoli-type surfers who venture into

Mexi
Muy Caro
Playa El Coyote, Baja
Photo: Trevor Cralle

Mexico and speak Spanish with a very poor accent. (P)

⋘⋘⋘⋘⋘⋘⋘⋘⋘⋘⋘⋘⋘

"Who's got the beaucoup dollares?" . . . "I got uno nicklea."

—*Jeff Spicoli (Sean Penn) in*
Fast Times at Ridgemont High (1982)

⋘⋘⋘⋘⋘⋘⋘⋘⋘⋘⋘⋘⋘

micro *n.* A perfectly shaped wave but unridable because of its small size. (Newport Beach)

mid-face turn *n.* Any minor directional change, for example between 60 and 130 degrees, that has little influence on speed.

mid-latitude cyclones *n.* Strong low pressure systems that track across the North Pacific in winter. Depending on how far north or south these storms are steered by the jet stream, California experiences a west, northwest, or north swell. (BB, October 1990)

mil *n.* Short for millimeter when applied to thickness of neoprene rubber. Usage: "My wetsuit is three mil." See FOUR/THREE.

mildude *n.* Surfer corruption of *mildew* —that nasty smell of fungus growth on a wetsuit or neoprene booties when they haven't been properly hung up to dry. Usage: "Oh, man, my suit is all mildude." (Coined by Trevor Cralle during a phone call between California and Maryland at 2 P.M. on November 15, 1993; inspired by Damien Russell) See BOOTIE JUICE.

milk, milking *v.* To get the most out of a wave, as in "milking speed and energy from small surf."

milky *adj.* Used to describe the whitewater section of a broken wave.

mindless *adj.* Used to describe insane waves that are beyond the wildest imaginings of the mind. (MM)

mind-surf, mind surfing *n.* When you look at a wave, or anything such as a hill, or cement wall, and imagine yourself surfing it. See SURF DREAMS, WAVE DREAMS.

miniboards *n.* Shortboards, which are usually teardrop or bullet shaped.

minigun *n.* A surfboard that is somewhere between a shortboard and a big gun in length.

minilog *n.* A shortened version of a longboard. (GTV)

minimum wave requirement *n.* A prerequisite, measured in WAVE HEIGHT to hold some surf contests. For example, the waves must be at least twenty feet high in order to hold the memorial Eddie Aikau contest at Waimea Bay; some years the event doesn't happen.

minitanker *n.* MINILOG.

minor maneuvers *n.* In competitive surfing, moves that are not in the category of major maneuvers but that have some influence on scoring potential. They are (in descending order of difficulty): TOP TURN, FOAM FLOATER, FOAM TURN, and FADE. (L&L) Also see MAJOR MANEUVERS, METHODS OF FINISH, and TRANSITIONAL MANEUVERS.

minus tide *n.* An extremely low tide that occurs during a spring-tide period.

micro
six inches high, Baja
Photo: Woody Woodworth

Beach Brolly, Sombrillas
Playa del Este, Havana, Cuba
Painting: Susan Matthews

Surf monkeys
San Diego, California
Photo: Trevor Cralle

Ken Collins
Santa Crucial, California
Photo: Mike Peralta

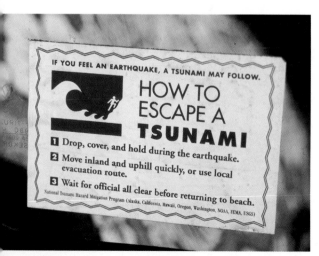

IF YOU FEEL AN EARTHQUAKE, A TSUNAMI MAY FOLLOW.

HOW TO ESCAPE A TSUNAMI

1 Drop, cover, and hold during the earthquake.
2 Move inland and uphill quickly, or use local evacuation route.
3 Wait for official all clear before returning to beach.

National Tsunami Hazard Mitigation Program (Alaska, California, Hawaii, Oregon, Washington, NOAA, FEMA, USGS)

Photo: Trevor Cralle

Edrick Baldwin
Hawaii
Photo: Mike Peralta

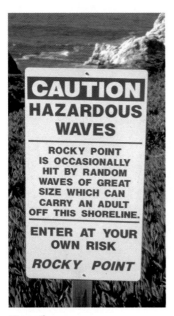

Hazardous seas
Photo: Trevor Cralle

Evan Slater
Maverick's
Photo: Mike Peralta

Dan Jenkin with lobsters
Santa Rosaliita, Baja California
Photo: Baja Collective

Flea
The Lane
Photo: Mike Peralta

Greg Noll at Pipeline, 1964
Photo: Surfer magazine, courtesy of Greg Noll

Surf contest
Pleasure Point, Santa Cruz, California
Photo: Trevor Cralle

Photo: Trevor Cralle

Freighters surf spot
Baja California
Photo: Liz Phegan

Mark Perko with recycled board
Photo: Lori Hanson

...niver
...nta Cruz, California
...oto: Courtesy of Jim Phillips

Kinstle in Mexico
Photo: Trevor Cralle

Santa Cruz, California
Photo: Trevor Cralle

...artin's Beach, California
...oto: Lee Micheaux

Lifeguard tower
Oahu, Hawaii
Photo: Camille Seaman

Woody
Santa Cruz, California
Photo: Trevor Cralle

Hot batch
Art: Jim Phillips

"Evening Glass Off"
Art: Bill Ogden
Gordon McCelland Collection

Waimea Bay warning
Hawaii
Photo: Jan Jenkin

n the Pope's living room"

: John Nickerson

pyright © 2000, Mullethead Surf Designs

Peter Mel
Maverick's
Photo: Mike Peralta

Joey Hutson
Salsa Brava, Costa Rica
Photo: Mike Peralta

Party wave
Maverick's
Photo: Mike Peralta

minute air n. Barely catching air. See BIG AIR, SOAR.

miragey adj. The effect when a wave looks huge from far away but is actually quite small by the time it reaches you. (MPZ) Usage: "It was really miragey out there today."

mixed tides n. A widespread phenomenon in the Pacific and Indian oceans, in which pairs of high and low tides are unequal in height, so that there is a **higher high tide**, followed by a **lower low tide**, and a **lower high tide**, and a **higher low tide** each day; caused by changes in the moon's and sun's positions with respect to the earth's equator. (CCRG, WB). See TIDES.

moana (mo-AH-na) n. Hawaiian for ocean.

mob n. An Australian term for a group of surfers—usually many. See CARVING UP THE MOB.

mo'bettah Hawaiian Pidgin English for "more better."

modern surfboard eras n. Specific periods in the history of surfing in Australia, identified with the kinds of board in use, include **1)** the solid board, from 1912 to 1938; **2)** the hollow board, from 1938 to 1956; **3)** the balsa-wood Malibu board from America, fiberglass covered and fitted with a fin, from 1956 until 1965; **4)** the American-invented polyurethane/glass-covered board, from 1965 to the present. (ASKC)

modern surfing n. A surfing era that was born in the 1940s and 1950s and that was characterized by the transition to lighter surfboards.

moke, big moke n. A local heavy surfer dude who may or may not be aggressive or in a good mood. (Hawaii; PDX, PZ)

MOLTO man (Man Of Late Take-Offs) n. Someone who consistently catches a wave late, thus making the drop-in very hairy. (ATRL)

mombro n. Your mom. What about **papabro** and **babybro**? (August 1993)

mondo adj. Used to describe huge surf conditions, of epic proportions. (ATRL) Usage: "It was mondo."

monkey hop v. Surfing straight out to the flats.

monster n. **1)** A gigantic wave. (MM) **2) monster surf** Huge waves. —**monsta** (Hawaiian Pidgin), **monster air, monsters**

"... waves that bulged and grew monstrous, like mountains ..."

—The Odyssey of Homer, translated by Richmond Lattimore (New York: Harper and Row, 1975)

monster
Peter Mel
Maverick's
Photo: Mike Peralta

monstering *adj.* Term used to describe huge surf by Cheyne Horan in the video *Biggest Wednesday.* **—monstrous reef pass suckout**

moon *n.* The earth's natural satellite whose gravitational pull is the primary force controlling the tides. It takes the earth twenty-four hours and fifty minutes to revolve, which is why the moon "rises" fifty minutes later each day. (CCRG) Tides are highest and lowest during a new and full moon. See SPRING TIDES, SURFER MOON.

Moondoggie A character in the book/movie *Gidget*, who lived in a grass shack on the beach and was based on a real guy named Billy Bangston. (CC) Sometimes misspelled "Moondawg" or "Moon Dog."

Morey Boogie *n.* The original Boogie Board invented by Tom Morey in the 1970s; developed from aircraft foam. See BODYBOARD, BOOGIE BOARD.

morning sickness *n.* Early in the day when the ocean is HEAVING and the waves are SICK.

most excellent *adj.* Supremely wonderful; used to describe waves and other favorable situations. (From the 1989 movie *Bill and Ted's Excellent Adventure*.)

Mother Bu MALIBU.

motorized skateboard *n.* Skateboard with a small motor attached; controlled by a hand-held throttle cable.

motorized surfboard *n.* Invented in the 1960s.

motorized surfboard
Mac Reed Collection
Photo: Trevor Cralle

mountains *n.* Used as a metaphor for waves. "Surfing is like mountain climbing, only in surfing the mountain chases you!" —Phil Edwards (1967)

Some lucky day each November
great waves awake and are drawn
Like smoking mountains bright
from the west.

—*Robinson Jeffers, "November Surf"*

mouth surfing *n.* The act of eating hot chile peppers.

"A bite brings on fiery pain.
Then comes a wave of relief.
One expert calls it 'mouth-surfing.'"

—*Anne Raver, The New York Times, October 11, 1992*

moves up *adj.* Said of a wave that becomes THICK and FAT. Usage: "The wave at Mav's really moves up on you after you catch it."

mow *v.* To eat; to MACK OUT.

multifin *n.* Any surfboard with more than one fin placement. **—multifin designs**

multiple stringers *n.* More than one stringer on a longboard, generally refers to two or three.

munch *v.* **1)** To get eaten up by a wave. (P) Usage: "I got totally munched on that last one." **2)** To scarf down some food.

munchie *n.* Australian for man-eating shark. (Victoria, Australia; RDTW) See GUMMIES.

Murph the Surf 1) The nickname of surfer-turned-jewel-thief Jack Murphy, who together with Allan Kuhn stole the Star of India sapphire from New York's American Museum of Natural History in 1964. **2)** A 1975 movie starring Don Stroud and Robert Conrad, based loosely on Murphy and Kuhn's adventures.

Murphy *n.* Rick Griffin's fictitious cartoon characterization of a typical gremmie, who made his debut in 1961 in the second issue of *Surfer* magazine.

mushburger *n.* A shapeless wave, sometimes caused by unfavorable winds. In other cases, though, a spot just doesn't have a good bottom contour and the waves are always mushburgers. (MW) See MUSHY.

mushing wave *n.* A wave that breaks in the top and dies quickly, resulting in a very short ride. (MF, 1967)

mushroom cloud *n.* The white, inverted-mushroom-shape cloud produced underwater by the impact of the falling crest of a large wave on its forward slope. Seen only from beneath the surface.

mushy *adj.* **1)** Applied to waves that are blown over by onshore winds. The walls collapse, creating much white water and making conditions poor for surfing. Usage: "The wave totally mushed out." **2)** Said of a slow, sloppy or rolling wave that has little power or speed. **3)** In general, used to describe poor-quality, small surf. (L&L) **4)** *n.* **mush dog, mush doggie** A wave that never breaks. **5) mush** Surf under one foot high that is barely ridable. (H&R) —**mush out** *v.*, **mushier** *adj.*

mysterioso *n.* **1)** An "adornment" or surf trick created by Mickey Muñoz in the late 1950s, in which he bent over and hid his head in his hands. Spelled "mysteriouso" in the first issue of *Surfer* magazine (1960). **2)** A jazz tune by Thelonious Monk.

mysto dude *n.* An introverted surfer who hangs by himself. (El Salvador, 1992)

mysto-spot *n.* A surf spot that breaks big when other places are flat.

My wave! A surfer's claim to own the wave he or she is riding; a presumption documented in the Surf Punks' song "My Wave." Also used to signal someone to stay out of the way. See GOT IT.

Murphy
Cover of Surfer magazine,
Aug–Sept 1962
Art: Rick Griffin

NO:

 **DIVING**

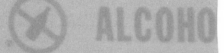 **ALCOHO**

 **GLASS C**

 **DOGS OR**

 **MOTOR VEH**

 **LITTERING**

 **OPEN FIRES**

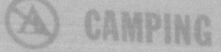 **CAMPING**

 **BASEBALL**

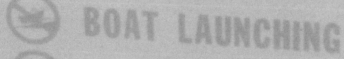 **BOAT LAUNCHING**

 **VENDORS**

nailed *v.* To be wiped out badly, to get dumped on—happens after a surfer "closes the lid" on a coffin ride. (MCR) Usage: "I got nailed by the lip."

nalu (na-LOO) *n.* Hawaiian for wave; the surf. See "Ancient Hawaiian Surfing Terms" in Appendix A.

nami nori (NAH-mee NOR-ee) *n.* Japanese for surfing.

napper *n.* Anyone sleeping on the beach. (California, San Onofre Surf Club, 1940s)

nar *adj.* Short for GNARLY. (SP) Usage: "Those waves look pretty nar out there." See GNAR-GNAR.

narlip *n.* A surfer's lip as he talks out of one side of his mouth. Sort of like a surfer's hairlip. Not to be confused with LIPNAR.

narly *adj.* GNARLY.

narrow nose *n.* A design used on a big-wave board so that offshore winds won't hold up surfers at the crest of the wave as they attempt to paddle into it.

NASA (National Association of Surfing Attorneys) *n.* A network of law students, lawyers, and activists who are dedicated to coastal zone environmental law. Founded in San Francisco in 1992 by Mark Masara. Publishes biannual journal, *SURFLAW*.

nasodrain *n.* When the large quantity of seawater that is lodged in one's nasal passages as a result of the previous surf session empties out through one's nostrils in the space of a nanosecond. (SFG, 1990)

natural, natural foot, natural-footer *n.* A surfer (usually a right-handed one) who rides with the left foot forward; the opposite of a goofy foot.
—natural rider, natural surfer

natural heater *n.* Urinating in a wetsuit. (Santa Cruz) Same as DOING A SAUNA, INTERNAL HEATING, PETER HEATER, URINOPHORIA.

natural high *n.* The feeling you get from surfing.

nautical mile, international nautical mile *n.* A unit of distance designed to equal about one minute of arc of latitude; its length is 6,076.115 feet (1,852 meters), approximately 1.15 times as long as the statute mile of 5,280 feet. (GVS) See KNOT.

neap tides *n.* Tides of less-than-average magnitude that occur at the first and third quarters of the moon, when the sun and moon are at right angles to each other with respect to the earth, so that the sun's effect on the tides partially cancels the effect of the moon. (CCRG, WB) See SPRING TIDES.

near drowning experience *n.* When you almost die from a really bad wipeout.

nectar *n.* **1)** The juice, or energy, of a wave. **2)** Any fruit juice, such as papaya,

natural foot
Art: Robbie Quine

nectar betty
Sasha Hrycenko
Photo: Trevor Cralle

passion fruit, or mango, especially after a surf; the **nectar of the goddess**. **3)** *adj.* Sweet, like nectar; used to describe an attractive female. Usage: "She's really nectar." **—nectar betty**

needle nose *n.* The sharp pointed tip of a surfboard. See SHARKY.

neoprene *n.* **1)** The rubber used in the construction and repair of wetsuits. **2) neoprene rubber cement** The substance used to glue together and repair wetsuit seams, booties, etc.

Neptune's Revenge What you get when you drink too much saltwater, derived from an instrumental surf tune by The Mermen (1990). See KING NEPTUNE.

net surfing, network surfing *n.* See SURFING THE INTERNET.

"**Consider the net a totally radical swell that allows you to swim out to cherry new waves. To surf the net, you need to get coastal access— i.e., a place to log on—and (often) pay a user fee. Information is accessible only from within the internet environment (much like the rippiest rides can only be had when you're deep inside the curl).**"

—*Stephen A. Mallery. "Tales of the CyBeer Surfer." Beer, September 1994*

---

newporsche (new-porsh) *n.* Newport Beach. Popularized in the Hollywood movie *Under the Boardwalk* (1988).

new wave *n.* **1)** The new wave of anything vs. the old wave. **2)** New Wave music of the late 1970s.

New Zealand swells *n.* Southern-hemisphere swells caused by low pressure systems off Antarctica that develop to full strength just south of New Zealand. Whether California receives a southwest or a straight south swell depends on how far east these storms continue to intensify. (BB, October 1990)

nibbler *n.* Anyone eating at or near the beach. (California, San Onofre Surf Club, 1940s)

night chargers *n.* People who surf at night, sometimes under a full moon. (Santa Cruz, 1992)

night session *n.* Surfing after dark.

night surfing *n.* A unique night-time experience, especially under a full moon. Tiny plankton (bioluminescent phosphorescence) that light up at night when disturbed can make a whole wave glow a bright lime green, adding a new dimension to tube riding. (W&B) This phenomenon occurs all over the world.

911 wave *n.* The kind of wave that makes you feel afterward like you want to go home in an ambulance. (El Segundo, California)

ninth-wave theory *n.* The notion that each ninth wave is the highest; generally not the case.

nip factor *n.* Cold ocean. Much in evidence when the water gets nippy. (Santa Cruz) Usage: "The nip factor today was way high."

nipple *adj.* Used to describe freezing cold water. (Santa Barbara) Usage: "It was nipple out there." —**nipson** (Newport Beach)

noah *n.* Rhyming slang for shark, as in Noah's Ark. (Australia, MW) Usage: "Did you see that noah out there?"

"No Beach Access" signs = Beach Access!

No Fat Chicks! A slogan perpetuating anorexia, bulimia, speed walking, the dieting craze, and possibly other serious disorders yet to be seen; originated around 1980 in Santa Monica and Malibu and is used by brainless, superficial types who want to live in a society of Barbie dolls.

no-hesitation situation *n.* The split second that you have in which to make that drop down the wave face; otherwise you enter the TOADS zone. (RO)

no ka 'oi (no-Kah-OY) Hawaiian for "the best." Usage: "Maui no ka 'oi." ("Maui is the best.")

no man *n.* Derogatory term for body-boarder. (Santa Cruz) Same as HALF MAN.

non *n.* A nonsurfer.

nonlocal *n.* Anyone who's not from the area. Same as UNLOCAL. See LOCAL.

no one out 1) A joyous sight—perfect surf and nobody around to crowd it up. **2)** Possibly also a sign of bad surfing conditions, like maybe there's a reason nobody's out surfing. See SHARK.

no-paddle takeoff *n.* Rocking into a wave and catching it without having to paddle the board (A&M) —an extremely difficult maneuver.

nor'easters *n.* **1)** The prevailing summer winds along Australia's east coast. (MW) **2)** A big storm in the Northeast of the United States.

North Shore The surf center of the planet Earth, located on Oahu, Hawaii; the proving grounds—site of a number of world-famous surf spots, including Haleiwa, Waimea, Pupukea, Pipeline, and Sunset. (GN).

north swell *n.* A swell that moves from north to south. (ORB)

north wind *n.* A wind that blows from north to south. (ORB)

nose *n.* **1)** The bow or front end of a surf-board. **2)** The tip of a board. **3)** The front third of a surfboard. (ORB)

nose channels *n.* 1970s design feature. See CHANNELS.

no see 'ums *n.* Invisible biting insects encountered on shore in Baja and other parts of the globe. Vanilla is said to keep them away.

nose guard *n.* A small, triangular sili-cone plastic cover that is glued onto

Cowell's Beach, Santa Cruz
Photo: Trevor Cralle

No Beach Access
Montara, California
Photo: Stephanie Gene Morgan

the nose tip of contemporary surfboards and acts as a shock-absorbing bumper. It was developed by Island Classic Surfboards shaper Eric Arakawa and partner David Skedeleski in response to the increasing number of injuries from pointed nose tips. Because of its softness, the nose guard can also improve the safety of blunted noses. (ORB)

nose kick *n.* The upward curve, or rocker, in the front third of a surfboard.

nose ride or **nose-ride** *n.* **1)** Riding a longboard by putting one or both feet on the board's nose. **2)** Shooting across a hollow wave while standing on the nose of a board. (A&M) —**nose riding, noseriding**

⚓⚓⚓⚓⚓⚓⚓⚓⚓⚓

"**You can take off and run to the noɅe quickly; take off and do a bottom turn, then go to the noɅe; take off, Ʌtall, then go to the noɅe; or bottom turn, Ʌtall, then go to a noɅeride.**"

—*Belén Connelly.* Surfinggirl, April 2000

⚓⚓⚓⚓⚓⚓⚓⚓⚓⚓

nose rider *n.* **1)** A longboard with a rounded nose tip that makes it suitable for nose riding; originally created by

Phil Edwards. **2)** A surfer who rides at the front end of a surfboard. (MM)

nose tip *n.* The pointed front end of a surfboard.

nose under, nosing *v.* To slip the front of a surfboard under water while riding a wave. Usage: "I was nosing under on that last section." See PEARL, PEARLING.

nose width *n.* A dimension used by shapers, measured twelve inches from the tip of the nose of the surfboard.

no surf The absence of rideable waves. See FLAT CALM.

⚓⚓⚓⚓⚓⚓⚓⚓⚓⚓

"**There'Ʌ never no Ʌurf.**"

—*Tony Ray.* Surfing magazine. April 1994

⚓⚓⚓⚓⚓⚓⚓⚓⚓⚓

No Surfing The sign that every surfer hates to see. Some beaches have posted times or restricted areas for surfing.

. . . not "I really like it . . . not"—a surfer's favorite way of turning a positive into a negative. Used on *Saturday Night Live* TV skit "Wayne's World."

NSSA National Scholastic Surfing Association; the governing body of

YAAAAAAAAAAAAAAAAAAAA AAAAAAA

amateur surf competition. Consists of seven conferences nationwide.

nuclear wave *n.* A wave generated by the explosion of a nuclear bomb. "Nuclear wave—if you can surf it, you can survive it" —John Leffingwell

(Maybeck High School, Berkeley, California, 1978)

nugs *n.* Rippable waves—waves you can really tear into. (Eastside, Santa Cruz; SFR, August 1990) See BUCKET O' NUGS.

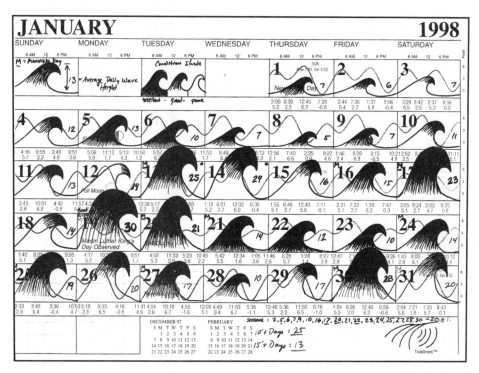

*Grant Washburn's
hand-drawn tide calendar*

ocean energy
Brian Bulkley
Photo: Don Balch

oatmeals *n.* Little mushy waves. (Florida; TDW)

ocean *n.* **1)** The entire body of saltwater that covers about 72 percent of the earth's surface. **2)** Any of the principal divisions of this body of water, including the Atlantic, Pacific, and Indian oceans, their southern extensions in Antarctica, and the Arctic Ocean. **3)** The source of a surfer's pleasure. See SEA.

~~~~~~~~~~~~~~~~~~~~~~~~~~~~~~~~~~~

The word **ocean** comes from the Latin *oceanus*, which came from the Greek *Okeanos*, in Greek mythology the god of the great outer sea thought of as a river encircling the earth. (AHD2, W9)

"Ocean . . . the source of all."

—Homer

"There are more atoms in a tea-spoonful of ocean than there are teaspoonfuls in the ocean."

—Liz Phegan's chemistry textbook

~~~~~~~~~~~~~~~~~~~~~~~~~~~~~~~~~~~

ocean awareness *n.* See OCEAN CONSCIOUSNESS.

ocean briefs *n.* Monologist Spalding Gray's term for surf trunks in his performance piece, book, and film entitled *Swimming to Cambodia* (1985).

ocean consciousness *n.* Being in tune with the ocean, regardless of the activity—surfing, sailing, scuba diving, body

surfing, living in close proximity to the beach, or whatever.

Ocean Day *n.* A national holiday celebrated in Japan.

ocean energy *n.* Wave power in action; the juice of a breaking wave.

ocean hit *n.* The natural high of being at the beach on a sunny day and smelling the fresh salt air.

ocean pulse *n.* What Cheyne Horan says governs the rhythm of the sets and allows one to anticipate the bigger waves. (L&L)

~~~~~~~~~~~~~~~~~~~~~~~~~~~~~~~~~~~

"My soul is full of longing
For the secret of the sea,
And the heart of the great ocean
Sends a thrilling pulse through me."

—Henry Wadsworth Longfellow,
"The Secret of the Sea"

~~~~~~~~~~~~~~~~~~~~~~~~~~~~~~~~~~~

ocean roar *n.* **1)** The sound of the surf. See ROAR OF THE OCEAN. **2) Ocean Roar** A California coastal community on Tomales Bay.

ocean spray *n.* Watery mist that blows off the tops of waves as they break. See OFFSHORE WIND, ROOSTER TAIL.

ocean wave *n.* **1)** Same as WAVE. **2)** A sculpted hairdo in the shape of a wave; the current craze is especially popular among African-American women around Miami, Florida. (February 2000) Also called **head wave.**

ocean wave
Yvonne, Key Largo
Photo: Damien Russell

off-the-lip
Terry Simms
Photo: Bud Clark

o-double *v.* To GO OFF, or surf radically; an abbreviation of "g double-o double-f," an expression that has fallen into disfavor. Usage: "Peter o-doubled his quarterfinal, but went down in the semis." (Santa Cruz; SFR, 1989)

off its tits An Australian expression for outrageous; said of great surfing conditions. Usage: "The reef was off its tits yesterday."

offset or **off-set** *n.* A surfboard with an asymmetrical shape. (MF, 1967)

offshore *adv.* **1)** Refers to the direction of the wind, as in "offshore breeze" or "offshore wind." **2)** Used to indicate the location of a surf spot, such as an offshore island. **3)** Indicates a favorable wind condition. (JRW)

offshore breeze *n.* A lighter form of OFFSHORE WIND.

offshore wind *n.* Wind blowing away from shore, off the land, or away from land to sea. In California, hot winds blowing offshore are called Santanas or devil winds. (Q&M) See SANTA ANA WINDS.

off-the-bottom *n.* A maneuver in which the surfer springs from the bottom of a wave face up to the top.

off-the-face *n.* Any maneuver performed on the front of an advancing wave face.

off-the-lip *n.* **1)** A maneuver performed by cutting sharply up the wave face to a near vertical stall on the lip, then quickly turning down again. **2)** Snapping the board off the top of a wave. (MM)

off the Richter *adj.* A term used by surfers to describe something very good, or off the scale, as in "totally off the Richter." (Australia and USA; MW) Same as OFF ITS TITS, AWESOME, OUTRAGEOUS, TO THE MAX. See RICHTER.

off-the-top *n.* **1)** Smashing off the top of a wave lip. **2)** Turning on the top portion of the wave. (L&L)

off-the-wall *n.* **1)** A banking maneuver off of the wave face. **2) Off-The-Wall** A Hawaiian surf spot. See OTW. **3) off the wall** The slogan on the back of Van's tennis shoes. **4)** *adj.* An early seventies expression meaning "outrageous."

Oflow *n.* Sitting on the beach, relaxing and allowing the sound of the ocean to

Oflow
Art:©2000 Mullethead
Surf Designs

flow into your mind. Usage: "I'm just catchin' the Oflow." (Coined by Damien Russell, Maryland, 1993)

OFOLS Old Farts On Longboards. (Jacksonville, Florida, 1993)

Oi! An exclamation like "Hey!" "Cowabunga!" or "Yo!"

oil, oily adj. Irish surf term for GLASSY.

oil spill, oil slick n. An environmental disaster that happens all too frequently today; usually caused by giant oil tankers running aground and disgorging their contents into the water. One of the consequences is damage to surf spots. See BLACK TIDE.

Two infamous oil spills that affected surfers were the huge Santa Barbara spill that coated beaches from Point Conception south in 1969 and the nearly 400,000-gallon oil spill of crude that stained the Orange County coastline in 1990.

olas n. Spanish for "waves." —**olas grandes** (big waves)

old man baggies n. Oversized surfing trunks. (A&M) See BAGGIES.

old surfer n. While some people have surfed into their 80s and 90s (See movie *Surfing for Life*), young surfers have a slew of derogatory put-downs. How old do you have to be to get labeled an "old surfer?" See BARNACLE FACE, CUT DOWNS FOR OLD SURFERS, CYCLOPS, SOUL BARNEY, STIFF-LEGGED HUNCHBACK, UNCLE FESTER.

olo board n. A long surfboard used exclusively by ancient Hawaiian kings. (A&M) *Olo* means "thick"—and the boards were up to twenty feet long and weighed as much as 180 pounds. (DM) They were made from wili wili, ula, or koa wood.

omega fin n. A skeg designed so it won't grab kelp.

one eighty n. A 180-degree turn.

180-degree forehand turn n. After fading in a backhand direction, a turn back to the original tracking direction (RA); this shift is usually necessary to continue riding the wave.

one man-one wave One of the interference rules put into

oil slick
Art: Rick Stover

force for the ASP circuit at the beginning of the 1985–86 pro surfing season. (L&L) It dictates only one person on a wave at a time.

"one more" *n.* As in one more wave. Usage: "Let me get one more wave and then I'll go in." Same as HANA HO. See LAST WAVE.

one-way board *n.* A board designed mainly for traveling in one direction. (MF, 1967)

onshore *adj.* Refers to the direction the wind is blowing. Usage: "It was completely onshore."

onshore breeze *n.* A light form of ONSHORE WIND.

onshore wind *n.* **1)** A wind that blows from sea to land. (ORB) **2)** A wind that blows from behind the waves. (MW)

on the die 1) Used to describe a subsiding wave. Usage: "The wave was on the die." **2)** Said of a surfer who's about to eat it. Usage: "I was on the die."

on the nose *n.* Surfing in polluted waters. (Australia; MW) Same as YUK, WOOFY, SURFING UNDER TURD. Usage: "It was on the nose out there."

ookei nami (OH-key NAH-me) *n.* Japanese for big wave.

open door *n.* A wave that has no close-out sections. (Australia; L&L) See PUERTAS ABIERTAS.

opposing current *n.* An ocean current that is flowing against the direction that a swell is traveling. An opposing current decreases wave lengths and increases wave heights, thus steepening the wave

face—the opposite effect of a following current. (DKM)

opposite talk *n.* Saying the opposite of what you mean, like "Qual" (Quality)—when it's not. (Monterey Peninsula surfers, 1980s)

. . . or what? A slang expression of enthusiasm. "Or what?" is the last phrase of a rhetorical question, and implies an affirmative answer. Usage: "Is that a great sunset, or what?" "Are we playing cards, or what?" (LMY)

OTA Optimum tanning angle—positioning one's body in direct line with the sun in order to absorb the maximum amount of sun rays.

OTW The abbreviation for OFF-THE-WALL, the Hawaiian surf spot where Shaun Tomson's tube riding was made famous in the 1978 movie *Free Ride*.

"Our Mother Ocean" (OMO) *n.* A monthly column in *Surfer* magazine on the environment; has the slogan "To Save Our Mother Ocean."

out *adv.* Used to mean "to go out surfing." Usage: "I went out today at Black's." —a **go out**

outboard *n.* The direction or side of a surfboard away from the wall of a wave. Usage: "I caught my outboard rail on the wave."

outer reef *n.* OUTSIDE REEF.

outers *n.* OUTSIDE.

out of control 1) Said of a surfer who is unable to control the board as he or she is coming down a wave. **2)** Heading for a wipeout. Usage: "He's out of control." **3)** Said of a gnarly wave. Usage: "That

THERE'S NOT MUCH OF A SHOULDER BUT IT'S A HECK OF A DROP !!

YOSEMITE FALLS SLIDE ??

wave's out of control."

out of sight *adj.* The greatest, terrific.

outrageous, outrageous to the max *adj.* Incredible; said of unbelievable waves, food, or women.

outside *n.* **1)** Seaward of the breaking waves. An **outside wave** is one that unexpectedly breaks outside of the surf zone. **2)** An area beyond which most set waves are breaking. (ORB) **3)** A position beyond the line of breaking waves or outside the lineup. (NAT, 1985) Same as OUT THE BACK. **4)** A warning cry. When you're out in the water and someone yells, "Outside!" it usually means there's a big set approaching the break. (MW)

outside break *n.* The area farthest from shore where the waves are breaking. See INSIDE BREAK.

outsider *n.* A wave that is approaching and developing shape beyond the normal wave zone.

outside rail *n.* The edge of the board closest to the shore. (L&L)

outside reef *n.* **1)** A reef farther out to sea, beyond the inner reef. **2)** A surf spot that breaks beyond the first reef. (GN) Also called OUTER REEF.

out the back *adv.* **1)** To be outside, or seaward, of the breaking waves. (Australia) **2)** To be behind where the waves are breaking.

oval office *n.* Inside of a BARREL.

overgunned *adj.* Riding a board that's too big for the surf, for instance, a seven-foot-plus surfboard in three-foot waves. (SFR, October 1983); the opposite of being underboarded. See UNDERGUNNED.

overhead *adv.* Used to describe waves higher than a surfer is tall—nice. **Double overhead** is even nicer. Usage: "It was double overhead for about two hours."

overlap *n.* The place along the rails of a surfboard where top and bottom layers of fiberglass converge; **double overlap** is stronger.

over the falls, over da falls 1) To be trapped in the plunging lip of a wave, hurled to the bottom, and sometimes sucked up the wave face and launched again—an unpleasant experience. Being poured over with the descending water, from the top of the breaking wave to the bottom, is like going over a waterfall. **2)** To topple off the very top of a wave instead of riding it out. (IDSM) **3)** To free-fall with the breaking lip of a hollow wave. (A&B) Usage: "I got sucked over the falls on that last one."

over the hill, over the hillers *n.* A derogatory expression for surfers who drive to Santa Cruz from San Jose or elsewhere in the San Francisco Bay Area via Highway 17 through the Santa Cruz Mountains.

Oz *n.* Another name for Australia, as in *The Land of Oz.*

*opposite: What's up bro,
ow's the surf?*
noto: Mike Peralta

paddleboard
13-foot hollow plywood
*Photo: Tom Sevais/
Surfer magazine*

Pacific High *n.* A very large high pressure system off the West Coast of California that influences weather.

Pacific Ocean *n.* The largest ocean in the world with a surface area of 63.8 million square miles; bounded on the east by the continents of the Americas, on the north by the Bering Strait, on the west by a line from the Malay Peninsula through Cape Londonderry in Australia and Tasmania, then along meridian 147E to Antarctica. The Pacific includes all adjacent semienclosed seas that connect with it. (GVS)

paddle 1) *v.* To lie in the center of a board and take deep rhythmic strokes through the water. (WWK) **2) paddling** *n.* A means of propelling a surfboard through water; arm stroking. (MF)

paddle back *n.* The journey back out to the lineup after riding a wave in. Usage: "The paddle back was horrendous." (Cabo, 1998) See PADDLE OUT.

paddleboard *n.* A square-sided hollow surf craft invented by Tom Blake in 1926 at Waikiki. It is usually constructed of plywood and is used in long-distance racing competitions.

paddle gloves, paddling gloves *n.* Gloves specially designed to create a wider paddling surface to help surfers catch waves; same as WEBBED PADDLING GLOVES.

paddle-in surfing *n.* As distinct from TOW-IN SURFING.

paddle out *v.* **1)** To stroke out through the incoming surf to the lineup. See OUT-SIDE. **2) Paddle out!** An exclamation used to signal fellow surfers that an outside set of waves is approaching. (Byron Bay, Australia, 1988) Same as OUTSIDE.

paddle out reentry *n.* A difficult-to-pull-off longboard maneuver requiring the surfer to stroke up the face of a wave that is just about to break and turn the board around with the advancing wave. (BBD)

paddler *n.* Someone who rides a paddleboard. (GN)

paddle rash *n.* Sore armpits from wetsuit chaffing during paddling. See BOARD RASH.

paddle ski *n.* South African term for a WAVE SKI.

paddle surf *v.* The traditional way to catch a wave; as distinct from being towed-in to the wave.

paddle takeoff *n.* Stroking with one's arms to catch a wave on a skim board. (TLH) See NO-PADDLE TAKEOFF.

paipo, paipo board (PAY-po) *n.* A small polyurethane-foam bellyboard used in the Hawaiian Islands.

pantyhose *n.* What surfers in north Queensland, Australia, wear out in the warm water to protect them from getting stung by a BOX JELLY.

papa nui (pa-pa NU-ee) *n.* A Hawaiian term that literally means "big surfboard" but is loosely applied to big surf or a big surf site.

paradise *n.* In the eyes of a surfer, the ultimate tropical island reef break.

paraffin *n.* A waxy-like substance that is commonly

paddle out
Art: Bob Penuelas

paddle gloves
*Rat
Santa Cruz
Photo: Mike Peralta*

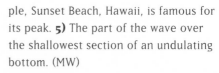

party wave
Maverick's
Photo: Mike Peralta

peak
Mark Foo's last ride
Maverick's
Aloha
Photo: Mike Peralta

applied on the deck of a surfboard to reduce slickness. Unlike modern surf wax, paraffin doesn't rip hair from the legs and chest. (DWK)

party wave *n.* When you yell it and everyone goes. (Santa Cruz) "Party Wave!" See BROTHERHOOD WAVE.

pass *v.* To sleep. Usage: "Are you gonna get passious?" (North San Diego County; LH)

passmodious *adj.* Really tired. (North San Diego County; LH)

patience *n.* The most important word in ding repair. (GCD)

PCH The abbreviation for Pacific Coast Highway, a section of California's Highway 1, which passes through Malibu.

peak *n.* **1)** The highest point of an advancing wave, marking the spot where the wave will begin to spill, break, or plunge. **2)** A narrow, humping wave that has little wall and that generally tapers fast from the middle or high point of the wave to almost flat on the shoulders; produced by a triangular reef or sandbank. **3)** A wedge-shaped wall of water that throws out as the wave breaks. **4)** The best spot for the takeoff; for exam-

ple, Sunset Beach, Hawaii, is famous for its peak. **5)** The part of the wave over the shallowest section of an undulating bottom. (MW)

peak break *n.* One of several kinds of surf breaks; distinguished by waves that form peaks at the point at which they begin to break. Usually associated with a reef or sandbar. See SURF BREAKS.

peaking tide *n.* The phase when the tide is approaching its highest or its lowest point.

peaking wave *n.* When a reef squeezes a wave inward and upward.

peak surf, peaking surf *n.* **1)** Waves whose tops form peaks. (MF) **2)** Waves that peak up due to the shape of the sea bottom. (WWK)

peak takeoff *n.* A takeoff on the highest and steepest part of a wave.

peak up *v.* (said of a swell) To begin to build up to a break. Usage: "The waves peak up at low tide."

peaky *adj.* Said of irregular wave crests caused by a cross swell (WB); hard to line up in. **—peaky beach break**

pearl, pearling *v.* **1)** To catch or bury the nose of the board in the water; usually occurs on a takeoff and is caused by the steepness of the wave or because the surfer has put too much weight toward the front of the board. (MM, A&M) Usage: "I pearled on that last one." Called in Australian going DOWN THE MINE (DSH) **2)** To nose the surfboard under a wave. (IDSM) **—pearl dive, pearl diving**

pebble clap *n.* Similar to COBBLE APPLAUSE only lighter. (Coined by Trevor Cralle at Brighton, England, 1997)

pecking order *n.* **1)** Seniority at a given surf spot. **2)** How you figure out whose turn it is to ride; determined by many factors, including paddling strength and just waiting your turn.

~~~~~~~~~~~~~~~~~~~~~~~~

The tradition of pecking order goes back to the earliest days of surfing. In the early 1960s, when there were more people capable of riding than there were waves, no one wanted to share waves. The pecking order at point breaks and reefs is easy to figure out because take-off areas are small and well-defined. At beach breaks or peaks that shift, pecking order begins with the person in the best position to get the best ride. If there's more than one surfer in position, whoever has waited longest for a ride (on an equal quality wave) should get it. A hyperjerk who out-positions someone who's been waiting longer has no respect for pecking order. (HJP)

~~~~~~~~~~~~~~~~~~~~~~~~

peel 1) *v.* (Of a wave) To break fast from end to end. (MM) **2) peeler** *n.* a fast, curling wave that curls perfectly without sectioning ahead. **3) peeling** *adj.* Typical of the way good surfing waves break.

(A&B) Usage: "Look at those peeling waves." —**peeling shoulders** **4)** sunburned skin may also peel.

peel-off *n.* CUTOUT; turning back off the shoulder of a wave to terminate a ride.

pee pool *n.* When you're sitting on the beach, and you pee in your trunks or wetsuit. Usage: "There's nothing better than relaxing in a pee pool before a sesh." (TWS, December 1999)

Pendleton, Pendleton shirt *n.* A brightly colored plaid wool shirt worn by some surfers; originally popular in the fifties and sixties but still considered a stylish article of clothing.

penie flash *n.* What you get when male surfers are changing and the towel around their waist falls down. (Santa Cruz) See SURF CHANGE.

peninsula *n.* A projection of land into a body of water, for example, the Palos Verdes or Monterey peninsulas in California.

penis puncher *n.* Waist-high shore-break. (Santa Cruz)

perfect *adj.* Said of nice waves. Usage: "It was a perfect six foot with no one out." —**perfect conditions**

perfection *n.* Perfect waves, perfect surfing days, flawlessness. As in "ranch perfection."

perfect wave *n.* A wave that files off, or peels, with mechanical perfection. (A&M) The movie *The Endless Summer* (1964) involved a search for "the perfect wave," discovered at Cape St. Francis in South Africa.

Pendleton
Photo: Tom Servais/ Surfer magazine

pintail
Photo: Tom Servais/
Surfer Magazine

═══════════════

"Remember, there are no perfect people, perfect relationships, etc., just perfect waves."

—Filenea Bahris (1990)

"One Day I'll Catch A Perfect Wave And Just Keep Riding . . ."

—Duke Kahanamoku

"I guess my perfect surf would be 4- to 6-foot, offshore rights with an initial barrel section that goes into a long, rippable wall."

—Serena Brooke, Surfer magazine, May 1999

═══════════════

period n. **1)** The time interval between the passing of two wave crests; same as WAVE PERIOD, SWELL PERIOD. **2)** The time between sets—a relatively calm period.

peroxide, hydrogen peroxide n. A bleach; commonly used in the 1960s to achieve instant surfer blonde.

peter heater n. Urinating in a wetsuit.

Petroleum Transfer Engineer n. An impressive-sounding job description for any surfer who works at a gas station; a euphemism for gas station attendant. (San Juan Capistrano; JRN)

pet the cat, petting the cat v. The motion of a surfer who crouches down and strokes the air or water to get through a section; doesn't create speed and has no functional purpose, but everyone does it. Usage: "Bro, you never saw Derek Ho pet the cat at

Pipe, right?" (New Jersey and East Coast; SFR, 1989)

pick up, picking up v. (said of the waves) To get bigger. Usage: "The surf is picking up." "It's picked up quite a bit." See UP.

pidgin n. A simplified mixture of two or more languages, used for communication between groups speaking different languages. In Hawaiian Pidgin English, for example, *da* means, "the," and so on.

pier n. An elevated structure projecting out into the ocean, most commonly used for fishing and boat access; sometimes blocks the wind.

pier break n. Waves breaking near or underneath a pier. See SHOOTING THE PIER.

pier hook n. A wave that is hooking or curling as it goes through a pier. Such a wave is very fast and permits little error when riding it.

pier out v. To hide behind the pier pilings while waiting for calm periods in which to make it out to the surf. (Manhattan Beach; anonymous body-boarder dudette, 1990)

pig, pig board n. A surfboard with an extremely pointed nose and the greatest width toward the rear (wide hips and broad tail).

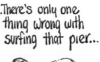
...There's only one thing wrong with surfing that pier...

pig dog n. A style of pulling in backside where you grab the outside rail of the board, making

Art: Jim Phillip

you look like a pig or a dog. (TWS, May/June 1999) See BACKSIDE RAIL GRAB, PIGLET PUT.

piglet pup *n.* A grommet's smaller version of PIG DOG.

pigment *n.* An opaque coloring agent for resin. (ORB)

pile drive *v.* To have your head slammed hard into the sandy bottom while bodysurfing. Usage: "I got pile driven at Sandy's yesterday."

piling *n.* A large cement or wooden pillar used in the construction of a pier. See SHOOTING THE PIER.

pillow surfing *n.* Sleeping. See SURF DREAMS, SURFED-OUT INSOMNIA.

piña colada *n.* **1)** A flavor for everything—surf wax, lip balm, suntan oil, etc. **2)** An alcoholic beverage containing pineapple and coconut juices mixed with rum.

Pineapple Express, Pineapple Connection *n.* Very wet Pacific storms fed from tropical moisture from Hawaii.

pineapple juice *n.* **1)** A rain squall in Hawaii. Same as LIQUID SUNSHINE. **2)** A tasty beverage made from the fruit of the pineapple.

pinline *n.* Decorative resin strips on a surfboard. Originally designed in the 1960s to disguise the cutline where the laminator wrapped fiberglass up and around from the bottom of the board, but evolved into an artform within an art. Laura Powers from Santa Monica was one of the best **pinliners**. The advent of widespread airbrushing in the

pier
Art: Jim Phillips

mid-1970s spelled the end of pinlines. (SFG, January 1992)

pintail or **pin-tail** *n.* A surfboard configuration characterized by a reduced-area tail section that comes rather sharply to a point.

pipe *n.* **1)** The inside curve of a wave that creates a tunnel. (MM) Same as TUBE, BARREL. **2) Pipe** Short for PIPELINE.

pipe cleaner or **pipecleaner** *n.* A surfboard that has been tube ridden. (SFG, February 1990) See TUBE RIDER.

piped *v.* Getting BARRELED.

pipeline *n.* **1)** A very long and large TUBE. **2)** The curl of a breaking wave that spreads onto each shoulder of the wave so rapidly that the rolling water resembles a pipe. (DSHJ)

Pipeline *n.* **1)** Probably the most famous wave in the world, located on the North Shore of Oahu, Hawaii, between Waimea Bay and Sunset Beach, off Ehukai Beach Park. **2)** Site of the annual Pipeline Masters surfing competition held in December. **3)** A classic instrumental surf tune by the Chantays from Santa Ana, California, in December 1962; it reached #4 on the charts in the spring of 1963. Other notable versions include those of the Ventures in 1962 and of Agent Orange in 1982.

pillow surfing
Nancy I. Kelly
Photo: Trevor Cralle

〜〜〜〜〜〜〜〜〜〜〜〜〜

Originally named by Bruce Brown, Pipeline was renamed Banzai Beach by John Severson. Then it became Banzai Pipeline, and now it's back to Pipeline—Pipe for short. Pipeline is famous for its tube ride; deep-water swells hit the extremely shallow reef very quickly, making the waves hollow. The first person to surf it was Phil Edwards in December 1961; Outside Pipeline was first ridden by Greg Noll on January 3, 1964. (GN)

〜〜〜〜〜〜〜〜〜〜〜〜〜

pipeliner *n.* Any surfboard that has been ridden at Pipeline, Hawaii. (SFG, February 1990)

Pipe shots *n.* A surf photographer's term for Pipeline pictures.

pit *n.* **1)** The crashing foam of a breaking wave adjacent to the smooth shoulder of the wave. See GETTING STUFFED IN THE PIT.

2) The Pit An area just north of the Malibu Pier, along a chain-link fence near a wall on the beach where the heavies used to hang out in the 1960s (KSO); known for its graffiti.

pitch *v.* A term used to describe the way the top part of a wave jacks up (gains height) and throws forward, caused by the wave suddenly moving from deep into shallow water. (MW) Usage: "Look at that pitching barrel."

pitched, getting pitched *v.* Getting thrown or tossed off one's board. (MDF)

pivot point *n.* The general area near the center of the surfboard that the surfer turns on.

pivot roll *n.* A surfing maneuver involving rolling with the wave.

pivot turn *n.* A very sharp turn.

planer, power planer *n.* A hand-held power tool used by shapers to remove foam from blanks quickly, easily, and accurately. (ORB)

planing *n.* A long, steady ride on a steep wave in which the board-to-wave angle is small. A portion of the forward end of the board may be partially supported by the flow of air rising up the face of the wave.

planing surface *n.* The bottom of the surfboard—the part that skims on the top of the water.

plank *n.* The name given to heavy, unmaneuverable boards, usually referring to the redwood giants ridden prior to the 1950s. **—redwood plank**

planshape *n.* The outline of a surfboard when viewed from above. (MF) Same as TEMPLATE.

Pipeline
Greg Noll
Pipeline, 1964
Photo: Surfer magazine
Courtesy of Greg Noll

plastic lei *n.* A mainland substitute for da reel deal. See LEI.

plow *v.* A surfer term for sexual intercourse. (Marin County, California)

plug *n.* **1)** A small cup cut into the surfboard so that a shock cord can be attached. See LEASH CUP. **2)** A piece of foam cut into a wedge to repair a surfboard.

plugged *adj.* Used to describe a crowded surf spot. Usage: "The place was really plugged." (GN)

plunging breaker *n.* A kind of wave where the crest falls in front of the lower part of the wave, rather than spilling down the face—the most dynamic, exciting manifestation of wave action on the ocean. (DKM)

pocket *n.* **1)** The portion of the wave inside the curl. **2)** The portion high on the wave wall as the lip begins to curl over. (RA) **3)** The part of a wave under the breaking lip. (NAT, 1985) **4)** The point on the wall of a breaking wave where the maximum power for surfing is found. **—deep pocket**

pocket beach *n.* A small, crescent-shaped beach inside a cove or between rocky headlands, often inundated at high tide. (CCRG)

pocket ride *n.* Surfing tight in the curl.

pocket surfing, surfing in the pocket *n.* Riding in or near the curl—fundamental to the modern shortboard era because the shortboards of today are incapable of maintaining their momentum out on the shoulder of a wave. (L&L)

point break
Rincon Point, California
Photo: Don Balch

pod 1) *v.* To pass out. Usage: "He's poddin'." "He's fully podded." **2) POD** *n.* Passed-out dude. (LH)

point *n.* Refers to a jutting piece of land or the surf breaking directly off of it.

point break *n.* A type of surf break where waves wrap around a promontory and peel as they break; sometimes occurs in combination with a reef break. Rincon Point, just south of the Santa Barbara/Ventura county line in California, is a classic example of a point break. See BEACH BREAK, SURF BREAKS.

Point Break (1991) Hollywood movie with bank-robbing surf mystic Patrick Swayze. Featured a dialogue on the pier between undercover detectives Keanu Reeves and Gary Busey on how surfers talk to each other. The skydiving scene was the best part of the movie.

point grinder *n.* **1)** A tubular wave that spits and breaks off of a point with a grinding, churning motion. **2)** In the movie *Big Wednesday* (1978), a girl from The Point who is widely acclaimed for her amorous activities. (A&M)

point surf *n.* Surf breaking off a point. (MF) Same as POINT BREAK.

plastic lei
Sonal Petal
Mid-Winter Luau
Photo: Trevor Cralle

Portuguese man-of-war

Art: Andrea McCann

pole set *n.* Waves breaking adjacent to or immediately inside of a large pole jutting out of the water at Ala Moana on Oahu, Hawaii.

political waves *n.* What surfers make when their salty playground is threatened by pollution and overdevelopment. (FLD)

pollution in the ocean *n.* In some areas, an inescapable part of modern surfing. Surfers variously describe the experience of surfing in polluted waters as YUK, WOOFY, FLOATIES, SHIT PIPE, SURFING UNDER TURD, ON YOUR NOSE, and SURFING WITH POO.

poly or **pollie** *n.* FOAMIE.

polyester resin *n.* A liquid plastic widely used in surfboard construction; mixed with a catalyst and accelerator to form the hard outer shell, or skin, of the board.

Polynesian Paradise (PP) *n.* A tropical malaise to which surfers are particularly susceptible. An attack of the PPs can mean almost total incapacitation for up to a week. Apart from surfing four to six hours a day, the victim lies motionless on the hotel-room floor watching television and drinking six-packs of beer. Speech, thought, or personal hygiene are out of the question until the fever passes. (JARR)

polystyrene *n.* A type of plastic foam used in surfboard construction.

polyurethane blank *n.* See FOAM BLANK.

polyurethane board, polyurethane foam board *n.* The modern surfboard. See FOAM.

polyurethane foam, polyfoam *n.* A type of plastic foam (a petro-

Art: Peter Spacek

leum by-product) that is commonly used in the construction of surfboards. (ASKC, 1965)

pop up, popping up *v.* (of waves) To jack up suddenly over a shallow spot.

Popeye *n.* Someone who exhibits above-average paddling strength, no doubt due to the regular ingestion of pounds of spinach. (Santa Monica; LJE)

popout or **pop-out** *n.* A relatively inexpensive mass-produced surfboard made in the early sixties by molding foam and fiberglass mat together. Popouts were cheap (because they involved little handwork), heavy, and weak; the process was abandoned, and the term is obsolete.

popping air off the lip *v.* To do an aerial; same as SLASHING OFF THE LIP. (RO) Usage: "Bro, I was fully popping air off the lip."

Portuguese man-of-war, man-o'-war (*Hydrozoa physalia physalis*) *n.* A stinging jellyfish indigenous to warm seas and having a bluish, bladderlike float from which are suspended numer-

pollution in the ocean
Photo: Stephanie Gene Morgan

ous long stinging tentacles capable of inflicting severe injury (AHd2); found off Florida, in the Caribbean, etc. Also called BLUE BOTTLE (in New Zealand and Australia). See LIT-UP.

poser, surf poser *n.* **1)** A would-be surfer; someone who only dresses the part. (MM) **2)** An imitation surfer. (JP) **—pousuer**

post-ocean crust *n.* The salt rock formations that dry and cake in the crevices of body parts when you don't shower after an ocean encounter. (Coined by Estrella del Mar, 1997) See SALT ITCH.

post-session nasal drip (PSND) *n.* A gushing of sea water out of the nasal passages; this almost always occurs after a grueling skim session while talking to an extremely fine girl. (Santa

Monica; RC) Same as FAUCET NOSE, NASODRAIN.

post-surf helmet *n.* Sea-sculpted hair after a session. (Coined by Chicha, 1993) See OCEAN WAVE.

potato chip *n.* CHIP or CHIP BOARD.

potench *adj.* Potential. Usage: "I think there's some potench for a south swell this week." (Santa Barbara, 1992)

pound, pounded *v.* To get slammed by a wave.

pound clown *n.* Surfer who rides shore pound for mindless glory, often getting deposited on the sand. (Westside, Santa Cruz)

pounder *n.* **1)** A hard-breaking wave; a wave that breaks with pounding ferocity.

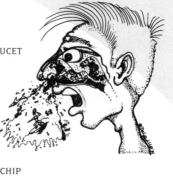

post-session nasal drip
Art: Karen T. Delgadillo

Portuguese Surf Glossary:

If you're charging in Brazil or Portugal, these words may come in handy.

beach: *praia*
dude: *dude* (pron. "dooj")
jellyfish: *águaviva or medusa*
ocean: *oceano*
point: *ponto*
reef: *recife*
sea: *mar*
seaquake: *maremoto*
shark: *tubarão*
surf: *reffaca or rebentação*

surfboard: *pranca*
surf wax: *cera*
tide: *maré*
high tide: *maré alta*
low tide: *maré baixo*
wave: *vaga*
big: *grande*
small: *pequeno*
wind: *vento*

2) A big perfect wave. **—poundah** (Hawaiian Pidgin)

pounding surf *n*. Hard-breaking waves.

pour it on *v*. To trim a board on a wave and assume a stance that achieves maximum speed and control.

pour over 1) *v*. What a wave does when it breaks. **2) pour-over** *n*. An over-the-falls wipeout, in which the surfer gets caught and goes over with the breaking wave into the white water.

powah surf *n*. A Hawaiian term for spots that get heavy surf.

power move *n*. **1)** Any impressive maneuver on a wave, such as a "power cutback." (CC) **2) power surfing** Making big moves. **3) power it** *v*. A seventies term for doing just about anything, as in "to power a sandwich."

power pocket, power section n. That part of the wave closest to the curl.

power set *n*. Big waves.

"Pray for Surf" A caption that appeared on many surfing publications in the 1960s.

predawn patrol *n*. Rolling in the dark toward the surf. See DAWN PATROL.

premium waves *n*. Waves with good size and shape and the potential for high scoring in competitive surfing contests. See WAVE SELECTION.

press, pressing *v*. **1)** When a rider on the outside (away from the curl) is crowded by a rider on the inside (near the curl). **2)** Any crowding while riding.

pressure ding *n*. COMPRESSION DING.

primo *adj*. Top rate. Usage: "The waves are gonna be really primo-bitchin' today."

Primo beer *n*. A Hawaiian brew that is no longer produced.

priority *n*. The right to the first or next wave in a surfing contest because you **1)** have won the toss of a coin; **2)** have paddled around the priority buoy; or **3)** have the position closest to the curl.

priority buoy *n*. A brightly colored float in the water outside the break and used in competitive surfing to determine who has the right-of-way on the next waves. Also called EIGHT BALL. See GETTING BEHIND THE EIGHT BALL.

The old rule for right-of-way was that whoever was on the inside had it. Then in 1982, Peter Townend and Ian Cairns unveiled the priority buoy system at the first Op Pro surf contest in California. Originally, after each surfer had completed one ride, the first to paddle back outside and around the buoy had the choice of the following waves. This changed with the 1984–85 ASP World Tour season, when the first priority for every heat began to be decided by the toss of a coin. Thereafter in the heat, the first surfer who paddles out and around the priority buoy has the right-of-way on the upcoming wave.

---

private beach *n*. An exclusive property right that in California and certain other areas of the world extends only to the MEAN HIGH TIDE LINE.

pro circuit board (PCB) *n.* A surfboard made from a foam-sandwich mold, developed by veteran super-shaper Bob McTavish in the late 1980s based on a technique first developed for use with sailboards. A double foam-layer shell is glued up using a vacuum mold and then injected with expanding polystyrene foam; then a polyester gel coat is sprayed on to give the board a color design. Because a mold is used, a perfect copy can be made of any surfboard or shaped blank and reproduced as a PCB. A high-density foam reduces the weight of the boards to about five or six pounds. (SFG, February 1990)

professional surfing *n.* Born in the late 1970s. See ASP.

projection *n.* Thrusting out of a turn. Usage: "Did you see the projection he got on that wave?"

prone out or **prone-out** *v.* **1)** To ride one's board to the beach by lying down and holding on to the rails, often done to get ashore safely through heavy surf. **2)** To drop back to a prone position to keep from being knocked off the board when paddling out. **3)** To straighten out in front of a wave and lie down on the board, rather than risk being separated from the board in the turmoil of white water. Usage: "I had to prone out through the white water."

prone position *n.* Lying outstretched and stomach down on a surfboard.

prone turn *n.* Angling one's board while lying down by dropping one foot in the water. The right foot will turn the board right; the left foot will turn it left.

Proplugs *n.* Dr. Scott's ear plugs (with leash) from Santa Cruz; worn for the prevention of SURFER'S EAR.

prosecuted *v.* To get wiped out to the fullest extent. Usage: "Guy got *prosecuted* on that wave." (LH) See SURF CRIMES.

protected *adj.* Describes any surf spot that is sheltered from wind by kelp, a cove, etc.

PSAA Professional Surfing Association of America; a domestic pro circuit founded by Joey Buran in 1985.

pseud *n.* Australian slang for PSEUDO. (JARR)

pseudo, pseudo surfer *n.* Someone who only pretends to be a surfer.

psyched out *v.* To be mentally incapacitated; to be overcome with fear. Generally refers to a surfer's reaction to big surf. See CLUCKED.

pterygium *n.* An eye ailment caused by exposure to sun and surf; the medical term for SURFER'S EYE.

Puertas Abiertas A surf spot on Isla Natividad off Baja; means "open doors" in Spanish. See OPEN DOOR.

puff *n.* WIND SQUALL.

pu in ʌai (POO-in-SIGH) Hawaiian Pidgin for PULL INSIDE. Has evolved many uses in the late 1990s: pull in, take it, go for it. "Eh, Carls, pu in sai, brah." Possibly derived from a surfer with a heavy Filipino accent. (Maui)

Bolinas, California
Photo: Trevor Cralle

puka *n.* Hawaiian for "hole"; used as a substitute for DING.

puka shells, ***puka-shell*** **necklace** *n.* An adornment worn by many surfers in the 1970s. Mike Purpus began wearing these tiny white shells in 1973. (SFG, November 1989)

pull back *v.* To abort a takeoff to prevent the nose of the board from going underwater. To sit up on the board and drag your legs to abort takeoff, as in "He pulled back." "Here's something you don't see every day: Brock Little pulling back." (SFR, February 1995)

pulled template *n.* A surfboard that, viewed from above, is narrower than normal. See FULL TEMPLATE.

pull in, pull inside *v.* To enter the barrel or the tube is to "pull in." Get in the barrel.

pull in to a deep grinding death barrel *v.* Turning the board into a particularly dangerous tubing wave with tons of murder power over a reef made up of beginners' skulls. (ABC)

pull into a wave *v.* To drop down the face of a wave and turn back up for a ride. Usage: "Dane is pulling into a monster wave."

pull off *v.* To succeed in making a maneuver. Usage: "Did you see me pull off that last move?"

pull out *v.* **1)** To steer a board over or through the back of a wave in order to end a ride. **2)** To exit a wave. (MM) **3)** To exit through the bottom of the wall of a wave, with board and body moving in the same direction. (L&L) **4) pullout**

n. A maneuver to guide the board out of a wave. (WWK) Same as CUT OUT.

pull root *v.* To masturbate; what surfers do when there are no waves. The term came up in a conversation with an Italian surfer that was carried on mostly in sign language. When asked what he did when there were no waves (which is almost always in Italy), he promptly responded with an up-and-down movement around his groin area. (P)

pummeled *adj.* Getting totally wiped-out by the surf.

Pump House Gang, The Tom Wolfe's second collection of essays (1968), named after a "California surfing elite" at Windansea, La Jolla. The book was critically attacked by surfers, who over the years have inspired such graffiti as "Tom Wolfe is a dork!"

pumping *v.* When huge powerful waves break in consistent intervals, or come one after another; going strong.

—pumpeen, pom-ping to da max (Hawaiian Pidgin)

pumping down the line *v.* To work one's board along the wave to extract the most energy out of a fast ride.

pump out *v.* To break vigorously, as in a point that "pumps out" some pretty unreal waves.

pump the board *v.* To extend a ride through small surf by swinging the board back and forth to keep up momentum. See HOP.

pump turn *n.* A hopping motion that generates forward momentum in a slow section of the wave. In surf contests, a pump turn lacks the scoring potential of other turns because it maintains horizontal direction and doesn't make a significant climbing or dropping direction change— that is, less than 60 degrees. (L&L)

punch through *v.* To negotiate an oncoming wave. See PUSH THROUGH.

punchy *adj.* Used to describe a wave that delivers a full blow; some waves are punchier than others. Usage: "The waves are a bit punchy." (Newcastle Surf Shop, Australia)

pushing the limits *v.* Going beyond one's personal limitations while surfing. **—pushing it to the max**

push through *v.* **1)** Originally meant to get your surfboard through a wave by climbing off the board and, holding on to the rear of the board, pushing it ahead of you through the wave; now means to get through the surf or white water by any means whatsoever. **2)** To paddle the board seaward through broken waves. **3)** To paddle out through the surf by ducking under incoming waves. (MM) Same as PUNCH THROUGH.

pushing it to the max

Art: *The Pizz*

quad
Willy Morris and Al Merrick,
Ventura, California, 1983
Photo: Bob Barbour

Q-cel *n.* A resin additive designed to take up maximum volume with minimum resin; makes an excellent filler to keep weight down. (QCD)

quad *n.* A 1980s term for a four-fin surfboard. The four-fin board has two normal size fins with two smaller fins in line behind them.

quakers *n.* Big waves. (Florida, TDW)

quaper (QUAY-per) *n.* A wave that is a quantum leap beyond a GAPER. Usage: "Dude, that wave was the full quaper. You were six feet back and you're still hair-dry!" (North San Diego County; SFR, 1989)

quash *v.* To make void; a legal term applied to the sport of surfing. (ECN) Usage: "That wave totally quashed me." See SURF CRIMES.

Quasimoto, The Quasimoto *n.* A hot-dog riding stance invented by Mickey Muñoz; performed riding on the nose of a surfboard in a crouched, hunchback position with one arm stretched forward and the other arm stretched to the rear.

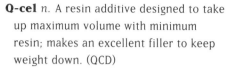

The term derives from the name Quasimodo, the hunchback of the title in Victor Hugo's novel *The Hunchback of Notre Dame.* However, in John Severson's First Annual Surf Photo Book in 1960

(the first issue of Surfer magazine), it was spelled "Quasimoto," and that spelling stuck. In surfing, the term is Quasimoto not Quasimodo.

queber *n.* GEEK. (MM)

Queen Mary *n.* A board too big for the rider, one that is usually very large and buoyant.

quick release pin *n.* A safety device located on some LEASH CUFFS that allows you to bail the tether to your board and escape dangerous situations, such as being trapped underwater or getting stuck in the rocks.

Quicks *n.* Short for any article of clothing made by Quicksilver.

quimby *n.* Pencilneck geek, dork, idiot (boogie boarder); mom drops you off at the beach in a station wagon, you get nosebleeds and have allergies. (Oxnard; TJ)

quiver *n.* An assortment or collection of different surfboards to accommodate varying wave conditions, like a quiver of arrows.

Quonset hut *n.* A prefabricated World War II shelter with a semicircular arching roof of corrugated metal that served as basic lodging for early big-wave riders at Makaha; also used for surf stomps in Southern California.

Quasimoto
Mickey Muñoz

Art: Mr. X ©2000
Mullethead Surf Designs

quiver
Jim Phillips,
Santa Cruz

R&D *n.* Research and development—what surfers do when looking for new surf spots, especially on expeditions to places like Baja.

rabbit-ear skeg *n.* A twin skeg, joined at the base and designed to increase holding power on sharp turns as well as minimize spinouts.

rack flyer *n.* A surfboard that you forget to tie down on the roof rack of your car and that becomes airborne when you drive away. (RBS)

rad *adj.* Super cool; short for RADICAL. Usage: "Those waves were rad!" **—way rad**

~~~~~~~~~~~~~~~~~~~~~~~~~~~~~~

According to Michael Girvin, "rad" was derived from a BMX trick called "a Radical," where the cyclist while airborne crossed the handlebar all the way to one side and then back straight before landing.

"Oh my god, rad."

—*Kiakima Simon, 1994*

"That is so fuckin' rad."

—*Laura Bozzolo, 1994*

"It's like beyond rad."

—*Liz Phegan*

"Stay rad!"

—*Michael Girvin*

~~~~~~~~~~~~~~~~~~~~~~~~~~~~~~

radical *adj.* **1)** Heavy-duty, extreme, outrageous. (WWK) **2)** PUSHING THE LIMITS; going for broke. (A&M) **3)** Used to describe a difficult surfing maneuver or an outrageous surfing style. (MM; NAT, 1985) **—totally radical, super radical, radical turn, radical bottom turn, unradical**

rack flyer
"Did I check the racks before I left?"
Art: I. B. Nelson

~~~~~~~~~~~~~~~~~~~~~~~~~~~~~~

"I just like to get radical."

—*Matt Archbold, 1987 (SFR, January 1990)*

"El Salvador was radical!"

—*Danny Minton. (Outside, September 1991)*

"I thought it was pretty radical."

—*Anonymous (Santa Cruz)*

". . . and the only thing you can do is do radness to get out."

—*Chicha, 1993*

"Surf radical is a orgasm total!"

—*Unknown surfer quoted in the Swedish Surfing Association's online magazine, Surfblåsk (1999)*

~~~~~~~~~~~~~~~~~~~~~~~~~~~~~~

radical controlled maneuvers *n.* The highest scoring component of the ASP criteria for judging a surf contest; RCMs for short.

rager
Simon Anderson after he won the Pipe in 1981, celebrating with Rabbit.
Photo: Don Balch

Walking around and posing may have been popular surfing moves in the sixties, but competitive surfing judges want to see more defined moves now. Originally two factors distinguished a radical maneuver: commitment and positioning. "Controlled" was added in 1985. (L&L)

radical maneuvers *n.* In competitive surfing, dynamic moves with a high degree of difficulty. (L&L)

radio wave *n.* As in "Catch a ride on a radio wave." —Lala Land, Los Angeles comedienne

radio weather channel *n.* The most accurate and up-to-date information available to most surfers, including the positioning of lows and highs, the size and direction of swells and seas, and wind velocities. (W&B) See WEATHER RADIO.

rage *v.* GO OFF; refers to a surfer. Usage: "I fully raged on that wave."

rail saver
Photo: Don Balch

rager *n.* A good surfer party. (CVG) Usage: "That was a real rager last night."
—raging

raging surf *n.* Really big waves.
—raging waves

rail *n.* The rounded side or outside edge of a surfboard. Usage: "Feel the rails on this board."

rail apex *n.* The point where the rail meets the tip of the surfboard nose.

rail design *n.* The shape of a surfboard rail; a crucial element in overall surfboard design in that the rails direct water flow and aid in turning. There are many different rail designs, but broadly they can be divided into hard rail (those with a sharply defined edge on the board's underside) and soft rail (those that are rounded above and below).

rail digging *n.* Same as BURYING A RAIL, DIGGING A RAIL.

rail grab *n.* Holding onto the outside rail of the surfboard with your hand while crouching and tracking in critical situations; adds to stability. (RA) See GRAB THE RAIL.

rail line *n.* The outside edge of a surfboard. (ORB)

rail radius *n.* The curve joining the top and bottom of a surfboard.

rail sandwich *n.* A surfboard between the legs. (A&M)

rail saver *n.* A flat nylon strap, one to two inches wide and eight to ten inches in length, used to prevent the leash from tearing into the rail. (ORB) A rail saver is attached between the board and the leash.

rail sandwich
Photo: Fred Swegles

rail shift *n.* The shifting of one's weight from one rail to the other, something done during every cutback but rarely accomplished in the tube. Same as RAIL-TO-RAIL TRANSITION.

rail slash *n.* Carving a sharp turn so that the rail digs into the wave and casts a spray.

"I hope the current phase of surf/body English is soon massacred by the surf media so we can all get on with doing some hard core rail slashes for the public instead of breakdancing performances for them and fooling ourselves."

—Mitch Thorson (TRKS, June 1989)

---

rail strips *n.* BONES.

rail-to-rail transition, rail-to-rail turn *n.* RAIL SHIFT.

rain *n.* LIQUID SUNSHINE (Maui), PINEAPPLE JUICE (Oahu). See PINEAPPLE EXPRESS, RAIN SQUALL, LIGHTNING.

rain squall *n.* A brief period of rain, usually lasting a few minutes or less; sometimes heavy, and sometimes accompanied by strong winds; a common occurrence in the tropics. Same as SQUALL. See WIND SQUALL. —**blinding rain squall**

"Just relax folks, it's pure pineapple juice."

—Surf contest announcer Lord Tally Ho Sanders describing a rain squall at Sunset Beach, Hawaii, in December 1982

---

raize *v.* To bother someone or give them verbal abuse. Usage: "If that guy raizes on me one more time I'm gonna rub Vaseline over his wax." (SFG, December 1981)

rake *n.* The way the fin area is arranged in relation to the fin base. (ORB) See FIN RAKE.

rakeback skeg *n.* A fin with its lower extremity or axis angled toward the rear.

Ranch, the *n.* A well-known collection of surf spots offshore of the Hollister and Bixby ranches between Santa Barbara and the Vandenberg Air Force Base.

rapper *n.* A wave that you ride into on a skimboard and get barreled in as it breaks over the top of you. (TLH)

rappin' *adj.* **1)** Used to describe a wave as

rail-to-rail transition
Art: I. B. Neslon

Real Surfers

Here are some views of what it takes to be a "real surfer":
Real surfers dress cool: have fixed dings: know how to ride bikes while holding surfboards: have been to Hawaii: have trouble choosing between girlfriends and waves: know how to surf with their hands (describe a ride): have made their own surfboards: have taken long, gnarly swims to shore: have cut school: can smell saltwater from more than a mile away: have stepped on sea urchins: have had at least one great tube ride: have surfed at sunup and sundown: have ridden skateboards: have had sunburned noses and lips: have done three-sixty maneuvers: love any food that comes from the ocean: have lived by the beach at least once in their lifetime: have had saltwater run out of their noses while kissing: hoot at surfing movies: have been the only ones in the water somewhere: know how to look at surfboards: have entered contests: have written surfing graffiti: go on surfaris: have surfing pictures in their rooms. (SGE, P)

"Real surfers don't wear pink wetsuits: never wash their cars: surf standing up: don't have green hair: are nice to young girls (trust me): don't gyro-spaz on the shoulder: never clean their wax and never ever buy it: puke on trail mix: don't have pink bodies: don't own a tie: don't straighten out: meditate in the tube (not on the beach): stay in the tube (not in the car): don't wear earrings (unless they're chicks): don't read GQ: can stay down longer: don't wear bun huggers: gag on sprouts: like it big and hairy: like it steep and deep: don't wear shoes: don't wear leather: don't wear gold chains: don't wear polyester: don't listen to Wayne Newton tapes: don't watch the news: hate the Dallas Cowboys (red neck team from Baja Oklahoma): aren't Seymoors: aren't into vinyl: don't make their beds: don't drive cars that use unleaded: don't smoke Camels: don't jog or diet: don't get caught: don't drink un-cola: don't use baby oil: don't wear designer anything: don't chicken out: don't sleep until noon and miss it: still surf when it's blown out: surf in the rain: can't read "no trespassing" signs: don't listen to the "mellow sound": think Fila is what you do to Italian girls: don't want any mercy (or give any): have fat chicks for lunch (but never dinner): don't do dishes: get down on the first date: never do laundry: don't read: don't write: can't spell: don't care: just surf."

—Corky Carroll, "Real Surfers," in Surfer magazine, May 1984

Corky Carroll
Photo: Tom Servais/
Surfer magazine

it pours over. (KTD) Usage: "The lip was fully rappin.'" **2)** Said of a swell that bends or wraps around a point. See WAVE REFRACTION.

rash guard *n.* A thin, short-sleeve stretch-lycra jersey worn to protect against skin irritation caused by the body rubbing against a wetsuit and a surfboard; can be worn as an undergarment beneath a wetsuit or by itself in warm water for sun protection. Some of the newer wetsuits have a rash-guard lining. See BOARD RASH.

rashie *n.* RASH GUARD.

rat holing *v.* When somebody drops in on a wave from behind another surfer as distinct from SHOULDER HOPPING, when they snake in front of the surfer. (John Lawson, Santa Cruz) See DOGSNIFF.

ratly *n.* Santa Cruz slang for young surfer. See SURF RAT.

rat pack *n.* Surfing competitors vying for top place or recognition. (L&L)

rat pack *v.* To surround someone in the water and beat 'em up. Usage: "OK, we're going to rat pack you now." (Windansea)

rave *n.* **1)** After a good session, five to ten minutes of indulgence during which surfers go on about the unbelievability of their performance and about what a great pity it is that no one saw the barrel roll three sixty they pulled off up the beach a bit. (JARR) **2)** *v.* To dance to techno, trance, and jungle music.

raw *adj.* Happening, hot, cool; similar to LIVE. Usage: "That's raw."

rawsome (raw + awesome) *adj.* Fusion said to have been invented in Berkeley in 1987.

"Very short-lived. I said it a couple times I think."

—Daniel Jenkin, 1993

---

rays *n.* **1)** Sun rays. Usage: "Let's catch some rays." **2)** STINGRAYS. **3) ray** A stingray bicycle used as a beach bomber or beach cruiser.

RCMs *n.* RADICAL CONTROLLED MANEUVERS.

reach-for-the-sky reentries *n.* Coming high off the wave with arms reaching straight up in the air—as if signaling a touchdown—and then dropping back down. See REENTRY.

really *adv.* Truly, as in "really primo-bitchin' surf."

real surfer *n.* Someone who meets a well-defined set of criteria concerning ocean, surf, and other life experiences. See "Real Surfers" on page 206.

rebound *n.* A turn off of the lip or white water of a wave. See RICOCHET.

rebound wave *n.* An outgoing wave, one going away from the beach. (TLH)

reckless abandon *n.* **1)** Surfing with wild style. **2)** A go-for-it attitude.

recovery *n.* Standing up again after having lost footing. (L&L)

red hot *adj.* Fantastic, awesome, the best, hard-core. Usage: "The surf here gets red hot in the summer."

rash guard
Yvonne Wu
Photo: Trevor Cralle

rebound wave
Skimboarder
Photo: Woody Woodworth

red-hot surfing *n.* Hard-core surfing; performing at a high degree of excellence.

redirection *n.* Changing direction while surfing. Usage: "Look at that scorching redirection."

red tide *n.* **1)** A misnomer for a phenomenon that is neither a tide nor necessarily red; the sea may take on colors ranging from dirty brown to reds and violets, or may show no discoloration at all. A "red tide" is caused by a high concentration of minute organisms called dinoflagellates, whose population explosion, or "bloom," produces a toxin that can kill off huge amounts of fish. It is also responsible for paralytic shellfish poisoning (PSP), which may be harmful to humans who eat shellfish during quarantine months. (OA, P) **2)** That time of month. (SP)

Red Triangle *n.* In Northern California, the offshore area between Monterey (including Santa Cruz), the Farallon Islands off San Francisco, and Tomales Bay in Marin County that has the highest number of reported great white shark attacks in the world. The area was dubbed the Red Triangle in 1986.

redwood plank *n.* A premodern surfboard generally used in the early 1900s and in the 1940s in Santa Cruz.

reeds *n.* **1)** A kind of pants worn by surfers that extend just below the knee. (IDSM) **2)** BAGGIES from the 1950s; made by the wife of a Huntington Beach lifeguard named Mr. Reed. (MCR) See SURF FASHION.

reef *n.* **1)** A line, ridge, or assemblage of rock, coral, or sand lying at, below, or near the surface of the water. **2)** A natural underwater formation that creates good waves. See CORAL REEF, INSIDE REEF, OUTSIDE REEF. **3) reefy** *adj.* "You have to get through this reefy section. . . ." (Larry Brown, 1993) See EATING REEF, GETTING REEFED.

reef break *n.* A surf spot where waves break over a reef.

reef configuration *n.* The underwater formation, or shape, of a reef. If you are familiar with a surf spot's reef configuration, you may be able to get in a better position to catch waves.

Reef Girl *n.* A regular in surfing magazines, appearing on behalf of Reef Brazil sandals and beachwear. After viewing multiple Reef Girls, one will notice that the advertiser chooses a consistent angle for photography of the subject. (The Swamis, 1998)

reefies *n.* Australian for reef sharks.

reef rash *n.* What you get surfing in the tropics when you scrape yourself on a coral reef. (KSO) See CORAL CUT.

reef surf *n.* Surf breaking on a reef. (MF) Same as REEF BREAK.

reef walkers *n.* Footware specially designed to protect feet from getting cut on sharp coral.

reeling *adj.* FIRING, GOING OFF, as in "The surf was reeling."

reentry *n.* **1)** A maneuver in which the surfer shoots to the very top of a wave, briefly skates along the top of the lip just ahead of the curl, and then drops back down along the face. The most difficult reentry is to go past vertical in ascent or to recross the path of the original vertical ascent when descending. **2)** An extreme version of a roller coaster, in which the surfer has all but kicked out and then radically cuts back into the breaking wave. See FLOATER REENTRY.

re-form *v.* **1)** (of a wave) To jack up and break again after crossing deep water and moving once more into the shallows. Waves often break on an outer sandbank or reef before moving across deep water and then re-forming, usually as shore breaks. (MW) **2)** When a wave becomes green again after having broken. (L&L) See BACK OFF, HUNTINGTON HOP.

refraction *n.* See WAVE REFRACTION.

reggae, reggae music *n.* **1)** Popular music that originated in Jamaica and has been adopted by many surfers worldwide. **2)** In Caribbean dialect, the feel-good irie vibes and heavy bass line roots dub riddim to accompany the natural soul lifestyle and help combat the dread forces of babylon (concrete jungles). **3)** Live and direct inna strictly massive ragamuffin surf posse stylee. **4)** Peace warrior sounds including those of Bob Marley, Steele Pulse, and Pato Banton.
—Jahwaiian (Hawaiian reggae music)

regular foot, regularfoot *n.* A surfboard stance with the left foot forward, right foot back. (ORB) Same as NATURAL FOOT.

release *n.* The separation of water flow from the bottom or rails of a surfboard; akin to breaking suction.

releasing and reengaging rails *n.* **1)** Bending and flexing the legs to exert pressure on the surfboard, allowing for ultimate maneuvering in critical situations. **2)** Also a bodyboarding maneuver, where it is done with the arms.

religion and surfing The "Spirituality of Surfing" has spawned many descriptions, such as GOING TO CHURCH, IN THE POPE'S LIVING ROOM, WHIRLING CATHEDRAL, etc.

"God must have been a Surfer. . . ."
> —Bill Dobbins (1917–1990)

"When I surf I dance for Krishna."
> —Ted Spencer, Tracks magazine, August 1974

"I can't hope to adequately capture the experience of surfing in words, just as it is impossible to describe a religious experience in regular language."
> —James David Meacham, III, from a 1994 sermon, "The Tao of Surfing"

"The moana is my religion."
> —Thomas Farber, The Face of the Deep (1998)

removable fin(s) n. Can be changed for different surf conditions and they're a lot less hassle while traveling.

rental n. A surfboard or wetsuit for hire, clearly marked "RENTAL"—a sure sign of a geek or hodad.

removable fins
Photo: Trevor Cralle

reo *n*. Short for REENTRY. (Australia)

reshape *v*. To reconstruct a surfboard by modifying its original shape.

resin *n*. In surfboard construction, the liquid plastic that is poured on fiberglass to bind it to the surfboard; used to laminate the fiberglass cloth to the foam.

resin fumes *n*. Extremely toxic vapors encountered during surfboard construction.

respirator *n*. A mask used to filter toxic fumes and dust from the air during the building and repairing of surfboards.

responsive *adj*. A surfboard performance characteristic. Usage: "Your board is really loose and responsive." —**responsiveness** *n*.

restaurant board *n*. A surfboard made specifically to hang as art.

reverse kickout *n*. The same as a KICK-OUT, except that the surfer executes a half spinner in kicking the board out of the wave.

reverse pullout *n*. **1)** Kicking out of a wave by quickly twisting the body to the rear, thus propelling the board over the top of the wave. **2)** Swinging the board around and off the wave in the direction opposite to that of the slide.

reverse takeoff *n*. A skeg-first takeoff in which the surfer lies on the board and, once in the wave, spins the board around and stands up, riding in the correct manner. (MM)

reverse 360 air *n*. A bodyboarding maneuver. See THREE SIXTY.

reverse twist *n*. A hot-dog peel-off with the board turning off the wave to one side and the rider's body twisting around the other way. Also called REVERSE PULLOUT.

revetment *n*. A structure built along the coast to prevent erosion and other damage by wave action. Similar to a SEA WALL. (CCRG) —**rock revetment**

rev-head *n*. A fool who thinks that cars are more important than surfboards. (Australia; JARR)

rhino *n*. **1)** A bodacious wave; the ultimate surfing experience. (CVG) **2)** A board over seven feet long and weighing over fifteen pounds. (H&R) **3) rhino chaser, rhino-chaser gun** See BIG GUN.

richter (RICK-ter) **1)** *v*. To do a hard turn; to go off. Usage: "Potter richtered his bottom turn, made it around the section and pulled into the barrel." (Australia and U.S.; SFR, 1989) **2)** Richter scale *n*. A scale, ranging from 1 to 10, used for expressing the intensity of an earthquake; developed by U.S. seismologist Charles Richter (1900–1985). See OFF THE RICHTER.

ricochet *n*. The end result of the most difficult type of cutback, where the surfer bounces the board off the breaking wave and again reverses horizontal direction. In competition, the difficulty of this move is determined by how far the board projects back into the breaking white water and how steep a vertical plane the board achieves. (L&L)

ride *v*. To surf a wave. Usage: "Hey bro, I saw that last ride you got."

rideable *adj.* SURFABLE. —**rideable waves** *n.*

rider on the inside *n.* The surfer riding closest to the breaking portion of the wave; this person has the right-of-way.

riding the crest of a wave, riding on the crest *v.* To be perched on the lip of the wave.

riding the crimson wave *v.* Said of females during their menstrual period; "I'm riding the crimson wave." Popularized by the movie, *Clueless* (1995). Same as SURFING THE CRIMSON WAVE.

riggin *n.* A surfer who won't stop talking. (MPZ) See YARNER.

right *n.* **1)** Any wave breaking in such a way that a surfer taking off must turn to the right to stay ahead of the curl. **2)** A wave that breaks from right to left, as viewed from shore, and from left to right, as viewed from out in the water. (MF) See LEFT. —**rights** *pl.*, **right-hander** (Australia)

righteous Something that's right on, KILLER. Usage: "Righteous, dude."

right-of-way *n.* The first rule of surfing etiquette—that a surfer already on a wave and riding has the right-of-way, especially if he or she is on the inside closest to the curl. Anyone else coming into the wave should respect this right. See INSIDE.

right point *n.* A point break that produces waves that break to the right.

right slide *n.* A ride where the surfer slides to the right on a wave that is breaking from left to right.

ring around the collar Said of the

collar of a wetsuit that is a different color than the rest of the suit. (SP)

ring fish *n.* Condoms that end up in the sea and on our beaches when sewage is not treated before it is discharged. (United Kingdom, 1990s)

rinse cycle *n.* See WASHING MACHINE.

rip *v.* **1)** To perform aggressive maneuvers on a wave; a complimentary term. Usage: "That dude really rips." **2)** To surf radically. **3) rippin'** or **ripping** Surfing hard. Same as RIP IT UP, RIP 'N' TEAR.

rip current, rip *n.* **1)** A powerful seaward movement of water created by waves breaking in rapid succession onto a beach, then rushing back through the lowest portion of the beach, thereby eroding an underwater exit channel in the sand. **2)** A narrow river of water moving seaward, the result of breaking waves and the subsequent accumulation of water in the near-shore zone. Generally accompanies big surf because the masses of water moving shoreward must have a way to get back out to sea. **3)** A current of water moving away from the beach. See LONGSHORE CURRENT.

A rip current is easily recognized by waves crossing diagonally over each other rather than rolling toward shore in parallel. The outward flow is sometimes called an OFFSET, RUNOUT, SEA PUSS, OR SEA PUSSY. It is sometimes mistakenly thought of as "undertow"—even though it doesn't drag you under the water but rather pulls you out to sea. It is also wrong to call it a RIPTIDE, since it has nothing to do with the tides.

ripe *adj.* Used to describe a perfect wave waiting to be surfed.

rip it up, ripping it up *v.* To attack a wave; same as TEAR IT UP.

rip 'n' tear *v.* To surf radically; same as RIP. Usage: "I saw you rip 'n' tear out there."

ripper *n.* **1)** Someone who tears it up when surfing. **2)** Used to congratulate someone on a great ride, as in "Ripper, dude!" **—rippah** (Hawaiian Pidgin)

riprap *n.* Boulders or rock rubble used to construct a jetty or revetment. (CCRG)

riptide *n.* A misnomer for RIP CURRENT.

riverbar break *n.* Waves breaking over a sandbar at the mouth of a river; can be dangerous because of the currents, including rips, that are common at river mouths. (WWK)

river bodyboarding, river boogie *n.* Using a special board to surf river eddies, or the reversing foam of river "holes"; works best on deep and narrow "drop-and-pool"-type rivers. Also called WHITE-WATER SURFING.

The bodyboard adapted for river running is cut big for high flotation (four and one-half feet long, two feet wide, and four inches thick), equipped with two sets of handles, a slick bottom coat of high-density polyethylene, and a scalloped hip recess. In addition, a river bodyboarder needs a drysuit to ward off the river's chill; soccer shin guards, skateboard kneepads, and a kayaker's helmet to prevent bangs from river rocks; and swim fins and webbed gloves to enhance propulsion. (MHG)

"Kayakers are separated from the water by their gear—they touch a paddle here, poke the bow over there. Very artistic. Bodyboarding is full immersion; it's more like wrestling. You go down on the mat with the river."

—Bob Carlson of Carlson Designs (1990)

river mouth *n.* **1)** Sometimes a good surf site due to the presence of sandbars. See RIVERBAR BREAK. **2)** Sometimes a feeding ground for sharks.

river surfing *n.* **1)** Riding a surfboard on river rapids while holding onto a line attached to an upstream bridge. In addition, as fast-running rivers flow over submerged obstacles, they sometimes form stationary waves that can be surfed. See STANDING WAVE. **2)** Surfing upstream on a tidal bore.

road trip *n.* A surfing adventure. See SURFARI, SURFIN' SAFARI.

roar of the ocean *n.* The sound of the surf. —**ocean roar**

"The three great sounds in nature are the sound of the rain, the sound of the wind . . . and the sound of outer ocean on a beach.

I have heard them all and that of the ocean is the most awesome, beautiful and varied. . . ."

—*Henry Beston*

---

rock dance, rock dancing *n.* A slippery walk over sharp, moss-covered rocks to retrieve a lost surfboard; often occurs at low tide. Your feet are at the mercy of sea urchins, pinching crabs, sea slugs, sea anemones, and barnacles—a miserable experience. (A&M, KSO)

rocker *n.* **1)** The gradual curve along a surfboard's fore-to-aft axis; the curvature of a surfboard in profile. A board with a lot of nose rocker has a pronounced upward curve toward the nose. **2)** The

lengthwise bottom curvature of a surfboard. (L&L) **3) flat rocker** A rocker with little or no curve. **4) full rocker** A surfboard with an exaggerated upward curve in the nose and tail. **5)** An Australian HODAD. **6)** A member of a motorbike cult opposed to surfies. (Australia; MF)

When viewed from the side, a surfboard is higher at both ends than in the center. This fact has given rise to a number of colorful names; in addition to *rocker*, there is BANANA, SCOOP, and SPOON. The curve is also called CAMBER and LIFT.

---

rocker block *n.* A hard foam block that attaches to the back of a thruster-style board and against which the back foot can be braced. (NAT, 1985)

rock in *v.* When you barely begin to paddle on a steep wave and you catch it with minimal effort. See NO-PADDLE TAKE-OFF, TWO-STROKE TAKEOFF.

rock reef *n.* A reef formed of rocks, as distinct from a CORAL REEF. This kind of reef is common in California.

rocks *n.* A part of the surfing landscape that one encounters in just about every surf session, such as during entry and exit from the water. Lost boards, for instance, are carried into hungry rocks that produce efficient board-digesting

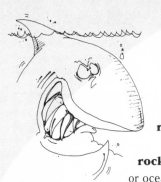

rogue shark
Art: Deano

enzymes. See ROCK DANCE, EAT THE ROCKS.

rock spider *n.* VALLEY. (Santa Cruz)

rocky *adj.* One kind of shoreline or ocean bottom. Surf breaking over a rocky bottom or beach performs differently from surf breaking over a sandy beach or a mud flat.

rocky point *n.* A headland with a rocky shoreline that may feature a point break.

rodney wave *n.* A wave where everyone drops in on you and you get no respect; named for comedian Rodney Dangerfield. (MCR)

rogue shark *n.* A shark that roams alone. *Rogue,* as applied to animals, also means "vicious and destructive" —which in some circumstances aptly describes shark behavior.

rogue wave *n.* **1)** A wave that appears unexpectedly and does not follow the pattern of previous waves. **2)** An unpredictably large wave in the open ocean, often in very deep waters, which sometimes exceeds one hundred feet in height. (SFR, June 1988) **3)** A mid-ocean freak wave that is formed when a series of waves, commonly called trains, get "in step" for a short time, often less than a minute, and jack up into a single wave; not to be confused with a tsunami. (SFG, October 1982)

roll, rollover *n.* A maneuver used to get out through the white water. In the face of an oncoming broken wave, the surfer rolls over with the board, so that the bottom of the board is facing up, and hangs onto the rails—sometimes wrapping his or her legs around the board—until the wave passes over, then turns the board right side up and continues paddling outside. **—rolling over** *v.*

roller *n.* **1)** A wave that does not curl or tube; instead, the white water slides down its face. **2)** A wave that breaks gently and evenly toward a beach or shoreline. Same as SPILLING WAVE.

roller coaster *n.* **1)** A surfing maneuver in which the surfer comes out of a fast bottom turn, slides up the face of the wave, and rebounds off the lip at the crest of the wave. **2)** A surfer's up-and-down movement on the face of a wave. (MM) See CLIMB AND DROP.

roll in *v.* Said of large, unbroken waves or swell moving toward shore. Usage: "Look at that swell roll in."

rolling surf *n.* Said of incoming waves approaching the shore.

rolling thunder *n.* Big ocean waves; taken from the name of a Great Plains Indian. (PZ)

roof of the wave *n.* The underside of the wave lip; the CANOPY.

roof rack *n.* SURF RACK.

room time *n.* Time spent in the tube. (DS) Same as CLOCKING IN THE GREEN ROOM, TUBE TIME.

roost *v.* To BAIL, fast. Usage: "Let's roost." "We're roosting." Santa Monica; TMA, 1985)

rooster, rooster tail *n.* **1)** An upward-curving spray of water directly astern of a fast-moving surfboard. **2)** The arching

rubbah slippahs
Courtesy of Leslie King

trail of spray that shoots up off the back of the board as the surfer carves into a good turn. (A&M)

rope *n.* **1)** An Australian term for a SURF LEASH. Also called LEG ROPE. **2)** A fiberglass product used in fin laminations and leash loops. (GCD)

roto-moto *n.* The performance of continuous spinners while surfing; a surfing maneuver.

rounded diamond tail *n.* A surfboard design feature.

rounded pin *n.* A surfboard design featuring a narrow, rounded tail; the standard by which all other boards are judged.

rounded square tail *n.* A surfboard design feature.

roundhouse, roundhouse cutback *n.* **1)** A maneuver in which the surfer cuts back into the wave and forces it to break, making an otherwise dull wave surfable. (JP) **2)** A cutback during which the surfer maintains speed and momentum through a turn of large radius (180 degrees).

—sweeping roundhouse cutback

roundhouser *n.* Any roundhouse maneuver.

round rail *n.* A surfboard rail, the cross section of which is round and thickened, and which generally produces a slow and stable, or stiff, response.

round tail or **roundtail** *n.* A surfboard design featuring a rounded tail section, as distinct from one that is squared off or pointed. (NAT, 1985) See ROUNDED PIN.

'round the island, 'round the world *n.* A tandem maneuver where the female partner is rotated 360 degrees around the male partner's shoulders or waist.

round toe booties *n.* As distinct from SPLIT TOE BOOTIES.

routed skeg *n.* A strong method of attaching a skeg in a routed slot.

routed stick *n.* **1)** A surfboard with inlayed, decorative stringers. (MCR) **2)** A cheap method of inlaying a nonfull stick.

router *n.* A high-speed precision power tool used to install leash cups and fin boxes.

rubbah slippahs *n.* Hawaiian Pidgin for rubber sandals; same as THONGS, FLIP-FLOPS, GO-AHEADS.

rubber arms *n.* **1)** The term for a surfer who doesn't paddle hard enough to get a wave because it's too large or too critical. **2)** The feeling you occasionally get in your arms when you're paddling for an unusually large wave and you're not quite sure you want it.

rubberneck An Australian term for KOOK. (1980s)

rubber suit *n.* A cold-water insulating suit made of sponge rubber; the old term for WETSUIT. (JKMJ, 1965)

rule *v.* To dominate the waves. Usage: "Let's rule, dude." (San Diego)

rumbled *v.* To get tossed in a wave. (TMA) Usage: "I was fully rumbled out there."

runback *n.* Fast back-stepping on a surfboard.

runup *n.* Fast forward-stepping on a surfboard.

round toe booties
Photo: Trevor Cralle

roundhouse cutback
Kaipo Guerrero
Photo: Rob Gilley

sacred *adj.* Used to describe something really cool; **sacy** (SAKE-ee)—if you're from Pt. Loma, California. (TJ)

safe zone *n.* An area of relative calm where the waves don't break. See CHANNEL, CHANNEL SITTING.

sailboard *n.* **1)** A specialized board that is similar to a surfboard but outfitted with a mast, boom, and sail; first tested in the waters off Waikiki by Tom Blake in 1935. (GTM) See WINDSURFER. **2)** A small light sailboat with a flat hull designed to carry one or two persons. **3) Sailboard** A name trademarked in 1962.

sailboarding, sailsurfing *n.* WINDSURFING.

salt itch *n.* What develops over time when you don't have access to a freshwater shower. (Coined by Trevor Cralle, Greek islands, August 3, 1997) See JUNGLE RASH, POST-OCEAN CRUST.

saltwater *n.* Same as SEAWATER.

~~~~~~~~~~~~~~~~~~~~~~~~~

"The cure for anything is salt water—sweat, tears, or the sea."

—Isak Dinesen (1885–1962)

~~~~~~~~~~~~~~~~~~~~~~~~~

sampan roll *n.* **1)** An area seaward of Waikiki Bay frequented by fishing sampans on their way to sea, where only the largest swells break in blue water. **2)** A 1960s term for any site where large swells break.

sand *n.* **1)** The more or less fine debris of rocks found at the beach, consisting of small, loose grains often of quartz and feldspar. Other kinds of beaches are covered with volcanic black sand or coral white sand. See BEACH. **2)** Unpleasant yellow particles that form a buffer zone between ocean and earth. Sand burns your feet on hot days, it gets into your board wax, and it can ruin an amorous adventure under the stars if it gets where it's not wanted. (JARR)

sailboard
Art: The Pizz

SAND Surfers Against Nuclear Destruction—an Australian group of concerned surfers.

sandals *n.* Open-air shoes favored by surfers, for example, THONGS, RUBBAH SLIPPAHS (Hawaiian Pidgin), ZORRIES, GETOGS, FLIP-FLOPS, and GO-AHEADS.

sandbank *n.* A submerged area of sand that causes waves to break. (NAT, 1985)

sandbar *n.* **1)** A submerged offshore deposit of sand or sediment created by littoral drift or wave action; also occurs at a river mouth. (CCRG) **2)** A mound or plateau of sand caused by wave action or sea currents and occasionally acting as an underwater reef, creating good surfing waves and causing them to break further offshore.

~~~~~~~~~~~~~~~~~~~~~~~~~

Sandbars form parallel to the beach, but are not permanent—they shift around seasonally. Winter storm waves erode the summer beach profile and deposit sands offshore.

~~~~~~~~~~~~~~~~~~~~~~~~~

sandbar break *n.* A kind of surf break caused by swell moving over sand deposits just offshore; can be unstable, given that sandbars shift seasonally with changes in weather. See SURF BREAKS.

sand biscuit *n.* Usually dog shit on the beach; occasionally human excrement (especially in Ventura).

sandboarding *n.* Sandboarders use waxed-up skimboards and other specialized boards to ride down huge sand dunes at places like Jockey's Ridge, a ninety-foot mountain of sand near Nags Head, North Carolina. Unfortunately, this activity is destructive to a dynamic yet fragile landform. Sandboarding is an offshoot of surfing that now incorporates snowboarding technology as well. It first appeared in the movie *The Endless Summer* (1964), which showed surfers in South Africa using longboards to slide down large dunes on the way to a remote break.

sand coat, sanding coat *n.* In surfboard construction, the resin layer that is sanded to blend and refine the contours of the board. (ORB) Also known as HOT COAT.

sand dune *n.* A mound, ridge, or hill of wind-blown sand, either bare or covered with vegetation; an aeolian landscape. Also called *dune.*

sander *n.* In surfboard construction, a power tool used by the shaper to smooth out ridges left by the planer and to sand out the board.

sand flea, sand fly *n.* Someone who avoids the water and just stays on the beach. (IDSM)

sanding agent *n.* A resin additive used to transform laminating resin into hot-coat resin. (GCD)

sanding block *n.* A small piece of wood with sandpaper wrapped around it, making it easier to sand certain areas of a surfboard.

sanding resin, surfacing resin *n.* A special resin used to fill in the texture and lap seams in the fiberglass cloth of a surfboard. This resin contains a surfacing agent, which floats to the surface once the resin is applied and blocks air, causing the resin to set up hard and tack-free. The resin is then sanded to make the board smooth. Same as HOT-COAT RESIN.

sand in the tub *n.* Sandy residue left in the bathtub after you rinse off your wetsuit in the shower.

sandpaper *n.* The magic wand of ding repair; comes in a wide range of grits. For instance, #60 grit paper takes down the excess resin and glass and leaves a good surface for a gloss coat to bond to. Among the **finishing sandpapers,**

#220 is used to take the gloss lines off, and #400 and #600 grit are used to prepare the gloss for buffing. (GCD)

sandruff *n.* Scalp full of sand, like dandruff only with grains of sand. (Coined by Trevor Cralle and Lee Micheaux, Santa Cruz Beach Boardwalk, March 24, 1992)

sandsliding *n.* SKIMBOARDING. (Hawaii; ELK)

sand spit *n.* **1)** A narrow, fingerlike embankment of sand deposited by littoral drift into the open water of a bay. **2)** The seasonal or permanent sand or sediment deposit at the mouth of a river. (CCRG)

sand surfing *n.* Sliding down the crumbling wave cut beach berm on your bare feet or with shoes on. (Coined by Bill Johns, Stump Beach, California, 1994)

sandwichable syndrome *n.* Getting crunched by a wave. (SFR, October 1983)

San Jose *n.* **1)** Northern California's VALLEY. **2)** A densely populated urban area east of Santa Cruz and south of San Francisco. See OVER THE HILL, VALLEY SURPRISE.

※※※※※※※※※※※※※※

"You can take a valley out of San Jose, but you can't take San Jose out of the valley." (MCR)

※※※※※※※※※※※※※※

San Jose leeches, San Jose module *n.* Santa Cruz derogatory terms for someone from San Jose, California. See OVER THE HILL, VALLEY SHEEP.

sano *adj.* Used to describe very, very clean waves. (MVA) Usage: "It's sano out there."

Santa Ana winds, Santa Anas, Santanas, Santa Ana condition *n.* **1)** Named for the Santa Ana Canyon in Southern California but occurring throughout the Los Angeles Basin, winds that form in fall and winter when the air in the interior deserts piles up against the transverse ranges and begins streaming down the mountain passes toward the coast. The air heats as it moves downhill, sometimes raising coastal temperatures to over 100 degrees. **2)** Hot, dry winds that blow offshore all day and create excellent surfing conditions; may also reach gale strength—up to sixty miles per hour—and create dangerous waves offshore. (CCRG) Also called DEVIL WINDS.

※※※※※※※※※※※※※※

"In the morning, standing at the bus stop, you know the waves are classic and you can smell the wind." (SFR)

※※※※※※※※※※※※※※

Santa Cruz *n.* A Northern California surfing community, first surfed by Hawaiian Prince David Kawononaokoa in 1885 and home of the Santa Cruz Surfing Museum. Surf spots include Steamer Lane and Pleasure Point.

Santa Monica Bay *n.* **1)** The site of numerous surfing communities, including the Palos Verdes Peninsula, Manhattan Beach, Redondo Beach, Hermosa Beach, Santa Monica, and Malibu. **2)** One of the most polluted bays in the world, especially during heavy rains, when millions of gallons of raw, untreated sewage run off into the bay.

sardine *n.* An old term for shark. (JKMJ, 1965)

Sargasso Sea *n.* A large tract of the North Atlantic that is covered by vast blankets of sargassum seaweed, for which the sea is named; fed by the Gulf Stream, which deposits seaweed transplanted by hurricanes from the reefs of Florida and the West Indies. (OA) See SURF SOUP.

satu lagi (SAW-two LAH-ghee) An Indonesia word meaning literally "one more," and in surfing means "Outside!" Usage: "That Indo guy's screaming *satu lagi* at us! I'll get the anchor, you start the motor!" (SFR, 1990) See HANA HO.

sausage board *n.* A special shape of surfboard rounded at both ends. (MF)

Save Our Surf (SOS) *n.* Environmental organization of surfers founded by John Kelly in the early 1960s in Hawaii.

scam *v.* To hit on someone—to look for and hopefully get together with someone you are attracted to. Usage: "Look, he's totally scamming."

scareamundo *adj.* Scary.

scend *n.* The back part of a wave.

—**wave scend**

schedy *n.* Schedule. Usage: "Check your schedy, brah." (Lewellen, San Rafael, California, 1994)

schooling tuna *v.* To dial in on some BUTTER. (Florida; TDW) Usage: "Let's go school some tuna."

scoop *n.* **1)** The turned-up shape in the nose of a surfboard. **2)** The camber, or uplifted shape, of the forward or rear portion of a surfboard. Also called SPOON, CUP. (DSHJ) See ROCKER.

scope, scope out *v.* To check something out, as in "to scope out the surf" or "to scope out a person you're attracted to." —**scopin'**

score *v.* To achieve or accomplish a goal, usually said in regards to waves, food, or babes. Usage: "I scored the full-on drumstick."

scoring criteria *n.* SURFING CRITERIA.

scorpion tail *n.* The tail scoop aft of the step on a hydroplane surfboard.

scraps *n.* INSIDE WAVES. Usage: "I'm gonna paddle in and pick off some scraps." See LEFTOVERS, GROMMET SNACKS.

scratch *v.* **1)** To paddle hard. Usage: "I had to scratch really hard to make that wave." **2) scratching over the top** To paddle rapidly and still barely make it over a huge incoming wave. (MM)

scratch-up zone *n.* In surfboard construction, an area just outside of the grind-down zone that gets scratched up during sanding and later covered with gloss resin. (GCD)

screaming *v.* Traveling fast down the face of a wave.

Art: The Pizz

screw foot *n.* Someone who rides a surf-board with the right foot forward, left foot back. (ORB) Same as GOOFY FOOT.

scrozzling (SCRAW-zuhl-ling) *v.* A move beyond groveling. Usage: "Yeah, I saw you scrozzling through that section, but I didn't think you'd make it, so I went." (Santa Cruz, SFR, 1989)

scrub *v.* Eat it. Usage: "I fully scrubbed."
—scrubbin'

scungies *n.* Trunks worn for surfboard riding. (Australia; MNL)

sea *n.* **1)** The ocean. **2)** A tract of water within an ocean. **3)** A relatively large body of saltwater partially or com-pletely landlocked. **4)** The condition of the ocean's surface, as in a "high sea." **5)** Something that suggests the sea in its overwhelming sweep or vastness, as in "a sea of wildflowers." (AHD2)
6) the seven seas All the major waters of the world.

sea anemone *n.* Any sedimentary marine animal of the phylum *Coelenterata*, having a flexible cylin-drical body and numerous tentacles surrounding the mouth and superficial-ly resembling a flower. Anemones come in bright and varied colors; some species in tropical waters are highly toxic to touch.

sea breeze *n.* **1)** A thermally produced wind blowing from a cool ocean surface onto adjoining warm land. (RHD) **2)** A light cooling breeze blowing onshore. **3)** A local wind rising as land heats up during the day.

Sea breezes bring wind chop to the majority of surf spots. They some-times die down an hour or two before sundown, allowing surfers to enjoy an evening glass-off. (S&C)

sea chariot *n.* SURFBOARD.

sea dwarf *n.* The size of a human male penis after a cold-water session. (TWS, January 2000) See GATOR MINI.

sea-going muffin *n.* BODYBOARDER —something you wash the dishes with. (Santa Cruz)

sea hag *n.* An ugly woman.

sea lice *n.* Jellyfish larvae that implant themselves under your skin from April to June in Palm Beach and other areas of South Florida. Wash off with water immediately before the sun bakes the larvae into your skin and causes you to itch all over. Surfers apply nail polish to exposed areas of skin before it spreads.

sea lion *n.* Known to bodysurf in groups, returning again and again to a good peak.

seal suit *n.* WETSUIT. Also called FROGSKINS.

sea puss, sea pussy *n.* A rip current found at open beaches; happens when waves breaking over a sandbar create an excess of water that has to flow out through a hole in the sandbar. (DSHJ) See RIP CURRENT.

sea rats *n.* Another name for sea gulls, because they crap everywhere and eat anything. (PZ)

sea snake
Art: Andrea McCann

seasick, seasickness
adj. When your equilibrium is thrown out of balance by the up-and-down bobbing or side-to-side rocking in, on, or under the ocean, which leads to an extremely uncomfortable dizzy feeling in the head and often culminates in vomiting. There are different measures an individual can take to prevent seasickness, such as taking two 250 mg capsules of powdered ginger an hour before going out to sea. See AQUA BOOT, TALKING TO THE SEALS.

sea snake, sea serpent *n.* Any of numerous venomous aquatic viviparous snakes (of the family *Hydrophidae*) found in warm seas. (W9) Although potentially deadly and a bit startling when encountered swimming around surfers in certain South Pacific surf spots, these snakes are not aggressive, and they have such tiny mouths that the only place they can bite is the webbed skin between the fingers of a surfer's hand.

sea state *n.* A condition in which waves are formed locally by winds blowing close to the coast; the crests are generally rounded and the waves are close together and travel slowly. (L&L) Usage: "I think we're getting a bit of sea state developing." —**sea state calm**

seat surfing *n.* At a concert or other event, burying one's ticket stub deep in one's pants pocket, and floating from unoccupied seat to unoccupied seat, each closer to the stage than the last.

While it appears anarchic to the ushers, seat surfing is actually a team sport, with thousands playing at the same time. (David Shenk and Steve Silberman, *Skeleton Key: A Dictionary for Deadheads,* 1994)

sea ulcer *n.* A sore usually on the feet or ankles that is a common problem among surfers; typically starts as a cut, often a deep one, then instead of healing shut, as most wounds do, it deepens and becomes encircled by a thick, rubbery kind of callus. A sea ulcer may last for weeks, months, or even years, all the while not looking particularly infected, but just never healing. The best treatment is to keep it clean and dry. (SFR)

sea urchin *n.* Any of a class (*Echinoidea*) of echinoderms usually encased in a thin brittle shell that is covered with movable spines.

Urchins can be quite abundant in rocky areas with shallow water, and if you lose your board and are forced to stand up and walk ashore, you may find your foot punctured by needle-like spines that can break off under the skin, emitting a poison and causing a wound that can hurt for months. The treatment is to dissolve the spines—which are composed of calcium carbonate—in any weak acid such as vinegar, lemon juice, or uric acid. This last suggests a

possible emergency procedure: urinate on the injured foot and the reaction may force the spines out.

sea wall *n.* A strong wall or embankment erected to prevent the encroachment of the sea and to protect the shore from erosion; serves as a **breakwater.**

sea wasp *n.* Any of various highly poisonous stinging jellyfish of the order *Cubomedusae,* found in tropical seas. (RHD) Surfers along Australia's northeastern coast wear pantyhose in the warm water to guard against their potentially lethal stings. Also called BOX JELLY or MARINE STINGER.

seawater *n.* Salty water in or from the ocean, large amounts of which are involuntarily swallowed by surfers during heavy wipeouts.

seaweed *n.* An algae generally divided into four groups: blue-green, green, brown, and red. Kelp is the familiar brown variety; mermaid's hair is a common blue-green species that lives on rocks and pilings. (OA)

Sebastian Inlet The most famous surf spot in Florida.

second break *n.* **1)** The area where waves break a second time, closer to shore than the first break. **2) Second Break** A specific surf site at Waikiki, Oahu, Hawaii.

second lip *n.* An additional wave lip that will sometimes form on the wave face, as commonly seen in the Waimea Shorebreak in Hawaii. See DOUBLE UP.

secret goo *n.* A very useful mixture of resin and fiberglass clippings used in ding repair. (GCD)

secret spot *n.* A relatively undiscovered surf site.

section *n.* **1)** A part of a breaking wave. **2)** The difficult part of a wave. (L&L) **3)** The fast part of a wave, where ten or fifteen yards of wall fold over at once instead of peeling off. (A&M) **4)** An area within a surf spot where the wave can be predicted to break in a certain way.

sectioning *v.* **1)** What happens when a wave breaks in front of a surfer, making it difficult to make the wave. **2)** When a wave breaks in two or more places at once, instead of peeling from one side to the other. **3)** When a portion of a wave breaks all at once, rather than peeling. (A&B) Usage: "The wave started sectioning on me just as I took off."

sectiony *adj.* Said of a wave that is not breaking evenly, or is breaking ahead of itself. Usage: "The waves are a little sectiony."

see-through wave *n.* A murky-free, clean curling wave that is back-lit by the sun.

sea wall
*Ocean Beach,
San Francisco*
Photo: Trevor Cralle

seismic sea wave *n.* A long-period wave generated by an underwater earthquake, landslide, or volcanic eruption; a TSUNAMI. Erroneously called a TIDAL WAVE. (CCRG)

seismograph *n.* An instrument that detects, measures, and records ground motion (for instance, the vibrations of earthquakes and disturbances from wave shock). This device is an excellent indicator of surf conditions. If the recorded lines are parallel to each other, little or no seismic activity is indicated and the surf is probably small or flat; if the lines are squiggly and crooked, probably the surf is up. Some colleges display seismographs in their earth sciences department.

semigun *n.* A big-wave surfboard modified to move at a slower speed and with somewhat increased maneuverability.

semipig *n.* A pig board modified to be less pointed in the nose and not quite as wide, or fat, in the rear.

seppo *n.* Short for Septic Tank Yank—a derogatory Australian term for an American. Some say the term originated way back, when some Americans visited Australia and noticed that when some Australians had to relieve themselves, they just let it run all over the place. So the Americans explained what a septic tank was, but the Australians turned it around on them and said, "Wha'd ya mean, mate, you have this big tank full of shit—and you keep it?"

Serfin *n.* The name of a Mexican bank, preferred by many a visiting surfer to Mexico.

session *n.* **1)** Any time spent surfing; **sesh** or **sess** for short. Also called SURF SESSION. **2)** An Australian term for a SET.

set, wave set *n.* **1)** A series of waves—two, three, or four in a row—generally arriving at regularly spaced intervals. **2)** The largest waves to come through on a particular day or during a particular session, usually three or four or seven or eight at a time, the groupings separated by intervals of relative calm ranging from less than a minute to a half an hour or more. **3)** A series of waves following rapidly one after the other. (Waves usually come in sets.)

Set waves come in many varieties: kitchen sets are waves you can really cook on; dining room sets are close out waves that you can eat; living room sets provide easy-chair types of rides—waves that anyone can ride; in bathroom sets everyone gets flushed on. (MCR)

set *v.* To be carried down the coast in an ocean current. Usage: "I was set down the coast."

set an edge *n.* DIG A RAIL. (L&L)

setious *n.* Very regular or long sets. Usage: "There's a setious on the horizon." (Santa Cruz)

setting the scale *n.* In competitive surfing, the practice of using the first ride that is scored in a heat as the

standard against which all subsequent rides in that heat are judged. On the ASP tour the scale is set using a scoring range of 1 to 10, with increments of one-tenth of a point to reduce the likelihood of a tie. (L&L)

set up 1) *v.* To incorporate a surfer's desired specifications into a surfboard design. Shapers can "set up" shortboards and longboards for various conditions by adjusting length, width, rocker, bottom contours, wide point placement, rail design, number of fins, and so on. **2)** A resin term; same as GO OFF. (GCD)

3) deep setup *n.* The position of a surfer way back in the tube.

set waves *n.* Big surf that is breaking consistently.

Seven Mile Miracle *n.* A stretch of coastline from Haleiwa to Sunset Beach along the North Shore of Oahu, Hawaii, that features the finest surfbreaks on earth, including PIPELINE and WAIMEA BAY.

sewer *n.* **1)** Watch out for sewer pipes spewing untreated toxic sludge at or near your favorite surf spot. **2) Sewer Peak** A surf spot on the Eastside of Santa Cruz, California.

Surfing Versus Sex

Although many surfers take up sex as a second sport, aesthetically speaking it is not in the same league. True, many of the maneuvers are similar, but the feeling of satisfaction and exhilaration that floods over the surfer when he penetrates the deepest recesses of a bitchin' barrel knows no rival. (JARR)

Is surfing better than sex? The first international surfing and sex survey by Wilson-Horsechester-Market Research included the following (GS, April 1990):

You wake up for an early because you know the surf is going off, but your partner wants to have sex. Do you:

a) Go surfing regardless 17%
b) Have a quickie and go surfing 77%
c) Forget surfing and spend all morning in bed 6%

In addition:
72% said their sexual appetite was increased during flat spells.
51% said they thought about surfing during sex.

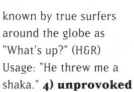

shaka
Art: Ri...

"NO DUMPING • DRAINS TO OCEAN"

—Slogan painted by sewer drains

sex *n.* An activity that competes with surfing as the number-one priority in a surfer's life. Or does it? See SURFING VERSUS SEX on page 225 and SURFING AS METAPHOR on page 281.

Sex Wax *n.* A brand of surf wax, Mr. Zog's Sex Wax, features the slogan, "The Best for Your Stick."

shacked, shacking, getting shacked 1) *v.* To get barreled, tubed, etc. Usage: "It'll be shacking." **2) shackable waves** *n.* A derivative of A-FRAME. See HOUSES, GARAGED. (California and Hawaii)

shacking the lip *n.* A combination maneuver, something between a cutback and an off-the-lip. (Newport Beach)

shaka, shaka brah *n.* **1)** Hawaiian Pidgin for "Right on!" **2)** A hand signal meaning howzit, hello, so long, great ride, I agree, take it easy, hang loose, and various other things. The shaka is made by wiggling a raised hand with only the thumb and little finger extended. **3)** An internationally understood sign

shaka
Benj-I, Maui
Photo: Trevor Cralle

known by true surfers around the globe as "What's up?" (H&R) Usage: "He threw me a shaka." **4) unprovoked shaka** When a total stranger gives you a friendly acknowledgment. Usage: "Hey, I just got an unprovoked shaka from that local on the bicycle at the shave ice stand." **5) double shaka** Usually given enthusiastically with a big smile.

6) driving shaka When you casually raise your pinkie and thumb together, while maintaining contact with the steering wheel with your three middle fingers. Some surfers add a slight backward head tilt simultaneously with the shaka for additional acknowledgment. (Maui 1999) **7) subtle shaka** A more casual form of the more enthusiastic wrist-shaking variety.

There are several explanations for the origin of shaka. The gesture is believed to have been invented by Hamana Kalili, a Hawaiian folk hero, fisherman, tug-of-war champion, hukilau (party) organizer, and resident of Laie (a tiny town on Oahu), who used the sign—not the word—as a sort of blessing and community calling. His right hand was missing three fingers; the thumb and the little finger were all that was left. Kalili is said to have lost

shacked
Ken Collins,
Sharks Reef
Photo: Mike Peralta

his fingers from (a) using dynamite to kill fish; (b) being smashed in the rollers at Kahuku Sugar Mill; or (c) being bitten by a ferocious shark.

The word shaka was used in the 1960s by Lippy Espinda, a Honolulu used-car salesman and TV movie host. But it may have derived from much earlier times, for instance from a Buddha named "Shaykanuma," who prayed with his fingers folded except for his little finger and thumb. And some old-time Japanese residents of Hawaii say that shaka dates back to the 1880s; they claim it means "Praise the Lord" and was used when someone did something good. (SFG, May 1986)

✿✿✿✿✿✿✿✿✿✿✿✿✿

shallow, shallow reef *n*. Refers to a spot in the ocean that's not very deep and may pose a hazard. See ROCK DANCE, SUCKING DRY.

shallow surf *n*. Waves breaking over a shallow area like a reef.

shape *n*. **1)** Refers to the configuration, or form, of waves—well-shaped, poor, fair, etc. Usage: "It was a perfect six foot with really good shape." **2)** The foam blank as completed by the shaper (ORB); **board shape**. **3)** *v*. To form or sculpt a foam blank into a specified surfboard shape.

shaper, surfboard shaper *n*. The craftsperson who shapes foam blanks into surfboards.

shark *n*. **1)** The animal many surfers dread—even though Duke Kahanamoku believed that the shark was his *aumakua*, his guardian. **2)** A type of elasmobranch fish that has existed for over 415 million years, comes in a variety of shapes and sizes, resides in various habitats, and sometimes travels far afield. Also known as, among many other names, *the landlords, hermann,* and (in Australia) *"the man in the gray suit"* (from the movie *The Endless Summer.*) See "A Few Facts about Sharks" on the next page. Also see HUMAN LURE, RED TRIANGLE, WHITE SHARK.

shaper
Art: Jim Phillips

✿✿✿✿✿✿✿✿✿✿✿✿✿

"I don't bother them, they don't bother me."

—Duke Kahanamoku on sharks

"I used to sleep naked with my ex on a waterbed without shaving my legs first; my nubs would be so sharp he'd wake up going, 'SHARK!, SHARK!'"

—Lala Land, Los Angeles comedienne

✿✿✿✿✿✿✿✿✿✿✿✿✿

shark appetizer *n*. Derogatory term for bodyboarder.

shark attack *n*. **1)** The reason that surfers dread sharks. **2)** Mr.

shark attack
Brent Laucher feeling happy to still be surfing, after a board meeting with the man in the gray suit at a shark-infested river mouth near the Oregon border

Photo: Trevor Cralle

Myths and Facts about Sharks

Sharks range in size from the tiny, six-inch bioluminescent spined pygmy shark up to the forty-five-foot-long, quite docile whale shark. The fastest known shark, the mako, has been clocked at up to twenty-two miles (thirty-five kilometers) per hour. Sharks have good vision and are sensitive to light, movement, and contrast—all important to their success as hunters. Prey is detected by sight, sound, and smell; sharks can detect odors from a hundred yards or farther away, and electrical reception and vibration from about six feet away.

Sharks that live near the sunlit surface or in shallow water are usually nocturnal, that is, active at night; others are crepuscular, active at dawn, dusk, or both (this is a busy time, when fish are waking up or settling down for the evening). A shark's eyes glow in the dark like a cat's.

A surfer may encounter a variety of sharks, including the fearsome great white (see WHITE SHARK), tiger sharks, hammerheads, and bull sharks. The large and ferocious tiger shark, a tropical species, has been known to eat anything in sight; it prowls reefs, bays, and river mouths in shallow, warm waters worldwide. Scientists think the broad, odd-shaped head of the hammerhead shark helps it steer and enhances its ability to see, smell, or detect the electrical fields given off by hidden prey. Dangerous bull sharks have been found 1,800 miles up the Amazon River and up the Mississippi River as far as Illinois.

Surfer terms for different shark species include **bronzies** (the bronze whalers), **formula ones** (for hammerheads), **terries** (for tiger sharks), and the surfer's favorite, **white pointers** (for great whites). (NHMLA)

Public hysteria over sharks was fueled by Steven Spielberg's movie *Jaws* (1975), which drove many beachgoers away from the ocean. Contrary to popular belief, however, sharks are not vicious man-eaters. Only about 27 of the more than 250 known species have attacked humans; these include the bull shark, gray shark,

Art: The Pizz

white-tip shark, blue shark, tiger shark, mako shark, white shark, and hammerhead shark. About one hundred people are attacked each year worldwide (twelve in the United States); in California, attacks average one per year.

Most shark attacks do not end in death, which results mainly from loss of blood and shock rather than from being eaten. In fact, sharks usually take one bite and swim away, leaving some 70 percent of their victims to survive. Most reported shark attacks occur in warm, tropical waters near large cities (where there are more people in the water), and most occur in shallow water (because there are more people near shore) or at the surface offshore. To a shark swimming below, the silhouette of a surfer floating on a shortboard may resemble the shape of a seal or a sea lion (its favorite foods). The increase in shark attacks in recent years is thought to be due in part to the growth in the marine mammal population brought about by the Marine Mammal Protection Act of 1973.

Some advice for prevention of shark attacks:

- Don't surf alone.
- Don't surf in murky water.
- Don't surf while wearing brightly colored clothing. (See YUMMY YELLOW.)
- Don't surf at night; some sharks see well in dim light and hunt by moonlight.
- Don't surf if you are cut or bleeding; sharks have a keen sense of smell and are able to detect one part of blood in one million parts of water (equivalent to one drop in twenty-five gallons of water). (GVS, NHMLA)

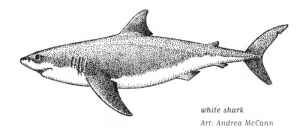

white shark
Art: Andrea McCann

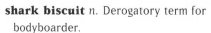

Zog's Shark Jerky with the slogan "Bite Back." **3) "Shark Attack"** A song by the Surf Punks.

"More people are killed in the United States by pigs (especially in the Midwest) than by sharks."

—Camm Swift (Natural History Museum of Los Angeles County, 1990)

"I would consider the whole thing to be an overwhelmingly positive experience. I'm glad it happened."

—Eric Larsen, white shark attack survivor, who lost half the blood in his body and required four hundred stitches (October 1991)

shave ice
Photo: Trevor Cralle

shark biscuit *n.* Derogatory term for bodyboarder.

Sharkbusters *n.* An airborne coastal beach and bay patrol based in Victoria, Australia, and founded by Ric D. T. Wilson in January 1988. From a single-engine airplane equipped with shark-alert sirens, the patrol looks for sharks near water users, as well as for major pollution and coastal abnormalities.

sharkin' *n.* To go surfing. (Texas; H&R) Usage: "Let's go sharkin'."

shark nose *n.* A surfboard shape with a pointed nose. (ASKC, 1965) See SHARKY.

sharky *adj.* **1)** Used to describe a surfboard with a sharp pointed nose, or a shark nose. Usage: "The nose is a bit sharky." (New Castle, Australia) **2)** Said

of a **shark-infested** area. **3)** Sharkey, Tennessee. Usage: "The waters there are supposed to be a little sharky."
—sharky thoughts

shave ice *n.* A Hawaiian snow cone—a popular surf snack.

A delicious Hawaiian treat made of finely crushed (shaved) ice, which is mounded in a paper cone and generously doused with long streams of flavored syrups. Some stands offer extras like ice cream or sweet milk on your cone. A straw and a thin, flat wooden spoon paddle are usually included. NOT AT ALL like the inferior mainland "snow cone," whose ice is way more coarse. A few tips on how to recognize a great shave ice:
1) The ice packing technique has to be loose and plenty; if packed too tight, it fails to create the goal of freshly fallen powder snow before any sun makes it into slush.
2) Having someone greet you from behind the counter in the friendly aloha style is key to the overall experience of bliss once your lips wrap around the globe of ecstasy.
3) A wide variety of flavors to choose from, like non-red lychee or lilikoi (passion fruit).

—Elizabeth Phegan reporting from Wilson's By the Bay, in Hilo, Hawaii, January 2000

---

shelf *n.* A reef or rock formation under-water that drops off sharply. Shore-bound waves hitting this shelf often jack up, creating a larger and faster-breaking wave than if the wave ran its normal course. Waimea Bay is a good example of a shelf type break.

shifting peak *n.* A wave breaking over a seabed dotted with many small bars or reefs, whose irregularity causes the breaking depth to change from wave to wave, so that the peak—and hence the takeoff point—is constantly shifting. Ocean Beach in San Francisco is a good example.

shifty *adj.* Said of waves that don't break in a consistent spot. Usage: "The waves are extremely shifty." See DISORGANIZED.

shine, shine it, shine on that *v.* Forget it now. (TMA) Usage: "Let's shine this place." "We fully shined it." "Shine on that. Come to the party." (California 1980s)

shiner *n.* Someone who says they'll meet you in fifteen minutes and then never shows up—they fully bail and shine you. (Nags Head, North Carolina, 1991)

shinner *n.* What you get when a skim-board hits your shin. (TLH)

shishi *n.* A local (Hawaiian) word of Japanese origin for urine; also an old Hawaiian remedy for removing embed-ded sea urchin spines and other marine-organism stings (to be used locally, not orally). (S&S)

shite hawks *n.* Seagulls; they feed off sewage. (United Kingdom) Also called SEA RATS.

Shit Pipe *n.* A Redondo Beach surf spot next to a sewage outflow pipe.

shoal *n.* A sandbar or reef formation that cre-ates shallow water.

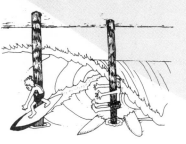

shooting the pier
Art: Robbie Quine

shoaling *n.* A process when deep ocean swells "feel the bottom" and mound upward as they strike a reef.

shoaling waves *n.* Waves that, because of the way they jack up and shift around in shallow water, are said to "feel the bottom" as they approach shore.

shock cord *n.* An early term for SURF LEASH.

shock wave *n.* A side-wake caused by the motion of a fast board across the face of a large wave.

shoot *v.* To ride a wave, as in "shoot the curl." (DSHJ)

shoot the curl *v.* **1)** Riding through the curling or tubing part of a wave; making a hot section. **2)** Catching a wave at exactly the right moment and riding it all the way in to the beach. Usage: "Did you see me shoot the curl?" **—shooting the curl** *n.*

shoot the pier *v.* To ride a wave in between and through the pilings of a wharf or pier, or to attempt such a ride. **—shooting the pier** *n.*

shoot the tube *v.* To ride through a tight curl, so that the breaking wave is actually arching over the board, the rider, or both. **—shooting the tube** *n.*

shoot the tunnel *v.* To slide very rap-idly through a tunneling wave, same as SHOOT THE TUBE, SHOOT THE CURL.**—shooting the tunnel** *n.*

shop rat *n.* Kid who hangs around a surf shop. (1997)

shore break or **shore-break** *n.*
1) Waves (usually small) breaking close to shore or directly on beaches. **2)** A breaker line caused by an abruptly shoaling bottom close to shore. The waves of such a break usually steepen and topple over quickly in shallow depths, and are therefore difficult and dangerous to ride. (DSH) Same as BEACH BREAK. **—whomping shorebreak**

shore pound *n.* A very hard-breaking wave, usually thick in the lip and hitting right on the shore.

shortboard or **short board** *n.* **1)** A lightweight surfboard designed for high-performance surfing; usually five to seven feet long. **2)** The Australian term for a general-purpose or hot-dog board. (JKMJ, 1965)

A ʌhortboard can be turned more eaʌily and iʌ quicker and more maneuverable than a longboard. It iʌ also ʌenʌitive to front/rear weight tranʌfer, which helpʌ in

negotiating a ʌteep drop in ʌmall ʌurf without pearling. A ʌurfer can generate ʌpeed by quickly maneuvering through critical ʌectionʌ of a wave.

Shortboard Revolution *n.* A trend toward using shorter boards that began in Australia in the late 1960s. George Greenough is the California innovator who most influenced the movement in Australia. (SFR, June 1988) Other names associated with shortboards are Bob McTavish and Nat Young.

shortboarder *n.* Someone who rides a shortboard.

short john *n.* A sleeveless wetsuit with the legs cut off above the knees, as distinct from a LONG JOHN. Usage: "I've got a short john in my trunk."

shorty *n.* SHORT JOHN.

shoulder *n.* **1)** The smooth hump of a breaking wave that moves ahead of the curl but has not yet become an actual wall. **2)** The unbroken section next to the white water, or next to the curling hook. **3)** The part of a wave that hasn't

broken yet (ORB); the flat, slow part of the wave. **4)** The smoothly rounded end or edge of a wave away from the soup. **5)** The section to either side of the peak of a wave. Usually, the peak breaks first, with the curl spreading progressively along the shoulders. (DSHJ)

shoulder city *n.* Waves that are shoulder-high. (JP)

shoulder hopper *n.* **1)** Someone who insists on sharing a wave, thereby breaking the taboo of one wave, one surfer. (CVG) **2)** A surfer who cuts in on another surfer's right-of-way. (MM) See DROPPING IN, SNAKING WAVES.

shoulder hopper
Art: Jimbo Phillips

"**Shoulder hopper, don't drop in on me.**"

—*Surf Punks,* "*Shoulder Hopper*" (1980)

shoulder surfers *n.* Police term for scammers who peer over the shoulders of people using cards to charge their calls at pay phones. Numbers are quickly memorized or recorded, and then they look for someone who wants to buy cheap phone time on someone else's card—such as an international visitor at an airport. (*Scientific American,* March 1994)

shoulder surfing *n.* Athletic celebration; "If the shoulder surfing he was doing in the end zone on the arms and shoulders of his 49ers teammates after the touchdown run was any indication, we can surmise that there were no hard feelings." (C. W. Nevius, *San Francisco Chronicle,* September 26, 1994)

shoulder turn *n.* Turning with the shoulders rotating in the direction of the turn.

shoulder zip *n.* A horizontal zipper that runs along the upper back of a wetsuit. (IBN)

shower *n.* **1)** A place to rinse your gear off. **2)** Unfortunately, for those of us who love the feeling of salt caked on our skin after a surf, increasing pollution of the ocean has made it almost a necessity to shower after a session to avoid irritated skin or getting sick.

shrack *v.* Hybrid of SHRED, SHRALP, and SPRACK.

shralp or **schralp** *v.* Kind of lame word used to describe someone who is SHREDDING

shoulder zip
Gabe Sermeno
Photo: Trevor Cralle

or TEARING IT UP. (SP) Usage: "Dude, you were fully shralping out there."

shred *v.* To tear up the waves while surfing; to ride the waves well. (H&R, JP) Usage: "Those guys were really shredding it up." See RIP. According to Michael Girvin, the term originated from skateboard trucks that became shredded on the coping of a swimming pool.

shrivel cockitus syndrome *n.* See GATOR MINI. (Santa Cruz)

shuffle, shuffling *v.* **1)** To move toward the nose of the board without crossing foot over foot, usually a sliding maneuver. **2)** To change position on a surfboard without a walking step. **3)** To slide up or down the board without letting one's feet leave the deck. (A&M)

sick *adj.* Australian for great, awesome, unreal. Usage: "Rincon could be sick."

side current *n.* CROSSCURRENT.

side drift *n.* See RIP CURRENT.

side fin *n.* Same as HELPER FIN.

sider *n.* A skimboarder's term for any beach where you can ride a rebound wave out and catch an incoming wave back in to shore. The Wedge in Newport Beach is a good example. (TLH)

side ride *n.* Riding a bodyboard lying on one's side, possible only on a very steep wave.

sideshore wind *n.* A wind that blows parallel to the waves, making them a bit choppy and causing them to break early.

sideslip *n.* The act of releasing the rail that is in the wave so that the surfboard slides sideways; somewhat like a skiing or snowboarding sideslip.

sideslipping or **side-slipping** *n.* The drift of the forward end of a surfboard diagonally down the face of a wave, a natural component of the motion of wave riding. **—sideslipping on the nose, sideslipping in the curl**

sidewalk surfin' *n.* **1)** A sixties term for SKATEBOARDING. (MM) **2) "Sidewalk Surfin'"** A song by Jan & Dean (October 1964) about the skateboard craze. Brian Wilson originally penned the tune for The Beach Boys as "Catch a Wave"; Roger Christian rewrote the lyrics.

side wedge *n.* Caused by wave refraction off a cliff, jetty, or groin.

Silver Surfer A Marvel comic book character.

Cameron Stover
Photo: Judith Cralle

Silver Surfer
Issue Number One
Courtesy of Jim Phillips

The Pizz

SIMA Surf Industry Manufacturers Association, formed in 1989.

Simmons, Bob A Southern California surfer with an engineering background who made major contributions to surfboard construction and who provided the link between the redwood board and the modern surfboard in the 1940s and early 1950s. He died in 1954, when his own board slapped him on the head at Windansea. (GN)

Simmons played a central role in the following innovations: 1) the transition to lighter-weight boards (he experimented with different materials, such as sandwiching balsa, plywood, and Styrofoam together); 2) the use of fiberglass (he was the first to combine lightweight materials and fiberglass); 3) the use of foam in a surfboard (he was the first person ever to try foam in a surfboard—polystyrene foam in 1950s).

single fin *n.* A surfboard with one fin.

*"One God
One Country
One Fin"*

—*California bumper sticker. c. 1992*

sinker *n.* Any ding in which there is a hole to be filled; the most common type of ding on earth. (GCD) See CRUNCHER.

sitting island pullout *n.* An ISLAND PULLOUT in the sitting position.

size *adj.* Refers to WAVE SIZE. Usage: "Malibu and Dume have size, but the tides aren't quite right."

sizeable *adj.* A decent wave height. "It's a sunny, blustery afternoon on the Bay of Biscay, and the swell, though sizeable, is bumpy and confused." —Rob Buchanan, "Mr. Sunset Rides Again," *Outside,* April 2000

sizzler *n.* Someone who is boisterous and at the same time conspicuously out of place; inappropriately vain. (Newport Beach; ALN)

skag *n.* **1)** A rare spelling of SKEG, the fin at the end of a surfboard. (IDSM) **2)** An ugly woman.

skankamangus *n.* A rather large woman walking down the beach. (Southern California)

skateboard *n.* Originally a skate mounted on a short piece of wood shaped like a miniature surfboard. Made of fiberglass in the 1970s and again of wood in the 1980s to the present.

skateboarding *n.* A pastime and sport that originated in Southern California in 1963 when an unknown creator put together a simple vehicle consisting of a small, short board with round ends and two pairs of roller skate wheels mounted to the underside. Like a surfboard, a skateboard is ridden standing

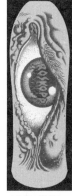

Art: Jim Phillips

Art: Jim Phillips

up or squatting down. Also called ASPHALT SURFING, SIDEWALK SURFIN'. See SURF-SKATE SYNTHESIS.

～～～～～～～～～～～～～～

The initial fad for skateboards lasted only about two years in the early sixties, though it was nationwide. Interest revived around 1975, again in Southern California, with the introduction of fiberglass boards whose polyurethane wheels allowed riders to move at great speeds and to perform athletic movements resembling those achieved on surfboards. Professional teams and championship tournaments soon came into being, as did a popular literature of magazines on the subject, such as *Thrasher*. Moves like "the McTwist," "hydro ollie-hop," and "fakie" and expressions like "boneless" and "boomin'" have grown out of the culture, which has also given birth to a punk skate band called McRad. (JDH)

Skateboarders do their thing in (or on) all sorts of places, including empty swimming pools, skate parks (in the 1970s) and presently, large drain pipes and half pipes, homemade backyard ramps, ditches, curbs—and, of course, streets and sidewalks. In the 1970s, Larry Bertlemann,

Buttons Kaluhiokalani, Mark Liddell, Dane Kealoha, and Cheyne Horan integrated skateboard moves into their surfing.

"Skateboarding Is Not a Crime."
—Popular bumper sticker

～～～～～～～～～～～～～～

skating *n.* **1)** PUMP TURN—a surfing maneuver that helps the rider traverse the slow part of a wave. (L&L) Usage: "I was skating through that last section." **2)** A bodysurfing technique using the hands as a planing surface. (MF)

skeg *n.* The fixed, rudderlike fin on the bottom rear of a surfboard that allows the surfer to steer; also provides directional stability and holds the stern of the board in the wave. The skeg was invented by Tom Blake in 1935. Also called FIN.

skeg first, skeg reverse *n.* Intentionally dropping into a wave tail first, just for the fun of spinning around with the board. (MVA, WWK)

skegged *adj.* Same as FINNED. Usage: "That scar on my foot is from when I got skegged in Baja."

skeggin' *adj.* Having great fun, as in a "skeggin' party" or a "skeggin' time."

skeg hum, skeg whine *n.* See WHISTLING SKEG.

Skegness *n.* A town in England. As far as known, it has nothing to do with surfboard fins.

skim *n.* To SKIMBOARD. Usage: "I skim."

skimboard or **skim board** *n.* A rounded plywood or fiberglass board two or three feet across, used to slide over the shallow water at the water's edge.

skimboarding, skimming *n.* Standing up on a flat board and riding it along the shoreline on top of a thin layer of water. Also called SANDSLIDING.

skin *n.* **1)** The outside layer of a foam blank. **2)** What you lose when dragged over the coral reef at Banzai Pipeline in Hawaii. (ATRL)

skin cancer *n.* Acquired from spending too much time out in the sun without the proper protection, such as sunscreen with a high SPF rating. Nature's way of telling us we're no longer needed.

skin it *v.* Surfing without a wetsuit, as in "Let's skin it." (CSD) Same as TRUNK IT, BARE BACK.

skitter board *n.* **1)** A fast, finless, flat-bottomed bellyboard or paipo board about forty-two inches long and thirty inches wide and around three-eighths of an inch thick—one of the fastest wave-riding devices. **2)** An old term for SKIMBOARD.

skurfing *n.* A combination of water skiing and surfing, where the rider is towed behind a speedboat on a **skurfer**, a specialized board with foot straps.

skysurfing *n.* Hang gliding. (From Dan Poynter's book *Hang Gliding: The Basic Handbook of Skysurfing*)

slab *n.* **1)** An extremely hollow, cold, thick, dark, spooky wave. (Marin County, California). **2)** PLANK.

slack, slack tide, slack water *n.* **1)** The period between the ebb and flow of the tide, when the water is relatively motionless. **2)** The quiet period between sets of waves.

slap-down *n.* What the front of your board does when you scratch over the top of a wave while paddling out.

slaps it off the top A phrase commonly used by surf contest announcers to describe a sharp turn at the top of a wave; same as WHACKS IT OFF THE TOP. Usage: ". . . and she slaps it off the top!"

slash 1) *n.* A radical, carving cutback, performed on the steep face of a wave. (MW) **2) slashing** *v., adj.* Usage: "I saw you slashing on the inside." "He ripped a slashing backside bottom turn." **3) slashing off the lip** Doing an aerial.

s'later "See you later."

sleeper, sleeper wave *v.* A wave that sneaks up on you and is larger than usual.

sleeper set *n.* SNEAKER SET.

slibity *n.* A police. (Half Moon Bay; PPJ)

slice, slicing *v.* **1)** To carve a turn or cut through a wave. **2)** To run over another surfboard. Usage: "I sliced his board."

slide *n.* **1)** A long track down a large wave from which a safe deviation is usually not possible without wiping out. **2)** A diagonal descent on a wave. (MM) **3) sliding** Movement across the face of a wave, as opposed to going straight in with the wave. **4)** *v.* To ride either left or right, on a track somewhat parallel to shore. See STRAIGHT OFF.

skimboarding
Wipeout, Maui
Photo: Don Balch

snowboarding

Top: Stephanie Morgan
Bottom: Trevor Cralle
Northstar, Lake Tahoe, California

Photos: Trevor and Stephanie

slimeball *n.* An undesirable person or obnoxious surfer. (JP)

sling off *n.* To maneuver out of a wave; to pull out. (JKMJ, 1967)

slip slops *n.* (South Africa) Mostly called "slops," they are what Australians call thongs, or sandals. Proper slops are made from rubber and have a strap between your big toe and its partner. (WVS)

slop *n.* **1)** Small, mushy, sometimes blown-out surf that is chopped up by crosswinds and tides but is otherwise surfable. **2)** Very poor surf. **3)** Wind-forced wavelets a maximum of two feet high. L&L) **4)** Unridable waves. (H&R)

slope *n.* The curvature of the face of an unbroken wave.

slopey *adj.* Used to describe steep waves. Usage: "The waves are really slopey." (T & C Surf Shop, Ala Moana, Hawaii)

sloppy *adj.* Characteristic of surf in an onshore wind, when waves collapse and are formless or irregular. Usage: "Sloppy surf today, bro." (MW, MF)

slot *n.* **1)** A hole in which a skeg can be affixed; same as FIN SLOT. **2)** The most desirable riding area of a wave, where the rider is in position to plane; a little less than halfway up from the forefront to the crest—that is, in the curl. To be slotted in is much preferable to being far out on the shoulder of a wave.

slot wave *n.* A wave in between the peaks of other waves, such as at Steamer Lane, Santa Cruz. (IBN)

slow motion wave *n.* A wave that appears to be breaking much slower than regular speed.

slow surf *n.* Slow waves, as distinct from ZIPPERS. In slow surf, you have to work really hard to catch a wave, and the ride usually doesn't last very long.

sluggo *n.* An Australian term for a G-string bikini.

smack *v.* To hit or rebound, as in "to smack the lip of a wave."

small craft advisory *n.* A warning broadcast on the weather radio indicating winds over twenty-five knots and surf that may become blown out.

smash, smashing *v.* SLASHING.

smerfect *adj.* Small and perfect (waves).

smog monster *n.* A derogatory term for an inland surfer. (Southern California; KH)

smokin' a pipe *v., n.* Speeding down the face of a wave in the tube. (MM) Usage: "I was smokin' a pipe out there."

smurf *n.* **1)** Small surf. (Texas; H&R) **2) smurfage** Many small waves.

"I wish I was smurph size."

—*Anonymous Santa Cruz grommet*

---

snake, snaking waves *v.* To drop down in front of another surfer who is already riding a wave. See SHOULDER HOPPER, RAT HOLING.

snake pit *n.* A wave full of shoulder hoppers. (San Francisco; JWN)

snap *n., v.* Riding directly into a wave and flipping around 180 degrees to begin riding the face. (JP) Usage: "Did you see that lip snap I pulled off?" "You really snapped it out there on the shoulder."

snapback or **snap-back** or **snap back** *n.* A move invented by Ian Cairns in the early 1970s; rather than easing into a long, sweeping cutback, you race out onto the shoulder and then jam the full force of your body weight back onto the inside rail so violently that the board virtually comes to a stop. (L&L)

snap off the face *n.* A surfing maneuver. See SNAP.

snapped board *n.* A surfboard that has broken into two pieces. Usage: "I snapped my board." See BROKEN BOARD.

snappy *adj.* Said of bitchin' waves or babes.

snap turn *n.* A radical change in direction. (L&L)

sneaker set *n.* A surprise group of larger-than-normal waves that come out of nowhere. (KSO) Same as SLEEPER SET.

sneaker wave *n.* SLEEPER WAVE.

snibbler *n.* Someone who tries to get everything for nothing—free lunch, free wax, free boards, etc. (Southern California; TMA)

snog, snog up *v.* A term with a flirtatious, sex-driven connotation—to encroach on someone's personal space, for example, when some slimeball is sleezing up to a girl at the beach. Not necessarily a bad thing to have happen if the person being **snogged** is interested in the person doing the **snogging**. (Newport Beach)

snowboarding *n.* Riding a specialized board on snow-covered mountain ski slopes. This surfing spin-off sport was featured in the opening sequence of the James Bond movie *A View to a Kill* (1985), where 007 surfs down the mountain.

A miniglossary of snowboarding terms follows: 1) BOARDHEAD Someone who snowboards all the time. 2) BOARDIN' Snowboarding, as in "Let's go boardin'." (RO) 3) LAME AIR Not very high. 4) LAWN-CHAIR AIR Going really high in the air, then falling on the snow and collapsing like a lawn chair. 5) HAIRSPRAY AIR Jumping so high that you puncture the ozone. (JGD) 6) FAKIE Riding backward or switch stance. 7) FASTIE Fast snowboarder. 8) KNUCKLE DRAGGER Derogatory term for a snowboarder (1991). 9) POW POW Powder. 10) STEEPS Steep snow slope.

snowsurfing *n.* An old term for SNOWBOARDING. (SFG, October 1985)

snuff, snuff out *v.* To WIPEOUT really fast; to be covered by the curl or tube and either disappear or be blasted off the board. Usage: "That wave totally snuffed me."

snurfing *n.* Surfing with a soft, Doyle board; not necessarily derogatory. Derived from Nerf ball—like snurf. (St.

soar
Ken Collins,
Santa Crucial
Photo: Mike Peralta

Malo, Oceanside,
California)

soaker *n.* **1)** A surfer who
never takes a wave; a DUCK or BUOY.
2) Someone who just sits out in the lineup
and **soaks up** the sun and the saltwater.

soar *v.* Getting major air over the lip.
Usage: "Dude, you soar." See MINUTE AIR.

So Cal SOUTHERN CALIFORNIA.

sofa surfing *n.* COUCH SURFING.

soft *adj.* Used to describe slow, gentle
surf that hasn't much energy. Usage:
"The waves are pretty soft today."

soft board *n.* **1)** A surfboard made of soft
sponge foam. **2)** A compliant surfboard
that is easily maneuvered. See SNURFING.

soft rack *n.* A surf rack made from foam
pads strapped across the roof of a car.

soft rail *n.* A rounded rail with a softer,
less defined edge that makes the board
looser.

soft wing *n.* A wing with a less defined
edge. **—soft-wing swallowtail**

sognar (sog-nar) *v.* When a dog that's
been playing in the ocean comes up and
shakes off on you; to get sprayed.
Usage: "I got **sognared** by my dog."
(Santa Barbara; TJ and his dog, Mort)

solid *adj.* **1)** Used to describe the feel of
a surfboard or a wave. Usage: "Your
board really feels solid." "That last wave
felt really solid." **2)** Looking like a good-
size wave; solid waves
are five to six feet.
(WWK) Usage: "It
was a solid six feet
out there today."

sognar
Art: Rick Stover

soul arch *n.* A back bend while surfing; a
wave rider's posture, as in a Lopezesque
soul arch (named for Gerry Lopez). Also
called ARCH.

soul barney *n.* **1)** A surfer who surfs in
his own way without caring about what
others think of his style or other competitive perceptions. **2)** A surfer in his
or her mid-30s and 40s. (Westside,
Santa Cruz)

soul surfer *n.* **1)** A surfer who surfs for
the joy of it. **2)** A noncompetitive surfer.
(MM) **—soul surfing**

sound *v.* **1)** To deliver harsh words to an
unwelcome surfer. Usage: "That dude
totally sounded me." **2)** To dive to the
bottom of the ocean. (JKMJ, 1965)

soup *n.* **1)** The turbulent foam created by
a wave's breaking; not very suitable for
surfing, and often dangerous in big surf.
Also called FROTH, SWASH, WHITE WATER.
2) A mixture of air bubbles and moving
water.**—soupy** *adj.*

soup bowl *n.* The white-water area
known as the BONE YARD.

south *n.* SOUTH SWELL. Usage: "There's supposed to be a **monster south** on the
way." See BIG SOUTH.

solid
A solid 10-foot-wave
—if not bigger
Photo: Don Balch

Southern California *n.* **1)** The mythological capital of the sport of surfing and its attendant lifestyles—a creation helped along by music and movies about surfing. George Freeth was the first person to surf Southern California, at Redondo Beach in 1907. (BHP) See CALIFORNIA MYTH. **2)** In a strict geographic sense, the area in California beginning at Point Conception and continuing to the Mexican border. As a social and stylistic boundary within the surfing world, however, the dividing line between the northern and southern part of the state is debatable; the transition begins somewhere around Santa Barbara and Oxnard. (SFR) Also called SO CAL.

southers *n.* A derogatory term for Southern California surfers.

south-facing beach *n.* Where the coastline is oriented in an east-west direction, such as at Malibu and Santa Cruz.

south swell *n.* A swell that moves from the south to the north. (ORB)

south wind *n.* A wind that blows from south to north. (ORB) Usage: "The wind has a little south in it."

spaghetti arms *n.* A condition caused by surfing for hours on end. In Australia when the classic point breaks are happening, you can't stop even after riding incredibly long waves because the good waves are so numerous you can't stand to see them go to waste. So you continue surfing for hours, and all that paddling makes your arms and legs tired and heavy. (MW)

Spanish for surfers See "Spanish for the Mexico-Bound Surfer" on page 242.

sparkle factor *n.* **1)** The diamondlike glistening of the sun's rays reflecting off the ocean, especially in the afternoon as the sun goes down. **2)** The glitter of moonglow on the ocean. **3)** Whether created by the sun or moon, one of the most pleasing visual sensations of being at the beach or floating in the lineup.

"Innumerable twinkling of the waves of the sea"

—*Aeschylus (525–456 B.C.) in* Prometheus Bound

sparkle room *n.* Inside the tube; same as GREEN ROOM.

spat out *adj.* The fortunate few who have been spat out of a tube with a burst of spray when compressed air caught in the swirling cylinder is suddenly released. (WVS) See TUBE SPIT.

specialty fins *n.* Fins designed for specific surfing conditions, such as the omega fin, which is designed so it won't grab kelp.

sparkle factor
Tex Wilson
Photo: Bob Richardson

speed bead n. A resin ridge near the rail on the bottom of a surfboard, the purpose of which is to direct water flow and increase speed. (ORB)

speed bump n. SPONGE. (SWH)

speed finish n. A thin layer of fiberglass applied to a surfboard to enhance high-performance surfing; makes the board lighter but doesn't last as long as a regular glass job.

speed run n. A skimboarding maneuver in which the skimboard rides out into an incoming wave and surfs it back onto the beach.

Spanish for the Mexico-Bound Surfer*

For many American surfers, a burning desire to escape the crowded conditions of the home break spells MEXICO. Travel is one of the most exciting aspects of surfing—and possibly the most educational part of life—but it requires some minimum language skills to maximize the possibility of positive contact with the natives of the country visited. Anybody who has ever traveled to Baja or mainland Mexico with a Spanish speaker knows the advantages of being able to communicate with the people. Most Mexicans have become used to the "stupid gringo" who travels south to take a cut-rate vacation, drink cheap beer, and buy souvenirs; so don't be surprised if you get treated less than warmly when you make requests to a Mexican in English.

The following simple guidelines will help you increase your chances of having good, even memorable experiences. Even if your Spanish is horrible, it's worth it to make an effort because it is the recognition of this effort that creates a bridge of understanding and shows that you are different from the *gringo típico* to whom the Mexicans have numbed themselves. As you will learn, Mexicans are very generous and hospitable to travelers who are hip to their culture and language. So don't be shy, put yourself on the line and try to speak what you know, even if you think it's really bad. (P) See pages 244–245.

"Pack Your Trash"
in Spanish, translated
by Bill Dawson

Art: Jim Phillips

*May be useful in Spain as well as Latin American countries.

speed shape *n*. A surfboard shape featuring an elongated nose and tail; developed around 1972.

speed tails *n*. A surfboard with a sleek shape designed for speed. (A&M) See SPEED SHAPE.

speedy *adj*. Said of a fast wave. See WAVE SPEED, MAALAEA, ZIPPER.

spent *adj*. Physically exhausted after a surf session. See KACKED, TAPPED.

SPF Sun protection factor—the rating number on sun screen tubes and bottles (2, 4, 6, 8, 10, etc., up to total blockout) that refers to the amount of time you can expect to be protected from the sun's harmful ultraviolet rays. For example, an SPF #8 rating means that you can stay in the sun eight times longer and be protected. Nonetheless, the time varies for each individual.

Spicoli, Jeff 1) A character played by Sean Penn in the movie *Fast Times at Ridgemont High* (1982). Pot smoking, long haired, and a poor student, personified one version of the modern surfer. Because of Spicoli, terms like *dude* and *gnarly* entered the mainstream. ("Hey, dude—let's party!") **2) spicoli** Someone who acts or looks like the character in the movie. Usage: "He's a total spicoli."

spider ding *n*. A small, cobweb-like fracture of the fiberglass skin on the rail of a surfboard. (BP)

spilling wave, spilling breaker, spiller *n*. **1)** A cresting wave that breaks forward gradually, crumbling at the top and spilling down the front. Such a wave breaks slowly and without the violent release of energy needed to fling the crest forward into the trough ahead. A good example is the surf at Waikiki in Hawaii. (WB) **2)** A wave that spills over instead of breaking clean. See FEATHERING WAVE.

Stocar

The Spanish verb "to stoke."

yo stoco (I stoke)

tu stocas (you stoke)

el/ella/usted stoca (he/she/ you stoke pl.)

nos stocamos (we stoke)

ellos/ellas/ustedes stoca (them/you stoke pl.)

stocado Stoked.

stoquito A little stoked.

stocando Stoking (gerund form).

El Stocador del fuego Fire stoker; said of anyone stoking the campfire.

La Stocadora A female stoker.

Spanish Pronunciation Made Easy

Pronunciation of vowels:

a	ah	as in *taco*
e	eh	as in *cerveza* (a key word)
i	ee	as in *hijo* (pronounced EE-ho)
o	oh	as in *hola* and *ola* ("hello" and "wave," respectively—very important words)
u	oo	as in *rubio* ("blonde," something Mexicans are fond of calling anyone who has light-colored hair)

Pronunciation of tricky consonants:

g	pronounced like *h* in English when followed by *e* or *i*, for example, *gente* ("people"); when followed by *a, o, u,* or a consonant, pronounced like *g* in *grommet*
h	always silent, for example, *hombre* ("man")
j	pronounced like *h* in Hawaii, for example, *jardin* ("garden")
ll	pronounced like *y* in *your*, for example, *Me llamo . . .*
ñ	pronounced somewhat like *ni* in *onion*, for example, *año, enseñor* ("year" and "to teach," respectively)
q	pronounced like *c* in English *come*; always followed by *ue* or *ui*, in which the *u* is silent, for example, *querer* and *quitar* ("to want" and "to remove" or "to take away," respectively); the sound of English *qu* is represented in Spanish by *cu*, for example, *cuenta* ("bill" or "check")
z	pronounced like *s* in English *surf* in Latin America, and like *th* in English *thruster* in Spain (Castilian Spanish), for example, *zapato* ("shoe")

"Silver Slider"
aka Silver Surfer
Courtesy of Jim Phillips

Key Words and Phrases

por favor: please

arrecife: reef

gracias: thank you

patinaje sobre las olas, surfear: surfing

de nada: you're welcome

lo siento: I'm sorry

tabla de surf: surfboard

ola: wave

cera de surf: surf wax

la playa: beach

grande: big

el tiburón: shark

pequeño: small

el pilluelo: sea urchin

océano: ocean

el viento: wind

canal: channel

terral: offshore wind

marea: tide

tubo: tube

alto: high

punta: point

bajo: low

¿ Dónde está . . . ?	Where is . . . ?
¿Cuanto cuesta?	How much does it cost, how much is . . . ?
La cuenta, por favor.	May I have the check, please?
¿Cómo se llama, usted?	What is your name?
Me llamo . . .	My name is . . .
¿De dónde es, usted?	Where are you from?
Yo soy de . . .	I am from . . .
Soy Norteamericano.	I am American. (It's important to say "norte" because in Latin America the people also consider themselves American.)

spinner *n.* **1)** A maneuver in which the surfer turns around 360 degrees on the board while riding a wave. This move is distinct from a three sixty, where the board itself is rotated in a full-circle turn. **2)** A 360-degree body spin or twist on a Malibu. (NAT, 1985)

spinning board *n.* The fate of a board thrown into the air by the force of a wave, aided by its buoyancy. Usage: "Look at that spinning board."

spin out *v.* What happens when the skeg and tail lose contact with the wave face, usually because of the sharpness of a turn or the tightness of the trimming, and the rider takes a spill. Usage: "Did you see me spin out on that wave?" **—spinout** *n.*

spiral V *n.* A vee in the tail section of the bottom of a surfboard that comes to a point under the backfoot area. (L&L) This design helps channel water away from the board.

spities *n.* Grommets who are spiteful and talk back. (Santa Cruz)

spitter *n.* A tubing wave that emits air and spray as it collapses. Air caught in a curl must go somewhere when a wave collapses; if there is an open end, the air and spray hiss out and the wave is called a "spitter." See TUBE SPIT.

splampted *n.* To get wiped out. (LH)

spleet *n.* GEEK or GOON. (Florida; TDW)

splitting peaks *v.* When two surfers take off in opposite directions from the main peak of the wave. Usage: "We were splitting peaks."

spock out, spock *v.* To check, peruse, or look over. Usage: "Hey man, spock this out." "Did you spock out that last cutback I did?" (SFG, December 1981)

sponge *n.* **1)** A degrading term for boogie boarders, who surf on soft, flexible foam boards. Also called *sponge heads, sponge people, sponge riders, spongers.* Usage: "Kind of a sponge problem out here, dude." (California) See BOOGIE FLAPPER. **2)** A leech.

spoon *n.* The upturned nose of a surfboard, whose purpose is to keep the board from pearling; made popular by Reynolds Yater. (MCR) Also called SCOOP, CAMBER, ROCKER.

spot *n.* The place where waves are generated; a SURF SPOT. Usage: "That spot is totally happening." **—hot spot**

sprack *v.* When you hit the lip so hard it actually makes a popping sound. (Santa Cruz) See SHRACK.

spray *n.* See OCEAN SPRAY.

spring suit *n.* A wetsuit with either long or short arms and short legs cut above the knee.

spring tides *n.* Tides that occur twice a month, at the new and full moons, when the sun and the moon are in line with the earth and their combined gravitational force produces tides that are of greater magnitude than average. The highest high tide and lowest low tide occur during spring tides.

squall *n.* A gust of violent wind, often accompanied by heavy rain, and lasting only a short while; a common occurrence

squid
Art: The Pizz

in the tropics. See WIND SQUALL, RAIN SQUALL.

squall line *n.* An advancing wall of rain. Usage: "Look at that squall line out over the water."

square *n.* **1)** An extremely hollow wave whose bottom drops quickly as the top pitches, stretching the wave face vertically and creating "corners" on the wave profile; can be dangerous to surfers, as in "You see the wave go square." The term originated in Australia but is also used in the U.S. (MW) **2)** One of the tail shapes of a surfboard; also the name of a surfboard with a square tail.

squared-off fin *n.* STRAIGHT-EDGE FIN.

square tail or **squaretail** *n.* A surfboard with the tail squared off, rather than rounded or pointed.

squash tail or **squashtail** *n.* A surfboard design. A squared-off tail looks like either a square tail with blunted corners or a pintail that's been dropped on the ground. (SFG, April 1987)

squatting island pullout *n.* An ISLAND PULLOUT made in a squatting position. See SITTING ISLAND PULLOUT, STANDING ISLAND PULLOUT.

squatting through *v.* To crouch down to avoid being caught by the curl of a wave as it pours over. Usage: "Did you see me squatting through that cover-up?"

squealy *adj.* Used to describe a surfboard that performs very loosely, in contrast to one that is stiff and has stable handling characteristics.

squeegee *n.* In surfboard construction, a rubber tool used to force resin into fiberglass cloth so that the cloth becomes saturated.

squid, squid head *n.* KOOK; sometimes spelled *skwid*. —**inland squid**

squid lid *n.* A derogatory term for the neoprene hood that some surfers wear in cold water.

squid lips *n.* **1)** GEEK. **2)** A term for an overweight surfer. (H&R) Usage: "Hey—outta my way, squid lips."

stable *adj.* A surfboard handling characteristic; said of a board that maintains **stability** on a wave, for example by holding on the wave face through a turn. The opposite of SQUEALY.

stacked, stacked up *v., adj.*
1) Describes the situation of several surfers grouped closely—one above another—in or on a wave. Usage: "Check out that wave—those guys are completely stacked." **2)** Said of a group of many parallel waves, or lines, coming toward shore. **3)** Crashed; wiped out. Usage: "I fully stacked it on the rocks." —**stacking it**

stall, stalling *v.* **1)** To slow one's forward speed in order to reposition oneself on the face of a breaking wave; similar to FADE. **2)** To slow the board when it has outdistanced a wave, usually by climbing up the wave's face, so that the curl can catch up with the surfer. **3)** To slow a board down and pull it out of a wave. (IDSM) **4)** To slow the board while waiting for the wave to steepen ahead. —**stall** *n.*

squid lid
Matt Albert
Photo: Trevor Cralle

247

stacked
Photo: Robert Brown

> To stall a board, the surfer steps back, shifting his or her weight to the rear of the board, and angles the board up toward the top of the wave. A bodysurfer can stall by raising head and shoulders.

stall out 1) *v.* To lose the wave by letting the nose of the surfboard ride too high. (DSHJ); **stalled out. 2) stallout** *n.* A stall held long enough to let the wave pass by.

standard *n.* **1)** A type of surfboard. Same as STOCK. **2)** A surfer who rides with the left foot forward; a left-foot-forward stance. Same as NATURAL. See GOOFY FOOT.

standard foil *n.* See FOIL.

standing island, standing island pullout *n.* **1)** An ISLAND PULLOUT made in a standing position. See SITTING ISLAND PULLOUT, SQUATTING ISLAND PULLOUT. **2)** A pullout in which the rider slashes through the back of a wave while standing toward the front or on the nose of the board.

standing up The normal surfboard position—standing on two feet as you ride a wave in to shore, as opposed to kneeling or lying on your stomach.

standing wave *n.* A spot on a river where water coursing over a rock consistently forms a wave that a surfer can ride while remaining in one place. This happens, for example, on the Snake River in Wyoming and on the Eisbach River in Munich, Germany. Same as STATIONARY WAVE. See RIVER SURFING.

stand up 1) *v.* The motion of a swell as it comes out of deep water and rises to break. (MW) Usage: "That swell really stands up on the outside reef." See JACK. **2) stand-up** *n.* A beginning bodyboarding move.

stand up, stand-up surfer *n.* Describes anyone who stands on two feet while riding a surfboard, as distinct from a BODYBOARDER, KNEEBOARDER, etc.

—stand ups (A group of surfers)

stand-up tube *n.* A tube large enough for a surfer to stand up inside of it.

—stand-up barrel

Statue of the Unknown Surfer
Santa Cruz, California
Photo: Trevor Cralle

star tail *n.* A surfboard tail that ends in two points, rather than in a single point, as in a pintail.

stationary wave *n.* STANDING WAVE.

Statue of Liberty *n.* A cutback or snapback right in the hook, in which the surfer's leading arm raises high like the Statue of Liberty's. (SFG, December 1981)

Statue of the Unknown Surfer *n.* A bronze sculpture, dedicated on May 23, 1992, located on the blufftop along West Cliff Drive above Steamer Lane in Santa Cruz. "Dedicated to all surfers, past, present, and future." Flower leis are frequently placed around his neck.

stay dry An expression meaning "Don't take that wave." (LH) Usage: "Dude, stay dry."

staying high in the section *v., n.* **1)** Riding in the upper portion of the wave crest as a means of gaining speed. **2)** Taking a track across the wave's lip in order to get the most out of the available energy. (A&M)

stay-wag *n.* A station wagon. (LWK) See LAND YACHT.

steamer *n.* An Australian term for FULL SUIT, a wetsuit with long arms and legs. (NAT, 1985)

steamer lane *n.* **1)** The general area where ships pass by offshore. **2)** Loosely, any place far out from the shore. **3)** A deep-water surfing site. **4) Steamer Lane** The Santa Cruz surf spot known locally as **Steamers** or **"the Lane"**; the site of the annual Cold Water Classic, a stop on the ASP World Tour.

steep *adj.* Said of waves or wave faces that incline sharply. Usage: "Man, that wave was steep." **—wave steepness, steep takeoff**

stellar *adj.* Golden. Usage: "Man, Geoff has the stellar set up with his pad in Bolinas—you can even check the surf from the bus stop."

step *n.* On a hydroplane surfboard, the line or shoulder differentiating the planing surface from the scorpion tail. See HYDROPLANE STEP.

stepoff *n.* **1)** A move to terminate a ride by walking back, one foot at a time. **2)** A stall or exit necessitated by coming to the end of a wave or reaching the shoreline. (L&L)

stern *n.* The rear end of a surfboard.

stern wave *n.* A wave formed by the wake of a motor boat. Same as BOAT WAKE. See WAKE SURFING.

stick *n.* **1)** A SURFBOARD. **2)** A STRINGER—a piece of wood, such as redwood, that is glued between two sides of a surfboard for strength; when preshaped, it helps the shaper to shape the board. Additional off-center or curved sticks are sometimes added for greater strength, weight, and design.

sticker placement *n.* The orientation and display of surf stickers and decals on your surfboard. Whether you have the "right" stickers or even the right number of stickers is viewed by some as a measure of how cool you are. See SURF STICKERS.

stiff *adj.* A surfboard handling characteristic that has to do with how easily

a board maneuvers; the opposite of LOOSE.

stiffener *n.* STRINGER or STICK. Usage: "We can add an additional stiffener to the board."

stiff-legged hunchback *n.* OLD SURFER. See CYCLOPS, UNCLE FESTER.

sting, stinger, stinger board *n.* **1)** A surfboard design that features pronounced wings and, consequently, a more forward pivot point. (SFR, June 1988) **2)** A shift in the template that alters the rail line. (ORB)

stingray *n.* An elasmobranch fish of the family *Dasyatidae* that has a flattened body, greatly enlarged pectoral fins, and a long, flexible tail armed near the base with a strong, serrated bony spine that can inflict a very painful puncture wound in the foot if the ray is stepped on. (S&C)

Photo: Tom Dodd

Stingrayʌ inhabit ʌandy bayʌ with flat bottomʌ, ʌo be extra careful when wading through ʌhallow murky water. One preventative technique iʌ the "Jake Shuffle" (named after a Long Beach fireman who invented it in Baja): ʌimply move your feet in ʌmall, ʌweeping circleʌ aʌ you walk out into the water, and the diʌturbance will cauʌe any rayʌ in the vicinity to ʌwim away.

---

stinkbug stance *n.* An awkward squatting position in which the surfer's rear end protrudes like a stinkbug's. (A&M)

stink eye *n.* A hostile, threatening, contemptible, or utterly curious way of looking at someone. (Hawaii; S&S) Usage: "Wow, you saw da stink eye she wen geev me?" (DSN)

stitches *n.* The means of sewing together the gash in your head after you get smacked or speared by a surfboard, or mauled by a coral reef.

stock *n., adj.* The basic board type, which today is the rounded pintail—the standard by which all others are judged; a very versatile design that can deal with a wide variety of situations. Usage: "He's riding a stock." "I bought a stock board." Same as STANDARD.

stokaboka or **stoka boka** *adj.* Superstoked. (1960s) —**cowabunga stokaboka**

stoked *adv., adj* **1)** Excited, thrilled, jazzed—usually about the surf; chock-full of enthusiasm or satisfaction; happy; also fired up, hyped, pumped, on fire. **2)** Feeling the ultimate in exhilaration; feeling high on life—can't wait to go surfing. **3)** An impressed reaction to something "boss." (IDSM) **4)** A reaction to the ultimate ride on the ultimate wave. (MM)

Art: Jim Ph

Usage: "I'm stoked!" "I was stoked to the max." **5) stoke** *n.* A term sometimes used to mention an encounter with marine mammals. Usage: "Did you see the pelican stoke I had out there?" "No, but I got seal stoked." **6) stoke** *v.* To feed a fire on the beach, or to feed hungry individuals. For instance, Pacific Northwest lumberjacks often stoke themselves with a huge breakfast. **7) stoker** *n.* Something that makes you feel stoked. Usage: "What a stoker." "That was a real stoker." **—surf stoked, stoke-a-rama, stoking, double stoked, super stoked, wave stoke** Additional usage: "I'm so stoked," or "I'm sooooo stoked." "Stokage in full affect." "Here's some stoke juice." "Yeaaahhh." "I was mega-stoked."

"To catch a wave was (and is) to stoke the fires of the heart and soul. Hence, the terms: to be stoked, the stoked life, degrees of stoke, and pure stoke."

—*John Grissim, Pure Stoke (1982)*

". . . and I'm just like stoked."

—*Female guest on the Ricki Lake Show, January 1998*

"It's the greatest feeling that you ever had. The sound of the water bumping against the nose of the board, it stokes you."

-*John "Doc" Ball, the oldest known American surfer at ninety-three (Surfing for Life 1999)*

Stoke-on-Trent *n.* A place on the east coast of England.

stomp patch *n.* DECK PATCH.

stoner-philosopher surfer *n.* Someone with a baked eye glaze that yarns about the surf.

storm *n.* A disturbance of the atmosphere marked by wind, rain, thunder, lightning, etc., and responsible for whipping up the surf. In weather language, storms are low pressure systems, which have unstable moving air and winds blowing counterclockwise around their center. (W&B)

storm-drain runoff *n.* A major contributor to ocean pollution, especially during heavy rains when raw, untreated sewage filled with bacteria and heavy metal residue spills into the ocean, putting surfers at risk of contracting hepatitis. See SANTA MONICA BAY.

storm front *n.* The leading edge of a storm; may bring good stuff.

storm peak *n.* Shifting takeoff point on a big wave during or right after a storm. (1994)

storm surf *n.* Waves generated by a local storm, which are usually big but not clean.

storm-surge waves, storm surges, sea surges *n.* Wind-driven waves

storm surf
Santa Cruz, Westside, winter, 1983
Photo: Woody Woodworth

caused by cyclones, superimposed on storm-swollen tides. Usually produces a systematic, pounding surf, but can also form single crests up to forty feet high and do incredible damage. (OA) Not to be confused with TSUNAMIS.

storm track *n.* The path a storm takes.

straight-edge fin *n.* An old concept (the squared-off fin—1968–1972) with a new application and a simple design premise—that straighter lines beget cleaner, more efficient release. The extra area at the tip increases holding power, so that the fin can be shorter and still hold in. (B, June 1983) Same as angular 757 fin.

straighten off, straighten out *v.* **1)** To turn from riding at a definite angle across a wave to heading directly toward shore or in the same direction as the wave is moving. **2)** To ride directly toward shore in front of the white water to escape the wave. (ORB)

straight in, straight off or **straight-off** *adv.* **1)** Refers to riding straight toward shore, without turning or angling, directly in line with the movement of the wave, rather than sliding across the wave. **2)** A term applied to the riding style of novices.

straightout "I mean it." "That's it." (TMA)

straight ride *n.* The last ride of a session—straight in to the beach. (SWA)

strap surfing *n.* Riding a surfboard with foot straps. Usage: "He strap surfed it." See TOE IN SURFING.

Strauch crouch *n.* A riding position developed by Paul Strauch in the Hawaiian Islands in the 1960s. Traveling parallel to the wave, in trim, the surfer moves forward on the board, crouches, not right on the nose but a few feet from it, then extends the forward foot and hangs it over the nose. (MF) Also called CHEATER FIVE, CHEATER FIVE NOSE RIDE.

stretched *adj.* Describes what happens to a swell that, because it is coming in at an angle, must bend around to fit the contour of a point; consequently it loses much of its size. See WAVE REFRACTION. Usage: "That swell is really stretched."

stretch five *n.* A longboard maneuver; same as CHEATER FIVE. (DSO)

stringer *n.* **1)** The wooden runner or runners (one-sixteenth to one-quarter inch thick) that most well-made surfboards have inside of them, aligned from front to back along the longitudinal centerline, for the purpose of strengthening the foam and fiberglass. The stringer sets the rocker; that is, it determines how much curvature (nose scoop) the surfboard will have. **2)** Narrow strips of wood, usually redwood, laminated into a surfboard, generally for strength or decoration. **3)** Thin pieces of wood glued down the middle of the foam core, or blank, to give lateral strength. (NAT, 1985) Also called STICK, STRIP.

Although stringers are commonly made of redwood, balsa, butternut, and spruce can also be used. Canadian cedar gives a rich dark effect or, if a blonde appearance is required for the finished job, Pacific maple (which is slightly stronger) can be used. (ASKC) Greg Noll was the first to use light-weight sticks (aircraft-grade spruce) for stringers, which he did to reduce the weight.

stringer line *n*. A line measured from the tip of the nose to the tail of a surfboard; a measure of the length of a board.

strip *n*. A narrow piece of wood used to reinforce a surfboard; sometimes used for decoration only. Same as STRINGER.

stripes *n*. Decorations applied on the outside of a surfboard.

stroking into a wave The act of paddling and taking off on a wave.

strong swell *n*. A swell that is well developed and bringing good waves.

stubbies *n*. Australian for shorts.

stub-vector *n*. Surfboard shape.

stuffed, stuffed in the pit *v*. To get wiped out in the surf. —**stuffed in the nose** (of the board)

S-turn *n*. **1)** A move intended to keep the surfer nearer the pocket, like an abbreviated cutback and fade, followed immediately by a turn in the original tracking direction. **2)** CLIMBING AND DROPPING.

style *n*. The distinctive quality in the way individual surfers ride the waves.

styling, stylin', stylish *adj*. **1)** Fully cool. Usage: "That's so styling." **2)** Used to compliment a fancy maneuver. Usage: "That was a way stylish cutback. "Dude, you were fully stylin' out there."

styrene *n*. A resin thinner.

submarine *n*. A board that is too small, short, or thin for the rider, so that he or she is floated partially under the surface. The opposite of CORK.

submarine canyon *n*. A steep, underwater, V-shaped valley cut into the continental shelf and slope. The part of a wave that comes in over the canyon moves at full speed when nearing the beach, while the part that is over the shallower fringes of the canyon slows down; this creates a bend in the swell—a bowl or pocket—where generally a large peak forms that is larger than the original swell, and the wave peels off in both directions from the center of the peak. (CCRG, W&B)

submerger *n*. A wave that forces the front end of a surfboard to pearl.

sub-surf *v*. Surfing a sea kayak under the wave.

sucked out *v*. To get carried away in a current. Usage: "I was sucked out to the point."

sucked over *v*. To be pulled back by the force of a breaking wave and creamed in the white water. (A&M) —**sucked over the falls**

suckey wave or **sucky wave** *n*. **1)** A wave that breaks extremely fast, throwing its lip out in front of itself and creating a space or tube; caused by the wave passing suddenly over a shallow spot and throwing forward. A suckey wave is like a DREDGING WAVE,

253

suckey wave
Troy Eckert,
Puerto Escondido, Mexico
Photo: Mike Peralta

only slightly less awesome. **2)** An extremely•hollow wave. (Australia; NAT, 1985; MW)

sucking dry *adj.* A wave that jacks up, leaving very shallow water in front of it. "The wave just **sucked dry**." See DRY REEF.

suck milk *v.* To WIPEOUT, EAT SHIT, drink white water. Usage: "Sucking plenty milk, brah." (Hawaii; BNJ, P, 1983)

suck out, suck up *v.* What happens when an advancing wave draws water into, and up, its face as it breaks. Usage: "That wave really sucks up at low tide near the jetty." **—hollow suckular tubes, heavy suckouts** *n.*

suck out barrel *n.* A tubing wave that breaks fairly close to shore very quickly.

sudden-death takeoff *n.* KAMIKAZE RUN. (A&M)

sunglasses
Amazon wahines
Photo: Trevor Cralle

The Tres Amigos
Photo: Camille Seaman

suitdooker *n.* Something that makes you dook in your suit, like a big wave. Anything that makes you drop one. You can easily take it out of surf context, i.e., "The on-coming semi in our lane was a total suitdooker." Usage: "Dude, those waves were suitdookable" or "She hard-core suitdooked you." (Baja Collective, 1993) **—suitdookey, suitdookage, The Suitdook Factor**

summer *n.* The time of year when the beach gets crowded and things start to heat up, as in "Summer Means Fun" (1964), a song originally by the Fantastic Baggys and later by Jan & Dean.

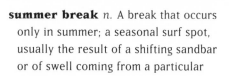

Summer without the beach is like a love affair without the lover.

—*Meg Stewart, Bondi (1984)*

summer break *n.* A break that occurs only in summer; a seasonal surf spot, usually the result of a shifting sandbar or of swell coming from a particular direction. See WINTER BREAK.

summer swell *n.* A south swell generated by storms in the South Pacific, most commonly between April and October, or by *chubascos* (hurricanes) off the coast of Baja California from June to November. The waves come in strong, clear lines, usually two to five feet high, but occasionally over fifteen feet. (S&C)

sun *n.* **1)** A source of gravitational pull on waves. Compared with that of the moon, however, it has little influence. **2)** The source of sun rays, celebrated in such music as "The Warmth of the Sun" by The Beach Boys and "We All Live for the Sun" by the Surf Punks. On the negative side, too much time spent in the sun can cause skin cancer. See TROPPO.

sunglasses *n.* Fashion articles that make you look cool and that filter out harmful ultraviolet (UV) rays. Also called *dark-glasses*, *shades*, etc.

sunnies *n*. Australian for SUNGLASSES.

sunscreen *n*. A protective lotion applied to the skin to minimize sunburn. See ZINC.

Sunset Beach A famous surf spot on the North Shore of Oahu, Hawaii, known especially for its peak. Originally called Pau Malu, it was later named after the Sunset Market just down the road. It was first surfed by Greg Noll and others in 1957 and is now the site of major surfing contests, including a leg of the HAWAIIAN TRIPLE CROWN.

Things move around a lot, depending on the size and direction of the swell. It's not like Pipeline, where there's one definite takeoff spot. It's faster and steeper, and there's so much more water. You can't halfway commit. You gotta put yourself right in the guts of it."

—*Jeff Hakman on the notoriously hard-to-read break; quoted in Rob Buchanan's, "Mr. Sunset Rides Again," Outside, April 2000*

sunset stroll *n*. If you're not out surfing the glass-off, then you should at least be walking along the beach.

suntan *n*. The deep golden-brown color that a surfer acquires from hanging out under the sun all the time; an indispensable part of the surfer image. See SKIN CANCER.

suntan lotion *n*. See SPF.

Sunset Beach
North Shore, Hawaii
Photo: Bob Barbour

suntan oil *n*. A means of greasing up before exposure to the sun that provides little or no protection against the sun's harmful rays.

Supertubes or **Super Tubes** *n*. A name given to various surf spots, for instance the ones in Ventura County, California, and in Peniche, Portugal.

surf *n*. **1)** The area of any body of water adjoining the shoreline in which the wave action is accelerated by reason of the decreasing depth of water approaching the shoreline. **2)** The line or mass of foamy water caused by the sea breaking against the shore or rocks. Variously called *sea*, *waves*, *breakers*, *rollers*, *whitecaps*, *white horses*, *billows*, *surge*, *spume*, *sea foam*, *froth*, *spindrift*, *spray*. **3)** The foam, splash, and sound of breaking waves. **4)** *v*. To ride the surf (as on a surfboard). **5)** A SURF SESSION. Usage: "I had some nice surfs last week." "I went out for a surf today." See the *Oxford English Dictionary*'s complete etymology of "surf" on page 256. Most frequently heard usage: "What's the surf like?" "Do you surf?" or "Are you a surfer?" **6)** "Free-style, partnerless dance of the early 1960s." —Tom Hibbert,

surf (sɜːf), *sb.* Also 8 surff. [Continues SUFF *sb.* in chronology and meaning, but the relation between the forms is not clear. (Not in general Dicts. before Todd, 1818.)

Both *suff* and *surf* are used particularly in reference to the coast of India, a circumstance which makes a native origin for the words probable.]

1. a. The swell of the sea which breaks upon a shore, esp. a shallow shore. (In recent use usually with implication of sense 2.)

1685 W. HEDGES *Diary* (Hakl. Soc.) I. 182 [At Fort St. George, Madras] This unhappy accident, together with ye greatness of ye Sea and Surf ashore, caused us to come aboard again. **1719** DE FOE *Crusoe* I. (Globe) 50 My Raft was now strong enough to bear any reasonable Weight; my next Care was.. how to preserve what I laid upon it from the Surf of the Sea. **1745** P. THOMAS *Jrnl. Anson's Voy.* 35 The Landing is bad by reason of pretty much Surf, and great Stones like Rocks. **1774** GOLDSM. *Nat. Hist.* (1862) I. xvii. 97 This rising of the waves against the shore, is called by mariners the surf of the sea. **1783** W. MARSDEN *Hist. Sumatra* (1811) 34 The surf..is used in India, and by navigators in general, to express a peculiar swell and breaking of the sea upon the shore. **1836** W. IRVING *Astoria* II. 100 Low bellowings..like the hoarse murmurs of the surf on a distant shore. **1840** E. E. NAPIER *Scenes & Sports For. Lands* I. p. xii, The progress of the neophyte..in that far land, from the moment when having crossed the 'surf'. [*Note.* An expression equivalent to entering or leaving India, as a person is never supposed to venture across this tremendous barrier of the Coromandel coast, unless on such momentous occasions.] **1886** RUSKIN *Præterita* I. 379 Half-a-mile of dangerous surf between the ship and the shore. **1906** MAX PEMBERTON *My Sword for Lafayette* xxiv, The distant thunder of the sea surf upon an angry shore.

b. with *a*. Also *transf.* (in first quot.).

1698 FRYER *Acc. E. India & P.* 14 A notable Fish..It might be in length forty Feet.. bolting out of the Water with a great Surf. **1748** *Anson's Voy.* II. ii. 134 The wind.. occasioned such a surf, that it was impossible for the boat to land. **1763** THOMPSON *Temple of Venus* i. 14 A dull promiscuous sound a-far..like..southern surffs upon an iron shore. **1803** WITTMAN *Trav. Turkey* 3 A military artificer was unfortunately washed off the vessel by a surf. **1840** MACAULAY *Ess.*, *Clive* ¶8 Fort St. George had arisen on a barren spot beaten by a raging surf. **1879** *A. R. Wallace's Australasia* xvi. 303 The southern coast..is exposed to a heavy and dangerous surf, which rolls in upon the shore at all seasons.

2. a. The mass or line of white foamy water caused by the sea breaking upon a shore or a rock.

1757 tr. *Keysler's Trav.* IV. 141 *note*, Salt..was not produced here as in other countries by a desiccation of the surf of the sea [tr. Tacitus *Ann.* XIII. lvii. *non ut alias apud gentis eluvie maris arescente unda*]. **1784** COWPER *Task* VI. 155 Light as the foamy surf That the wind severs from the broken wave. **1833** TENNYSON *Dream Fair Wom.* viii, White surf wind-scatter'd over sails and masts. **1882** 'OUIDA' *Maremma* I. 78 She played with the sails, with the surf, and with the crystals of the salt.

b. *transf.* and *fig.*

1847 LONGF. *Ev.* II. iii. 24 Just where the woodlands met the flowery surf of the prairie. **1873** LOWELL *Above & Below* II. i, To behold The first long surf of climbing light Flood all the thirsty east with gold.

3. *attrib.* and *Comb.*: Simple attrib., 'of or pertaining to surf', as ***surf barrier***, ***-beach***, ***-beat***, ***-billow***, ***line***, ***-rock***, ***-sound***, ***-thunder***; locative, as ***surf-bathe*** vb., ***-bather***, ***-bathing***, ***-fish*** vb., ***-fisherman***, ***-fishing***, ***lifesaver***, ***lifesaving***, ***-rider***, ***-riding***, ***-swimmer***, ***-swimming***; ***surf-sunk*** adj.; instrumental, as ***surf-battered***, ***-beaten***, ***-bound***, ***-showered***, ***-tormented***, ***-vexed***, ***-washed***, ***-wasted***, ***-worn*** adjs.; similative, as ***surf-white*** adj.; also **surf-bird**, a small, plover-like bird, *Aphriza virgata*, found on the Pacific coast of America; **surfboard**, a long narrow board on which one rides over a heavy surf to shore; hence as *v. intr.*, to ride on a surfboard (also *fig.*); **surfboarder**, **surfboarding** *vbl. sb.*; **surf-boat**, a boat specially constructed for passing through surf; hence **surf-boatman** = *surfman*; **surf-bum** *slang*, a surfing enthusiast who frequents beaches suitable for surf-riding; cf. *ski bum* s.v. SKI *sb.* 2 b; **surf-casting** *vbl. sb.*, fishing by casting a line into the sea from the shore; so (as a back-formation) **surf-cast** *v. intr.*, **surf-caster**; **surf-clam**, a large clam, esp. *Mactra* (or *Spisula*) *solidissima*, found on the Atlantic coast of the United States (*Funk's Standard Dict.* 1895); **surf-coot** = *surf-duck*; **surf day**, a day marked by rough surf along the shore (see quot. 1854); **surf-duck**, a North American species of sea-duck of the genus *Œdemia*, esp. *O. perspicillata*, found sometimes in Great Britain; **surf-fish**, any one of the numerous species of the family *Embiotocidæ*, abundant on the coast of California; **surf-grass**, any of several species of marine grass of the genus *Phyllospadix* (family Zosteraceæ), having thickened rootstocks and slender stems and growing underwater on rocky shores in temperate regions; **surf-man** *U.S.*, a member of the crew of a surf-boat; hence **surfmanship**; **surf music**, a variety of rock music which celebrates the sport of surf-riding; **surf-perch** = *surf-fish*; **surf-ride** *v. intr.* [back-formation from *surf-riding* above] = *surfboard* vb. above; also *fig.* and as *v. trans.* and *sb.*; **surf safari** = SURFARI; **surf-scoter** = *surf-duck*; **surf-shiner**, a small California fish, *Cymatogaster aggregatus* (Webster 1911); **surf-smelt**, a species of smelt, *Hypomesus olidus*, found on the Pacific coast of the United States; **surf-whiting**, the silver whiting, *Menticirrus littoralis*.

1940 V. BRITTAIN *Testament of Friendship* xii. 192 You'll look at the Rhodes Memorial and the Union Buildings..; you'll..*surf-bathe at Durban.., and then you'll begin to think you know everything. **1893** KATE SANBORN *S. California* 163 *Surf bathers go in every month of the year. **1884** *Encycl. Brit.* XVII. 461/1 Conveniences for *surf-bathing. **1902** *Temple Bar* May 579 Like *surf-battered swimmers. **1932** N. PALMER *Talking it Over* 137 *Surf-beaches of any size are rare in the world. **1966** *Weekly News* (N.Z.) 19 Jan. 11/1 Mt. Maunganui is probably one of New Zealand's best-known surf beaches. **1977** *Herald* (Melbourne) 17 Jan. 14/4 Within 16 km of Wollongong are 17 superb surf beaches. **1873** 'MARK TWAIN' *Gilded Age* lx. 543 A receding of tides, a quieting of the storm-wash to a murmurous *surf-beat. **1974** *Encycl. Brit. Micropædia* IX. 689/2 Surf beat, ocean waves of uncertain origin, with the relatively long periods of 1 to 5 minutes. These low-frequency waves appear to be related to the interaction of normal wind waves and swell. Surf beat is believed responsible for the generation of seiches in bays. **1801** CAMPBELL *Lochiel's Warning* 82 Like ocean-weeds heaped on the *surf-beaten shore. **1890** 'R. BOLDREWOOD' *Col. Reformer* (1891) 154 The deep-toned ceaseless roll of the *surf-billows. **1872** COUES *N. Amer. Birds* 245 *Aphriza*, *Surf Bird. *c* **1826** RICHARDS in Gosse *Ocean* vi. (1849) 285 Those who were standing on the beach saw the *surf-board ..floating on the water. **1931** T. E. LAWRENCE *Let.* 14 July (1938) 729 Here is a final report..on the little surf-board target. **1934** WEBSTER, *Surfboard, v.i.*, to ride the surf on a surfboard.—*surfboarding, n.* **1938** E. HEMINGWAY *Fifth Column* (1939) III. iv. 103 Or what about Malindi where you can surfboard on the beach. **1962** *Coast to Coast 1961–62* 63 He wished he could stand up and walk away from Pammie and go out with the surf-board riders. **1962** M. MCLUHAN *Gutenberg Galaxy* 248 (*heading*) Heidegger surf-boards along on the electronic wave as triumphantly as Descartes rode the mechanical wave. **1953** *Pop. Mechanics* July 157 Hitching a ride on a beach-bound ocean wave with a featherlight surf-board is rated tops in water sports by practiced *surf-boarders. **1969** *Britannica Bk. of Year 1968* 801/1 *Surfari*, a group of surfboarders who travel together in search of good surfing areas. **1964** *Sunday Mail Mag.* (Brisbane) 17 May 1 *Surfboarding was virtually forgotten until the late 1930's. **1856** DICKENS *Wreck Golden Mary* (1898) 22, I gave..the word to lower the Long-boat and the *Surf-boat. **1883** J. D. CAMPBELL *Fisheries China* 5 (Fish. Exhib. Publ.) The catamarans or surf-boats of South Formosa. **1886** *Encycl. Brit.* XXI. 804/2 The Madras surf boats. **1880** *Scribner's Mag.* Jan. 323 It is an erroneous notion that the experience of the sailor qualifies him for a *surf-boatman. **1884** *19th Cent.* Feb. 239 The noisy tumult of a *surf-bound shore. **1958** *Surf-bum [see PETITE *a.* 2]. **1971** Surf-bum [see PIPE-LINE *sb.* c]. **1975** *Country Life* 16 Jan. 131/2 *Surf-cast for corvina..on a California beach and you will probably have to show your California fishing licence. **1968** 'S. JAY' *Sleepers can Kill* xxiv. 248 When you've walked through to the beach, you'll see a *surfcaster, fishing by himself. **1928** *N.Y. Times* 8 Oct. 21/4 Charles Vollum of Philadelphia became *surf casting champion of the United States today at the annual tournament of the Dover Fishing Club of Philadelphia. **1963** *Weekly News* (Auckland, N.Z.) 8 May 56/6 Pukehina surfcasting beach. Near Te Puke, Bay of Plenty, one of the best surfcasting beaches in New Zealand. **1979** *Angling* July 45/3 As a contemporary guide to the basics of general shorefishing it gives excellent surfcasting instruction. **1884** *Bull. U.S. Nat. Museum* No. 27. 260 Hen Clam, *Surf Clam, or Sea Clam. Florida and Gulf of Mexico to Labrador. **1949** [see SKIMMER *sb.* 1 c]. **1978** *Times* 29 July 3/6 More than two weeks after the wreck..we saw millions of dead molluscs, urchins, razor and surf clams. **1885** SEEBOHM *Brit. Birds* III. 610 To the hunters on Long Island it [the Surf-scoter] is known as the 'Spectacled Coot' and '*Surf-Coot'. **1854** G. W. PECK *Melbourne & Chincha Islands* 187 Often when the mornings are still, and the surface of the sea undisturbed by a ripple, the surf will be rolling tremendously on the narrow beaches. .. These are called '*surf-days', and special allowance is made for them in the charter parties of vessels loading at the islands. **1950** J. S. LEARMONT *Master in Sail* 60 Surf days did not count as working days. These surf days are peculiar to the northern part of the coast of Chile. **1808–13** A. WILSON & BONAPARTE *Amer. Ornith.* (1832) III. 70 Black, or *Surf Duck, *Anas perspicillata*... This duck is peculiar to America, and..confined to the shores and bays of the sea. **1882** JORDAN & GILBERT *Fishes N. Amer.* 585 Embiotocidæ. The *Surf-fishes... Fishes of the Pacific coast of North America, inhabiting bays and the surf on sandy beaches. **1940** O. H. P. RODMAN *Handbk. Salt-Water Fishing* iii. 99 We will make a definite statement in regard to wetting down your cutty hunk line before you really start surf fishing. **1979** 'A. BLAISDELL' *No Villain need Be* vii. 120 They like to surf-fish, and they claim rain.. drives 'em in toward the beach. **1920** HEILNER & STICK *Call of Surf* i. 5 Those great and goodly fish which so frequently take into their capacious jaws the bait of the *surf fisherman. **1967** O. E. MIDDLETON in *Coast to Coast 1965–66* 123 The surf-fishermen leaned out over the shallows. **1920** HEILNER & STICK *Call of Surf* i. 4 *Surf fishing is by no means a new development of the angler's art..but only of late years has it begun to achieve real popularity. **1949** S. K. FARRINGTON *Fishing the Atlantic* iv. 82 Surf fishing at Narragansett should be a revelation. **1923** L. ABRAMS *Illustr. Flora Pacific States* I. 94 *Phyllospadix torreyi* S. Wats. Torrey's *Surf-grass. **1981** *Sci. Amer.* Mar. 92/1 The sea grasses number 12 genera and ..about 50 species... Eelgrass and surfgrass are familiar examples in temperate regions. **1977** *N.Z. Herald* 8 Jan. 1-6/4, I have been talking to the wife of a *surf lifesaver, and she spoke of the apparent indifference people show on being saved from drowning. **1968** W. WARWICK *Surfriding in N.Z.* 1 It is difficult to imagine how closely it was once associated with the *surf lifesaving movement. **1887** O. J. HUMPHREY *Wreck of Rainier* 33 When the *surf line was hauled tight the boat would run on the line and be kept head to the sea. **1923** H. BELLOC *Sonnets & Verse* I. 28 Above the surf-line, into the night-breeze; Eastward above the ever-whispering trees. **1965** P. L. DIXON *Compl. Bk. Surfing* 142 If the dory broaches in the surf line and turns over, bail out and get clear of oars and falling boat. **1880** *Scribner's Mag.* Jan. 322/2 The keeper [of the surf-boat] commands the crew of six *surfmen. *Ibid.* 334 Until 1871..*surfmanship was not a standard of qualification. **1965** *N.Z. Listener* 17 Dec. 4/1 The million-dollar industry of *surf music, surf movies and surf-wear. **1977** *Sounds* 9 July 28/2 The Turtles started out playing surf music at High School hops in LA. **1889** *Amer. Naturalist* Oct. 923 *Micrometrus aggregatus*, one of the viviparous *surf-perches. **1953** 'S. RATTRAY' *Bishop in Check* 101 One-half per cent of them play tennis—or swim, or *surf-ride. **1958** *Listener* 2 Oct. 494/1 This motorization wave is not something on which the rich alone can surf-ride. **1973** *Times* 1 June (Australia Suppl.) p. i/3 The Whitlam Government has been in office just six months tomorrow. For the Prime Minister it has been 'a surf ride so far'. **1976** *National Observer* (U.S.) 19 June 1/3 Now, surf-riding his victory in the California Presidential primary last week, he's racing to a showdown with Gerald Ford. **1882** *Hawaiian Almanac* 52 At one time they sent their champion *surf-rider to compete with chiefs in the sport at Hawaii. **1981** L. LEAMER *Assignment* iii. 43 They take this drug. They have learned this from these hippie surf-riders. **1882** *Hawaiian Almanac* 52 Among the various sports and pastimes of the ancient Hawaiians..the principal one..is that of surf-bathing, or more properly speaking, *surf-riding. **1898** JEAN A. OWEN *Hawaii* iii. 81 Surf-riding on boards is still much practised. **1800** COLERIDGE *Piccolom.* I. xii, The *surf rocks of the Baltic. **1962** *Austral. Women's Weekly* 24 Oct. (Suppl.) 3/4 **Surf safari*, a trip around different beaches to find a good surf. **1835** JENYNS *Man. Brit. Vertebr. Anim.* 240 O[*idemia*] *perspicillata*, Steph. (*Surf Scoter.) **1882** JORDAN & GILBERT *Fishes N. Amer.* 294 Hypomesus, Gill. *Surf Smelts... H[ypomesus] pretiosus... Surf Smelt... Pacific coast, from California northward; abundant, spawning in the surf. **1828** CAMPBELL *Death-boat Heligoland* 22 Now *surf-sunk for minutes, again they uptossed. **1845** GOSSE *Ocean* vi. (1849) 283 The cry of 'A Shark!' among the *surf swimmers will instantly set them in the utmost terror. **1858** R. M. BALLANTYNE *Coral Island* xxv. 305 'What sort of amusement is this *surf swimming?'.. 'Each man..has got a short board or plank, with which he swims a mile or more to Sea, and then, gettin' on the top o' yon thunderin' breaker, they come to shore on the top of it.' **1890** 'R. BOLDREWOOD' *Col. Reformer* (1891) 150 The wind is..from the south, we shall have the *surf-thunder in perfection. **1829** POE *Dream within a Dream* ii, I stand amid the roar Of a *surf-tormented shore. **1852** MUNDY *Antipodes* (1857) 24 Green turfy knolls sloping abruptly to the *surf-vexed beach. **1861** L. L. NOBLE *Icebergs* 180 The bleak, *surf-washed rocks. **1854** H. MILLER *Sch. & Schm.* xxiv. (1858) 532 The picturesque *surf-wasted stacks of the granitic wall of rock. **1897** MARY KINGSLEY *W. Africa* 391 The young women..with their soft dusky skins,..pretty brown eyes, and *surf-white teeth. **1882** JORDAN & GILBERT *Fishes N. Amer.* 933 M[enticirrus] littoralis... *Surf Whiting... South Atlantic and Gulf coast. **1878** GEIKIE *Geol. Sketches* ii. (1882) 34 Weather-beaten or *surf-worn sheets of rock.

surf (sɜːf), *v.* [f. the sb.] **1.** *intr.* To form surf. *rare.*

1831 J. WILSON in *Blackw. Mag.* XXIX. 141 The breakers surfing on a lee-shore. **1832** *Ibid.* XXXII. 131.

2. To go surf-riding; to surf-ride. Also *transf.* and *fig.*

1917 *Chambers's Jrnl.* Apr. 280/2 The depth of the lagoon is trifling.., and this it is which makes surfing there so safe and enjoyable. **1932** *Ibid.* Aug. 462/2, I had snaps, too, of the children, riding or surfing, and of the whole family in their ocean-going yacht. *a* **1957** R. CAMPBELL *Coll. Poems* (1960) III. 83 Over its surge in red tornadoes rolling My heart goes surfing on the waves of fire. **1965** *N.Z. Listener* 17 Dec. 4/5 Once a person is bitten by this surfing bug he seems to become insatiable. He surfs every day he can, the whole year round. **1970** *Motor Boat & Yachting* 16 Oct. 29/1 *La Russhe* surfed handsomely down the backs of the heavy swell and buried herself into the short steep seas on the way. **1976** M. BIRMINGHAM *Heat of Sun* iv. 51 Biriwa has..a comparatively safe beach..where you can surf when the tide is right.

3. *trans.* **a.** To ride (a boat) on the surf. **b.** To surf-ride at (a specified place).

1965 P. L. DIXON *Compl. Bk. Surfing* 18 Dories, canoes, sailing catamarans, and a few special motorboats can be surfed by experts. Where waves break far from shore and spill gradually forward. **1967** W. MURRAY *Sweet Ride* vi. 85 Ten years ago..no one surfed this place but him. **1968** *Surfer Mag.* Jan. 56/1 Paulo surfed a beach break off the famous Rio Copacabana called Posto Six Pier.

Hence **'surfing** *vbl. sb.*, surf-riding, surfboarding.

1955 A. ROSS *Australia 55* xv. 214 The essential art of surfing is timing. **1959** H. HOBSON *Mission House Murder* xviii. 119 When they'd had enough surfing, they brought the boards back up the beach. **1963** *Wall St. Jrnl.* 22 July 1 Surfin' music is characterized by a heavy echo guitar sound, supposed to simulate the roar of the surf. **1971** 'D. HALLIDAY' *Dolly & Doctor Bird* i. 2 Skin diving, rum punches, calypso night-clubs, surfing, dancing, gambling.

surfari
Art: The Pizz

*Rockspeak!
The Dictionary
of Rock Terms,*
Omnibus Press,
London (1983)

Surf 1) A small coastal town (elevation 10) in Santa Barbara County, California. **2)** A brand name of laundry detergent, popular among surfers.

surfable *adj.* Used to say whether or not waves are ridable. Usage: "Are they surfable?" The opposite of UNSURFABLE.

Surfabout *n.* A famous Australian surfing competition.

surface chop *n.* A ruffled ocean surface; caused by local winds. Also called **surface chops.** Waves upon waves that can bounce a surfer into the air.

surfadelia *n.* Psychedelic surf music. (*SF Weekly,* November 5, 1997)

surf ads *n.* Advertisements from the surf industry in surfing magazines.

surfari *n.* **1)** A caravan of surf-hungry surfers. **2)** A surfing trip. (MM) See SURFIN' SAFARI. **3) The Surfaris** A 1960s surfin' band with hits such as "Wipe Out!"

surf art, surfing art *n.* Art created by people who surf. Examples are giant wall murals painted on the outside of surf shops, surf graffiti, and furniture made from surfboards. In recent years, collecting surf paintings has become increasingly popular.

surfatorium *n.* WAVE POOL.

surf band *n.* A group that plays surf music, such as Dick Dale and The Deltones.

surf beach *n.* "It's a surf beach" as distinct from a beach with no rideable surf.

surf beat *n.* **1)** The action and impact of sets of waves crashing against the shore. **2)** The sound of surf music.

surf betty, surf bettys *n.* BETTY. (1994) See LONGBOARD BETTY.

surfboard *n.* **1)** A narrow, somewhat rounded board used by surfers for riding waves into shore; sometimes spelled *surfboard.* (DM, 1962) **2)** A kind of wave vehicle; a form with which to communicate with a wave. **3)** A long narrow buoyant board used in the sport of surfing. (W9)

surfboard bonk *n.* Getting hit on the head or smacked in the face by a loose board, as in "Dude, what happened to your nose?" (August 22, 1995) See CHEWIN' THE PLANK.

surfboarder *n.* A surfer. (W9)

surfboard hum *n.* See BOARD HUM.

surfboarding *n.* SURFING.

surfboard polo *n.* A sport probably invented by the Kahanamoku brothers (Louis, Sam, and Sargent) in 1929 at Waikiki, where it became the rage during the 1930s. The game was similar to water polo, except that it was played on surfboards. (GTM)

surf art
"Birth of Venus" by Tim Smith; mixed media on surfboard

surf betty
Siri Cota,
Santa Cruz
Photo: Mike Peralta

surf bomb
Will Natilla
Photo: *Don Balch*

surfboard rack *n.* SURF RACK.

surfboard riding *n.* Surfing. —**surf board riding** (WPA Guide to Los Angeles, 1941)

surfboard stand *n.* A structure used for ding repair, usually padded with a chunk of old rug or a discarded wetsuit. (GCD)

surfboard width See WIDTH.

surf boat *n.* An old four-door car that is so big and awesome it barely fits in a lane on Highway 1. See LAND YACHT, MAUI CRUISER.

surfboat *n.* A boat made especially for use in the surf. (MF)

surf bomb *n.* A clunker car. (BP)

surf-bot *n.* A robot that surfs.

". . . We don't actually surf ourselves. That's what the robots are for."

"You just control them from the beach."

"Right on. Surf-botting is tougher than it seems. Not just any hodad can do it."

—*Surfing Samurai Robots* (1988) by Mel Gilden

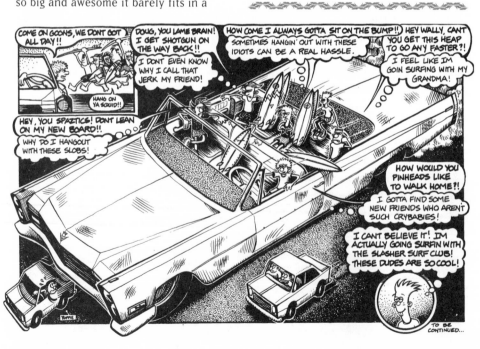

surf bomb
Art: *Bob Penuelas*

Art: Surf Toons Magazine, 1967

surf breaks *n.* Places where waves are breaking. There are several kinds of surf breaks, depending on the ocean bottom contour or the obstructions causing the waves to break: **1) beach break, shore break** Where the surf breaks close in to shore and sometimes directly onto the beach. **2) peak break** Waves that form peaks as they begin to break; usually formed in conjunction with a reef. **3) pier break** Surf generated by pier pilings in the water. **4) point break** Surf that breaks in along a line that wraps around a rocky point. **5) reef break** Surf that breaks over a rock or coral reef. **6) sandbar break** Surf that breaks in sections over sand deposits just offshore of the beach or at a river mouth.

surf bum *n.* Someone who lives only for surfing. "Ride the waves, eat, sleep, not a care in the world" —Kahoona in the movie *Gidget* (1959)

surf bumps
Photo: *Surfer's Medical Association*/Surfer *magazine*

surf bumps *n.* Gnarly looking calcium deposits that develop on various parts of the body as a result of constant contact with a surfboard. A common location is below the kneecap, where they are caused by resting on the knees while paddling a surfboard, but they also form on bottom ribs and the tops of feet and toe joints just from lying down on the board. Surf bumps were frequently cited as the reason for classifying surfers 4-F during the Korean War. (A&M; DWK) Same as SURF KNOBS, SURF KNOTS. See VOLCANO.

surf bunny *n.* **1)** A sixties term for a surfer's girlfriend. **2)** A female surfer, usually deeply tanned, with sun-bleached, windblown hair. Sometimes called BEAVER. (IDSM) **3)** A girl who hangs around with surfers; usually not a surfer herself, but attracted to boys who surf. Also called BEACH BUNNY.

surf cam or **surfcam** *n.* A camera placed at various surf spots around the world. Live feeds allow you to check the conditions from your work or home computer. Same as WAVE CAM.

surf camp *n.* An organized camp for surfers of all ages; became popular in the 1980s.

surf carnival *n.* Lifeguard competition in Australia.

surf cartoons *n.* Cartoons with stereotypical characters and situations centering on the surfing scene. John Severson, the first acknowledged surf illustrator, published drawings in *Surfer* magazine in 1961. He established a panoramic genre—capturing a day's worth of action in a single frame—that was copied by a whole generation of surf artists. Rick Griffin set the standard in the early 1960s. Among the broad stereotypes drawn by many surf cartoonists are the clueless kook, the pampered surf star, the superhuman wave warrior, the rabid local, the cosmic soul surfer, and the average Joe. (SFR) See CAPTAIN GOODVIBES, MURPHY, WILBUR KOOKMEYER.

surf cats *n.* Surfers.

surf change *n.* The act of changing into, or out of, your clothes, surf trunks/bathing suit, or wetsuit, with or without a towel, sometimes in full view of the public.

Art: Surf Crazed Comics by Roy Gonzales and Salvador Paskowitz, 1991

~~~~~~~~~~~~~~~~~~~~~~~~~~~~

"When I was in high school we used to love to come hang at the beach and watch the surfers change in the parking lot. Still do."

—*Pia Hinckle,* San Francisco Bay Guardian,
December 7, 1994

~~~~~~~~~~~~~~~~~~~~~~~~~~~~

surf chaser *n.* An Australian term for a surfer's jalopy. (JKMJ, 1965)

surf check *n.* An appraisal of the surf at one or more spots to determine its quality, where to go out, etc.

surf chicks or **surf chix** *n.* Female surfers. See BETTY.

surf chowder *n.* Any warm, nourishing seafood soup, usually clam chowder.

"Surf City" *n.* **1)** A hit surfing tune about a mythical place in California, where the ratio of females to males is two to one. Written by Brian Wilson and sung by Jan & Dean (June 1963). It was Jan & Dean's first #1 hit. **2) Surf City** A mythical concept. **3)** A nickname given to Huntington Beach, California, by the surf and mainstream media. However, the historical evidence suggests that "Surf City" was a nickname for Santa Cruz, California, long before Huntington Beach (i.e., Surf City Produce Company, etc.). **4)** The incorporated Surf City, New Jersey, where people surf. **5)** The incorporated Surf City, North Carolina, where people surf. **6)** A designation, as in "Oh yeah, it's a **surf city.**" **7) Surf City, USA** The prototypical surf town.

Surf City
Surf City,
North Carolina

Photo: Trevor Cralle

surf classic *n.* Any well-known instrumental surf tune, such as "Miserlou" by Dick Dale & The Del-Tones, "Pipeline" by the Chantays, "Wipe Out" by The Surfaris, "Walk—Don't Run" by The Ventures. See SURF STANDARD.

surf club *n.* Any organization of surfers, such as a longboarding club.

surf conditions *n.* The state of the surf—how the waves are breaking at any particular time. Usage: "Let's check the surf conditions." Or simply, "How are the conditions?"

surf contest *n.* An amateur or professional competition, usually held over a period of several days or a week; may be delayed or postponed if the swell is poor. Popular professional contests include the OP Pro, Stubbies, and Pipeline Masters. See ASP, SURFING CRITERIA.

surf cord *n.* SURF LEASH.

surf craze *n.* A general reference to the period during the first half of the 1960s, when the sport grew tremendously.

surf crimes *n.* Legalese applied to surfing; originated in Southern California in

surf check
Art: Bob Penuelas

262

surf dog
ick Stover

the late 1980s; popular among grommets. Usage (to describe a really heavy wipeout): "That bailiff took him straight to the slammer." Also called LEGALESE GROMMETSPEAK. See PROSECUTED, QUASH, WITNESS.

surf culture *n.* A pervasive subculture, one that thrives over much of the globe. (BC, Spring 1990)

surfcut *n.* Any hip or stylish-looking haircut on a surfer. See BOWL CUT, SURF DREADS.

surf day *n.* Any day in Peru when the surf is too large for freighters to dock at piers to load or unload their cargoes. (1960s)

surf dog *n.* **1)** BEACH DOG. **2)** A veteran surfer.

Surfdom *n.* The kingdom of surfing. (MM)

surf dreads *n.* Bleached-blonde dreadlocks—a surfer hairstyle that became popular in the 1980s.

surf dreams *n.* The surfing you do in your mind at night while you're asleep. See WAVE DREAMS.

"I had the most amazing surf dreams last night."
—*Camille Seaman, 1998*

"I had an 'I-Can't-Surf-Dream' last night."
—*Mike Massucco, La Fortuna, Baja. December 1999*

Koda, the surfing dog
Bolinas, California
Photo: Camille Seaman

surf dude, *n.* A male surfer.

surfear *v.* Spanish for "to surf." (Puerto Rico)

surfed out 1) *adj.* How someone looks—tan, bleached hair, salt caked on the skin, etc.; the surfed-out look **2)** *adv.* How someone feels after a long surf session-tired. Usage: "I'm surfed out."

surfed-out insomnia *n.* One of the most delightful causes of sleeplessness is from surfing six to eight hours in one day, which so dramatically alters your body chemistry that it somehow keeps you from sleeping. You'll sweat a lot, toss and turn, and are constantly thirsty, and not very hungry. But even though you're not asleep, you'll be dreaming of all those great waves you got. (SS) See PILLOW SURFING.

surfer *n.* **1)** Someone who surfs. **2)** In Chinese, "he who dances upon the water." (MGE) **3)** An endangered marine mammal. (SJN) **4)** In the Southern California surfer mystique, someone with sand between the toes, eyelids caked with salt, bleached-blonde hair, and a lifestyle that includes being surrounded by girls in string bikinis. (SMH) —

surfer
Jay Moriarity
Photo: Mike Peralta

263

Margo Oberg, Hawaii
Photo: Bob Barbour

total surfer, as in "He's a total surfer."**5)** Drug slang for PCP.

surfer blonde *adj.* The sun-bleached color of a surfer's hair acquired naturally while surfing in the ocean. Same as BEACH GIRL BLONDE.

surfer boy *n.* SURFER.

surfer dude *n.* SURFER.

surfer girl *n.* **1)** Any female who surfs. **2) "Surfer Girl"** A romantic ballad by The Beach Boys (1963) showcasing the harmonic influence the Four Freshman had on Brian Wilson. **3)** *Surfer Girl* A magazine devoted to women's surfing.

surfer hold, the *n.* A professional wrestling move, where the victim is seated on the ground with his legs outstretched; his arms are stretched out straight behind his body. The opponent has his foot on the victim's back for leverage.

surfer hoots *n.* Screams of encouragement or appreciation while surfing, such as "eeeyuuuu!" "aaaahooo!" "ahoooo!" "aawh wooo!" "AWOOO!" or "OWOOOOO!"; also yelled at the surf flick when someone gets a hot ride.

surfer image *n.* As perpetrated by the media, the negative image of a surf bum. However, any true surfer knows that there are many different surfer types. (BP)

"Surfer Joe" The character in a 1963 Surfaris' song of the same title, about a guy who surfs Doheny, gets drafted into the Marines, and has his long blond locks cut off; written and sung by Ron Wilson, drummer for the Surfaris; the flip side of "Wipe Out."

surfer moon *n.* **1)** A full moon. **2) "The Surfer Moon"** A song by The Beach Boys. (1963)

surfero, surfera *n.* Spanish for "male" and "female surfer," respectively.

Surfers Against Apartheid *n.* A group of professional wave riders who boycotted surfing competitions in South Africa from 1985 until Apartheid was dismantled during the early 1990s. (FLD)

Surfers Against Sewage (SAS) *n.* British environmental organization that campaigns for the cessation of all marine sewage and toxic waste discharges and represents not just surfers, but twenty million people who use the British coastline every year. Formed in May 1990.

Surfer's Cross, the *n.* Worn by surfers in the late 50s and early 60s. Also called the Iron Cross. See SURF NAZIS.

surfer's ear *n.* A condition in which the channels to the inner ear constrict in cold water, and over a period of time a bony growth closes the ear canal, sometimes causing intermittent deafness. Surfer's ear can be prevented by keeping the ear canal warm and dry with ear plugs.

Surfers' Environmental Alliance (SEA) *n.* A grassroots environmental organization with responsibility in protecting the coastal environment. SEA was formed by a group of surfers who wanted to do something to protect the ocean, beaches, coastlines, and keep this planet a safe place to surf. If you own a surfboard, just enjoy the beauty of the ocean, or are concerned about

surfer girl
Andrea Orvik,
Bolinas, California
Photo: Camille Seaman

Surfer's Cross
Kine Kahuna Collection
Photo: Trevor Cralle

preserving our planet's largest natural resource, then there's a place for you to get involved with SEA.

⚜⚜⚜⚜⚜⚜⚜⚜⚜⚜⚜

Contact:
Surfers' Environmental Alliance
P.O. Box 3578
Santa Cruz, CA 95063

Website:
http://www.damoon.net/
sea/index2.html

SEA-NJ
1032 Woodgate Ave
Long Branch, NJ 07740
732-870-9065
email at: brianshozen@yahoo.com

⚜⚜⚜⚜⚜⚜⚜⚜⚜⚜⚜

surfer's eye *n.* A condition caused by excessive exposure to the sun's glare and the irritation of salt water, in which soft tissue forms on the white of the eye and begins to grow over the cornea. The medical term is *pterygium.*

surfer's knee, surfer's knobs, surfer's knots *n.* Tumorlike growths of connective tissue just below the knees, on the tops of feet, and often on the toes; caused by pressure on the skin and tissue exerted by the surfboard. Same as SURF BUMPS, SURF KNOBS, SURF KNOTS. See VOLCANO.

Surfer's Medical Association (SMA) *n.* A San Francisco–based organization of surfing doctors interested in the prevention and treatment of surfing-related injuries; founded by Dr. Mark Renneker ("Doc Hazzard") in 1985.

surfer's nicknames *n.* Names given to famous surfers, sometimes in recognition of their surfing style. Examples are "Buffalo" (Richard Keaulana) because of his shaggy reddish-brown hair; "Da Bull" (Greg Noll) for his tenacity and aggressiveness in big waves; "Da Cat" (Mickey Dora); "Burrhead" Drever; "MR" (Mark Richards); "PT" (Peter Townend); "Bugs" or "Rabbit" (Wayne Bartholemew); and "The Animal" (Nat Young).

Surfers Paradise A built-up beach strip in Queensland, Australia.

surfer's ribs *n.* Extremely sore rib cage from paddling; also called SURF RIBS. See BOARD RASH.

surfers rule 1) Common graffiti in the 1960s claiming a beach as surfer territory. (DWK) **2) "Surfer's Rule"** A song by The Beach Boys. (1963)

surfer's squat *n.* **1)** A dance. **2)** A stance on a surfboard.

"Surfer's Stomp" *n.* A 1962 song by the Marketts from Balboa, California. Also recorded by the Belairs as "The Surfer's Stomp." See SURF STOMPS.

surfer stomp *n.* A dance step popular in the early 1960s. See SURF STOMPS.

Surfeteria, Lucy's *n.* A restaurant/bar in Manhattan, New York.

surf etiquette *n.* An unwritten water etiquette; code of conduct in the water; rules

*Courtesy of Surfers'
Environmental Alliance*

of the ocean road; the law of the sea, etc. See also BEACH ETIQUETTE, PECKING ORDER.

<hr />

A simple version includes:
**1) When paddling out through the surf and someone is surfing toward you on a wave, DON'T ATTEMPT TO MOVE OUT OF THEIR WAY—you will crash into each other like approaching strangers who make eye contact. Instead, simply HOLD YOUR COURSE, stop paddling and glide while the (hopefully) more experienced surfer maneuvers around you.
2) NEVER take off and attempt to catch a wave that somebody else is riding. This is the worst thing an inexperienced surfer can do and it could lead to trouble—verbal and/or physical harm. There are, of course, exceptions when you see multiple surfers on the same wave; for example, you may have an understanding with a friend that you're going to share it (see BROTHERHOOD WAVE, PARTY WAVE).**

<hr />

surf fashion *n.* Fashion trends inspired by surfer clothing, which has been an influence in the fashion world for many years. The first surfwear trend started with the cutoff sailor pants worn by Dale Velzy and his cohorts at the Manhattan Beach Surf Club in the 1950s.

(GN) Other surfer fashions include jams, reeds, Hawaiian shirts, and Day-Glo neon clothing. And don't forget J.C.'s/ Percells—1960s surfer footwear.

surf fever *n.* **1)** A condition prevalent along all coastlines of the world *Symptom:* a burning desire to go surfing. *Cause:* a lack of waves. *Treatment:* to go surfing-the only known cure. **2) *Surf Fever*** A 1960 John Severson surf flick.

surf-film humor *n.* Every surf flick has its classic moments of comedy. Try watching one of the Runman videos for some hilarious laughs.

surf flick *n.* Surf movie.

surf forecasting *n.* See WAVE FORECASTING.

surf god *n.* The legendary god of the waves, KAHUNA in Hawaii, HUEY in Australia.

surf grass (*Phyllospadix scouleri*) *n.* A sea grass found in and around Pacific Coast tidepools; encountered by surfers on their way to the surf.

surf guitar
Art: Jim Phillips

surf groupie *n.* Someone, usually a female, who hangs out around surfers. As Corky Carroll said in 1989, "A real surf groupie has sand in her butt."

surf guitar *n.* An instrumental reverb guitar imitating the hypnotic crashing of waves, pioneered by Dick Dale; consists of tremolos and reverbs (echoes). See SURF MUSIC.

surf hamburger *n.* **1)** A swimmer who gets banged up in the undertow. (*Los Angeles Times*, August 1990) **2)** The term was shortened to **surfburger** by Tom Dalzell in honor of his son's battles with the waves at Malibu. **3)** Note: There's a restaurant in San Francisco called Surf Burgers.

surfhead *n.* SURFER or BOARDHEAD.

surf hearse *n.* **1)** An old hearse rehabilitated for carrying surfboards. **2)** Any jalopy used to transport surfers and boards to and from the beach.

3) "Surfin' Hearse" A song by Jan & Dean (1960s).

surf helmet *n.* Lightweight, plastic hard-shelled helmet used to prevent head injuries.

surf hog heaven *n.* Where you are when you are really superstoked. Corky Carroll coined this term.

surf hound *n.* Same as WAVE HOUND.

Surficas Kneeboardicus *n.* KNEEBOARDER. (SFG, March 2000)

surfie *n.* Australian for SURFER.

surfie groupie *n.* "A girl who sleeps with as many surfing celebrities as possible." (*G'Day! Teach Yourself Australian in 20 Easy Lessons* by Colin Bowles, 1986)

surfin' *n.* **1)** A near mythic concept that embodies all the elements of a certain kind of "California Dreamin'"-sun, sand, surf, blondes in bikinis, and so on. See SURFING. **2) "Surfin'"** The Beach Boys' first hit tune, recorded in December 1961.

"Surfin' Bird" *n.* A song by the Trashmen of Minneapolis, Minnesota (December 1963); one of the most repetitive songs ever recorded. The Ramones did an excellent version of the song in 1977.

surfing *n.* **1)** A combination of water torture and simulated womb regression practiced by masochists and misfits. (JARR) **2)** A water sport in which the participant stands on a floating slab of wood resembling an ironing board in size and shape, and attempts to remain perpendicular while being hurtled toward the shore at a rather frightening speed on the crest of a huge wave. (Especially recommended for teenagers and all others lacking the slightest regard for life or limb.) (TBB, 1963) **3)** In general, a sport in which one attempts to ride a surfboard toward the shore. **4)** Riding across the face of a wave standing on a board especially made for the purpose.

surf helmet
Celia Oakley
Photo: Trevor Cralle

"Surfing is the art of harnessing that ocean energy, and in doing that the surfer momentarily becomes a sea creature, moving in rapport with the waves."

—*Richard Wolkomir*, Oceans *magazine, June 1988*

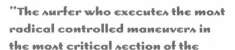

Plus léger qu'un bouchon j'ai dansé sur les flots.
Lighter than a cork I danced on the waves.

—*Arthur Rimbaud (1854–1891), Le Bateau Ivre, 1871*

"A most supreme pleasure."

—*Capt. James Cook, on surfing, 1777*

"Surfing is the most important thing in the world."

—*Dr. Geoff, Tracks magazine, December, 1984*

"I don't think you've even lived until you've surfed."

—*Lorrin "Whitey" Harrison (1912–1993)*
California surfer on "Invention,"
Discovery Channel, December 7, 1993

"It's like trying to put into words feelings communicated in a musical score."

—*Kent Nagano,*
Japanese-American conductor/surfer
People, October 24, 1994

surfing competition *n.* See COMPETITIVE SURFING, SURF CONTEST.

surfing criteria *n.* In competitive surfing, the factors by which a ride is judged. A good ride has four components: **1)** radical controlled maneuvers (RCMs); **2)** the most critical section; **3)** the biggest or the best waves; **4)** the longest functional distance. (L&L) Also called SCORING CRITERIA.

surf legend
Mickey Dora
Photo: Ron Stoner/
Surfer magazine

surf instructor
Trevor Cralle with his niece Cassie Stover, Waikiki, Hawaii
Photo: Judith Cralle

"The surfer who executes the most radical controlled maneuvers in the most critical section of the biggest wave and/or best waves for the longest functional distance shall be deemed the winner."

—*ASP Rule Book*

surfing fads *n.* See PUKA SHELL NECKLACE, SURFER'S CROSS.

surfing in Nebraska *adj.* Used to describe an individual who's totally vacant. Nothing going on upstairs. Usage: "Bro, I think that dude's surfing in Nebraska."

surfing museums *n.* Places that store surfing paraphernalia and memorabilia of surfing and surf culture. Two of the more permanent ones in California are the Santa Cruz Surfing Museum and the Huntington Beach International Surfing Museum. In addition, many museums come and go, but there are also many private collections, especially in California, that can be tracked down by word of mouth through local surf shops.

surfing spin-off sports *n.* Activities inspired by and sometimes imitating surfing maneuvers but done in other settings, for example sandboarding, snowboarding, and windsurfing.

surfing the crimson wave *v.* See RIDING THE CRIMSON WAVE.

"Surfing the Internet" *n.* The term was coined by Jean Armour Polly in 1992. See SURFING AS METAPHOR, page 281.

surfing under turd Surfing in polluted waters; same as ON THE NOSE, YUK, WOOFY. (Australia; MW)

surfing with poo Surfing in an area full of excrement. See FLOATIES. (Australia; SAB)

surfin' safari *n.* **1)** A trip in search of surf, generally considered to be more than just a short drive—an expedition. See SURFARI. **2)** *Surfin' Safari* The Beach Boys' second album and hit tune (September 1962); A Brian Wilson–Mike Love composition.

surf instructor *n.* A surfer who teaches a novice how to surf. See SURF LESSONS.

surfish *n.* A blend of surf slang and English; a term coined by Dr. John Cohen in *Surfer* magazine (September 1984). See "Surfish as a Second Language" on page 17.

surfistas (surf-EES-tahs) *n.* Portuguese for "surfers." (Brazil)

surf jousting *n.* A game to play when the surf is flat, where two people on longboards paddle hard towards each other from a distance like knights in armor. A split second before the boards narrowly pass each other, the surfers stand up, push and shove each other, and try to make the other person fall off! Invented in Mexico at Playa Coyote, Baja California, 1993. Same as BOARD JOUSTING.

surf kite *n.* A board specifically designed for KITE SURFING with two or four flying lines; four offers more control. Board sizes vary according to use, skill, weight, and conditions. Larger boards are used for cruising and light wind.

Small boards, including wakeboards, are used for speed and tricks. There are also water relaunchable kites that are helpful for learning.

surfin' safari
Art: Jim Phillips

surf knobs, surf knots *n.* SURF BUMPS.

surf leash *n.* A three- to four-foot elastic cord connecting a surfboard to a rider's angle (via a Velcro cuff). The cord is affixed to the top side of the surfboard's tail and to the surfer's trailing foot. Originally, leashes were attached to the nose of the board and the wrist of the surfer. Leashes were a new concept and innovation in the late 1970s. They were a great breakthrough in surfing, serving both as a safety device to keep the surfer close to his board as well as allowing surfers to surf in previously impossible breaks with rugged shorelines. (SFR, June 1987) Also known as LEASH, LEG ROPE, DING STRING, SHOCK CORD.

surf legends *n.* Surfers who have made a name for themselves in the history of surfing, for example, Lance Carson ("No Pants Lance"), Mickey Dora ("Da Cat"), Greg Noll ("Da Bull"), and Jack Murphy ("Murph the Surf"). See SURFERS' NICKNAMES.

surf lessons *n.* Being taught how to surf by a SURF INSTRUCTOR, be it your friend or professional. Most people who

269

surf knobs
Art: I. B. Nelson

teach surfing make it way too complicated. Contrary to what you may hear, the basic act of surfing really isn't that hard given proper instruction. Of course the total surfing experience is made up of various simple and complex elements, and no beginner should automatically assume that he or she can just paddle out anywhere and give it a go.

Free Bonus Basic Uncomplicated Simple Surf Lesson:
1) Never turn your back on the ocean, unless paddling to catch a wave.
2) Start paddling for the wave before it reaches you.
3) As soon as you feel the wave pushing you along, stop paddling, and pop up into your stance.
4) When you wipeout, always cover your head and protect your face with your hands.

surflets *n.* Special words for emotions, actions, or moments that only surfers experience. The term was coined by Eric Fairbanks at *Surfing* magazine (1990); possibly it was inspired by the HBO TV "sniglets." See NASODRAIN, URINOPHORIA.

surf lice *n.* Tiny marine organism. See SEA LICE.

surf lore *n.* See SURF STORIES.

surf mag *n.* Any magazine on surfing. See SURFZINE.

surf movie
Barefoot Adventure (1960)
™ & © Bruce Brown Films
Dave Kinstle Collection

surf monkey
San Diego, California
Photo: Trevor Cralle

surf mama *n.* 1) A female surfer. 2) The ocean, same as THE BIG MAMA.

surfman *n.* BOARDMAN.

surfmanship *n.* An unwritten code of "fraternal and noncompetitive coexistence" that guides surfers in sharing waves. (NWT)

surf mat *n.* A rubber mattress inflated and used to ride the waves. (Australia) Also called MAT, SURF-O-PLANE.

surfmobile *n.* SURF VEHICLE.

surf-mom *n.* Female parent of a grommet; drives 'em to beach. (Sausalito, California, 1992) See MOMBRO.

surf mongrel *n.* A hyper young surfer. (Australia)

surf music
Art: Jim Phillips

surf monkey *n.* Super tacky plaster-of-paris, air-brushed chimpanzee in a striped suit on a surfboard; a favorite purchase while waiting in line to cross from Tijuana back across the U.S./Mexican border. Locally called *chango.*

surf movies *n.* **1)** A genre of independently made films pioneered by Bud Browne in the 1940s and 1950s. It was further developed by Greg Noll, John Severson, and Bruce Brown in the late 1950s and early 1960s, and included such feature-length documentaries as Brown's *The Endless Summer* (1964). Also including some zonko surf-flick titles over the years, such as *Barefoot Adventure, Cat on a Hot Foam Board, Five Summer Stories, Free Ride.* In the early days, surf movies were screened with live narration. They were then, and still are, always accompanied by hooting and howling from the audience. **2)** Hollywood's version of the surf culture, including films like *Gidget* (1959), *Beach Party* (1963), *Beach Blanket Bingo* (the "Beach" movies starred Annette Funicello and Frankie Avalon), and *Ride the Wild Surf.* **3)** And in a class by itself, *Big Wednesday* (1978) by John Milius. In this film, Hollywood rendered the California surf culture from the perspective of a real surfer.

surf music *n.* **1)** A sound representational of the ocean landscape, associated with the late fifties and early sixties and created by two main "families" of musicians: the *Orange County* bands descended from Dick Dale, who generally used more reverb (**full reverb surf music**), and the *south bay* bands descended from the Belairs, who tended to use less reverb. Examples of surf music range from "Walk—Don't Run" by the Ventures to the spy-surf theme sound of "Outer Limits" by the Marketts to "Mr. Moto" by the Belairs. Also known as *instro.* **2)** Rock 'n' roll music from California in the early 1960s, characterized by close treble harmonies and with lyrics that celebrated the exhilaration of surfing and beach life. The Beach Boys are a prime example. **3)** Any music you can surf to—Jimi Hendrix, Led Zepplin, Ramones, Santana, punk, reggae, electronica, etc. See HAWAIIAN MUSIC, SURF GUITAR.

surf music
Jim Thomas,
Burning Man, 1996,
Black Rock Desert, Nevada
Photo: Trevor Cralle

With the introduction of the "reverb" unit by guitar maker Leo Fender in 1962, lots of lead guitars took on the big, hollow, tubular tone of the reverb. The Fender reverb gave the guitar a slippery, "wet" sort of tone, which naturally served to solidify the music's identification as "the sound of surfing." Some of the most memorable surf sounds (such as the Chantays' "Pipeline," the Surfaris' "Wipe Out," the Pyramids' "Penetration," and Dick Dale's "Miserlou") were literally drenched in reverb.

surf music
The Mermen jamming
with Henry Kaiser
during the "Latinia"
into "Cabash" segue
Photo: Trevor Cralle

The surf sound peaked in 1963; the advent of the Beatles in early 1964 and the "British Invasion" marked what is generally regarded as the end of the surf music era. Yet original surf music still has the energy, simplicity, and rawness of the setting that inspired it. (PJN)

". . . and you'll never hear surf music again" was Jimi Hendrix' phrase from the song "Third Stone from the Sun" on the album Are You Experienced? There are Hendrix tunes in which the influence of surf music is obvious including "Drifting" and "Pali Gap."

The only musical genre inspired by a sport.

"Surf Music is an infectious instrumental form of rock 'n' roll characterized by magical energy and imagery, and a strong sense of melody. It's a melding of Latin, Middle Eastern, Hawaiian, Country, and American Southwest styles in nifty capsules of melodic danceable joy. Positive vibes ooze from this guitar centered world of reverb and tribal rhythms."

—Phil Dirt, host of the long-running radio show Surfs-Up! heard every Saturday night at 7 p.m. on "The Wave of The West," KFJC 89.7 FM, Los Altos Hills, California

surf music revival *n.* A resurgence of instrumental surf music in the late 1970s and early 1980s, led by groups like Jon and the Nightriders, the Surf Raiders, the Halibuts, and Agent Orange. Surf music exploded in the 1990s.

Surf naked! An exclamation on T-shirts and bumper stickers, meaning something like "Go for it!" (North Carolina 1981)

surf nazis *n.* **1)** Originally, young gremlins of the 1960s, who took to wearing German Luftwaffe officers' coats for warmth on the beach on cold winter days; they also adopted the iron cross and the swastika as their emblems. (MCR) **2)** Loosely applied, refers to hyper young surfers. **3)** *Surf Nazis Must Die* (1987).

> "The swastika became a symbol of some surfers just because it pissed off some people. It was a rebellious act. That's why Mickey Dora painted swastikas all over his boards. Most surfers didn't even know what it meant. It was just another way of shaking the pillars of society; something we excelled in doing."
>
> —*Greg Noll, Da Bull (1989)*

Surf Ninjas *n.* 1993 Hollywood movie about two surfers who discover they are long-lost princes; Kwantzu Dudes!

surf-n-turf *n.* A generic term for any dish with meat and seafood.

surfology *n.* The study of good surf—identifying where the surf will be good and understanding why it will be good at some breaks in certain conditions and not in others. Elements that allow surfers to predict and find good surf include swell direction, wind, tides, land and underwater topography, and wave size. Satellite photos are also useful. (W&B)

Surfonics *n.* SURFSPEAK. The term was coined in January 1997 by San Diego's Kevin Moi at Wireless Flash News after he read a review of *The Surfin'ary* in the *Reader,* San Diego's local independent newspaper. Surfonics is a play on the term "Ebonics," an alternative to standard English proposed by the Oakland, California, Board of Education, which argued that Black students some-

times speak with a language that is partially derived from their African and West Indian heritage. The Board said that this language structure—well studied by scholars—ought to be respected and not simply dismissed as bad English. See BROBONICS.

surf-o-plane or **surfoplane** *n.* An inflatable rubber mat used in Australia in the 1950s. (MF) Same as SURF MAT.

surform *n.* A hand plane with removable blades used in shaping foam, fiberglass, and resin.

surf party *n.* A full-on raging good time, as seen in the "Crashers!" scene in the movie *Big Wednesday* (1978).

surf photography *n.* An area of photography that often requires the photographer to be positioned in the breaking wave in order to shoot the surfer coming down or through. Doc Ball was the first acknowledged **surf photographer;** other pioneers include John Severson, Bud Browne, and Bruce Brown. Today there are many surf photographers, among them Robert Brown, Jeff Divine, Aaron Chang, Rob Giley, Don King, and Woody Woodworth.

*surf
photographer*

Brain Bielmann

Photo: Bill Romerhaus

*surf
photographer*

In-water shot

Photo: Bob Barbour

surf poetry *n.* Poetry about the sea and the surfing experience.

Once more upon the waters!
yet once more!
And the waves bound beneath me
as a steed
That knows his rider.

—Lord Byron (1788–1824)
Childe Harold's Pilgrimage, *canto 3, stanza 2*

---

surf progression *n.* A specific set of chords played on a ukulele. (Kauai)

surf punk *n.* **1)** A young surfer. **2)** A surfer who is part of the punk rock scene—reads *Maximum Rock 'N' Roll* and *Thrasher* magazines, has spiked hair, listens to punk music, and so on.

Surf Punks *n.* A satirical rock music group from Malibu, formed in 1977 and led by Drew Steele and Dennis Dragon, which mirrored events experienced in the water and on the sand. Their observations of the Southern California beach and surf scene are mixed over a richly layered soundtrack; their songs include "My Beach," "My Wave," and "Locals Only."

"By over-simplifying our statements, I thought the surfing public would interpret the message as an obvious parody targeted at the beach communities. But I was wrong. Many of the younger surfers took on "My Beach—Go Home" as their anthem. However a few did understand and appreciated the comedic aspects of the show."

—Dennis Dragon (SFR, May 1983)

---

surf puppy *n.* Beginning surfer. Usage: "Eh, surf puppy, you go surf ovah deah." (Oahu, Hawaii, 2000)

surf rack, surfboard rack *n.* A metal, foam pad, or wooden apparatus attached to the top of a car and used to carry surfboards. Also called ROOF RACK. See SOFT RACK.

surf rasta *n.* A term loosely applied to any surfer who sprouts dreadlocks, listens to reggae music, enjoys living naturally, but doesn't necessarily subscribe to the Rastafarian religion. Usage: "He's a total surf rasta." See REGGAE.

surf rat *n.* A young and enthusiastic surfer. See RATLY.

surf rebel *n.* A surfer *with a cause,* who lives for surfing, and nothing else. Same as WAVE REBEL.

surf report *n.* **1)** An accounting of up-to-date regional surfing conditions given on local radio stations each morning. **2)** A telephone report offered by many lifeguard services. **3)** *The Surf Report* An informative publication put out by *Surfer*

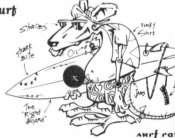

surf shop
Art: Jim Phillips

maga-
zine and
offering
monthly
sum-
maries
and
forecasts of worldwide surfing conditions. For various other sources of information about the surf, see "Where to
Get Surf Reports" below.

surf rider, surfrider *n.* SURFER.

Surfrider Beach *n.* A surf site located
within Malibu Lagoon State Beach and
popularized by surfing movies in the
early 1960s; one of the finest surfing
spots in California, especially during
summer when strong southwest swells
refract around a rock reef at Malibu
Point and break over a gently sloping
sandy bottom, offering long rides.

Surfrider Foundation *n.* A California-
based nonprofit organization founded in
1984, dedicated to the preservation and

Where to Get Surf Reports

One of the most accurate sources of information about the surf is the
marine weather channel on a weather radio, which sometimes provides information about the swell that you can't see just by looking at
it. Information found on the newspaper weather page is reasonably
accurate but always seems to be a day or so behind. A toll call to various 976 telephone numbers can provide you with surf predictions
using state-of-the-art meteorological technology. Turn to TV weather
on the news only as a last resort. (W&B; SFG, March 1990)

In addition, surf shops and lifeguard stations usually post some or
all of the following information daily:

A sample surf report
- skies: "clear," "hazy," "foggy," "partly cloudy," "overcast"
- swell: "2–4," "4–6," and so on (height given in feet)
- swell direction: "SW" (southwest), "West," "NW" (northwest)
- wave shape: "clean," "good," "fair," "poor"
- air temperature: "72"
- water temperature: "68"
- wind speed: "15–25" (knots or miles per hour)
- high tide: "12:00," "12:01"
- low tide: "6:00," "5:58"

Art: Jim Lucas.
Big Stick Surfing
Association

enjoyment of ocean waves and beaches worldwide. Its projects include protecting and improving beach access, promoting a long-range surf enhancement program, stopping encroachment of coastal structures, and supporting clean surfing conditions by advocating full sewage treatment and strict enforcement of toxic dumping regulations. See page 361 for contact info

surf riding or **surf-riding** or **surf-riding** *n.* The sport of riding the surf on a surfboard (W9); SURFING.

surf rock *n.* A type of music in the 1960s.

surf rocking *n.* Dancing, grooving to the music.

"Surf Route 101" *n.* A song by Jan & Dean about driving a woody up and down the coast. (1960s)

surf run *n.* A long trip in the car with the destination of catching some waves, for example, a "Mexico surf run."

surf sacrifice *n.* The ceremonial burning of a surfboard on the beach, usually an old or discarded board; not recommended for today's environmentally conscious surfer.

surfsailing *n.* WINDSURFING.

surf sista
Gretchen Back,
Santa Cruz
Photo: Mike Peralta

surf snack
Flea and Noi Kaulukukui
with octopus string
San Bartolo, Peru
Photo: Mike Peralta

surf scene *n.* The situation at the beach. Rent a few contemporary surf videos to check out the cultural pulse of the current surf scene.

surf scooter *n.* One means of transport to the beach—a Vespa or other type of motorcycle, but almost never a moped.

surf scoter (*Melanitta perspicillata*) *n.* An abundant sea-going duck that floats in flocks and rides waves; a sea duck.

surf scruff *n.* Facial stubble from not shaving; an element of the surfed-out look.

surf's down An expression meaning flat surf, which is possibly even unridable.

surf session *n.* See SESSION.

surf shop *n.* **1)** A store that sells surfing equipment and beach apparel; known for the intoxicating smell of surf wax, neoprene rubber wetsuits, and fiberglass surfboards. **2)** The original "Surf Shop," a name registered to Jack O'Neill in 1962, which later became a generic term. (SCSM) In the early 1960s, the common surf shop was also a surfboard factory. (GN)

surf shorts *n.* A surfer's swimsuit. Also called BOARDSHORTS, SURF TRUNKS.

Surfside *n.* A residential beach community located on the south spit of Anaheim Bay within the city of Seal Beach, California. Surfside Beach, adjacent to the Pacific Coast Highway, was an excellent surf spot until the early 1960s, when the beach was rebuilt after heavy storms.

surf sista, surf sistas *n.* Female surfer(s).

surf site or **surfsite** *n.* **1)** A location where waves break in a form suitable for surfing—the result of swell interactions with the bottom and wind interactions with the water surface. **2)** A spot composed of a takeoff area, a riding area, an end-of-ride area, a board-recovery area, a return path, and an access route. (JRW) Also called SURF SPOT.

surf-skate synthesis, surf-skate crossover *n.* The transference of terminology and maneuvers between surfing and skateboarding. Examples are aerial and face plant. (SFR, November 1983)

surf ski *n.* An Australian paddleboard invented in 1933 by Dr. G. A. Crackenthorp of Manly Surf Club in Sydney. Surf skis have a lot of scoop in the nose, are very long (about nineteen feet), and narrow (about seventeen inches), and have a rudder. The rider sits on the board with feet in holders and propels the craft with a double-bladed paddle—occasionally standing while surfing. Surf skis were very popular in Australia before Malibu boards arrived. (DM) Sometimes called *racing ski*. *Not a* WAVE SKI.

surf-skate
crossover
Art: Jim Phillips

277

surf slippers *n.* AQUA SOCKS.

surf snack *n.* Anything you munch before or after a session; **plate lunch**. (Hawaii) See BURRITO, FISH TACO, HAKENVEESMO, GRINDS, SHAVE ICE.

surf-skate
synthesis
Art: Jim Phillips

surf sound *n.* **1)** The music of American surf bands in the early 1960s; **California surf sound**. (IDSM) See SURF MUSIC. **2)** The sound of powerful ocean waves, crashing against the beach or onto the water surface. Same as OCEAN ROAR, ROAR OF THE OCEAN.

surf soup *n.* **1)** An unappealing condition of the water surface when southeast winds off of Florida blow a Sargasso Sea–like mat of algae into the surf zone—it's like paddling through pea soup. (TDW) **2)** SURF CHOWDER.

surf spot *n.* SURF SITE, such as Padang Padang on the island of Bali. ("The spot's so good they had to name it twice.")

surf spot names Names used by surfers to identify specific surf spots; may be confined to surfer use initially but usually spreads into general use after a while. Surfers name spots for a variety of reasons; for example, Garbage Pit, Hawaii, is named for the pollution in the area, and K38 in Baja California, Mexico, is so named because of the location of the break near roadside signpost K38. See Appendix D, "Major Surf Spots around the World."

surf standard *n.* An instrumental surf tune, like a "jazz standard," that is covered by many surf bands such as "Mr. Moto" by The Belairs. See SURF CLASSIC.

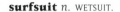

surf stickers *n.* Sticky-backed decals displaying the logos of surf-industry equipment. Stuck on surfboards, cars, gas pumps, and road signs; also good for temporary ding repair.

surf stoke 1) *n.* Adrenaline stoking the body's fire. (JGM) **2) surf stoked** *adj.* Usage: "I was completely surf stoked." See STOKED.

surf stomps *n.* Dances in the early 1960s named after the popular dance style, the stomp, which became known as the **surfer stomp**. Another indigenous "surf" dance was trippin', a creation of Dick Dale's crowd. Together the two dances became a sort of surfer "tribal ritual"; these dances were exclusive to the folk culture of surfing. (PJN) See SURFER'S STOMP. **—surf stomping**

surf totem
*"Ulola," the author's
Mother Ocean surf totem
sculpted by
Briana Caufman*

Photo: Paul McEntyre

"It was an intense experience to be among hundreds of surfers all doing nothing but stomping their sandals on the dance floor to the pulsating beat of the band!"

—Paul Johnson (1987)

surf stories *n.* Stories exchanged among friends, usually about a hot ride or a surf trip adventure; an important element of surfing. See TALK STORY.

surf strap *n.* A stretch band used to secure surfboards to the roof rack or a soft rack to the car roof.

surfsuit *n.* WETSUIT.

surf's up A statement indicating that the waves are breaking at a high level, ideal for surfing. (IDSM) "Surf's Up!"

surf talk, surfer talk *n.* Same as surf slang, surf lingo, surfspeak, etc.

"We're all equal in the ocean," he explained. "That's surfer talk, but it makes a weird kind of sense."

—Ackerman, in Hunter S. Thompson's
The Curse of Lono (1983)

surf tattoo *n.* Became popular in the late 1980s and early 1990s.

surf time *n.* The natural rhythm of the ocean expressed in sets and lulls. An apparent contradiction exists between the surfer's laid-back attitude and the need to consult a watch to know when the best tides are.

"Watches and clocks irrelevant mechanisms of measure here, time organizing itself into sets and lulls, sets and lulls."

—Thomas Farber, On Water (1994)

Surftones *n.* A surf band from Newport Beach. (1980s)

surf totem *n.* Any item or object that you pray to in order to help conjure up the surf. See CHESTER.

278

surf vehicle
Photo: Dennis Junor

surf town *n.* Any small coastal community that has a beachy feeling about it.

surf trip *n.* A road trip in search of waves. See SURFARI, SURFIN' SAFARI.

surf trunks or **surftrunks** *n.* A swimsuit designed especially for surfing; made of heavy-duty fabric, double stitched, with pocket for a bar of wax in the rear. Also called BOARDSHORTS.

surf tunes *n.* SURF MUSIC.

surf types *n.* See SURF BREAKS.

Surfurbia *n.* Historical architecture professor Reyner Banham's term for the seaside communities of Redondo Beach, Hermosa Beach, and Manhattan Beach in Southern California. Also called **Surfurbs.**

surf vehicle *n.* **1)** A mode of transport to and from the beach, such as a VW Bug or a microbus (combi). **2)** A rusted-out heap if you surf in the tropics. See BAJA BUG, CRUISEMOBILE, SURF BOMB, SURFWAGON, WOODY.

surf vid *n.* SURF VIDEO.

surf video *n.* A means of seeing surf movies in your very living room; available in almost every surf shop these days. Unfortunately, watching videos can't duplicate the feeling of watching a surf movie on a big screen together with a screaming surfer audience.

surfwagon *n.* A woody or other station wagon used for transporting surfboards. Also known as STAY-WAG.

SurfWatch *n.* A computer software product that filters sexually explicit material on the Internet.

surf wax or **surfwax** *n.* Specialized wax spread on the surface of a board to give better traction, so the feet won't slip. Also called WAX.

surfwear *n.* Surfer apparel such as neon boardshorts, long-sleeve T-shirts, and wetsuits. See SURF FASHION.

surf widow *n.* A surfer's wife or girlfriend. (San Francisco) "When a woman meets a surfer, she thinks she's lucky. He's tall, blond and handsome. Eventually she gets jealous of the surf. It can be hard sharing your husband with the ocean." —Kathleen Bergerson (CVG, 1988) "I had a boyfriend who was a surfer; it kinda broke us up. I'd never see him. He quit his job and moved to Australia to surf. I guess I'm jealous of the water." —Heidi, at a party in San Francisco, 1997

surfy 1) *n.* An Australian term for a surfer or surfer type; also spelled *surfie,* as in "a barefoot, surfie-looking dude." (CC) **2)** *adj.* Abounding with surf; forming surf or like surf. **—surfier, surfiest**

surfwear
Classic long-sleeve surf T-shirt
Photo: Trevor Cralle

"Police will maintain a constant alert today on Sydney's 15 beaches to prevent gang warfare between Rockers and Surfies."

—*Sun-Herald, March 10, 1963*

surfy head *n.* A surfer. (Australia; MON)

surfzine *n.* Generally refers to the more underground, self-published type of

swallowtail
Photo: Tom Servais/
Surfer magazine

surfing publication, as distinct from a glossy SURF MAG.

surf zombie *n.* Someone who is totally obsessed by a strange power so that all they wanna do is surf (there's no fighting it); a state caused by a new swell. You can spot surf zombies by their fried eyeballs and leaky sinuses. The term derived from a Wilbur Kookmeyer cartoon, "Surf Zombies."

surf zone *n.* The area affected by wave action, extending from the shoreline high-water mark seaward to where the waves start to break. (CCRG)

surge, surge channel *n.* A narrow gap in rocky intertidal areas along the coastline through which waves surge; if timed right, can be used to carry a surfer on a board to or from a surf spot. (But beware of sharp creatures such as barnacles along the way.)

SW What everyone in Australia calls *Surfing World* magazine.

swallowtail, swallow tail *n.* A surfboard tail design featuring two pintails side by side. (NAT, 1985)

Swami's *n.* **1)** A surf spot in Encinitas, California. **2)** Name of a really great, but sadly now defunct, San Francisco–based surf band in the 1990s; originally formed in Santa Barbara, their theatrical live shows usually featured someone playing the coconuts.

swan *n.* FLYING SWAN.

swash *n.* Incoming water, water moving up the beach; the opposite of

BACKWASH. (TLH) Usage: "I rode the swash up to the berm."

sweeping cutback *n.* A long, drawn-out turn.

sweet *adj.* Cool; said of anything you like. (PZ) Usage: "That's sweet."

sweet ride *n.* **1)** A nice ride. **2)** *The Sweet Ride* A Hollywood surf movie.

sweets *n.* A group of good-looking girls.

sweet spot *n.* **1)** The area on a surfboard that feels comfortable when you stand over it and that allows for ultimate maneuvering. **2)** A really good surf spot.

swell *n.* **1)** Unbroken waves; either one unbroken wave or all of the waves coming from one particular storm. **2)** A large, unbroken wave, usually of distant origin. **3)** Any wave before it breaks. **4)** Waves generated by wind in a particular storm. Two or more different swells may be present simultaneously. (S&C) **5) good swell** Regular, well-shaped waves created by distant storms and breaking consistently for several days.

Swells move in the open ocean at about thirty-five miles per hour; they move more slowly in shallow water. Once they hit shore, they may continue coming for a day, a week, or even a month, depending on the intensity of the distant storm and various other factors. For example, a storm in the North Pacific may send waves to the

Swami's
Art: I. B. Nelson

Surfing as Metaphor

"Truth be known, there's no surfing the Internet: surfing is surfing; no aspect of a network of computers is the ocean."

—*Thomas Farber,* The Face of The Deep *(1998)*

Originally a sport and an artform, these days surfing has evolved into a metaphor used to describe just about anything, including a person exploring, browsing, and jumping from site to site on the Internet's World Wide Web. How did this evolve?

The first use of the surfing metaphor was by Brian Wilson with the 1964 Jan and Dean tune **"Sidewalk Surfin'"** which was appropriate since skateboarding has many cross-over aspects. Many extensions followed, such as **windsurfing** (1969), **snowsurfing**—a short-lived term for snowboarding (1985), **sky surfing** or **air surfing** (1991)—Skydiving with feet strapped to a board, **ice surfing**—on frozen lakes, and **kite surfing** (both in the late 1990s).

One of the earliest abstract references or true metaphors, as opposed to an extension of the sport, may have come from the late, great Hawaiian comedian Rap Reiplinger back in the 1970s. On his album, *Poi Dog*, the routine "Loving you is surfing you" describes making love to a woman as if he were surfing a wave with surfing and sexual maneuvers and positions intertwined.

"Loving you is surfing you."
—Rap Reiplinger

Photo: Alan Tieger
www.bodyscapees.com

In the 1980s, the surfing metaphor appeared in Dan Poynter's *Hang Gliding: The Basic Handbook of Skysurfing.* In Fresno, California, throughout the 1980s, **bumper surfing**—the act of riding on the rear bumper of an automobile in a standing position while trying to keep your balance as the car zooms around the streets—was popular.

But it was **channel surfing**—using the TV remote control to quickly switch from one channel to another or flicking back and forth between several programs— that really caught the attention of mainstream popular culture in the late 80s.

This was followed by **train surfing**—this is the very dangerous practice of riding on the rooftops of electric passenger trains in Rio de Janeiro, Brazil; this is what a **subway surfer** does in New York, or what they call **tram surfing** in Grenoble, France.

The 1990s saw the explosion of surfing as everything, with a seemingly infinite list of activities being likened to the sport of surfing, including—but certainly not limited to—**elevator surfing**, the practice of riding up and down an elevator shaft on the top of an elevator; and **the surfer hold,** a professional wrestling move.

The term **surfing the Internet** was coined by Jean Armour Polly in 1992. This was followed by **information surfing**—navigating the information revolution through the libraries of the world, and **cyber surfing.** A cyber surfer is one who "surfs" the Internet. A computer hacker becomes a **bit surfer.**

A 1992 article in the *New York Times* describes the act of eating hot chile peppers as **mouth surfing.** Originally called "stage diving," and later, "head walking," Vice President Al Gore even tried **crowd surfing** on election night 1992. A San Francisco nightclub features the sign **"No Head Surfing."** There's also **pillow surfing**—sleeping (1993).

David Shenk and Steve Silberman, in *Skeleton Key: A Dictionary for Deadheads* (1994), list the following two terms: **dirt surfers**—Deadheads who have relaxed their standard of personal grooming to the extreme, and **seat surfing**—burying one's ticket stub deep in one's pants pocket and floating from unoccupied seat to unoccupied seat.

Shoulder surfers is a police term for scammers who peer over the shoulders of people using cards to charge their calls at pay phones. Numbers are quickly memorized or recorded, and then the "surfers" look for someone, such as an international visitor at an airport, who wants to buy cheap phone time on someone else's card (*Scientific American,* March 1994). As athletic celebration: "If the shoulder surfing he was doing in the end zone on the arms and shoulders of his 49ers teammates after the touchdown run was any indication, we can surmise that there were no hard feelings" (*San Francisco Chronicle,* September 26, 1994).

"I'm riding the crimson wave" (said of females during their menstrual period) was popularized by the movie *Clueless* (1995).

Theater surfing " . . . you go into a multiplex cinema . . . " (1994) **Couch surfing**—crashing around on other people's sofas. (1994) **Finger surfing**—navigating telephone message boards by pushing buttons on a Touch-Tone phone (1995). **Ego surfing**—searching for your own name on the Internet (1996). **Grate surfing**—running and sliding on slippery land-based surfaces (1997). **Dial surfers**—people who scan the radio, searching for stations (1998). **Vocal surfing**— speaking commands into a microphone to surf the Internet (1999).

Last year we saw an article entitled "**Style Surfing:** What to Wear in the 3rd Millennium" by Ted Polhemus, as well as **employee surfing**—hiring and firing. National Public Radio invites listeners to "Surf over to our website . . ." When will it ever stop? Finally, in the late 1990s, a radio commercial for Prodigy set the record straight: "You're not surfing. You're sitting at a desk in front of a computer."

Many real surfers despise the use of surfing as metaphor. However, since surfing is the ultimate activity, we surfers should all be honored that normal people have recognized it in a playful way. The above mentioned "surfing" terms are all listed individually throughout the main A–Z section of *The Surfin'ary.* Please send any additional surfing metaphors to the address listed on page 360. More quotes on surfing as metaphor:

"There are far too many negative connotations attached to "surfing" for schools to emphasize that aspect of the Net."

—Jamie McKenzie, Director of Media and Technology,
Bellingham, Washington, "The Research Cycle," 1995

"The surfing metaphor used with relation to the Internet is based on analogy with channel surfing on TV (so it's a metaphor of a metaphor!). That's a shame: real surfing is a more powerful metaphor for systems designers: how to create programs, learning activities, social structures, etc. that can ride the fluid, moving, ever-changing wave of the underlying functionality, content, and interface of the rapidly evolving digital library."

—Michael B. Twidale, Computing Department, Lancaster University,
"Supporting the Users of the Digital Library," October 28, 1996

Eliza Laffin
Ripping online
Photo: Trevor Cralle

". . . the 'surfing' metaphor was recently killed by the Loma Prieta—inspired AT&T ad showing multicultural business types riding a horrific sinewave of asphalt through the middle of downtown Manhattan. Who wants to surf their way through flying chunks of pavement?"

—Michael Sippey, "War of the Words," May 16, 1997

"The abundance of new users and new sites on the World Wide Web has lead to the popularization of a 'surfing' metaphor for information seekers on the Web. The metaphor lends itself to visualizing a user moving more or less effortlessly over a wide sea of information, twisting and turning as the currents and his interests dictate.

"Despite the appeal of the metaphor, there are no real environments for web surfing, or browsing. Most people experience the web as a contextless set of links, each page supplying tens or sometimes hundreds of options for further exploration. Even those sites which categorize their links, do not usually indicate how the links may relate. Users simply go from page to page, following whatever link seems best. This depth-first wandering provides no organization and no means of relating one discovery to another."

—Alan Wexelblat, "An Environment for Aiding Information-Browsing Tasks,"
© 1996 AAAI Spring Symposium on Acquisition,
Learning & Demonstration: Automating Tasks for Users (Gil, Birmingham, Cypher & Pazzani, eds.)

North Shore of Hawaii that are ten
feet the first day, twenty feet the
second day, and twelve feet the
third day, all with good shape.

≈≈≈≈≈≈≈≈≈≈≈≈≈≈≈≈

swell characteristics *n.* The multitude
of qualities that any given swell may
exhibit, such as pumping in consistently
or not being well defined.

swell classification *n.* Identifying the
type of swell, "west swell," "south
swell," etc. Detecting this from the
beach is a fine art; there aren't any hard
and fast rules.

swell direction *n.* **1)** The direction
from which the swell is coming.
2) Usually the first thing to check when
deciding where to surf, since it can
cause one spot to have better surf than
another on any particular day. Surf
spots break differently with different
swells; for example, Cardiff reef in
Southern California will break on any
swell, but it peels and has more bowls
when the swell comes in from a norther-
ly direction. (W&B) **—north swell,
east swell, south swell, west
swell, southwest swell**, etc.

swell period *n.* The time it takes for two

swells to pass a given point; the longer
the period, the stronger the swell. (BB,
October 1990) Same as PERIOD, WAVE PERIOD.

swell window *n.* **1)** A gap between offshore islands that allows swells to pass
unobstructed to shore and break with
full force. Also called WINDOW. **2)** The
direction from which surf can come and
reach the shore; islands, points, and
peninsulas may block swells from
reaching certain areas. (W&B) An **open
window** means that nothing is blocking the swell.

swim *v., n.* What you do to retrieve a
surfboard that got away. Usually necessary with boards, such as longboards,
that don't have leashes. Usage: "I had
about fifteen swims today." (GN)

switchfoot *n.* A surfer who rides with
either the right foot or the left foot forward, depending on which direction the
waves are breaking, in an effort to face
the wave at all times.

switch-stance *n.* The ability to ride
frontside on both rights and lefts. (ORB)

Swizzle *n.* A nine-foot longboard made
out of polypropylene, coated with
fiberglass and capped with rubber
ends; invented by Tom Morey in the
late 1990s.

Pleasure Point,
Santa Cruz

Photo: Trevor Cralle

tabis (TAH-beez) *n.* Hawaiian split-toe booties—the neoprene equivalent of toe socks. (ECN)

tablista Hawaiiano *n.* Literally a Hawaiian surfer, but loosely applied to any visiting California surfer in El Salvador in the 1960s. (PDX)

tablistas (tab-LEES-tahs) *n.* A Spanish word for "surfers." (Peru)

tag *v.* To leave's one signature as graffiti under a bridge at a local surf spot. (PZ) Usage: "Yeah, we tagged our names over by the river mouth."

tail *n.* **1)** The stern or back end of a surfboard. **2)** The rear third of a surfboard. (ORB) Also called REAR or BUTT.

tail block or **tailblock** *n.* The back or tail section of a surfboard.

tail corner *n.* A sharp edge in the tail of a surfboard that allows water flow to break away.

tail curve *n.* A rounded place in the tail of a surfboard that holds water flow.

tail design *n.* The shape of the rear end of a surfboard. Tail designs include single-winged swallow, double-bump rounded square, round, double-winged rounded swallow, single-bump rounded pin, rounded diamond, square, winger, flyer, stinger, and screwdriver. (ORB) Same as TAIL PLANSHAPE.

tail-drift *n.* Tail slide.

tail fin *n.* SKEG.

tail flutter *n.* Instability in the tail of a surfboard, which sometimes happens on bigger waves when the tail goes out of control and the board slaps up and

takeoff
Photo: Woody Woodworth

down; caused by too wide a tail or a board bottom that is too flat, or by riding too far to the rear of the board.

tail hook *n.* A metal hook attached to the tail of an old-style paddle board.

tail kick *n.* The part of a board from the rear edge of the fin(s) to the tip of the tail. See ROCKER.

tail patch *n.* A sticky-backed foam pad affixed to a surfboard deck and used as a wax substitute to give added traction. Same as DECK PATCH.

tail planshape *n.* TAIL DESIGN.

tail-side floater *n.* FLOATER.

tail width *n.* The distance across the tail of a board, measured twelve inches from the tip(s) of the tail.

take gas *v.* **1)** To have trouble, especially the kind that leads to a wipeout. **2)** To get trapped in the curl of a wave and lose one's board; to wipeout. Usage: "I saw you taking gas out there."

takeoff or **take-off** *n.* **1)** The act of catching a wave. **2)** In general, the start of a ride. (A&M) **3)** In competitive surfing, the beginning of a ride, defined as the space of time between the hands leaving the rails and the commencement

talking story
Art: Jim Phillips

of the first maneuver or turn. (L&L)
4) The moment of truth for surfers and astronauts alike. Surfers probably have a marginally better chance of coming back alive, but you wouldn't know it to see their eyeballs as they peer down the face of a concave monster. (JARR) See LATE TAKEOFF (late drop-in), TOADS.
—**screaming takeoff 5) take off** *n.* To paddle into a breaking wave in order to ride it, to catch a wave or begin a ride, to launch.

takeoff point *n.* The exact spot where the waves are consistently breaking in such a way as to provide a good ride.

taking the drop *n., v.* **1)** Coming over the top of a wave in order to take advantage of its velocity to stay ahead of the curl and avoid being wiped out. (IDSM) **2)** Dropping down the face of a wave. See FREE FALL. Usage: "Taking the drop at the Wedge is insanely gnarly."

taking the whip *v.* Going over the falls. (CSD) Usage: "You were taking the whip in that shore break."

talking to the seals *v.* Vomiting; same as AQUA BOOT. Usage: "I got seasick this morning and started talking to the seals."

talk story, talking story 1) *v.* Hawaiian Pidgin for sitting around with friends and telling stories. **2)** *n.* Accounts of surfing adventures. Every surfer has stories to tell; some surfers talk more than others. See RIGGIN, SURF STORIES, YARNER.

> "I love 'talking story.' Surfers sometimes take as much pleasure from sitting around talking about surfing as they do actually surfing."
>
> —*Fred Hemmings, The Soul of Surfing*

tan 1) *v.* To make or become brown by exposure to the sun. **2)** *n.* The brownish color that sun rays impart to the skin. **3)** *adj.* Having a SUNTAN. (AHD) Usage: "Nice tan."

tandem, tandem surfboard *n.* A large surfboard used for tandem riding. Tandem boards are usually extra wide and at least nine feet long, to give increased stability and compensate for the weight of two riders.

tandem surfing *n.* **1)** Two people—usually a man and a woman—riding a wave together on the same surfboard. **2)** Two bodysurfers riding a wave together, one on the back of the other.

tank, tanker *n.* A very old and heavy longboard.

288

tandem surfing
Steve Farwell and
Chrissy Morrison
Photo: Bob Barbour

tanning center *n.* Skin-cancer ward. (SP)

tapered *adj.* Used to describe rails that gradually blend smoothly into the contour of the surfboard.

tapped *adj.* SPENT. Usage: "I was so tapped after that sesh."

tar *n.* Sticky, black gobs of oil that adhere to your feet when you step in it on the beach. The beaches of Santa Barbara are notorious for this stuff.

taste or **tasty** *adj.* Said of fine-looking waves or babes. (MVA) Usage: "Oh, dude, that's taste."

T-band *n.* A surfboard whose wood stringer and wood tail block form a T.

tea bag *n.* Bodyboard with a leash.

Team Barney *n.* A surfer who's acting kookish.

team riding *n.* Derogatory term for LONGBOARDING—as in,"Yeah, we're sponsored." Usage: "Look at those geeky team riders who think they're cool." (Santa Cruz)

tear, tear it up *v.* To shred waves, to surf very hard; same as RIP IT UP, RIP 'N' TEAR.

teardrop *n.* A surfboard shape, one with a wide tail. (1967)

ted *adj.* **1)** Bloated from eating too much. Usage: "Dude, I'm ted." **2) get tedly** To eat a lot. (North San Diego County; LH) Usage: "Let's get tedly."

Teenage Mutant Ninja Turtles *n.* Sewer-dwelling amphibians who co-opted valley and surf lingo ("Cowabunga!" "Go for it," "radical," "pizza dude," "awesome," "gnarly"). Originally comic-book characters, then stars of a Saturday morning TV cartoon show, they were later brought to life through animatronics for a 1990 Hollywood blockbuster movie. The immense popularity of these "heroes on the half shell" was capitalized on by more than three hundred products in the marketplace, including sugary children's cereal, stuffed animals, and bubble gum trading cards.

template *n.* The silhouette or outline curve of a surfboard, viewed from the top or bottom; same as PLANSHAPE.

ten over *n.* A riding stance where the surfer is so far forward that both feet extend over the nose of the board. Also called HANGING TEN. (IDSM)

"Tequila" *n.* **1)** An instrumental surfy tune (except for the word "Taaah-KEEEY-laaah") originally performed by The Champs; later popularized by The Ventures in 1960. Pee Wee Herman did the best dance to it in *Pee Wee's Big Adventure.* **2) tequila** Mexican liquor made from the desert agave plant.

terlines *n.* Form-fitting nylon trunks designed for swimming; used by many Australian surfers.

textured deck *n.* A nonslip surface on the top of a surfboard.

thaw-out *n.* A quiet period after a winter surf session during which the only sound heard is the chattering of teeth and the cursing of the elements. You can tell a thaw-out is ending when the surfer is able to manipulate his tongue in such a manner as to form the words, "Unzip me, please." (JARR)

theater surfing *n.* "You go into a multi-plex cinema . . . " (Noah Levy, Berkeley High School, California 1994)

thick *adj.* Characteristic of some waves; can apply to the whole wave but usually relates to how big the lip is. A thick wave will pound you heavily or smack you in the face with full force. Usage: "That lip was really thick." See THIN.

thickness flow, thickness foil *n.* Refers to the distribution of foam along the length of a surfboard—from the nose to the tail—as seen from the side.

—nose thickness, middle thickness, tail thickness

thicky, thickies *n.* A type of wave with a thicker than usual lip and sometimes a big barrel. "He towed me into a big old thicky, and I began to fade deep into the bowl." —Skindog (SFG, March 2000)

thin *adj.* Characteristic of some waves; applies mainly to the wave lip, which may be said to "peel thinly." Distinguished from THICK or SQUARE WAVES.

thongs *n.* Approved footwear for surfers, worn for all occasions all year round, often teamed with socks in winter. The beauty of the thong is its versatility. It can be used as a musical instrument, weapon, fly swatter, and sex aid. Any establishment that won't let you in wearing thongs is run by nerds. (JARR) Same as FLIP-FLOPS.

thrash, thrashing *v.* **1)** To rip or shred on a wave. Usage: "Did you see me thrashing on that wave?" **2) thrashed** To get wiped out. Usage: "I got com-pletely thrashed on that last wave."

—thrashed-out

thrasher *n.* A surfing show-off.

three-sixty *n.* **1)** A maneuver in which the surfer turns the board 360 degrees. **2)** A modern maneuver in which the surfer continues the bottom turn up through the lip; the fins then break loose, and the board and surfer continue around in a 360-degree loop on the same wave. (NAT, 1985) Not the same as a SPINNER or 360 SPINNER.

360 air *n.* A three-sixty board spin in the air.

360 curtain floater *n.* A three-sixty board spin on top of the white water.

360 spinner *n.* A move in which the surfer, not the board, does a quick 360-degree pirouette while standing on the moving board. Same as SPINNER.

throat *n.* An anatomical nickname for a hollow wave; a TUBE.

through the back *n.* A move to get through a wave before getting sucked over the falls. Usage: "I saw you made it out through the back." See OUT THE BACK.

through-the-lip el rollo *n.* A body-boarding maneuver. Sometimes spelled *thru-the-lip*. See EL ROLLO.

through-the-lip rebound *n.* A maneu-ver normally attempted at the conclusion of a fade toward the main curl, at which point the surfer rides through the curl, instead of turning back to the original direction, and then takes the drop with the soup. Between hitting the curl and regaining a track in the original direction, the surfer has to turn the board through more than 180 degrees. (RA)

throwing the brains *n.* When male surfers expose themselves in front of their friends. (North San Diego County)

throwing the fin *n.* Hitting the top of a wave and exposing a fin. (MM)

throwin' the tools in the shed *v.* Heading into a barrel from which there is little hope of exiting. Usage: "Did you see me throw my tools into that shed? I knew I'd get worked, but I had some business to do in the green room." (Ocean Beach, San Francisco, 1999) See CLOSEOUT BARREL.

thruster *n.* Australian Simon Anderson's revolutionary three-fin surfboard design (revealed in 1981), which incorporates a very wide winged, rounded square tail. The wide point is located at or within a few inches of center; the nose is extremely narrow. The two side fins are toed in and canted out, the third fin is set only a few inches from the tip of the tail. Board characteristics are loose and fast; boards are from five-and-a-half to six-and-a-half feet long. They are called thrusters because they tend to come out of a turn with a little more thrust. (CC) Also called TRI or TRI-FIN. **—thrusties** (STM)

thruster
Ken Collins,
Santa Cruz
Photo: Mike Peralta

thunder crusher *n.* A gnarly wave. (A&M) See DUMPER.

tiburón *n.* Spanish for "shark"; this is a significant term for anyone surfing in Mexican waters. (BBD)

tidal bore *n.* **1)** A phenomenon that occurs where rivers enter the ocean via long funnel-shaped bays; in such estuaries, especially during high spring tides, the broad front of the incoming tide is restricted by the narrow channel and the shoaling water so that it abruptly increases in height, and a visible wave front, or bore, develops. When conditions are right, this bore can be ridden upstream. See RIVER SURFING. **2)** A person who talks about nothing but the height of the tide in relation to the surf and can tell you at any given time of day when the best tide is. (IBN)

thruster
Simon Anderson
with thruster
Photo: Peter Crawford/
Surfer magazine

"Well, something had to be done about those bloody twin-fins."

—*Simon Anderson, 1981 (SFR, January 1990)*

The bore of the Amazon is said to attain a height of twenty-five feet, giving it the appearance of a waterfall traveling upstream. It moves at a speed of twelve knots per hour and extends for three hundred miles. Other famous tidal bores are those of the Chientang River in northern China and the River Severn in England. (WB)

∿∿∿∿∿∿∿∿∿∿∿∿

tidal pull or **tidal flow** *n.* EBB and FLOW—the tide coming in and going out.

tidal wave *n.* In the ocean, a train of waves generated by an earthquake, volcanic eruption, underwater landslide, or nuclear explosion, containing a huge amount of energy and moving at high speed—up to 400 miles per hour in the open ocean. Can be tremendously destructive when they reach shore, inundating low-lying areas, because they steepen and increase in height on approaching shallow water. (WB)

∿∿∿∿∿∿∿∿∿∿∿∿

This popular term is entirely misleading in that the phenomenon it identifies has no connection with the tides. Consequently, American oceanographers adopted the Japanese word *tsunami*, which is still in general use, even though it merely means "tidal wave" in Japanese. A more descriptive term that applies to waves caused by earthquakes is *seismic sea wave*.

∿∿∿∿∿∿∿∿∿∿∿∿

tide book *n.* A reference book available at most surf shops that, in addition to a tide table with times and feet for high and low tides, contains such other useful information as the phases of the moon, times for sunrise and sunset, a wind chill factor table, and clam chowder recipes.

tide correction factor *n.* Amount of time subtracted or added to the tide tables based on your location in relation to the section of coastline covered in your TIDE BOOK.

tide graph *n.* The daily tidal range plotted on a graph.

tide range, tidal range *n.* The difference in feet or meters between high and low tides. For example, at Fistral Beach in Cornwall, England, the notorious tides can cause the break to shift in or out fifty yards during a single heat in a surf contest; during the annual Fosters Contest, numerous competitors fail to score their minimum waves simply because they "get lost" and out of position for the sets. (L&L) The Bay of Fundy, Nova Scotia, has a tidal range of sixty-five feet.

tides *n.* **1)** The periodic rising and falling of sea level as a consequence of the earth's rotation and the gravitational forces (or pull) of the moon and, to a lesser extent, the sun. Because these astronomical motions are very regular, tides are highly predictable. Tides are also influenced by the ocean's bottom topography. (CCRG) See TIDE BOOK. **2)** An important indicator as to when a surf spot is breaking best. See EQUATORIAL TIDES, MIXED TIDES, NEAP TIDES, SPRING TIDES, TROPIC TIDES.

tide book
Photo: Trevor Cralle

"The tide is turning [i.e., chang-ing]."

tide wave *n.* TIDAL BORE.

tint *n.* A transparent coloring agent for resin. (ORB)

tip *n.* **1)** The pointed front end of a surf-board. Also called NOSE TIP. **2)** Cabo San Lucas at the southern tip of Mexico's Baja California peninsula. Usage: "We're going to the tip." (BMS)

TK *adj.* Totally killer. Usage: "TK, dude."

to da max Hawaiian Pidgin for all the way, 100 percent. Usage: "Da surf is pompeen to da max."

TOAD Take Off and Dissolve—said of San Francisco's surf spot "The Dump," which is located offshore of the municipal dump and is off-limits to surfers. The lineup is inundated by toxic pollution (after a rainstorm the water turns purple from the dump runoff), and tons of bro-ken rebar (rusty World War II antisub-marine spikes) and concrete litter the paddle-out zone. (SFR, March 1991).

TOADS Take Off And Die Syndrome—a late takeoff that results in a heavy wipeout. Like a toad crossing the road, the surfer just goes for it and gets squashed. (DWK)

toast, toasted *adj.* A term for California surfers who are "burnt-out," usually from too much sun. (New Jersey; KAH) Usage: "Look at him, man, that dude is toast." See TROPPO.

toe socks *n.* Worn with flip-flops in the 1970s.

toes-on-the-nose, toes over *n.* Riding the forward tip of a surfboard with toes hanging over the nose. See HANG FIVE, HANG TEN.

toilet lid, lid rider *n.* Derogatory term for a bodyboarder. (Australia) See ESKY LID.

tombolo *n.* A bar of gravel or sand con-necting an island or rock with the main-land or with another island. (CCRG)

tombstone 1) *n.* A surfboard that is bro-ken completely in half. **2)** *v.* Usage: "Sorry bro, I **tombstoned** your board."

tonar *adj.* Totally gnarly. Usage: "I went to this party, man. It was tonar." (South Bay, early 1980s)

tool, wave tool *n.* A surfboard. (MM)

too many guys out Said of way crowd-ed surfing conditions.

toothpick *n.* An Australian surfboard from the 1940s and 1950s, usually sixteen feet long by fifteen inches wide, that was used primarily as a racing board and rel-atively little for wave riding. Toothpicks were constructed of plywood with a light timber frame. (NAT, 1985)

TOADS
Art: Robbie Quine

tourist
Photo: RSM Archive

top of the wave *n.* WAVE CREST—what Jack London described as the "giddy summit." (1907)

top rack *n.* A surfboard rack for carrying boards on a car. Also called ROOF RACK, SURF RACK.

top-to-bottom *adj.* **1)** Used to describe a wave that pours out in front when it breaks, with the initial point of contact matching the height of the wave. **2)** The term for a very thick, hollow wave, for instance a "top-to-bottom barrel." (MW)

top turn *n.* **1)** A simple turn at the top of a wave. (NAT, 1985) **2)** In competitive surfing, a turn performed in the top one-third of a wave that does not extend into the lip of the wave, as in a reentry, and does not reverse the surfer's horizontal direction by more than 130 degrees. (L&L)

totally *adv.* Completely, entirely, utterly, absolutely—as in "totally bitchin'," "totally radical," "totally awesome," "totally intense," "totally insane," and, all by itself, *"Totally."* "Oh, like totally." —Cassie Bauer, 1994

totally covered *adj.* TUBED.

tourist *n.* A visitor to the beach, a valley or nonlocal; **tour** for short. (MCR, MM) **—touristy-type cars**

"Hootervillus Touristimostus is a species of tourists found in Hawaii, who probably just bought a matching set of aloha wear from a Waikiki tourist trap for self and spouse. The male of this species is easily recognized by his brightly colored Hawaiian-print short pants with black socks and dress shoes. The female's favorite color seems to be red since she spends many hours sunning herself to get the desired color change—perhaps it is related to a mating ritual. One of this species' favorite migratory areas is Hanauma Bay, where the first day is spent sunning, swimming, and snorkeling. The second day is often spent in the hotel room or emergency room recovering from reef cuts and second-degree sunburns."

—Ken Suiso and Rell Sunn,
A Guide to Beach Survival *(1986)*

tourista *n.* What you get when you go on a surf trip to Mexico—the runs (diarrhea), an intestinal disorder characterized by abnormal frequency and fluidity of fecal evacuations. Also called *Montezuma's revenge* or *mud slide.* A LOG JAM (constipation) is the opposite of tourista. (PZ) **—the squirts** or if you're in Egypt, **mummy tummy**

touron *n.* TOURIST. Usage: "Check out all the tourons." (Ocean City, Maryland)

tow-board *n.* A gun-shaped surfboard equipped with foot straps.

tow day *n.* When the surf is too big for paddling.

tow-in surfing

294

Skinny towing
in Peter Mel,
Maverick's

Photo: Mike Peralta

tow-in surfing n. Using a specialized surfboard with foot straps, the surfer holds on to a waterski-type tow rope and is pulled by a Jet Ski into a huge wave that is too big to paddle into. The tow line is dropped as soon as the wave is caught. Pioneered on Maui in the early 1990s by Laird Hamilton, Buzzy Kerbox, Gerry Lopez, and others. See JAWS. **—tow-in, tow-ins** v.

townie n. VAL. Usage: "Yeah, townies." (Jacksonville, Florida, 1993)

tow surfing n. See CANAL SURFING.

"He'd grown up in the 1950s in Chico, in the northern Central Valley, stealing cars and joyriding through cherry orchards, tow-surfing the irrigation canals by ropes tied to the bumpers."

—*Daniel Duane.* Caught Inside: A Surfer's Year on the California Coast *(1996)*

track n. The line in which the surfboard is traveling, and which the surfboard usually wants to continue traveling even though you may be trying hard to turn it.

tracker n. A surfboard shape, circa 1968.

tracking v., n. **1)** Surfing along the length of the wave wall. (RA) **2)** Making long trails with the surfboard's wake. (MVA) Usage: "I was really tracking on that wave."

trade winds n. **1)** A system of winds that blow regularly in one direction or another, occupying most of the tropics. (AHD) **2)** The prevailing winds in the Caribbean, the Hawaiian Islands, and the South Pacific.

At most of the good Hawaiian surfing beaches, the trade winds blow offshore. (See KONA WINDS.) In the northern hemisphere they blow from the northeast and in the southern hemisphere from the southeast. In some places they blow six months a year in one direction and six months in the opposite direction.

trail arm, trailing arm n. The arm that the surfer extends to the rear while surfing. (MF)

trail foot, trailing foot n. In a normal stance, the foot toward the tail of the board.

trailing edge n. The rearmost edge of a surfboard or piece of water-riding equipment.

train surfing n. The very dangerous practice of riding on the rooftops of electric passenger trains in Rio de Janeiro, Brazil; what a **subway surfer** does in New York.

tourists
Art: Rick Stover

tram surfing *n.* Riding on top of a tram without falling off. (Grenoble, France; P)

tranny *n.* TRANSPLANT. Usage: "Hey, look at all the trannys."

transfer *n.* The act of exchanging boards on a wave, accidentally or on purpose.

transitional maneuver *n.* A competitive surfing term used to describe moves that come in between minor maneuvers and major maneuvers; they have little influence on scoring potential. They are (in descending order of degree of difficulty): MID-FACE TURNS, PUMP TURNS, FOAM PUMP TURNS, FACE PUMP TURNS, TRIM, FOAM TRIM or GROVELING, STALLING, RECOVERY, and PRONE OUT. (L&L) Also see METHODS OF FINISH.

transplant *n.* People who move to the beach after you do. Usage: "Dude, I've lived in Cali for two months longer than you, you transplant." (TWS, October 1999) See TRANNY.

treacherous *adj.* **1)** Characteristic of hazardous waves or babes. **2)** Said of a potentially dangerous situation. Usage: "It's fully treacherous out there."
—**treacherous surf**

tri *n.* A tri-fin surfboard. (Australia)

tribalism *n.* See LOCALISM. (MM)

tri-fin or **trifin** *n.* A three-fin surfboard. Often referred to as a THRUSTER.
—**tri-finned**

trim *v.* **1)** To ride across the face of a wave laterally or almost parallel to the wave's line and to the shore. **2)** To steer the board so that it planes best across the face of a wave. **3)** To orient oneself on the surfboard so that it can go, or plane, as fast as possible. Trimming involves placing one's body weight so that the board sits correctly in the water (has the maximum practical area in use as a bearing surface on the wave face) and is able to exploit the wave's speed to the fullest. It is most relevant to riding a Malibu. **4)** To achieve the best speed and balance. **5)** *n.* The status of the surfboard when a surfer is trimming; the positioning of the board on a wave. Usage: "He was in trim." (MF)

tri-plane hull *n.* A double concave planing surface, which consists of a shallow concave on each side of the stringer that extends from the center of the board to the fin(s).

Triple Crown of Surfing *n.* See HAWAIIAN TRIPLE crown.

triple overhead *adj.* Said of really big waves. See DOUBLE OVERHEAD.

trippin' *n.* A surf dance that sprang from Dick Dale's crowd at the Rendezvous Ballroom in Newport Beach in the early 1960s ("Let's Go Trippin'"). (PJN) See SURF STOMPS.

tropical cyclone *n.* HURRICANE.

tropical depression *n.* A storm grade below a tropical storm in strength, but stronger than a tropical wave.

tropical storm *n.* A storm grade below a hurricane, but stronger than a tropical depression.

tropical wave *n.* A storm grade below a tropical depression.

tropics *n.* **1)** The area of the globe between latitude 22 1/2 degrees north (the tropic of

Cancer) and 22½ degrees south (the tropic of Capricorn). **2)** The home of many of the world's finest surf spots, including Hawaii, parts of Australia, Indonesia, and Fiji. Tropical waters are rich with potentially dangerous and poisonous marine life, more so than temperate waters.

"Toto, we're not in Kansas anymore."

—*Dorothy in* The Wizard of Oz

---

tropic tides *n.* Tides of maximum range, occurring twice a month when the moon is over the tropic of Cancer or the tropic of Capricorn. These tides are particularly large in summer and winter when the sun is respectively highest and lowest in the sky. (CCRG)

troppo *adj.* **1)** Australian slang for too much time spent in the surf and sun. Usage: "You look a mite troppo, mate." (SFR, June 1987) Possibly derived from the Italian word *tropo,* meaning "too much." **2)** Having a bad sunburn or skin disorder (peeling, redness). See TOAST.

trough *n.* **1)** The low point between the crests of two waves. **2)** The bottom of the wave. (ORB) **3)** The space between two waves, two wives, or two paychecks. (JARR)

trough-to-crest transition *n.* Surfing from the bottom of the wave up to the top.

true foil *n.* The cross section of a fin, viewed straight on (or, in technical

terms, 90 degrees to its height). See FOIL.

trunk it, trunkin' it *v.* Wearing only surf trunks while surfing—no wetsuit. (CSD) Same as SKIN IT, BARE BACK. Usage: "The water was so warm we were trunkin' it."

tsunami (sue-NAW-me) *n.* A series of waves (not a single wave) caused by a sudden movement along a large portion of the ocean floor. Means "tidal wave" in Japanese, although the waves it describes have nothing to do with tides. They should also not be confused with storm-surge waves. Same as SEISMIC SEA WAVE. See TIDAL WAVE.

A tsunami does not materialize as a wall of water on the horizon but is perceived as a rapid and drastic lowering of sea level, followed by an equally drastic elevation of sea level (sometimes twenty feet or more). Evidence suggests that one such wave in Indonesia reached a height of one thousand feet! Wave length may be several hundred miles, with periods ranging from fifteen minutes to an hour or more. Tsunamis travel very fast, up to four hundred miles per hour.

---

tube, tubing wave *n.* **1)** The tubular or barrel-shaped form of a breaking wave created by the plunging lip throwing out in front of the advancing wall. **2)** The hollow, cylinder-like tunnel formed by a wave curling forward as it breaks over itself. **3)** A perfect wave, one that encloses a surfer; the inside section of a hot wave. **4)** The space inside a tubing wave. **5)** A saltwater tunnel. (WLK) Same as PIPELINE, BARREL. —**tube socks, boob tube, test tube,** etc.

"Time is expanded inside the tube."

—Shaun Tomson

"[A tube is] the G-spot of surfing. Where the pleasure is. A tube is the product of wind, water and topography. A bit of ocean that rears up close to shore and spills over in a cylindrical motion. And just what is so special about it is known only to those who have experienced the view from the inside, which hasn't stopped hundreds of surf-stoked wood-be Herman Melvilles from waxing lyrical about it."

—Phil Jarratt, The Surfing Dictionary (1985)

tube chip n. Any tortilla chip that resembles a curling wave—usually encountered while "dropping in" to some *salsa picante* at a Mexican restaurant.

tube city n. A surf session with plenty of tubing waves. (BSM)

tubed v. To be riding inside the hollow section of a wave. (MM) See GET TUBED.

Everyone has been tubed at least once in his or her life—inside either of a pair of slender ducts, called the fallopian tubes, that connect the ovaries to the uterus in the human female reproductive system; first described by Gabriello Fallopio (1523–1562).

Possibly the first description of a tubing wave: "And Neptune made for thee a spumy tent..."

—John Keats, British romantic poet. (1795–1821), "To Homer," 1818

tube farting n. "Everyone knows that farting in bed is one of life's greatest pleasures. Who doesn't enjoy letting go with a real sheet stainer and then pulling the blanket over their head to inhale that concentrated personal aroma."—Brian Bile on "Tube Farting," January 1981 (TKS, May 1987)

tubefest n. Heaps of barrels to surf, as in a "Mexican tubefest." See WAVE FEAST.

tube normal n. A tube ride that often results in a wipeout because the wave collapses over the surfer; primarily a surf-contest term.

tube radical n. **1)** A ride during which the surfer is completely covered up and emerges out of the tunnel before the wave collapses. **2)** The highest-scoring ride in a surf contest.

tube rat *n.* A surfer who frequently gets tubed. (C&M)

tube ride, tube riding *n.* **1)** A ride during which the rider disappears behind the curtain of a breaking wave—the ultimate sensation of surfing. **2)** The highest-scoring ride in a surfing contest. The degree of difficulty is measured by the size and hollowness of the wave and by the length of time in the tube. Crumbling tubes score less than dry tubes, where the surfer is completely enclosed. (L&L)

tube rider or **tuberider** *n.* **1)** A surfboard that has been tube ridden. (SFG, February 1990) Same as PIPE CLEANER. **2)** A surfer. **3) "Tube Rider"** A song by the Surf Punks.

tube spit *n.* Spray forced by pressure out of a hollow wave when it collapses, sometimes ejecting the surfer out of the tube onto the shoulder of the wave. (RO)

"... when the spit comes rushing from behind and lifts you off the board and lifts your board off the water and in some ways, you're actually flying along, you're off the surface of the water, flying along inside the tube—that's an incredible sensation, to be actually in flight. And another sensation too is the decompression, when the spit fires past you in the tube, and you're inside a compression chamber and you feel the pressure on your ears and incredible force as you're riding along almost inside a vacuum, and sometimes, when you're really deep, spit flies past you and reverses and comes back and hits you in the face."

—*Shaun Tomson, South African surfer*
(SFR, April 2000)

Tubesteak, Tubesteak Tracey, Old Tubesteak The nickname of Malibu surfer Terry Tracey, whose character was portrayed in the *Gidget* movies as Kahoona, a self-described surf bum who lived in a grass shack on the beach.

tube suit *n.* A wetsuit with short legs and no arms. (Australia; NAT, 1985)

tube time *n.* The number of seconds you spend in the barrel.

tubeward *adv.* Refers to surfing toward the tube.

tubular *adj.* **1)** Used to describe a tube-shaped wave. **2)** Valleyspeak for cool, as in "totally tubular."

tube spit
Art: Bob Penuelas

twin fin
Mark Richards
Photo: Jeff Divine/
Surfer magazine

tuck *n.* A crouching position on the surf-board, used for shifting body weight and gaining speed. (A&M)

tuck dive *n.* A maneuver used to duck under an incoming wave; same as DUCK DIVE, PUSH THROUGH.

tucked away, tucked in the tube *v.* To be surfing deep in the tube. See COVERED.

tucked-in bow, tucked-in stern *n.* A surfboard designed with a narrow bow or stern.

tucked-under edge rail *n.* A surf-board design feature. See CHINE RAIL.

tunneled *v.* TUBED; GET TUBED. **—tunnel-ing wave**

tunnels *n.* Exploratory observation communicated between females at the beach to indicate when a male who is wearing shorts is sitting in such a way that he is exposing his private parts. (Huntington Beach; anonymous, 1989)

tunnel skeg *n.* A tubular fin designed to minimize spinouts.

turbo fin *n.* A skeg that is curved through its entire height.

turkey *n.* BARNEY.

turn, turning *v.* To change a board's course on a wave. The surfer leans in the new direction, and the board follows beneath his or her feet. (A&M, MF)

turning radius *n.* The distance required for a surfboard to complete a turn; a performance characteristic. A shortboard has a much smaller turning radius than a longboard, allowing the surfer to go higher up the wave, come screaming down, pull off a radical turn, climb back up, then shoot down again, etc. (CC)

turnpiked *v.* What happens when you get stuck on a wave and can't get off and are forced to take it all the way in or face a heinous paddle-out through tons of white water. Usage: "I just got turnpiked. It took me fifteen minutes to get back out here." (Ocean Beach, San Francisco; BTV)

turn turtle *v., n.* Flipping the board upside-down and hanging on underwater as the wave passes over it. Usage: "I had to turn turtle." See ROLL.

tweeked *adv.* How you feel, for instance: **1)** Thrashed—if you get rumbled in a wave. **2)** High—after smoking a joint. **3)** Hyper—from drinking too much coffee. (PZ)

twin fin or **twinfin** *n.* **1)** Any board with two fins. (L&L) Mike Eaton is credit-

ed with the twin-fin breakthrough in 1976. (CC, WLK) **2)** A shortboard (5'8" to 6'8") with a wide tail for maneuverability and a fin near the rail for stability in radical turns. The wider tail provides more planing area and lift, which allows for more speed from less wave. This design is especially suited to smaller surf (under six feet).

"The twin-fin is the ultimate surf-board."

—*Mark Richards, circa 1980*

twinnie *n.* TWIN FIN. (Australia; SFG, February 1990)

twinzer *n.* Four-finned surfboard shape invented by Willy Jobson with two smaller fins mirrored a few inches outside and forward of two normal size fins.

twirlie *n.* SPINNER. (Australia; JPD)

two-legged piranha *n.* Feeding surfer. See HAKENVEESMO.

two-stroke takeoff *n.* When you give a couple of quick paddle strokes and you're dropping down the face of a wave. See NO PADDLE TAKEOFF, ROCK IN.

two wave hold-down *n.* When a surfer wipes out and is held underwater while a second wave passes overhead. See HELD DOWN.

typhoon *n.* A tropical cyclone, or hurricane, that originates east of the Philippines or in the China Sea.

Full on stoked
Art: The Pizz

Ugg Boots *n.* Sheepskin footwear created by Brian Smith; a part of Australian surf culture since the 1960s—later popularized by California surfers. A faintly ridiculous form of winter footwear favored by surfers, made from sheepskin and named for women's reaction to them when teamed with a formal suit. (Australia; JARR) **—ughies**

ukulele *n.* A small four-stringed guitar popularized in Hawaii; originally from Portugal. See HAWAIIAN MUSIC, SLACK KEY GUITAR.

ukuletion (OO-koo-LAY-tion) *n.* Emotional elevation due to the influences of ukulele music. A kind of ear candy, as in "Stokin' on the ukuletion." Term coined by California surfer Mark Perko, which is also the title of his first album of ukulele music.

ule (OO-lee) *n.* **1)** Hawaiian for penis. **2)** A jerk, analogous to the usage of *dick,* as in "What a dick."

ulola *n.* Sanskrit for "large wave" or surge.

ultimate cannon *n.* A very fast big-wave board; the fastest of the gun class of surfboard. (JKMJ, 1965)

ultralight riders *n.* Surfers who ride today's superlight type of shortboard. (W&B)

Uluwatu *n.* **1)** The world-famous left-ride surf spot off the southern tip of Bali, Indonesia; **Ulu** for short. **2)** Balinese for "place of the living dead" (SFR, June 1987) or "evil waters" (SFG, March 1990).

unbroken wave *n.* A developing wave, one that hasn't begun to break. Also known as GREEN WAVE.

Uncle Fester *n.* Derogatory term for an OLD SURFER. Named after the pale, bald-headed man with dark rings under his eyes in the television series *The Adams Family.*

uncontrolled *adj.* **1)** Refers to any wipeout, fall, or ungainly exit resulting in loss of board control. **2)** Said of any maneuver where the surfer falls before completion; such unfinished maneuvers are considered wipeouts in surfing competitions, and they detract from the wave score. (L&L)

uncool *adj.* Not happening; not nice. Usage: "That's *so* uncool." "That's *totally* uncool."

uncrowded, uncrowded break *adj.* Room to surf—what every surfer longs for.

underboarded *adj.* Using a surfboard that is too small for the size of the waves. Usage: "He's way underboarded." (Santa Cruz)

undergunned *adj.* Having too small of a surfboard for the conditions. Same as UNDERBOARDED. See OVERGUNNED.

underheel rail grab *n.* A move in which a surfer riding in a squatting position reaches behind his or her legs and grabs onto the rail.

undersea canyon *n.* SUBMARINE CANYON.

under-the-lip snap *n.* **1)** A standard surfing maneuver. Same as SNAP. **2)** An intermediate bodyboarding maneuver. (BB, December 1990)

undertow *n.* **1)** A misnomer—there's no such thing; one of the most ubiquitous myths of the seashore. (WB) See BACK-WASH. **2)** A subsurface current of water moving beneath and in a different direction from the surface water; said especially of a seaward current beneath breaking surf. Common in areas where incoming waves prevent the water's returning to the sea in a usual surface current. See RIP CURRENT.

underwater takeoff *n.* Bodysurfing maneuver that involves pushing off a sandy bottom ocean floor and launching yourself in the wave and emerging on the wave face. Mastered by lifeguard and champion bodysurfer Mark Cunningham.

un-go-outable *adj.* Dismal surfing conditions. See GO-OUTABLE.

unlocal *n.* NONLOCAL. As the slogan says, "No unlocals." See VALLEY.

unmakable section *n.* An area down the line from the surfer where the wave has already broken, making it impossible to get around or through the white water. See FLOATER.

unmakable takeoff *n.* A situation where the wave is too close to breaking for a reasonably safe departure to be made.

unreal *adj.* Absolutely wonderful; far out. (MVA) Or, if you're in Hawaii, "Onreal, brah."

unreal waves *n.* Big waves.

unrideable *adj.* The ocean conditions with no measurable waves to surf.

unspoken surf *n.* Various aspects of the total surfing experience that can't be conveyed or described with words. Hence the phrase: "Only a surfer knows the feeling." Read Thomas Farber's Foreword to the Second Edition of this book.

unstoked *adj.* BUMMED, CHAPPED.

unsurfable *adj.* Unridable.

up *adj.* Said of the surf when it's big, or good for surfing. Usage: "Surf's up!" See also PICK UP. "Maybe it'll come up" or "Maybe the surf will come up overnight."

"The swell finally came up after virtually a month sin olas [without waves]."

—*Cathy Oretsky (1969-1995)*
The Diary of a Gringa Betty *(1996)*

Up and riding! An exclamation used by surf contest announcers, such as Lord Tally Ho Sanders on Hawaii's North Shore, to alert spectators that a surfer has caught a wave. (1982)

updraft *n.* A wind rising up in the face of a wave, caused by the displacement of air by the moving wave.

upright bottom turn *n.* A turn that the surfer carves out of the bottom of a wave while standing straight up on the board.

upwelling *n.* A process by which surface waters that have been driven offshore by winds are replaced near shore by deeper, colder, nutrient-rich water; happens, for example, along the California coast in summer. Usage: "The upwelling near the submarine canyons makes it foggy and cold." See FOG.

urinophoria *n*. The deliciously warm sensation that comes when one's elimination process fills one's wetsuit with its product. (SFG, 1990) Same as INTERNAL HEATING, PETER HEATER.

uvana (oo-VA-na) *n*. Hawaiian for sea urchin.

urinophoria
Art: John Nickerson
© 2000 Mullethead
Surf Designs

V or **vee** *n.* **1)** The slight V-shaped configuration of a surfboard's bottom (often near the tail section) designed to minimize drag. **2)** A faceted planing surface. **3)** A bottom contour whose rear half is thicker on the stringer line than at the rails. (L&L)

vail Valleys Against Ignorant Locals—an organization formed in the early 1980s by surfers in the San Fernando Valley who "got pissed at local fags who think the ocean is only for people lucky enough to live by it." (Palmdale; SFG)

val 1) *n.* Short for VALLEY—a person who lives inland. **2) valish** *adj.* Having val characteristics. Usage: "That's so valish."

valley *n.* **1)** A derogatory term originally applied to the San Fernando Valley just north of LA and to anyone living there who came to the beach; has come to mean any place inland or anybody living there. The perceived distance between the beach and the valley varies depending on the person you're talking to. **2)** Outside two-mile limit and over the hill. (SP) See CAJON ZONE, LOCAL/VALLEY SWITCH, SAN JOSE. —**valley goons, valley boys**

"**Linguistically, the Valley is the foun-
tainhead of a very annoying and vir-
ulently infectious teenage patois.**"

—*Dave Hickey, introduction to*
The World of Jeffrey Vallance (1994)

valley cowboys *n.* A term for INLAND SURFERS in the late fifties and early six-

ties; the first use of *valley* in this context. Cowboy Phil Anderson was one of the first really good surfers to come out of the Valley. (MSO, A&M)

"Valley Girl" *n.* Frank Zappa's 1982 smash hit from the album *Ship Arriving Too Late to Save a Drowning Witch*. The lyrics consisted of words and dialogue heard by Zappa's daughter, Moon Unit, at the Sherman Oaks Galleria shopping mall in the San Fernando Valley, and included such expressions as "grody to the max," "Barf me out," and "Ohmigod, gag me with a spoon." Driven by the prominence of valspeak, surfing slang moved inland and burst onto the national—even international—scene.

valley
Valley voodoo doll
Art: The Pizz

"**Okay, fine . . .
Fer sure, fer sure
She's a Valley Girl
In a clothing store.**"

—*From* Valley Girl

"**She is funny and extremely articulate. This is not a Valley Girl.**"

—*Barbara Walters on Monica Lewinsky,*
February 22, 1999

valley go home Common graffiti seen in Santa Cruz and other areas along the California coast.

valley lifeline *n.* A derogatory term for a SURF LEASH. (SP) Also called KOOK CORD.

valley sheep *n.* People from San Jose who say "du-u-u-u-de" (spoken like sheep). (Santa Cruz; SP)

valley surprise *n.* Since around 1980, the name of an infamous turn on the return trip from Santa Cruz to San Jose along Highway 17—a major valley route to the ocean. There is some argument within the surfing community as to whether the actual turn is the first, second, or third hairpin turn encountered on the descent from the summit in the Santa Cruz Mountains into the Santa Clara Valley. (MPN, MCR)

valspeak, valleyspeak, valley-girl slang *n.* A special language that, according to the media, is confined to the San Fernando Valley—in other words, a media myth. In fact, many of the words and phrases associated with valspeak, for instance *gnarly, rad, radical to the max*, are surf terms that moved inland, transported by vals who were hanging out on the beach. The word *tubular*, for example,

valley sheep
Art: Rebecca Fish

which surfers invented to describe a well-curved wave, was co-opted to mean "very good" in valspeak. (CC)

Vans The brand name of a canvas deck shoe popular with surfers; carries the slogan "off the wall" on the heel. Styles include Hawaiian print.

V-drive *n.* High-cut bikini. Usage: "Hey, man, check out all the V-drives." (Southern California, 1980s) See BUTT THONG.

vee bottom *n.* **1)** The revolutionary 1960s concept of having two planing surfaces on the back third of a surfboard. Same as V or VEE. **2)** Refers to a girl wearing a bikini that rides up at the sides. (JARR) See V-DRIVE.

Velcro *n.* A nylon fabric that can be fastened to itself; invented by Switzerland's George de Mestral in 1948. Has many uses in the surfing industry including surfer's watchbands and leash-strap "cuffs" used to secure a leash to the rider's ankle.

Velcro watch band *n.* A surf standard that has worked its way into the mainstream. Jim Ganzer, artist, surfer, and founder of Jimmy Z. clothing company, introduced Velcro closures on surf clothing after experiencing the discomfort of hooks and snaps while lying on his surfboard. Mr. Ganzer describes the sound of ripping Velcro as "a modern mating call." The sound has been celebrated in the ZZ Top song "Velcro Fly." (DSL)

Ventures, The An instrumental surf band in the 1960s. Their hits included the theme of the TV series *Hawaii Five-o*.

venturi effect *n.* The tendency of fluids to increase in speed as they flow from a larger area through a smaller one (ORB); an important concept in surfboard design.

vert *n.* Short for VERTICAL, as in "going beyond vert."

vertical *adj.* Refers to the perpendicular orientation of a surfboard relative to the ocean horizon, achieved while riding up to the top of a wave. **—getting vertical**

vertical takeoff *n.* A steep drop down the face of a wave. See NO-PADDLE TAKEOFF.

vibe *v.* A derogatory term for giving someone, usually a nonlocal, the silent treatment. Usage: "She vibed me out." See BAD AIR. **—getting vibed, bad vibes, cold vibes**

vibe of the day, vibe of the session *n.* The atmosphere created by and how surfers react to each other—whether by sharing waves and taking turns or hogging waves; yelling at one another or not; sitting around and talking about girls or a party or making other small talk; long- and shortboarders getting along or not. The assortment of people in the water at a given time changes the vibe. One jerk in the water often ruins it for everyone; sometimes he's told off by the majority. The attitude around surf contests always reduce the vibes, never enhances them.

victory-at-sea conditions *n.* **1)** When the surf is big and stormy; derived from the title of the 1959 documentary *Victory at Sea* on the course of World War II at sea, which was adapted from the PBS TV series that always opened with a battleship pounding through some very mean seas. (W&B, EPZ) **2)** When the elements win. Go back to bed, go to work or school, or rent a surf movie video. There will be no surfing today. (JARR)

visual emergency *n.* Australian term for good-looking girls. See NECTAR.

V-Land Short for Velzyland, a surf spot on the North Shore of Oahu, Hawaii, named by Bruce Brown in 1958 after Southern California surfboard builder Dale Velzy.

vocal surfing *n.* Speaking commands into a microphone to surf the Internet.

volcano *n.* A surf knob with an open wound that, because of constant knee paddling, is never allowed to heal; common to longboard riders in the 1960s. (DWK)

VW barrel, V-Dub barrel *n.* A tube that's so big you can drive a Volkswagen through.

VW Bug *n.* A legendary surf vehicle. Surfmobile history was made when the first Volkswagens arrived in the U.S. in 1949. (SFG, November 1989) See BAJA BUG.

VW Bug
Lee Micheaux
Photo: Trevor Cralle

waffle boarder *n.* Derogatory term for bodyboarder.

wag *n.* A jerk, loser, nonsurfer. (East Coast)

wahine (wah-HEE-nee) *n.* A Hawaiian girl or woman.

"Waikiki style" surfboard *n.* Big longboard.

Waimea Bay *n.* A big-wave surf spot and contest site on the North Shore of Oahu, Hawaii; first surfed by Greg Noll in 1957 and later described by him as "Waimea's hang-on-to-your-balls super drop." The swell coming out of the very deep water creates high, wall-like waves. The **Waimea Shorebreak** is known for its pounding.

"The drop at Waimea feels as good as 20 ten-second tube rides put together. The feeling of conquering one drop there is better than anything, any wave, anywhere in my life."

—Mark Richards, January 1984 (TKS, May 1987)

Waimea stance *n.* Riding a longboard squatting with your feet spread wide and your butt sticking out; Same as STICKBUG STANCE.

waist-high *adj.* Said of a wave that's as high as the top of your surf trunks.

waiting for waves *v.* Surfers spend a lot of time in the water waiting for waves, laughing, talking story, and making up surf lingo.

waiting period *n.* A fixed window of time over which a specific surf contest may be held. For example, some events may have up to a five-month waiting period. The contest officials will wait and hope for the best possible conditions to hold the event. The surfers must wait, twitching in anticipation for the phone call in the middle of the night announcing the contest is on. See MINIMUM WAVE REQUIREMENT.

waiting room *n.* The area beyond the breakers where surfers wait for incoming waves. (MM) Same as LINEUP.

wake boarding *n.* See WAKE SURFING.

wake surfing or **wakesurfing** *n.* Riding the stern wave behind a boat—done standing on a surfboard, just as with an ordinary wave. See SKURFING.

walking *v., n.* Moving about on a surfboard. (MF)

walking the board *v., n.* Walking back and forth on the board to maintain control. Usage: "I was walking the board."

walking the dog *v., n.* Moving back and forth on a surfboard to alter speed. (MM)

walking the plank *v., n.* **1)** Walking forward and backward on a surfboard while riding a wave. **2)** An old pirate term; referred to a method of executing unwanted visitors. (PZ)

wall *n.* **1)** The steep forward portion of a wave. **2)** The glassy face of a wave. **3)** The face of a wave before it has broken. **4)** The steep unbroken wave face extending along the shoulder. (L&L) See WALL UP.

walking the plank
Photo: Don Balch

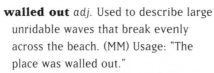

walled out *adj.* Used to describe large unridable waves that break evenly across the beach. (MM) Usage: "The place was walled out."

wallhangers *n.* Hand-shaped, wooden surfboards built primarily for display at surf shops and restaurants. (GN) Same as RESTAURANT BOARD.

wall-of-death *n.* A maneuver in which the surfer banks off the crest of the wave. (Australia; RA)

wall surf *n.* A wave face that seems to stand up vertically like a wall. (MF)

wall up *v.* What happens when a wave is steep and not breaking from right to left or left to right. Usage: "The wave walls up on the inside." —**walled up** *adj.*

wally *n.* BARNEY. Originally slang from England for a jerk or loser. (KSO)

wana (VAH-nah) *n.* Hawaiian for sea urchin. Same as UVANA.

wanker *n.* An individual displaying the classic symptoms of a complete lack of any common intelligence whatsoever. Windsurfers are sometimes referred to as wind wankers. (England; LJE) See GYRO WANKER.

wanks, wanketh *v.* Sucks. Usage: "It wanks." "It wanketh." (LH)

wannabee *n.* A neophyte or inexperienced surfer; a former hodad. (CVG) See WISH WAS.

warm ocean *n.* The amazingly warm ocean temperature in the tropics that makes you smile every time you jump in. About 78 degrees, sometimes higher. Makes it hard to get back into Northern

wake boarding

*Ron Parks
Note double wake
from two boats
Lake Austin, Texas*

Photo: George Parks

California waters—which average a chilly 48 to 52 degrees, not to mention areas further north where you have to wear a dry suit.

warm-water wax *n.* A kind of wax made especially for use in warm water; has different properties from cold-water wax. Also called SUMMER WAX. SEE WINTER WAX.

warp *v.* **1)** When an approaching big wave bends in such a way as to alter the usual look and feel of a surf spot. Usage: "It warped the Bay." (1998) **2)** *n.* Strands that run the length of fiberglass cloth. (ORB) See WELP.

washing machine *n.* An analogy for what it feels like to get held under and tumbled beneath a wave—like getting caught in the rinse cycle of a washing machine. Usage: "I was caught in the washing machine for the longest time." See HELD DOWN.

wasted *adj.* **1)** Exhausted, tired after a surf session. **2)** Screwed up, polluted, drunk. (A&M) **3)** Feeling high, lit, stoned.

water *n.* The liquid that descends from the clouds as rain, forming streams, lakes, and seas, all of which provide some form of wave to surf on; a major constituent of all matter.

water bed *n.* A bed whose mattress is a plastic bag filled with water. (W9, 1853)

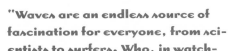

Surfers are fond of water beds as places to rest or sleep close to their liquid medium.

water dog *n.* Anyone who spends a lot of time in the ocean, be it surfer or dog. See SURF DOG.

waterlogged *adj.* A condition that may afflict a surfboard if its fiberglass skin is broken or cracked, allowing the foam to become saturated. A waterlogged board gets heavy. (ASKC) See FOAM ROT.

waterman *n.* A surfer or anyone else who participates in water sports, but also windsurfs, sails, scuba dives, etc.

water time *n.* Time spent in the ocean. See ROOM TIME, TUBE TIME.

watery hollows *v.* Tubing waves. (MWV, 1990)

wave, waves *n.* **1)** Undulating or rippling water, the three main natural causes of which are wind, earthquakes, and the gravitational pull of the moon and the sun. (WB) **2)** A moving pulse of energy; a horizontally moving ridge of water the particles of which move in closed curves. **3)** A requisite for surfing. (JRW) **—permanent wave, political waves, new wave, ultimate wave 4)** A giant collective undulation of stacked water molecules. **5) Waves, North Carolina. 6)** Surfers don't make waves, they ride 'em. **7)** Sound travels in waves. **8) wave, the** *n.* When sports fans stand up in alternating unison and wave their arms. The undulation travels around the stadium. **9) Wave** A small coastal town just north of Rincon Point in Santa Barbara County, California.

"Waves are an endless source of fascination for everyone, from scientists to surfers. Who, in watching, is not mesmerized by the ongoing cycles of surge and rush, flow and ebb, storm and calm?"
—Drew Kampion, The Book of Waves (1989)

"Waves: horizontally mobile transient vortexes."
—Thomas Farber, On Water (1994)

"Once more upon the water! Yet once more! And the waves bound beneath me as a steed that knows his rider."
—Lord Byron, Childe Harold's Pilgrimage, canto 3, stanza 2

wave Scott Cameron, Hawaii Photo: Terry Dix

wave action *n.* The continuous pounding of surf against the shore. See WAVE SHOCK.

wave anxiety *n.* Fear of a big wave. See CLUCKED.

wave attack *n.* A radical style of surfing. Usage: "Look at that dude's wave attack."

wave Santa Cruz Photo: Trevor Cralle

wave back *n.* The slope behind the wave face. The back of the wave. See BACK.

〰️〰️〰️〰️〰️

"A sudden, violent wind blew ribbons of mist twisting off wave backs like spindrift in a blizzard."

—*Daniel Duane.* Caught Inside: A Surfer's Year on the California Coast *(1996)*

〰️〰️〰️〰️〰️

wave cam *n.* SURF CAM.

wave catcher *n.* A surfboard that catches waves really easily with minimal effort. Usage: "Bro, your board's a total wave catcher."

wave characteristics *n.* The multitude of possibilities exhibited by ever-changing ocean waves, which fluctuate from spot to spot in response to numerous variables (bottom topography, swell direction, tides, etc.). Wave descriptions are seemingly endless and include pumping, gnarly, tubing, jacking, and so on.

wave collapse *n.* The action of a tubing wave that can no longer hold up. See TUBE SPIT.

wave crest *n.* See CREST.

wave-cut bench *n.* MARINE TERRACE.

wave dreams *n.* "I had a wave dream about being on a boat and having the wave turn to sand." —Elizabeth Phegan. See SURF DREAMS.

wave face *n.* The unbroken surface of a wave. (L&L)

wave feast *n.* Heaps of surfable waves. See TUBEFEST.

wave forecasting *n.* The art of predicting what the surf will be like. Same as SURF FORECASTING.

〰️〰️〰️〰️〰️

"Wave forecasting is an art based on thermal imaging, satellite-relay information, variable forces, and a flip of the coin."

—*Fully McFullon, letter to* Surfer *magazine, January 1992*

〰️〰️〰️〰️〰️

waveforms *n.* Waves.

wave height *n.* The vertical distance measured from the trough to the crest of a wave. (WB) See WAVE SIZE, WAVE STEEPNESS.

wave hog *n.* Someone who aggressively tries to steal every wave instead of sharing.

wave hound *n.* SURFER. Same as SURF HOUND.

wave jumping *n.* When a windsurfer rides at high speed in the face of a wave and catches air, sometimes soaring to spectacular heights.

wave knowledge, wave judgment *n.* A crucial aspect of surfing. It takes years to accumulate the experience needed to deal with the multitude of situations the sea pres-

Art: Jimbo Phill

ents—to know, for example, when to take off.

wave ledge *n.* The somewhat rounded lip of the wave as it begins to pitch out.

wave length *n.* The distance between two wave crests measured in seconds— the time it takes for one trough to pass a given point such as a buoy. (W&B) "Are we on the same wavelength?"

wavelet *n.* A little wave; a ripple. (W9, 1810)

wave lip *n.* The top part of a wave that throws out in front and over the wave face. Also called LIP.

wave magnet *n.* Any spot, often an island, that attracts good surf; the moon is a wave magnet. Even a person can be a wave magnet. Usage: "Kevin is a total wave magnet."

wave model *n.* Computer-plotted projection of storm tracks.

"Wave of Mutilation" *n.* 1980s song title by The Pixies.

wave of the future *n.* A movement that is viewed as representing forces or a trend that will inevitably prevail. (W9, 1940)

The wave of the future is coming and there is no fighting it.

—*Anne Morrow Lindbergh (b. 1906)*
The Wave of the Future (1940)

---

wave-os *n.* Waves. Commonly said playfully while in Mexico; obviously not meaning "eggs" (*huevos*) in this case.

(George's California Surf Museum)

wave period *n.* See PERIOD.

wave pool or **wavepool** *n.* An artificial chlorinated surfing pool in which ridable waves are produced by a wave machine. (L&L) Located at inland water-theme parks, such as Allentown Wave Pool, Pennsylvania (site of the World Inland Surfing Championships in 1986) and Big Surf in Tempe, Arizona.

wave possession *n.* In competitive surfing, the issue of who has priority on a specific wave. Some associations still use the "first rider up" rule, but the majority have gone to "the rider on the inside"—the distinction is crucial! See INTERFERENCE RULE(S).

wave quota *n.* An individual's sufficient number of caught waves. Usage: "I haven't had my wave quota yet." (Mark Warren, 1993)

wave rebel *n.* SURF REBEL.

wave refraction *n.* A deflection from the path that waves are traveling, brought about by a number of factors. Refraction implies a change in both direction and speed—a common phenomenon at point breaks.

"On entering shallow water, incoming waveforms are increasingly influenced by the offshore submarine topography and are refracted such that the wave crests tend to parallel the depth contours. Waves arriving at straight coastlines with parallel depth contours and a sloping beach are slowed and experience a reduction in wavelength; the crests of the waves, however, remain parallel to the beach. Waves traveling obliquely toward a beach with parallel depth contours are refracted so that the crests become more aligned with the beach. Along an irregular coastline, waves are refracted toward promontories and away from indentations in the coast, a phenomenon that aids in selective erosion and a tendency toward a straight coastline, which explains why indentations can provide shelter from waves advancing toward the coast."

—The New Grolier Electronic Encyclopedia
(Danbury, CT: Grolier Electronic Publishing, 1990)

wave rider or **waverider** n. SURFER.

wave riding n. SURFING.

Wave Rock n. A natural rock formation in Australia that looks like a giant frozen wave. See LAND TUBED.

Wave Runner n. Brand name of JET SKI popular for tow-in surfing.

wave sailing n. WINDSURFING.

wave sailor n. WINDSURFER.

wave selection n. In competitive surfing, the waves you *want* to catch and the waves you *don't* want to catch. (L&L)

wave shape n. See SHAPE.

wave shock n. The force of waves as they strike the coast; measured by a seismograph.

wave size n. **1)** A measurement relative to a surfer's body height, made at the first opportunity to compare the standing height of the person against the wave face—generally at the first bottom turn. (L&L) The various wave sizes relative to body height are ankle slapper, knee slapper, waist high, shoulder high, head high, overhead, double overhead. **2)** The height of a wave as measured from the back of the wave, calculated by doubling the height of the back to get the height of the face. See WAVE HEIGHT. Usage: "It was a solid two foot, brah." (Maui) or "two-foot Hawaiian," which is equivalent to about 4 to 5 feet by mainland standards.

One theory about wave size has it that an imperial foot (twelve inches) is different from a surfer's foot, which supposedly is much larger. This means that in Hawaii, for instance, twenty-foot surf is called ten-foot plus. At Hawaii's Banzai Pipeline, the roar of the wave helps surfers judge the size. Whatever the method of measurement, waves are always biggest in places where the coast faces into the swell. (ASL, April 1990; WLK, W&B)

"Ask ten surfers how to measure a wave and you'll get ten different explanations."

—Corky Carroll (1989)

"Not all waves are the same size."

—NOAA weather radio storm broadcast
stating the obvious (November 11, 1997)

"It's not the size of the wave, it's the motion of the ocean."

—Anonymous

"Waves are not measured in feet or inches, they are measured in increments of fear."

—Buzzy Trent

How Big Is Big?
"How do Hawaiians judge penis size? From the front or the back?"

—Barbie Dahl from New York,
letter to Surfer magazine, February 1995

wave-size threshold *n.* A personal limit to the size of a wave that a surfer will attempt to ride. (L&L)

wave ski *n.* A cross between a kayak and a surfboard; used to ride breaking waves and unbroken swell. *Not* a surf ski.

A wave ski has a hand-held double ended paddle for power, a seatbelt and foot strap for control and safety, and (usually) three adjustable fins. Wave skis range from seven to ten feet in length and twenty-two to twenty-five inches in width, and they weigh twenty to thirty pounds. The sport has been very popular in Australia for over twenty years. The most popular types of wave skis are foam-filled fiberglass; foam-filled plastics are next in popularity, followed by hollow fiberglass. Fiberglass skis are slightly lighter and more performance oriented; plastic skis are a little heavier but very rugged.

wave-ski surfer *n.* Someone who rides a wave ski.

wave speed *n.* The speed at which a wave travels in open water; swells travel at about thirty-five miles per hour before reaching shallow water. Over distance, waves die out and are replaced by following waves at such a rate that the group advances at just half the speed of the individual waves. (DKM)

wave spies *n.* A derogatory term for surf photographers because they expose little-known surf spots to the masses. (SP3)

wave-size threshold
Art: Deano

317

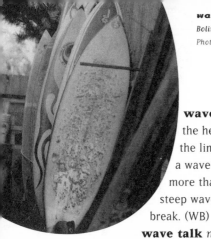

wave steepness *n.* The ratio of the height of a wave to its length; the limit is about 1:7. For example, a wave seven feet long can be no more than one foot high; when small steep waves exceed this limit they break. (WB)

wave talk *n.* Talking about the surf.

wave train *n.* A succession of similar waves at equal intervals. (W9, 1897)

wave vehicle *n.* Any of various surfriding crafts, such as a surfboard, surf mat, and bodyboard.

wavy *adj.* **1)** Rising or swelling in waves; abounding in waves, "wavy hair." **2)** Marked by undulation; rolling. **—waviness** *n.* (W9 1562) **—Wavy Gravy and the "Wavettes"**

wax *n.* **1)** A mixture of paraffin, beeswax, incense, and coloring that is rubbed on the deck of surfboards to aid traction. By rubbing it on and building up a coarse, beaded surface, one neutralizes the inherent slipperiness of wet fiberglass. (NAT, 1985; SFG, March 1990) **2)** Another name for a sanding agent.

wax buildup *n.* Dirty old wax that has clumped together. See GUNGA.

wax comb *n.* **1)** A thin plastic blade with one serrated edge that is used to score grooves into a fresh wax job or rough up an old wax coat, greatly increasing traction. (NAT, 1985) Most wax combs have a sharp edge that can be used to scrape off wax buildup. Same as WAX SCRAPER. **2)** The only type of comb that many surfers use or own.

wax down *v.* Same as WAX UP. "We're waxing down our surfboards. . ." —The Beach Boys, "Surfin' USA" (1962).

waxing off the top Sliding across the lip of a wave on a surfboard, a term coined by Peter Townend.

waxing poetic *n.* See SURF POETRY.

waxing the button *v.* Female masturbation term.

wax job *n.* The end result of applying surf wax to the deck of a surfboard.

wax pocket *n.* A rear pocket on a pair of surf shorts designed expressly for carrying a bar of surf wax.

wax rash *n.* BOARD RASH.

wax scabs *n.* Old, dirty wax that has built up. (SFG, March 1990) Same as WAX BUILDUP. See GUNGA.

wax scraper *n.* A plastic scraper that can be used to scrape off wax scabs after a board has been left in the sun for a while to soften the wax. (SFG, March 1990) Same as WAX COMB.

wax substitutes *n.* Substances or materials used instead of paraffin or other surf waxes. Examples are aerosol spray-on waxes and stick-on grip strips or pads.

wax up, waxing up *v.* To apply wax to a surfboard. Same as WAX DOWN.

wax yo stick *v.* Applying wax to a surfboard. (Hawaii, 1991)

way *adv.* An intensifier commonly used in California to make adjectives way more cool sounding. (P) **—way cool, way rad, way stoked** Early usage: "way famous," "way big," and "way fast." (Fullers, Big Sur, 1966)

way back *adv.* In the tube. **—getting way back**

way upper crust *adv.* At the top of a wave. (MM)

WCT *n.* World Championship Tour for professional surfers. Features the top forty-four male surfers determined by the previous year's ratings, plus four "wildcards" (surfers granted special invitations to compete). The women's WCT features the top sixteen female surfers plus a varied number of local and overseas qualifiers. See WQS.

weather radio *n.* An indispensable tool for all surfers—a surfer's best friend; provides continuous broadcasts of weather conditions and updated forecasts approximately every three hours. (WS)

webbed gloves, webbed paddling gloves *n.* PADDLE GLOVES; first used in a pro competition by Glen Winton in 1986. (SFG, November 1989)

wedge *n.* **1)** A heavy, peaking wave. (NAT, 1985) **2)** A pie-shaped piece of foam or wood used in repairing a surfboard; it is forced into the damaged opening in the surfboard and glassed over. Also called PLUG. **3)** *v.* When two waves coming from somewhat different directions merge when they meet. The wedging part of the two waves usually breaks a great deal harder than the breaking part of either wave by itself. **4) The Wedge** The famous and dangerous surf spot, popular among bodysurfers and bodyboarders, located at the southern tip of the Balboa Peninsula, Newport Beach, California.

wedging *adj.* A wave characteristic, as in "a wedging wave." See WEDGE, WEDGY.

wedgy *adj.* Used to describe how a swell refracts, or breaks up, and then stands up over a shallow bottom in a compact, peaky fashion. (Australian; MW)

weed *n.* **1)** A small person; a GROMMET. **2)** A large plant grown in a quiet corner of your garden and used under medical supervision to improve your surfing. (JARR)

weekly *n.* Refers to a "weekly chick"—a nonresident female who rents an apartment near the beach for a week or two and takes pictures of people she meets to show off at home as souvenirs. Usage: "I had about six or seven weeklies this summer." (Newport Beach)

weighting/unweighting, weight-on/weight-off *n.* Altering the amount of body weight acting downward on the board during a ride; can be accomplished for short periods by quickly flexing or extending the legs. (RA)

well-shaped wave *n.* Any wave that is suitable for surfing.

welp *n.* Strands that run the width of fiberglass cloth. Also referred to as *fill*. (ORB) See WARP.

west *n.* A wind or swell direction. Usage: "It's got way too much west in it."

Westie loop *n.* A flip negotiated while holding onto a skimboard; named after Kurt Westgaard, who was the first person to do it. (TLH) Same as WIDDLEY.

west swell *n.* A swell that travels from west to east. (ORB)

weather radio
Photo: Trevor Cralle

wetsuit
Wetsuit removal with
help from amigos
Photo: Baja Collective

west wind, westerly *n.* A wind that blows from west to east. (ORB)

wet dreams *n.* See SURF DREAMS.

wetsuit or **wet suit** *n.* A neoprene rubber suit used by surfers as insulation against cold water. Wetsuits are usually one-eighth inch thick (about three millimeters). The seams are glued together, or sometimes glued and stitched. The higher-quality suits are glued, stitched, and taped. They are designed to fit snugly but to allow a thin layer of water to enter, so that the water can be warmed by body heat and keep the user warm.

wetsuit
Debbie Hailu
Photo: Baja Collective

Wetsuits were pioneered by Jack O'Neill in the 1950s at Ocean Beach, San Francisco, where the water is cold year-round. He experimented by wearing sweaters from the Goodwill out in the ocean, then navy jackets sprayed with Thompson's water seal, and later, unicellular foam (PVC). (SCSM)

wetsuit chaffing *n.* See RASH GUARD.

wetsuit crotch-suck syndrome *n.* When your crotch feels like it's been vacuum-packed inside the pelvic portion of your wetsuit at least once during each session. (Mark C. Suction, San Francisco, 1994) "If a wetsuit fits, the peter gets pinched." (SFR, February 1995) Also called **Severe Urethane Crotch-Suction Syndrome (SUCSS).** "I just experienced the SUCSS." Treatment: Let a little water in through the neck of the wetsuit and work it down to the pinched region for relief.

wettie *n.* An Australian term for wetsuit.

wet wetsuit (getting back into one) *n.* Going through chilly torture to experience something awesome again.

whacks it off the top A common phrase used by surf contest announcers to describe various maneuvers performed on the wave lip or top of a wave.

whale *n.* BEACHED WHALE.

whatever *pron.* Everything or anything, as in "Whatever, dude." Or, if you're a valley girl, "What*ever.*"

"What up, bra? What up, bro?" "Hey, what's happening?" (Topanga, California)

whatever
Photo: Trevor Cralle

whine *n.* The sound of the skeg or tail of a surfboard cutting through the water at high speed. Also called SKEG HUM, WHISTLING SKEG.

whipturn or **whip turn** *n.* A maneuver in which a surfer taking off on a wave swiftly snaps the board into position.

whirlie *n.* A lesson taught to foul-mouthed young surfers. First the kid gets a warning, then if the bad words continue, an older surfer holds him by the feet, head-dips him into a public toilet, and flushes it to give his hairdo a whirlie. (La Jolla Shores; HJP)

whistling skeg *n.* A fin with a square afteredge that cause it to whistle at high speeds. Also called SKEG HUM, SKEG WHINE.

whitecaps *n.* **1)** The tops of waves or swell blown off at sea, forming spume or spindrift. **2)** A wind-blown chop or wave with its crest broken into white foam; generally rolls a short distance and backs off.

white-elephant break *n.* Really big surf on an outer reef. (GN)

white shark (*Carcharodon carcharias*-Latin for "having jagged teeth"): *n.* The world's largest predatory fish and the most feared species of shark. Popularly known as **great white shark**, they are also called *white* (in Australia) and *whitey* (in Santa Cruz). SEE RED TRIANGLE, SHARK, SHARK ATTACK.

White sharks are responsible for all shark attacks on humans between Santa Barbara, California, and Washington State. They populate all the cool ocean waters of the world—for example, the colder waters off of southern Australia and Northern California. Averaging five feet long and fifty pounds at birth, they don't reach sexual maturity until they are around fourteen feet long and weigh some three thousand pounds. (Males grow to fourteen-and-a-half feet, females to nineteen-and-a-half feet.) White sharks never sleep; they simply swim and eat. Their average speed is three to four knots per hour; their favorite food is seal or sea lion. They attack from below, take one bite, and retreat until their prey bleeds to death. In California, most white shark attacks occur between July and October; the slow months are February to April. (LMZ, MW, NHMEA)

white water or **whitewater** *n.* **1)** The turbulent, foaming, bubbling water and froth created by the breaking of a wave. **2)** The broken part of a wave. Also called SOUP.

white-water surfing *n.* RIVER BODYBOARDING.

white-water takeoff *n.* When the surfer begins riding on a wave that has already broken.

widdley, double widdley *n.* WESTIE LOOP.

wide point or **widepoint** *n*. Refers to the widest part of a surfboard, which may be located anywhere from two inches behind center to eight inches ahead of center. The location influences the board's turning characteristics. The further ahead of center the wide point is placed, the longer and more drawn out the board's turns will be. A wide point in back of center makes the board turn more quickly and sharply.

wide turn *n*. Riding out in front of a wave and gradually making a wide arc to turn back up the wave face.

width *n*. A surfboard dimension measured at right angles to the length of the board, usually near the center at the widest point. Typically, boards are from nineteen to twenty-one inches wide. Wider boards contain more foam, providing more flotation and making it easier to paddle and to catch waves earlier. The increasing planing area efficiently uses the energy from small and slow waves, providing more speed than a narrower board.

wiggle *n*. PUMP TURN. (Australia; L&L)

wild time *n*. A surf session with plenty of fast-breaking critical waves.

wilma *n*. A female DWEEB; from the character of the same name on *The Flintstones*.

wind, wind force *n*. A prime factor in creating surf; can ruin a good surf if it's blowing onshore, or make it even better if it's blowing offshore.

Windansea A La Jolla surf break written about by Tom Wolfe in *The Pump House Gang* (1968).

wind chill factor *n*. The effect of wind in lowering an already cold temperature even further. Tide books contain wind chill factor tables.

wind chop *n*. Waves produced by onshore winds blowing in the immediate vicinity of a surf spot as in "two-foot wind chop"; characterized by a bumpy-looking sea, whitecaps, and unhappy surfers. Wind chop can ruin the quality of excellent surf within minutes. (S&C) See BLOW-OUT, BLOWN OUT.

wind lift *n*. The strong updraft caused by an offshore wind blowing up the face of a wave. Wind lift can make it very difficult to drop in, and sometimes blows the surfer and board back over the top. (A&B)

wind line *n*. A distinct change in the appearance of the ocean surface at a certain place (for instance, ruffled on one side and smooth on the other), indi-

windsurfer
Art: Jim Phillips

cating that a stronger wind is outside the surf break or approaching it.
—**advancing wind line**

windmill *v.* Paddling really hard and fast in an attempt to catch a wave. (GN) Usage: "I had to windmill to catch that wave." Jack London referred to the "windmill stroke" in 1907.

window *n.* See SWELL WINDOW.

wind peaks *n.* Waves with a short wave length caused by strong, local winds; very narrow and generally choppy.

wind speed *n.* The velocity of wind, as measured in miles per hour (mph) or knots per hour. A guide for measuring the speed of wind without instruments follows:

CALM—smoke rises vertically
1-12 mph—just feel wind on face, leaves in motion
13-24 mph—raises dust or loose paper, small branches move
25-30 mph—large branches move, wires whistle
30-40 mph—whole trees in motion, hard to walk against

—*Adapted from the "Easy Read" Tide Book (1989)*

wind squall *n.* A gust of wind lasting only a short while—a common occurrence out on the ocean in the tropics. Also called PUFF. See SQUALL, RAIN SQUALL.

windsurfer *n.* **1)** Either a board or the rider who windsurfs. **2) Windsurfer** A trademark for a sailboard.

windsurfing *n.* The sport of wave riding and wave jumping using a surfboard mounted with a mast and sail, equipped with footstraps, and having a larger than normal fin area. Developed in 1969 by two Southern Californians, Hoyle Schweitzer and Jim Drake, windsurfing is popular on inland lakes as well as on bays and the open ocean. Also called SURFSAILING. See SAILBOARD.

wind swell *n.* **1)** Waves created by local wind conditions. Such swell doesn't normally perform well at reef and point breaks because it is not influenced much by bottom formations. Because the waves have shorter intervals, they do not feel the bottom until they are in relatively shallow water. (W&B) See SEA STATE. **2)** Small, uneven peaky surf produced by prevailing winds within a few hundred miles offshore; the waves are four to five feet year-round, but most noticeable in the spring. Such winds are often a little stronger after the passage of a cold front. (S&C) —**west wind swell**

wind waves *n.* Waves caused by local winds. The three factors influencing the size of wind waves are wind velocity, the duration of time the wind blows, and the extent of open water across which it blows (the fetch). (WB)

windwankers *n.* A term used by keen surfers to describe wave sailors (windsurfers) whose egos are advanced beyond their skills. (Australian; MW)

wipeout
Photos: Robert Brown

windward *adj.* Refers to the side of the island that the wind and waves reach first; as distinct from LEEWARD.

wing, winger *n.* **1)** A design feature on the rail of a board. Same as BUMP WING. **2)** Small appendages on the rail of a surfboard, from three to fourteen inches from the tip of the tail. One, two, or three pairs of wings may be used. **3)** A protective edging of redwood or other wood along the bow and sides of an old-style surfboard.

winged keel, winged keel fin *n.* A fin invented by Cheyne Horan that is similar to Ben Lexcen's design of the America's Cup sailboat keel of the same name. See X-FIN.

wing tail, wing-tail board *n.* The predecessor to the sting, or stinger board; invented by Steve Walden in 1973.

winter swell *n.* Swells generated by storms in the North Pacific from October to April; usually anywhere from three to six feet to fifteen to twenty feet high. Some of these storms lie south of due west, others are father

north. The west swells are more common during the fall months. (S&Q)
—west swell, north swell

winter wax *n.* A type of surf wax designed especially for cold-water surfing conditions. See WARM-WEATHER WAX.

wipe out *v.* **1)** To fall off one's board while taking off on or riding a wave. Same as TAKE GAS. **2)** To be knocked off a board either by a crashing wave or another surfer. **3)** In general, to fall off a surfboard. **4) wipeout** or **wipe-out** *n.* Any situation where the forces of a wave overcome the skills of a surf rider; falling because of loss of control of the board. **5) "Wipe Out"** A song by the Surfaris (June 1963) that went to #2 nationally, making it the highest charting surf instrumental of all time. (PJN)

wired 1) *v.* Figured out; understood-to have a surf spot wired is to understand its individual nature, to know which swell, wind, and tide conditions suit the break best. Some spots are hard to wire. (MW) **2)** *adj.* Feeling great. (RO) Usage: "I was so wired after that tube ride."

WISA (rhymes with Lisa) Women's International Surfing Association.

wish was *n.* Someone who wants to be a surfer. (PZ) Same as WANNABEE. Usage: "He's just a wish was."

witness *v.* To look, see, view, or watch over something. Usage: "Did you *witness* that wave, dude?" (LH) See SURF CRIMES.

womb *n.* The womb of the ocean—inside a hollow breaking wave. Same as GREEN ROOM, GREEN WOMB.

woody
Santa Cruz
Photo: Trevor Cralle

woody
Art: Jim Phillips

woody or **woodie** *n.* **1)** A vintage wooden-paneled, surfboard—carrying station wagon, for example, a 1934 Ford. **2)** The old car, usually a station wagon, that a surfer uses to haul boards to the beach. So named because of the wood paneling used on the sides of station wagons in the 1930s, 1940s, and early 1950s. (IDSM) **3)** An erection—morning timber. Usage: "I've got a total woody."

woofy *n.* Polluted water—and you can thank the antiquated Sydney sewage system for the introduction of this word. Same as ON THE NOSE, YUK, SURFING UNDER TURD. (Australia; MW)

work *v.* **1)** To attack or take on a wave. Usage: "He's really working the inside." **2)** To cause injury to a car or person.

wipeout
Photos: Robert Brown

Usage: "That asshole totally worked me just because I took off in front of him." **3)** *n.* An activity for people who don't surf. (DS) Positive connotation: Usage: "I hope the sunset just works it." (Chicha, Baja, 1993)

"They say that a bad day at surf is better than a good day at work!"

—*Cheyne Horan*

"Work is for people who don't surf."

—*Anonymous*

---

worked, getting worked *v.* Thrashed about in the soup. (MM) Usage: "I got worked on that wave."

World Tour *n.* In competitive surfing, the series of annual worldwide surf contests organized by the ASP and culminating each December in the Hawaiian Triple Crown held on the North Shore of Oahu.

WQS *n.* Due to the huge number of male pro surfers around the world, the ASP created the World Qualifying Series in 1992 to give surfers everywhere the chance to gain ratings points and put themselves in position to reach the highest level—the WCT. The top sixteen WQS—rated surfers at the end of the year will join the top twenty-eight for the World Championship Tour the following year. See WCT

WSA Western Surfing Association. (U.S.)

X-board *n.* A small, surfboard-shaped special controller peripheral used with the Sony Playstation video game "Surfing H3O." It snaps over the top of the Dual Shock2's twin analog sticks and is intended to provide greater control. (November 2000)

X-fin *n.* A surfboard fin design described by inventor Scott Bucknell as a cross between a propeller and wings. The design was influenced by Australian guru Cheyne Horan's winged keel fin (which was inspired by Ben Lexcen's America's Cup sailboat keel), but instead of a single foil, it has two foils crossed over to form an X and requires two fin boxes. (SFG, February 1990)

X marks the spot An olde pirate term used on treasure maps to indicate the location of a buried treasure chest. This doesn't have much to do with surfing, but we needed to add more entries to this X section.

x-fin
Photo: John S. Callahan

Xmas Swell *n.* An Australian phenomenon that has created a cargo-cult mentality among surfers. Almost without fail, king (high) tides and other seasonal factors produce good waves for the festive season, which is just as well because few surfers will have been good enough during the year to expect anything from Santa. (JARR)

X-stringer *n.* Flared stringers that cross over each other, usually inlaid.

G·R·R·R·R!

Art: Karen T. Delgadillo

SURFER X-ING

North Shore Highway,
Haleiwa, Hawaii
Photo: Bud Clark

yabba-dabba-doo! A surfer's exultant cry, à la Hanna-Barbera cartoon character Fred Flintstone. (ASKC, 1965)

yak slappers *n.* Derogatory term for SEA KAYAKERS.

yar *n.* Another pirate term adopted by surfers to get someone's attention, as in "Yar, dude."

yarner 1) *n.* Someone who tells stories for hours on end, with basically no apparent objective or point. (ALN) Similar to riggin. See FOSSIL **2) yarn** *v.* To spin yarns or talk forever.

"Ya Shoulda Been Here Yesterday" *n.* A Surf Punks song implying, "You missed some really good surf."

yeah *adv.* What the surfer audience says at a surf flick during the projection of a hot ride, usually a tube ride, wipeout, or takeoff on a giant wave.

Year of the Ocean *n.* 1997 World's Fair in Portugal.

Yeeeoooow! A surfer yell (upon taking off on a giant wave). (GN)

yellowed board, yellowed out *n.*, *adj.* Generally an old surfboard where the foam core beneath the fiberglass skin has turned a yellowish color due to extended exposure to UV rays from the sun. Usage: "This cyclops with a walrus mustache and his yellowed out board almost ran me over."

Yemaya *n.* West African ocean goddess of mother love (as opposed to romantic love). She is celebrated in places like Cuba, and in Brazil (Yemaja), where every year the beaches of Rio de Janeiro are jam packed with shrines in the sand with thousands of candles.

yoga maneuvers *n.* Longboard maneuvers. (Santa Cruz) Same as MEDITATING.

"You guys reeeally missed it" A phrase repeated throughout the movie *The Endless Summer* (1964), referring to surf that had been so good or big the day or week before.

You Should Have Been Here an Hour Ago: The Stoked Side of Surfing or How to Hang Ten Through Life and Stay Happy A great title for a book by Phil Edwards (1967) that has become a collector's item.

yowja
Art: Karen T. Delgadillo

"There are uncounted millions of people right now who are going through life without any sort of real, vibrant kick. The legions of the unjazzed. But surfers have found one way. God knows, there are other ways. Each to his own special danger. Skiing is not enough. Sailing is near. Ski jumping is almost. Automobile racing has got it. Bullfighting makes you dead. The answer is surfing."

—*Phil Edwards*

yowza! The orgasmic shriek of a surfer emerging from the green cathedral. There, we've got it all in one: surfing, sex, religion. (Australia; MW)

yuk *n.* Surfing in polluted waters; same as ON THE NOSE, SURFING UNDER TURD, WOOFY. (Australia; MW)

yummy yellow *n.* A shark's favorite color of wetsuit. (1980) Some sharks seem to avoid dull-colored objects; they are attracted instead to bright colors, such as yellow or orange, which are often used for life jackets so that the jackets can be easily seen by rescue crews. (NHMLA)

yuppie surfer *n.* An upwardly mobile surfer. (1980s)

Art: The Pizz

Art: John Nickerson
©2000 Mullethead
Surf Designs

zero break *n.* **1)** The general area where the biggest waves break beyond the first break. **2)** The outermost line of breakers on a day of exceptionally large surf.

zigzag or **zig-zag** *v.* To change rails while dropping down the face of a wave. (MM) **—zigzagging**

zinc, zinc cream, zinc oxide *n.* **1)** A type of sun block that rays can't penetrate; applied to the nose and lips for maximum protection. White originally, but now available in fluorescent colors as well. **2)** A sun-protection ointment designed to make you look ridiculous while keeping your skin in place. (Australian; JARR)

zip board *n.* MALIBU BOARD.

ziplocked *adj.* Tucked inside a barreling wave. (W&B)

zipper, fast zipper *n.* A fast wave that breaks quickly and peels off like a zipper. See INSIDE ZIPPER.

zipperless wetsuit *n.* A wetsuit that is secured with one Velcro shoulder strap.

zoners, zonies *n.* A semiderogatory nickname for surfers from Arizona. (San Diego County)

zonked *adj.* **1)** Excited, as in "totally zonked." (CC) **2)** Exhausted. Usage: "I was completely zonked after that surf."

zoo *n.* **1)** Used to describe a crowded surf or beach area, or too many surfers in the water. Usage: "Man, it's a zoo out there." **2) Zooport** An occasional name for Newport Beach, California, so called because of its crowded surfing conditions.

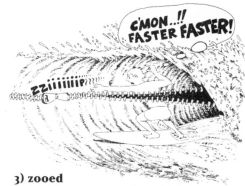

jipper
Art: I. B. Nelson

3) zooed *adj.* Usage: "The beach was fully zooed with inland kooks." **—way zooed** (supercrowded), **zooed out** (crowded to the max)

zorries *n.* Inexpensive, stamped-out rubber sandals. Also called *sleepahs* (Hawaiian Pidgin) and *slaps.* Same as FLIP-FLOPS, GO-AHEADS, etc.

Zuma, Zuma Beach *n.* Named after a Chumash Indian tribe, Malibu's largest beach and popular surf spot, officially called Zuma County Beach; attracts hoards of crowds in the summer, hence the nickname **Zooma**

zup "What's up?"

Zupe *n.* Zooed-out Newport Beach.

jipperless wetsuit
Kevin Parker
Photo: Camille Seaman

joo
Art: I. B. Nelson

A p p e n d i x

Ancient Hawaiian Surfing Terms

The earliest known surfing terms sprang from the Hawaiian people. Surfers of the kingdom of Hawaii had words for every aspect of the sport. Names for some of their
favorite surfing locations illustrate this: *nuumehalani,* a surf site on Oahu, meaning
"the heavenly site where you are alone"; *po'o,* a Kauai location for many ancient surf
competitions, meaning "to hollow out"; *uo,* a Maui surf site that translates as "a nimble
threading of a needle"; *hamakuapoko,* a well-surfed Oahu location that means "sky
clouds of fragrance"; and *kahalaia,* the "site of four winds" at Hilo. Specific words
detail specific surf situations. *Ahua* means a place close to shore where a broken wave
rises and breaks again; *lauloa* is a wave crest that breaks from one end of the beach to
the other; *kakala* is a swift, curling wave. (GFF) Also see Hawaiian and Hawaiian
Pidgin English surfing terms in the main text.

ahua (ah-HOO-ah) *n.* A place close to shore
where a broken wave rises and breaks
again. Also known as KIPAPA or PUAO. (F&H)

alaia (ah-LAI-ah) *n.* A thin wooden surfboard, wide in the front and tapering
toward the back, made of koa or bread-
fruit. Also called OMO. (F&H)

hamakuapoko (ha-ma-KOO-ah-PO-ko) *n.*
A well-surfed Oahu location, literally
"sky clouds of fragrance." (GFF)

he'e (Hay-ay) *v.* To slide, to surf (F&H); to
slip or flee. (P&E)

he'e nalu (Hay-ay NA-lu) **1)** *v.* To ride a
surfboard. **2)** *n.* Surfing; literally "wave
sliding." (F&H) **3)** *n.* Surf rider. (P&E)

he'e pu'ewai (Hay-ay POO-e-wai) *v.* To
ride toward the mouth of a stream or up
a stream. (F&H)

he'e umauma (Hay-ay oo-MAU-ma) *n.*
Bodysurfing. (F&H)

hee (Hay-ah) *n.* **1)** A flowing, as of liquid.
2) The menses. **3)** A flight, as of a routed
army. **4)** The squid, so-called because of
its slippery qualities. (ADW, 1865)

hee (Hay-ah) *v.* **1)** To melt; to run or flow,
as a liquid. **2)** To slip or glide along. **3)** To
ride on a surfboard. **4)** To flee; to flee
through fear. (ADW, 1865)

heenalu (Hay-ah NA-lu) *n.* Hee and nalu,
the surf. (ADW, 1865)

heihei nalu (Hay-hay NA-lu) *n.* A surf-board race. (F&H)

honua nalu (ho-NU-ah NA-lu) *n.* The base of the breaker.

huia (hu-E-ah) *n.* An especially high wave formed by the meeting of two crests, said to characterize the surf of Kaipaloaoa, Hawaii. (F&H)

iki (E-key) *n.* The collision of a returning wave with an incoming wave; this phrase may have been coined on the west side of Oahu, where these situations are common. (SFR, January 1990)

kaha (KAH-ha) *v.* To surf; to bodysurf. (F&H)

kaha nalu (kah-ha NA-lu) *n.* Bodysurfing. (F&H)

kahalaia (Kah-ha-LAYa-ah) *n.* The "site of four winds" at Hilo. (GF)

kakala (kah-KAH-la) *n.* The surf in which an *alaia* board is used; a curling wave. (F&H)

kiko'o (key-CO-oo) *n.* A twelve- to eighteen-foot surfboard that is hard to handle but good for surf that breaks roughly. (F&H)

kioe (key-O-e) *n.* A small surfboard. (F&H)

kipapa (key-PAH-pah) *n.* **1)** The prone riding position. **2)** A place close to shore where a broken wave rises and breaks again. (F&H)

kulana nalu (ku-LAH-nah NA-lu) *n.* The place where a surfer paddles to catch a wave; usually the most distant line of breakers. (F&H)

lala (LAH-lah) **1)** *v.* To surf diagonally to the wave front. **2)** *n.* Diagonal surf. **3)** *n.* A wave front; a wave to the right.

lala muku (LAH-lah MOO-koo) *n.* **1)** A wave to the left. **2)** The seaward side of a cresting wave. (F&H)

lauloa (lah-oo-LO-ah) *n.* One of two kinds of surf ridden (the other is *'ohu*); a long wave that crests and breaks from one end of the beach to the other. (F&H)

lele wa'a (lay-lay WAH-ah) *n.* Canoe leaping—leaping from a canoe with a surfboard to ride the wave. (F&H)

muku (MOO-koo) *n.* **1)** The side of a wave near the crest. **2)** The broken section of a wave. **3)** A wave to the left. See LALA MUKU. (F&H)

nala ha'i lala (NAH-lah HA-e-LAH-lah) *n.* A wave that breaks diagonally. (F&H)

nala nui (NAH-lah NU-e) *n.* A big wave. (SCSM)

nalu (NA-lu) **1)** *v.* To form waves. **2)** *n.* A wave; surf. **3)** *adj.* Full of waves; wavy, as wood grain. (F&H) Usage: *"Ke naluo nei ka moana."* "The ocean is full of waves." (P&E)

nalu (NA-lu) *adj.* Roaring; surfing; rolling in, as the surf of the sea. (ADW, 1865)

nalu (NA-lu) *n.* **1)** The surf as it rolls in upon the beach; a sea; a wave; a billow. **2)** The slimy liquid on the body of a newborn infant. (ADW, 1865)

nalu (NA-lu) *v.* **1)** To be in doubt or sus-pense; to suspend one's judgment. **2)** To speak secretly, or to speak to oneself; to think within oneself. **3)** To talk together or confer concerning a thing. **4)** To think; to search after any truth or fact. (ADW, 1865)

nalu puki (NA-lu PU-key) *n.* A wave that shoots high. (F&H)

nalunalu (NA-lu NA-lu) *adj.* oRough; of sea with high waves; forming high waves. (F&H)

no ka pakaka ale (no ka pa-KAH-kah AH-la) *v.* Gliding on the surf; probably refers mainly to canoe surfing. (F&H)

nuumehalani (NU-oo-MA-ha-LA-ne) *n.* A surf site on Oahu; means "the heavenly site where you are alone." (GFF)

'ohu (O-hoo) *n.* One of two kinds of surf ridden (the other is *lauloa*); a low, small wave that rises without breaking but with enough strength to carry a board. Also called OPU'U. (F&H)

olo *n.* The long heavy surfboard reserved for chiefs. (F&H)

omo (O-mo) *n.* ALAIA. (F&H)

onaula-loa (o-na-OO-la LO-ah) *n.* A wave of great length and endurance. (F&H)

onini (o-NEE-nee) *n.* A surfboard used by experts, difficult to manage; a thick board made of *wiliwili*; perhaps the same as an *olo*. (F&H)

opu'u (o-Poo-oo) *n.* A large surf, a swell. (F&H)

owili (o-WE-lee) *n.* A thick board of *wili-wili*; perhaps an *olo*. (F&H)

pa-ha (PAH-ha) *n.* A surfboard. (F&H)

papa he'e nalu (pa-pa HAY-ay NA-lu) *n.* A surfboard; literally, "a board for sliding waves." *Ha'awi papa he'e nalu*: To give a board with the understanding that it would be returned. Boards were apparently loaned rather than given. (F&H)

po'o (PO-o) *n.* A Kauai location for many ancient surf competitions; means "to hollow out." (GFF)

pu'ua (poo-OO-lah) *n.* A surfboard. (F&H)

uo (OO-o) *n.* A Maui surf site: translates as "a nimble threading of a needle." (GFF)

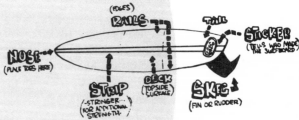

Art: Rick Griffin.
courtesy of Greg Noll

A p p e n d i x **B**

Wave Terms

Note: For definitions of terms, see dictionary.

Wave Characteristics or Conditions

big and stormy

bumps

bumpy

choppy

churly-churly

churning

clean

closed out

cranking

disorganized

dredging

fair

fast

fat

flat

glassy

good

heaving

miragey

mushy

poor

punchy

shifty

slopey

slow

snappy

soft

solid

steep

suckey

tasty

thick

thin

top-to-bottom

treacherous

tubing

tubular

wedgy, wedging

Big Waves

behemoth

big smoker

billow

brown boardshorts material

hair ball

honker

huge monolith

loomer

macker

mondo

monster

mountain

quaker

rolling thunder

white elephant break

Kinds of Waves

A-frame barrel

ankle slapper

bait wave

barrel

biscuit

body whomper

bomber

bone crusher

boomer

brotherhood wave

burger

chaser wave

comber

cruncher

double bubble

double humper

double overhead

dribble

dumper

family wave

fringing wave

gaper

ghost wave

gnarler

grinder

Gulliver wave

humper

in-betweener

inside zipper

knee slapper

micro

mushburger

mush doggie

oatmeal

party wave

pipe, pipeline

plunging breaker

pounder

ripple

rodney wave

rogue wave

roller

see-through wave

shoaling wave

shore pound

slab

sleeper wave

slop

slot wave

smurph, smurphage

sneaker wave

spiller, spilling wave

square

standing wave

stand-up tube

stationary wave

storm surf

submerger

suck out barrel

thicky

thunder crusher

tidal bore (tide wave)

tsunami

unbroken wave

wavelet

Things That Waves Do

acid drop

avalanche

backlash

back off

backwash

bowl

break

build

close out

collapse

curl

dissipate

double up

dredge

fat-out

feather

fire

flatten out

go off

hold up

hollow out

hydrocoffin

jack up

line up

max out

peak

suck dry

warp

A p p e n d i x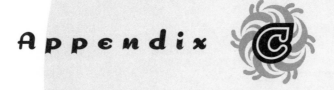

Surfing Synonyms: Different Ways to Say the Same Thing

Note: For definitions of terms, see dictionary.

**bodyboarder
(derogatory)**

boogie flapper

dick-dragger

doormat

esky lid

flatman

foam flapper

half man (when drop
knee)

Maxi-pad cowboy

no man

sea-going muffin

shark appetizer

shark biscuit

speed bump

sponge

sponge head

sponge people

sponger

sponge rider

tea bag

toilet lid

waffle boarder

cool

bitchin'

guava

happening

hot

in thar

killer

live

rad

raw

sacred, sacy

stylin'

sweet

cool it

chill out

gel

mellow out

**crowded surfing
conditions**

mob

plugged

too many guys out

zoo, zooed out

**freezing-cold
ocean water**

arctic

brisk

burly

nip factor

nipple

nipson

goofy foot

dangle foot

goof, goofy footer

screw foot

339

grommet

beach grem

gremlin, gremmie, gremmer

grom, grommer

helgi

ratly

surf mongrel

surf nazi

surf punk

surf rat

weed

heavy surfboard

barge

log, logger

plank

tank, tanker

hot

cool

filthy

killer

outrageous to the max

unreal

inland surfer

flatlander

inlander

inland squid

rock spider

smog monster

tourist

tranny

unlocal

val, valley, valley cowboy, valley sheep

in the tube

clocking in the green room

covered, covered up

going to church

in the curl

in the Pope's living room

in the tunnel

in the womb (the womb of the ocean)

oval office

room time

shacked

throwin' the tools in the shed

ziplocked

kook

abb

barnacle

barney, barn, barnyard

darryl

dewey, duey

dip

dork

drip

dweeb (dweeby)

dwid

egg, eggroll

geek, geekster, geek-a-mo

gilligan

goob

goon

kahuna tuna

kak

kookster

quimby

rubberneck

spleet

squid

wally

wanker

wilma

leash

cord

ding string

leggie

leg rope

rope

shock cord

surf cord

surf leash

leash (derogatory)

dope rope

goon cord

kook cord

valley lifeline

lip (of the wave)

axe

curtain

guillotine

hammer

pseudo surfer

dismo

freeway surfer

highway surfer

poser, pouser

pseud

wannabee

wish was

really good surfing conditions

classic

epic

firing

foffing

going off

honing

insane

off its tits

off the Richter

pumping

raging

reeling

sano

ripping

killing it

lacerating

shralping

shredding

slashing

slicing

smashing

tearing it up

thrashing

runny nose (after surfing)

faucet nose

nasodrain

post-session nasal drip (PSND)

someone who never takes a wave

buoy

decoy

duck

mallard

soaker

stealing another person's wave

dropping in

rat holing

shoulder hopping

snaking waves

tube

barrel

churning cathedral

glasshouse pipe

green room

pipe or pipeline

surfing in polluted waters

floaties

on the nose

surfing under turd

surfing with poo

woofy

yuk

urinating in a wetsuit

doing a sauna

internal heating

natural heater

peter heater

urinophoria

vomiting

  aqua boot

  talking to the seals

wipeout

  beef

  biff

  bombing out

  clam-shelled

  creamed

  down the mine

  dump

  eating it

face plant

gassed

greased

hammered

launched

nailed

over the falls

pearling

pitched

prosecuted

pummeled

quashed

rinse cycle

rumbled

scrub

splampted

stacked

sucking milk

taking gas

taking the whip

thrashed

turnpiked

tweeked

washing machine

Art: Bob Penuelas

Appendix D

Major Surf Spots around the World

This is not an attempt to name every single surf spot on the face of the earth. Some of the places listed below may have several different breaks within the spot that have also been given individual names. Some of the place-names in the list represent general areas or regions where there are numerous surf spots. Surf spots within a given country are generally listed from north to south.

Angola

Argentina

Australia

   East Coast

     Queensland

      Gold Coast

       Burleigh Heads

     New South Wales

      Byron Bay

      Newcastle

      Sydney

      Narrabeen

      Dee Why

      Manly

     Victoria

      Torquay

       Point Danger

       Bells Beach

   Western Australia

     Margaret River

Bahamas

Barbados

Brazil

   Rio de Janeiro

Canada

   Vancouver Island

Canary Islands

Chile

China

Costa Rica

Dominican Republic

Easter Island

Ecuador

El Salvador

   La Libertad

England

   Cornwall

     Newquay

     Porthleen

   Devon

   South Wales

   Porthcawl

   Gower Peninsula

   Freshwater

Fiji

   Tavarua

France

   Biarritz

     Anglet

     Grand Plage

     Côte de Basque

   Guethery

   Laffantania

Indonesia

   Bali

     Kuta Reef

     Nusa Dua

     Padang Padang

     Uluwatu

   Java

     Grajagan, "G-Land"

Ireland

   Northern Ireland

   Rossnowlagh

Israel

Tel Aviv

Jamaica

Boston Bay

Japan

Tokyo

Kenya

Malinda

Marquesas

Mauritius

Mexico

Baja California

K35, K38, K39

Todos Santos

Scorpion Bay

Mainland Mexico

Mazatlán

San Blas

Mexican Pipeline

Morocco

Hassan Surf

New Zealand

North Island

Piha Beach

Panama

Gulf of Panama

Peru

Punta Rocas

Philippines

Portugal

Ericeria

Figuera Da Foz

Lisbon

Peniche

Puerto Rico

Rincon del Mar

Reunion

Samoa

Seychelles

South Africa

Cape Town

Durban

Bay of Plenty

Dairy Beach

Cape St. Francis

Seal Point

Spain

El Duque

Mundacca

Sri Lanka

Tahiti

Tasmania

United States

California

Santa Cruz

Steamer Lane

Pleasure Point

Santa Barbara

Rincon

Los Angeles

Zuma

Malibu

Huntington Beach

Newport Beach

Trestles

San Diego

La Jolla Shores

Windansea

Pacific Beach

Ocean Beach

Imperial Beach

Tijuana Sloughs

Alabama

Gulf Shores

Florida

Sebastian Inlet

Hawaii

Oahu

Makaha

Waikiki

Sandy Beach

North Shore

Pipeline

Sunset

Waimea

Maui

Honolulu Bay

Maalaea

Massachusetts

Cape Cod

New York—
Long Island

Gilgo Beach

North Carolina

Cape Hatteras

South Carolina

Texas

Galveston

Corpus Christi

South Padre Island

Virginia

Virginia Beach

Uruguay

Vietnam

SURFBOARDS

ALL GREG NOLL BOARDS ARE MADE FROM THE BEST QUALITY
MATERIALS AND ARE GUARANTEED AGAINST TURNING YELLOW,
FOAM EXPANDING, OR BREAKING IN TWO (UNDER NORMAL CONDITIONS...)....

BOARD PRICES

0' TO 9' FEET	$100⁰⁰
9'1" TO 9'6" FEET	$105⁰⁰
9'7" TO 10' FEET	$110⁰⁰
10'1" TO 12' FEET	$120⁰⁰
ISLAND BOARDS (OUR SPECIALTY)	
10' TO 12' FEET	$130⁰⁰

INCLUDED IN ALL ABOVE **FREE** ARE : 1 REDWOOD CENTER STRIP
1 EXTRA DURABLE GLASS FIN
(ALL BOARDS ARE GLASSED WITH **20** OZ FIBERCLOTH)

EXTRAS .... PIGMENT ....

PANELING 1 SIDE ...	$10⁰⁰
TWO COLOR PANEL ...	$15⁰⁰
SOLID COLOR	$10⁰⁰
SINGLE COLOR TAPE OFF.	$10⁰⁰
TWO COLOR TAPE OFF.	$15⁰⁰

CENTER STRIPS ...

1½ INCH BALSA	$5⁰⁰
2½ INCH BALSA	$10⁰⁰
MAHOGANY, TEKE, ASH ...	$18
⅛ INCH REDWOOD INLAY (CURVED OR STRAIGHT)	$18

LOCATED AT...
1402 PACIFIC COAST HWY., **HERMOSA BEACH PHONE** 8 FRONTIER 6-4898

Circa early 1960s
Art: Rick Griffin,
courtesy of Greg Noll

Bibliography and Selected References

This section is divided into the following categories:

Books on Surfing

Coastal and Ocean Books

Books on Hawaiian Language and Hawaiian Pidgin English

Surfing Periodicals

Articles in Other Periodicals

Newspaper Articles

Unpublished Surfing Research Papers

Comics

Record Album Lyrics and Liner Notes

Surf Punks

English Dictionaries

Books on Slang

Miscellaneous Books

Books on Surfing

Aaberg, Dennis, and John Milius. *Big Wednesday*. New York: Bantam Books, 1978. Glossary of Surfing Terms, pp. 208–214. "From bail to wipe out: a unique guide to all great surfing terms."

Abbott, Rick. *The Science of Surfing*. Cardiff, England: John Jones Cardiff, July 1972.

Abbott, Rick, and Mike Baker. *Start Surfing*. Melbourne, Australia: Stanley Paul, 1980. Glossary, pp. 85–86.

Ahrens, Chris. *The Surfer's Travel Guide: A Handbook to Surf Paradise*. Cardiff-by-the-Sea, CA: Chubasco Publishing Company, 1995.

_____ *Joyrides: Surf Stories Volume Two*. Cardiff-by-the-Sea, CA: Chubasco Publishing Company, 1999.

Allen, Jim. *Locked In. Surfing for Life*. Everyday handbooks series; no. 316. Cranbury, NJ: A. S. Barnes and Co., 1970. Glossary, pp. 193–96.

Anderson, Michael V. *The Bad, Rad, Not to Forget Way Cool Beach and Surf Discriptionary*. Oceanside, CA: Oceanside Printers, 1988. Southern California surfer talk.

Ball, Doc. *California Surfriders, 1946: A Scrapbook of Surfing and Beach Stuff*. 2nd ed. Redondo Beach, CA: Mountain and Sea Books, 1979. Originally published as Ball, John H. *Surf Riders of California*. Los Angeles: Norman Whale, 1947.

Blair, John. *The Illustrated Discography of Surf Music 1961–1965*. 2nd ed., rev. Ann Arbor, MI: Pierian Press, 1985. "A Surfing Dictionary," pp. 123–25.

Blake, Tom. *Hawaiian Surfboard*. Honolulu, HI: Paradise of the Pacific, 1935. Reprinted as *Hawaiian Surfriders 1935* by Mountain and Sea in 1983.

_____ *Hawaiian Surfriding: The Ancient and Royal Pastime*. Flagstaff, AZ, 1961.

Bloomfield, John. *Know-how in the Surf*. Rutland, VT: Charles E. Tuttle Co., 1965. "Glossary of Surfing Terms," pp. 203–205. Originally published in Sydney, Australia, 1959.

Breaking Free. Available from Mountain and Sea Books, Redondo Beach, California.

Brennan, Joe. *Duke of Hawaii*. New York: Ballantine Books, 1968.

Burt, Rob. *Surf City, Drag City*. Dorset, England: Blandford Press, 1986. "Glossary of Surfing Terms," pp. 20–21.

Calish, Rus. *Paumalu: A Story of Modern Hawaii*. San Clemente, CA: Paumalu Press, 1979.

Cameron, Kirk, and Zack Hanle. *Surfer's Handbook*. New York: Dell Publishing Co., 1968.

Carroll, Corky, with Joel Engel. *Surf-Dog Days and Bitchin' Nights: Confessions of One Outrageous Surf Dude*. Chicago: Contemporary Books, 1989.

Channon, Bruce. *Surfing Wild Australia: Looking for Energy out on the Edge*. Mona Vale, New South Wales, Australia: Australian Surfing World, 1984.

Cleary, William. *Surfing: All the Young Wave Hunters*. Signet Book. New York: New American Library, 1967.

Colendich, George. *The Ding Repair Scriptures—The Complete Guide to Surfboard Repair*. Soquel, CA: Village Green Publications, 1986. "Glossary: A Few Key Terms," p. 88

Conway, John. *Adventure Sports Surfing*. Harrisburg, PA: Stackpole Books, 1988. Glossary, pp. 120–21.

Dalley, Robert J. *Surfin' Guitars—Instrumental Surf Bands of the Sixties*. Surf Publications, 1988. (6209 Oakbank Dr., Azusa, CA 91702.)

Dewey, Nelson. *How to Body Surf*. Sidney, British Columbia, Canada: Saltaire Publishing Co., 1970.

Dixon, Peter L. *The Complete Book of Surfing*. New York: Ballantine Books, 1965. Glossary, pp. 212–16. Rev. ed. New York: Coward-McCann, 1967.

_____ *Men and Waves: A Treasury of Surfing*. New York: Coward-McCann, 1966.

_____ *Where the Surfers Are: A Guide to the World's Great Surfing Spots*. New York: Coward-McCann, 1968.

_____ *Men Who Ride Mountains*. New York: Bantam Books, 1969.

Drummond, Ronald Blake. *The Art of Wave Riding*. Hollywood, CA: Cloister Press, 1931.

Duane, Daniel. *Caught Inside: A Surfer's Year on the California Coast*. New York: North Point Press, 1996.

Edwards, Phil, with Bob Ottum. *You Should Have Been Here an Hour Ago: The Stoked Side of Surfing or How to Hang Ten through Life and Stay Happy*. New York: Harper & Row, 1967.

Farber, Thomas. *On Water*. Hopewell, NJ: The Ecco Press, 1994.

_____ *The Face of the Deep*. San Francisco, CA: Mercury House, 1998.

Farrelly, Midget, as told to Craig McGregor. *The Surfing Life*. New York: Arco Publishing, 1967. "Glossary—Surfing Terms," pp. 19–92.

Filosa, Gary Fairmont R., II. *The Surfer's Almanac: An International Surfing Guide*. New York: E. P. Dutton, 1977. "Surfer's International Lexicon," pp. 180–98.

Finney, Ben, and James D. Houston. *Surfing—The Sport of Hawaiian Kings*. Rutland, VT: Charles E. Tuttle Co., 1966. "Ancient Hawaiian Surfing Terms," pp. 105–106.

_____ *Surfing: A History of the Ancient Hawaiian Sport*. San Francisco, CA: Pomegranate Artbooks, 1996.

Gardner, Robert. *The Art of Body Surfing*. Philadelphia: Chilton Book Co., 1972.

George, Sam. *Surfing: A Way of Life*. New York: Mallard Press, 1990.

Gleasner, Diana C. *Illustrated Swimming, Diving and Surfing Dictionary for Young People*. Englewood Cliffs, NJ: Prentice-Hall, 1980.

Grigg, Ricky, and Ron Church. *Surfer in Hawaii*. Dana Point, CA: John Severson Publications, 1963. "Surf Jargon Glossary," pp. 64–65.

Grissim, John. *Pure Stoke*. New York: Harper & Row, 1982. Glossary, pp. 156–58.

Halacy, Jr., D. S. *Surfer!* New York: Macmillan, 1965. "Surfing Glossary," pp. 213–17.

Hemmings, Fred. *Surfing: Hawaii's Gift to the World of Sports*. New York: Grosset and Dunlap, 1977. "Illustrated Surfing Glossary," pp. 100–18.

_____ *The Soul of Surfing*. New York: Thunder's Mouth Press, 1997.

Holmes, Paul. *Surfabout: The Complete Story of Professional Surfing and the World's Richest Contest*. Darlinghurst, New South Wales, Australia: Soundtracts Publishing, 1980.

Houston, James D. *A Native Son of the Golden West*. New York: Daily Press, 1971.

How to Surf for the Beginner. Honolulu: South Sea Sales, 1964.

Jamieson, Noel. *The Surfboard Riders Repair Manual*. Available from Perigian Beach Surf Shop, 1982.

Jarratt, Phil. *The Wave Game*. Broadway, New South Wales, Australia: Soundtracts Publishing, 1977. An inside look at professional surfing.

_____ *The Surfing Dictionary*. Sun Books. South Melbourne, Australia: Macmillan, 1985. An illustrated cartoon book.

Jenkins, Bruce. *North Shore Chronicles*. Berkeley: North Atlantic Books, 1990.

Jennar, Howard. *Making a Surfboard, the Complete Manual*. Darlinghurst, New South Wales, Australia: Mason Steward Publishing, 1985. Glossary, pp. 93–94.

Jury, Mark. *Surfing in Southern Africa*. Struik Publishers, 1989. P.O. Box 1144, Cape Town 8000, South Africa.

Kahanamoku, Duke, with Joe Brennan. *Duke Kahanamoku's World of Surfing*. Cremorne, Sydney, Australia: Angus and Robertson, 1972. "Glossary of Surfing Terms," pp. 169–79. First published in New York: Grosset and Dunlap, 1968.

Kampion, Drew. *The Book of Waves*. Santa Barbara, CA: Arpel Graphics, 1989.

Kelly, John M., Jr. *Surf and Sea*. New York: A. S. Barnes and Co., 1965. Glossary, pp. 279–98.

Kinstle, James S. *Surfboard Design and Construction*. Long Beach, CA: Natural High Express Co., 1975.

Klein, Arthur H. *Surfing*. New York: J. B. Lippincott, 1965. "Words about some surfing words," p. 236. Reprinted in London: Kaye Ward, 1967.

Kuhns, Grant W. *On Surfing*. Rutland, VT: Charles E. Tuttle Co., 1963. Glossary, pp. 113–23.

Levin, Wayne. *Through A Liquid Mirror*. Honolulu, HI: Editions Limited, 1997. Photographs by Wayne Levin with an Introduction by Thomas Farber.

London, Jack. *Learning Hawaiian Surfing: A Royal Sport at Waikiki Beach, Honolulu, 1907*. Hawaiian Memorial ed., Honolulu, HI: Boom Enterprises, 1983. First published by Crowell Publishing Co., 1907.

Lorch, Carlos. *Lopez: The Classic Hawaiian Surfer*. 1982. Available from Mountain & Sea, Redondo Beach, Calif.

Loveridge, Richard. *A Guide to the Surf Beaches of Victoria.* Melbourne, Australia: Globe Press, 1987.

Lowdon, Brian J., and Margaret Lowdon, Ph.D., eds. *Competitive Surfing—A Dedicated Approach.* Torquay, Victoria, Australia: Movement Publications, 1988. Glossary, pp. 293–95; Appendix A, "Manoeuvre Definitions," pp. 296–98.

Lueras, Leonard. *Surfing: The Ultimate Pleasure.* An Emphasis International Book. New York: Workman Publishing Co., 1984. "A Surf Filmography," pp. 216–221.

Lueras, Leonard and Lorca. *Fielding's Surfing Indonesia.* Redondo Beach, CA: Periplus Editions, 1996.

MacLaren, James. *Learn to Surf.* New York: The Lyons Press, 1997.

Margan, Frank, and Ben R. Finney. *A Pictorial History of Surfing.* Dee Why West, New South Wales, Australia: Paul Hamlyn, 1970. Glossary: "A General Guide Is," pp. 313–19.

Masters, Ted. *Surfing Made Easy.* Van Nuys, CA, 1962.

McClelland, Gordon. *Rick Griffin.* Surrey, Great Britain: Paper Tiger, 1980.

McGinness, Laurie. *Surfing Fundamentals.* Terry Hills, Sydney, Australia: A. H. and A. W. Reed, 1978.

McKissick, Mitch. *Surf Lingo—A Complete Guide to a Totally Rad Vocab!.* Balboa, CA: Coastline Press, 1987. A cartoon book with glossary, pp. 81–86.

Morris, Vic and Joe Nelson. *The Weather Surfer: A Guide to Oceanography and Meteorology for the World's Wave Hunters.* San Diego, CA: Grossmont Press, 1977.

Muirhead, Desmond. *Surfing in Hawaii: A Personal Memoir.* Flagstaff, AZ: Northland Press, 1962. With notes on California, Australia, Peru, and other surfing countries.

Nelson, William Desmond. *Surfing: A Handbook.* Philadelphia: Auerbach Publishers, 1973. Glossary, pp. 219–27.

Nentl, Jerolyn Ann. *Surfing.* Mankato, MN: Crestwood House, 1978.

Noll, Greg, and Andrea Gabbard. *Da Bull—Life Over the Edge.* Bozeman, MT: Bangtail Press, 1989.

Olney, Ross. *The Young Sportsman's Guide to Surfing.* New York: Thomas Nelson and Sons, 1965. Chapter VIII, "Surf Talk," pp. 86–94.

Orbelian, George. *Essential Surfing.* 3rd ed. San Francisco: Orbelian Arts, 1987. First published in 1982. "Fiber Reinforced Plastics Glossary," pp. 231–38; "Essential Surfing Glossary," pp. 239–42.

Patterson, O. B. *Surf-riding: Its Thrills and Techniques.* Rutland, VT: Charles E. Tuttle Co., 1960.

Pearson, Kent. *Surfing Subcultures of Australia and New Zealand.* St. Lucia, Australia: University of Queensland Press; Hemel Hempstead, England: distributed by Prentice-Hall International, 1979. pp. 136–43.

Penuelas, Bob. *Wilbur Kookmeyer and Friends.* Del Mar, CA: Yipes Publishing, 1990.

Petersen's Surfing Yearbook Number Two. Petersen Publishing Co., Los Angeles, 1965. "Glossary of Surfing Terms," p. 224.

Petersen's Surfing Yearbook Number Three. Petersen Publishing Co., Los Angeles, 1966.

Pohl, Henry F. *Conquering the Surf: Lifesaving and Surfboarding.* New York: Hoffman-Harris, 1944.

Pollard, Jack. *The Surfrider.* New York: Taplinger Publishing Co., 1968. "The Surfer's Vocabulary," pp. 16–21. First published as *The Australian Surfrider.* Sydney, Australia: K. G. Murray Publishing Co., 1963. "The Language of the Surfer," pp. 16–22.

———. *How to Ride a Surfboard.* Wollstonecraft, New South Wales, Australia: Pollard Publishing Co., 1976.

Prytherch, Reginald J. *Surfing—A Modern Guide*. London: Faber and Faber, 1972. Glossary, pp. 129–33.

Renneker, Mark, Kevin Starr, and Geoff Booth. *Sick Surfers Ask The Surf Docs and Dr. Geoff*. Palo Alto, CA: Bull Publishing Company, 1993.

Severson, John Hugh, ed. *The Surfer—John Severson's First Annual Surf Photo Book*. Dana Point, CA: Severson Studios, 1960. Reprinted in Dana Point, CA: Surfer Publications, 1973.

_____ *Modern Surfing Around the World*. New York: Doubleday, 1964. "Surfing Terminology," pp. 162–86.

_____ *Great Surfing: Photos, Stories, Essays, Reminiscences and Poems*. New York: Doubleday, 1967.

Shackleton, Roger, and John Christensen. *All About Wave Skis*. Brookvale, New South Wales, Australia: Surfside Press, 1985.

Shaw, Stephen M., ed. *Surfboard*. Rev. ed. La Mesa, CA: Transmedia, 1983. Formerly published as *Surfboard Builders' Manual* (1963) and *Surfboard Builders' Yearbook* (1971).

St. Pierre, Brian. *The Fantastic Plastic Voyage: Across the South Pacific with Surfers and a Camera*. New York: Coward-McCann, 1969.

Stern, David H., and William S. Cleary. *Surfing Guide to Southern California*. Volume one of International Surfing Guidebook Series. Malibu, CA: Fitzpatrick Co., 1963. 2d ed. Los Angeles: Mountain and Sea Books, 1977.

Sufrin, Mark. *Surfing: How to Improve Your Technique*. New York: Franklin Watts, 1973. Glossary, pp. 59–61.

Surf. How to—The Complete Guide to Surfing. Darlinghurst, New South Wales, Australia: Mason Stewart Publishing, 1983.

Surfboard. La Mesa, CA: Aileen S. Brown, 1981.

Surfboard. How to Make Your Own. North Sydney, Australia: Australian Surfing Kit Co., 1965. "A Glossary of Surfers' Terms," pp. 17–18.

Surfing the Big Wave. Available from Mountain and Sea Books, Los Angeles.

Surfing the Chain of Fire. Australian Surfing World. Available from Mountain and Sea Books, Los Angeles.

Thomson, Carl. *Surfing in Great Britain*. London: Constable, 1972.

Timmons, Grady. *Waikiki Beachboy*. Honolulu: Editions Limited, 1989.

Wardlaw, Lee. *Cowabunga! The Complete Book of Surfing*. New York: Avon Books, 1991.

Warren, Mark. *Mark Warren's Atlas of Australian Surfing*. North Ryde, New South Wales, Australia: Agnus and Robertson, 1988. Glossary, pp. 228–29. "An Introduction to Surf Talk," p. 29.

Warshaw, Matt. *Surfriders: In Search of the Perfect Wave*. New York: HarperCollins, 1997.

Warwick, Wayne. *A Guide to Surfriding in New Zealand*. Wellington, New Zealand: Viking Seven Seas, 1978. Glossary. (The third revised ed. does not have a glossary.)

Wegener, Tom, and Bill Burke. *Southern California's Best Surf: A Guide to Finding, Predicting, and Understanding the Surf of Southern California*. Redondo Beach, CA: Green Room Press, 1989.

Werner, Doug. *Surfer's Start-up: A Beginner's Guide to Surfing*. San Diego, CA: Tracks Publishing, Second Edition 1999.

_____ *Longboarder's Start-up: A Guide to Longboard Surfing*. San Diego, CA: Tracks Publishing, 1996.

White, Graham. *Surfing*. Sydney, Australia: Paul Hamlyn, 1977.

Wright, Bank. *Surfing California: A Complete Guide to the California Coast.* Redondo Beach, CA: Mañana, 1973.

_____. *Surfing Hawaii.* Redondo Beach, CA: Mountain and Sea, 1972.

Young, Nat. *Nat Young's Book of Surfing.* Sydney, Australia: A. H. and A. W. Reed, 1979. Glossary, p. 87.

_____ *Surfing Australia's East Coast.* Sydney, Australia: New Century Press, 1980.

_____ *The History of Surfing.* Palm Beach, New South Wales, Australia: Palm Beach Press, 1983.

_____ *Surfing & Sailboard Guide to Australia.* Palm Beach, New South Wales, Australia: Palm Beach Press, 1985.

_____ *Surfing Fundamentals.* Palm Beach, New South Wales, Australia: Palm Beach Press, 1985. Glossary, pp. 126–28.

Coastal and Ocean Books

Bascom, Willard. *Waves and Beaches.* Garden City, NY: Anchor Books, 1980.

California Coastal Access Guide. California Coastal Commission. Jo Ginsberg and Erin Caughman, eds. Rev. ed. Berkeley: University of California Press, 1991.

California Coastal Resource Guide. California Coastal Commission. Joanne Ginsberg and Madge Caughman, eds. Berkeley: University of California Press, 1987.

Dutton, Geoffrey. *Sun, Sea, Surf and Sand: The Myth of the Beach.* New York: Oxford University Press, 1985.

Gross, M. Grant. *Oceanography.* 4th ed. Columbus, OH: Charles E. Merrill Publishing Co., 1980.

Groves, Don. *The Oceans: A Book of Questions and Answers.* New York: John Wiley and Sons, 1989.

Hendrickson, Robert. *The Ocean Almanac.* New York: Doubleday, 1984.

Suiso, Ken, and Rell Sunn. *A Guide to Beach Survival.* Haleiwa, HI: Honolulu Water Safety Consultants, 1986.

The Times Atlas of the Oceans. Alastair Couper, ed. New York: Van Nostrand Reinhold Co., 1983.

Books on Hawaiian Language and Hawaiian Pidgin English

Andrews, Lorrin. *A Dictionary of the Hawaiian Language.* Lahaina, Maui, Hawaii, 1865.

Carr, Elizabeth Ball. *Da Kine Talk: From Pidgin to Standard English in Hawaii.* Honolulu: University of Hawaii Press, 1972.

Pukui, Mary Kawena and Samuel Elbert. *Hawaiian Dictionary.* Honolulu: University of Hawaii Press, 1971.

Pukui, Mary Kawena, et al. *The Pocket Hawaiian Dictionary.* Honolulu: University of Hawaii Press, 1975.

Simonson, Douglas (Peppo), et al. *Pidgin to the Max.* Honolulu: Peppovision, 1981.

_____. *Pidgin to da Max Hana Hou!* Honolulu: Peppovision, 1982.

Speak Hawaiian. Honolulu: Paradise Products, 1973.

Art: I. B. Nelson

Surfing Periodicals

Action. Imperial Beach, California.

Australia's Surfing Life. Burleigh Heads, Queensland, Australia.

Beach Culture. Dana Point, California.

Beach Happy. San Clemente, California.

Beach 'n' Waves. San Diego, California.

Bodyboarder International Magazine. Oceanside, California.

Body Boarding. San Clemente, California.

Breakout. Bimonthly. Carlsbad, California.

Cross Step. Dana Point, California.

Groundswell. Honolulu, Hawaii.

H2O The Magazine of Waterfont Culture. Malibu, California.

H3o Hawaiian Heavywater. Aiea, Hawaii.

International Surfing. Bimonthly. Hermosa Beach, California. See *Surfing.*

The Juice. Santa Cruz, California.

Kema. Dana Point, California.

Local. Santa Cruz, California.

Longboard Magazine. San Clemente, California.

Longboard Quarterly. San Clemente, California.

Making Waves. Huntington Beach, California. Newsletter of the Surfrider Foundation.

Riptide. Burleigh Heads, Queensland, Australia.

Skimboard. South Laguna, California.

South Swell. Jacksonville, Florida: South Swell Publishing.

Surf. Milano, Italy.

Surfer. Monthly. Dana Point, California. See "Eastside Speak" in *Sections* (August 1990): 78.

Surfer Girl.

The Surfer's Journal. San Clemente, California.

The Surfer's Path. Bude, North Cornwall, England.

Surf Guide. Monthly. Santa Monica, California.

Surfing. Monthly. San Clemente, California. See "Surfspeak—Beach Blanket Babble," Vol. 17, no. 12 (December 1981): 19.

Surfing Illustrated. Quarterly. Hermosa Beach, California.

"You'll like this place, it's all fresh baked daily."

Art: I. B. Nelson

Surfing Medicine. Published by the Surfer's Medical Association, San Francisco.

Surfing World. Monthly. Sydney, Australia.

Surfin' Life. Tokyo, Japan.

Surf Magazine. Sidcup, Kent, England.

Tracks. Monthly. Darlinghurst, New South Wales, Australia: Mason Stewart Publishing. See McTavish, Bob. "Pods for Primates: A Personal History of Surfboard Design." In *The Best of Tracks,* 1976, pp. 120–32.

Transworld Surf. Oceanside, California.

Tres 60. Santurce, Vizcaya, Spain.

Wahine. Long Beach, California.

Wave Length. England.

Wave Rider. Bimonthly. Cocoa Beach, Florida.

Waves. Waterloo, New South Wales, Australia.

Wind Surf. Paris, France. See "Do You Speak Surfer?" No. 18, 1990: pp. 16–17.

Articles in Other Periodicals

"Still Surfin' After All These Years" by Jonathan Kirsch, *New West.* Vol. 6, no. 5 (May 1981): 90–91.

"Surfin' Safari Revisited" by Laura Bernstein and Jill Johnson Keeney, *New West.* Vol. 6, no. 5 (May 1981): 92–99.

"Surf Wars" by Frank Bies, *New West.* Vol. 6., no. 5 (May 1981): 100–105.

Thrasher, San Francisco, California.

"Surfing on California Beach is a Favorite Summertime Sport." *Life.* Vol. 9 (August 1940): 50–52.

"Waves of Semiosis: Surfing's Iconic Progression" by Pierce Julius Flynn, *The American Journal of Semiotics,* Vol. 5, No. 3 & 4 (1987): 397–418.

"Waves & Thrills at Waikiki." *National Geographic.* Vol. 67, no. 5 (May 1935): 597.

"Surfboarders Capture California." *National Geographic.* Vol. 86, no. 3 (September 1944): 355.

"'Hey Man, My Wave!': The Authority of Private Language." *Poetics Journal.* No. 6 (1986): 3–5. Reprinted from a talk given by Michael Davidson at New Langton Arts, San Francisco, March 22, 1984.

"The Development and Diffusion of Modern Hawaiian Surfing" by Ben Finney. *The Journal of Polynesian Society,* Vol. 69, no. 4 (December 1960).

"Hitch-hiking on the Big Waves," *Popular Mechanics.* Vol. 77, no. 2 (February 1942): 72–75, 166.

"Surfboarding in Oceania: Its Pre-European Distribution" by Ben Finney. *Sonderdruck aus Wiener Völkerkundliche Mittelungen VII.* Jahrgang-Bd. II, Nr. 1–4.

"The Mechanics of Waves and the Art of Surfing" by Richard Wolkomir. *Oceans.* (June 1988): 36-41.

Newspaper Articles

Greth, Carlos Vidal. "Surfing in the City." *San Francisco Chronicle.* People Section, B3–B4, June 24, 1988. Glossary, "Official Argot of the Surf-Stoked."

Pine, Jon. "Surfing's Developed a Colorful Language." *Contra Costa Times* (Concord, CA), June 12, 1989, 8B. Glossary.

Stillman, Deanne. "Surf's Up Again: On Screen, On Canvas, and On the Radio." *New York Times.* September 2, 1990, Arts & Leisure, Section 2.

Zamora, Jim Herron. "Why Valley Girls and Mutant Turtles Sound Like Surfers." *The Wall Street Journal.* September 27, 1990.

Unpublished Surfing Research Papers

Digman, Debra. "Oral Testimonies of Santa Cruz Surfers: The Creation of a Culture." University of California, Santa Cruz, 1972. Special Collections GV840.S82M6 Santa Cruziana Archives.

Irwin, John Keith. "Surfers: A Study of the Growth of a Deviant Subculture." Master's Thesis, Department of Sociology, University of California, Berkeley, 1965.

Levine, Alice. "Stories of the Santa Cruz Surf Culture." University of California, Santa Cruz, 1972. Special Collections GV840.S82M654 Santa Cruziana Archives.

Lux, Anna Kathryn. "Surfing in Santa Cruz as Told through a Life History." University of California, Santa Cruz, 1987. Special Collections GV840.S8 L89 1987 Santa Cruziana Archives.

Spencer, C. Philip. "A Surfing Oral Tradition in Santa Cruz: 'Tales and Things'." University of California, Santa Cruz, 1975. Special Collections GV840.S82S67 Santa Cruziana Archives.

Comics

Silver Surfer, New York: Marvel Comics.

Surf Crazed Comics. San Clemente, CA: Paskowitz.

Tales from the Tube. Art-directed by Rick Griffin, 1973.

Wave Warriors. San Clemente, CA: Herbie Fletcher and Astroboys Productions.

Record Album Lyrics and Liner Notes

The Beach Boys, *Surfing U.S.A.* Album glossary. Capitol Records, 1961.

The Belairs and "The Origins of Surf Music: 1960–1963," with a written historical perspective by Paul Johnson. Los Angeles, CA: Iloki Records, 1987.

Golden Summer. Los Angeles: United Artists Records, 1976.

Surf Punks

My Beach, Surf Punks Glossary 1. New York: Epic/CBS, 1980.

Locals Only. Surf Punks Glossary 2. Malibu, CA: Day-Glo Records, 1982.

Oh, No! Not Them Again! Surf Punks Glossary 3. El Segundo, CA: Enigma Records, 1988.

Art: Jim Ph

English Dictionaries

The American Heritage Dictionary. 2nd college ed. Boston: Houghton Mifflin Co., 1985.

Oxford English Dictionary. New York: Oxford University Press, 1971.

Random House Dictionary. New York: Random House, 1987.

Webster's Ninth New Collegiate Dictionary. Springfield, MA: Merriam-Webster Inc., 1989.

Books on Slang

Blowdryer, Jennifer. *Modern English: A Trendy Slang Dictionary*. Berkeley: Last Gasp of San Francisco, 1985.

Munro, Pamela, ed. *U.C.L.A. Slang: A Dictionary of Slang Words and Expressions Used at U.C.L.A.* U.C.L.A. Occasional Paper in Linguistics, #8, Dept. of Linguistics, University of California at Los Angeles, 1989.

_____ *Slang U*. New York: Harmony Books, 1989.

Partridge, Eric. *Smaller Slang Dictionary*. New York: Dorset Press, 1961.

Miscellaneous Books

Bragonier, Reginald, Jr., and David Fisher. *What's What in Sports—The Visual Glossary of the Sports World*. Maplewood, NJ: Hammond, 1984. "Surfing," p. 161.

Hart, James D. *A Companion to California*. New York: Oxford University Press, 1978.

Javna, John. *The TV Theme Song Sing-Along Book Volume 2*. New York: St. Martin's Press, 1985.

Nicholson, Margaret. *The Little Aussie Fact Book*. Long Beach: Australia In Print, 1989.

The World Almanac and Book of Facts 1991. New York: Pharos Books, 1991.

Art: The Pizz

A note about sources used in compiling this dictionary: Like all dictionaries, *The Surfin'ary* draws on many sources. Although every effort was made to give credit for specific material, this wasn't always possible. Some definitions combine information from several sources; some terms are so widespread in their use and meaning that it would be senseless to attribute them to a single source. Nevertheless, all sources that contributed (knowingly or unknowingly) to this book are listed in either the bibliography or one of the credits sections. Concerning the editorial policy followed in compiling this book, except for verbatim quotations (which are clearly indicated and attributed), all material in this book has been edited, even when a source is cited.

Art and Photography Credits

Artists and Illustrators

Glenn Bering	Charles Lawrence	The Pizz	Rick Stover
Karen T. Delgadillo	Jim Lucas	Robbie Quine	*Surfer* magazine
Jen Delyth	Andrea McCann	Dean Rankine ("Deano")	John Van Hammersveld
Tony Edwards	I. B. Nelson	Rick Rietveld	Malcolm Wilson
Rebecca Fish	John Nickerson	Peter Schroff	George Woodbridge
Roy Gonzales	Bill Ogden	John Severson	Mr. X
Rick Griffin	Bob Penuelas	David Sirgany	
Keith Hunter	Jim Phillips	Tim Smith	
John Iwerks*	Jimbo Phillips	Peter Spacek	

To order your own copy of the Toadally Tubed Surfing Flipbook by John Iwerks (see page 57), send $9.00 plus $1.00 postage to John Iwerks, P.O. Box 1551, Santa Barbara, CA 93102. Toadally Tubed is printed in color, measures 3 x 5 inches, and contains 105 pages. Each book is personally hand assembled and hand bound.

Photographers

Nina Aldrich-Wolfe	Jeff Divine	Mike Peralta (www.mikeperalta photography.com)	*Surfer* magazine
Rolf Aurness	Tom Dodd		Surfers Medical Association
Don Balch	Kirwan Fox	Mark Perko	Fred Swegels
Bob Barbour	David Gelles	Liz Phegan	Jack Thomas
Grant Bennett	Rob Gilley	Mac Reed	Alan Tieger
Bishop Museum	Dan Jenkin	Bob Richardson	Leslie Werner
Elise Brewin	Dennis Junor/Creation Captured	Bill Romerhaus	David Wilson
Robert Brown	Don King	Damien P. Russell	John Witzig
John S. Callahan	Leslie King	Camille Seaman	Woody Woodworth/Creation Captured
Sherry Carlson	Tai Sing Loo	Tom Servais	
Bud Clark	Stephanie Gene Morgan	T. Severin	
Judith Cralle	I. B. Nelson	John Severson	
Trevor Cralle	O'Neill, Inc.	Ron Stoner	
Peter Crawford			

Jim Phillips

Additional Credits

Major Contributors

Ad the Rad Lad

Bernie Baker

Tim Baker *Tracks*, magazine

Bruce Brown

Corky Carroll

Will Church, via speakerphone, Santa Cruz Surf Shop

Michael Davidson, Department of Literature, University of California, San Diego

Peter Dixon

Dr. Dume, *Surfer* magazine

Eric Fairbanks, *Surfing* magazine

Nathan Fletcher

Chris Gallagher

Matt George

Sam George

Jay Gould

Tex & Lynn Haines, Victoria Skimboards

Harold Hawkins and Tony Ramarez, c/o Total Control Surfboards, Corpus Christi, Texas

Greg "The Gardner" Histed, aka "Frank"

Lisa Hybarger

Hal Jepsen

Matt Kechele

Dave "The Wave" Kinstle, aka "Flaco"

Rich Maile and Felix Alfaro, O'Neill Surf Shop, Santa Cruz

Ben Marcus, *Surfer* magazine

Gordon T. McClelland

Michael Martin

Paul "Mango" McEntyre

Anthony James Misner

Julie Moniz, Santa Cruz Surf Shop (also Tina George and Mike Courtney)

Bev Morgan

Ellen Nachtigall

I. B. Nelson

Greg Noll

Paco (Dan Jenkin)

Bob Penuelas

Mike Peterson

The Pizz

Laura Platt

Robbie Quine

Mac Reed

Lisa Roselli

Santa Cruz Surfing Museum

Richard Schmidt

Ken Seino, Chairman of the Boards for Cowabunga Surfware

Tom Servais

Allan Seymour

Ward Smith

Marcel Soros, Natural Progression

Drew Steele

Michelle Anne Stevens

Toby at Arrow Surf & Sport, Santa Cruz

Peter Townend

Greg Travers, Ocean Energy, Santa Cruz

Matt Warshaw, *Surfer* magazine

Additional Contributors

Sunny Abberton

Victor Abubo

The Agigian Sisters—Amy & Laura Michele

Matt Allen

Nicole Andlinger

Aqua Culture Surf Shop, Half Moon Bay, CA

Kevin Ascher

Lloyd Austin

Brian Baird

Dick Banfield

Mark Barbour

Steve Barilotti, *Surfer* magazine

Rich Bass

Benjah

Maya Berger ("Earth Puddle")

Big Stick Surfing Association

Katherine Bishop

Jeff Braverman

Dan Bush

Anton Calderon

Tyler Campbell

Tom Carroll

Bob Carlson of Carlson Designs

Sherry Carlson

Ted Cassidy

Gerry Chalmers

Richard Chester and Verne McCall

Karen T. Delgadillo

Chris Denney

Damian Dhar

Dennis Dragon

Mary Duffy

Lawrence J. England

Paul Feldman

Mike Ferreira

Rebecca Fish

Marcy Fleming

Toni Francavilla

Noah Franzblau

Justin (Santa Cruz grommet) Gamino

Rob Gilley

David Gilovitch, *Surfing* magazine

Cork Golston

Michael Golston

M. Gonzalez

Lulie Haddad

Jim Halperin (Jimbo)

Kini Harvey

Bob Hasier and Co.

Phillip Hellsten, President, Old Wave Surfing Association

Jared Hermann

Bob and Jennifer Hightower

Edwin A. Hoey

Keith Hunter

Todd Jacobs, Channel Islands National Marine Sanctuary

Dr. Scott Jenkins, The Surfrider Foundation

Jodster (Hollywood, Florida)

R. Jones

Val "Skate" Jones

Carlos Kende, Northern Mexico Coordinator, Association Mexicana de Surfing A.C.

Erik Larson

Dru Lewis

Tamara Lipper

Brock Little

Tony "Delgado" Litwak

Mike Locatelli

Toni Logan

Jorge MacFarland with Scorpio Surfing Tours

of Isla Natividad (Chula Vista)

Gary MacVicar

Ariel Marks

Paul McHugh

Lee Micheaux

Ira Miller

Mickey Muñoz

Barney Q. Nietschmann, Department of Geography, University of California, Berkeley

Margot O'Neill

Jill Ornstein

Ron Orton

A. Paskowitz

M. Paskowitz

Eric Penzower

Steve Pezman, *Surfer* magazine

Denny Plyer

Douglas Powell, Department of Geography, University of California, Berkeley

Rusty Preisendorfer

Rosemary Prem

R.C., Santa Monica, California

James D. Rawls

Rich & Dunc, Glenalta, South Australia

Kelly Richardson

Dave Romyn

Joe Ryan

Tim Ryan

Dennis Salles

Santa Crucial posse

Aaron Santell

Michael Schutz

Adel Shephard

Ken Shirriff

Scott Shurtz

Brad Smith

Jason Smith

Lynn Smith

Butt Stains (Long Beach)

Kirk Steers

Steve, Surf Side Sports, Newport Beach

Shaun Tomson

Jonathon Toste

Bob Travis

Non Travis

Two Hindu Surfers

A. D. Vernon

Mark M. Wagner

Jos Walton

Stuart and Devin Watson

Ernest Weekly

Steven White

Dave Williams

Rick D. T. Wilson

Todd Wolf and the Boca Surf Cafe crew, Florida

Mike Worth (Big Wednesday)

Yo Skankin' Dub Masters

. . . and a few others

Art: The Pizz

New Contributors to the Second Edition

Dennis Aaberg
Anda Abramovici
Matt Albert
Ryan Alfonso
Chuck Allison (Ocean City, New Jersey)
Mark Andre (Santa Cruz)
David Arnson of the Insect Surfers
Jack Barclay
Bryan Beyer
Jon Blair
boardz.com
Elise Brewin
Mary Ann Brewin
Pat Briggs ("Slack Key Pat")
Tony Cox, Ocean Energy
Tom Dalzell
Kim Darwin
Molly DeCoudreaux
Jenny Della Santa
Dave & Bev Dyk
Shanta Eastman
Tom Farber
Derek Ferrah (Hawaii)
Laurie Fork
Reed Foster
Spencer Franklin
Mr. Full On (Outer Banks)

Ed Garberry
David Gelles
Wayne & Brenda George
Robert Hakim
Brad Halfacre (Tasmania)
Denise Halferty-Neff
Art "Ski" Halperin
Jiro Hanaue
Charli Haynes
Clayton Horton ("Claytonious")
Supa-Dave Howlett
Issac, The Campbell Soup Kid
Jake (of Birdmen of Alcatraz)
John from Newport Beach (met on St. Kitts in 1994)
Louise Keoghan
Nate Knight
Lala Land
John Lawson (Santa Cruz)
Noah Levy
Matt Liverman ("Skibo")
Amber Mace
Julie Mammano
Mark Masara
Joe Matera
Luke Maura (Santa Cruz)

Sally & Kevin McClure
Katie Miller
Stephanie Gene Morgan
Julie Mott
Fred Nelli
The Not When The Surf's Up Construction Company, North Shore, Oahu
Jason Olaine ("Scrappy")
Paradise Surf Shop, Santa Cruz
Johann Pauwen
Harley Perleman
Liz Phegan
Mary Rackin
Sasha Radovich
Jackson Rahn (Santa Cruz)
Mark "Doc" Renneker
Ramona Reposa
Don Redondo
John Robinson (Santa Cruz)
Johnny Rocco
P. Damien Russell & Mullethead Surf Designs (Maryland and Florida)
Kim Smeaton
Charles Souza

Don Strout at Surflink
Dave Suther
Michael Tarsha
Jim Thomas and The Mermen (Alan & Martin)
Toronja
John Ugoretz
Gretchen Walker
Mark Walsh
Jay Ward
Ben Warwus
Dick Wayman
Kelly Williams-Richards, Perfection Surfboards, Garden City Beach, South Carolina
Wingnut
Reeve Woolpert

And the following at The Lane, Fall 1991:
Jason Christian
Matt Collins
Dameon DeWorken
Errol Levine
John Mueller
Jack Mullis
Tyler Smith

We'd love to add your name to this list—see next page for details.

A Note to the Reader

A Call for Submissions

Every conceivable effort has gone into making this book as complete as possible, but undoubtedly some terms and definitions were not uncovered and, regrettably, have been left out. This book, like any dictionary, will forever be "a work in progress."

Perhaps this collection of surfing terminology will inspire individuals like yourself to dig up old glossaries and recall forgotten or obscure terms, and maybe even create and introduce new words and phrases. Please send all comments, criticisms, corrections, and, of course, any new terms or expressions to the address below for inclusion in a future revised and updated edition.

A Note about Submissions

Send in anything—technical shaper's terms, wave descriptions, surfboard design features, derogatory slang, surfing maneuvers—whatever.

Ideally we'd like to get the following information, although anything that you send will be greatly appreciated.

1) Surfing term, phrase, or expression; a key to pronunciation (if not obvious).

2) A thorough and detailed definition or definitions; can be serious or funny or both.

3) Usage: Give at least one example of how the word is used in a sentence (surfing context).

4) Source: name of person(s) or publication(s) to be credited. (Anonymous contributions are also welcome.)

All contributions should be sent to:

Trevor Cralle, Editor
The Surfin'ary
c/o Ten Speed Press
999 Harrison Street
Berkeley, CA 94710 USA

You may also email me at: trevor@california.com
We are always looking for interesting photos or illustrations.
We want your feedback!

Stand Up for the Waves That Stand Up for You

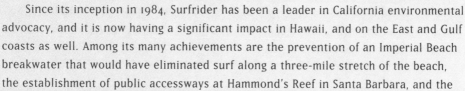

The Surfrider Foundation

The Surfrider Foundation is a nonprofit organization established for the protection and enhancement of the world's coastal and ocean environment through conservation, research, and education. Surfrider is dedicated to preserving the natural state of our waves and beaches, improving recreational opportunities, and assuring a clean and healthy marine environment for all people.

Since its inception in 1984, Surfrider has been a leader in California environmental advocacy, and it is now having a significant impact in Hawaii, and on the East and Gulf coasts as well. Among its many achievements are the prevention of an Imperial Beach breakwater that would have eliminated surf along a three-mile stretch of the beach, the establishment of public accessways at Hammond's Reef in Santa Barbara, and the initiation, under the Clean Water Act, of a citizen suit against two pulp mills in Humboldt County, the largest such suit to be brought to date.

Our beaches and waves are beseiged by more complex problems than ever before. Our ocean is used as a dump. The Blue Water Task Force was established to combat this situation. It is a grassroots program of water quality testing along our nation's shorelines. Designed to insure compliance with state and federal water-quality standards, it calls for harsh civil penalties against violators.

By joining the Surfrider Foundation, you are standing up for the waves that stand up for you. For more informaton, contact the Surfrider Foundation at 122 South El Camino Real #67, San Clemente, CA 92672, (800) 743-SURF (7873), www.surfrider.org.

Art: Jim Phillips

☼ About the Author

Trevor "Coconut" Cralle (KRAWL-ee, rhymes with "Bali") is a native California surfer with a degree in cultural geography from the University of California, Berkeley. Trevor is also a surf linguist and surfing lexicographer. He has worked for the California Coastal Commission, where he was one of the principal writers of the *California Coastal Resource Guide*, and the revised *California Coastal Access Guide*. He is also the author of *Flinging Monkeys at the Coconuts: A Traveler's Companion of Quotations* (Ten Speed Press, 1992). Trevor is an all-American swimmer, a scuba diving and surf instructor, and an underwater video cameraman. In addition to traveling in over fifty countries, he has sailed through the South Pacific on a thirty-nine-foot sloop, co-led marine educational field trips to Mexico, and is a windsurfing and lifeguard instructor and the head counselor at summer water sports camps on the islands of Antigua and St. Kitts in the Caribbean.

Trevor "Coconut" Cralle
Photo: Leslie Werner